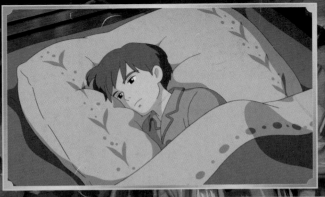

Shawn

A 12-year-old human boy. He has come to stay in the old house where his mother grew up in order to regain his health. He finds Arrietty and talks to her.

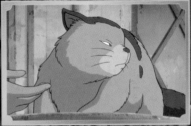

Nina

Jessica's pet cat, who is always dangerously on the prowl.

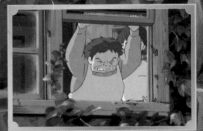

Hara

The maid at Jessica's house. She has lived and worked there for many, many years. She is full of curiosity.

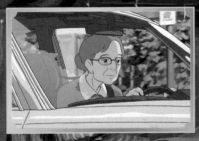

Jessica

Shawn's aunt who owns the old house in the country. She has a gentle personality.

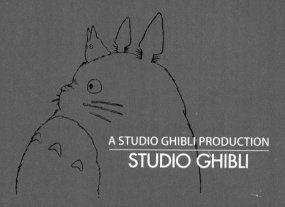

A STUDIO GHIBLI PRODUCTION
STUDIO GHIBLI

Studio Ghibli, Nippon Television Network, Dentsu, Hakuhodo
DYMP, Walt Disney Japan, Mitsubishi, Toho and Wild Bunch
PRESENT

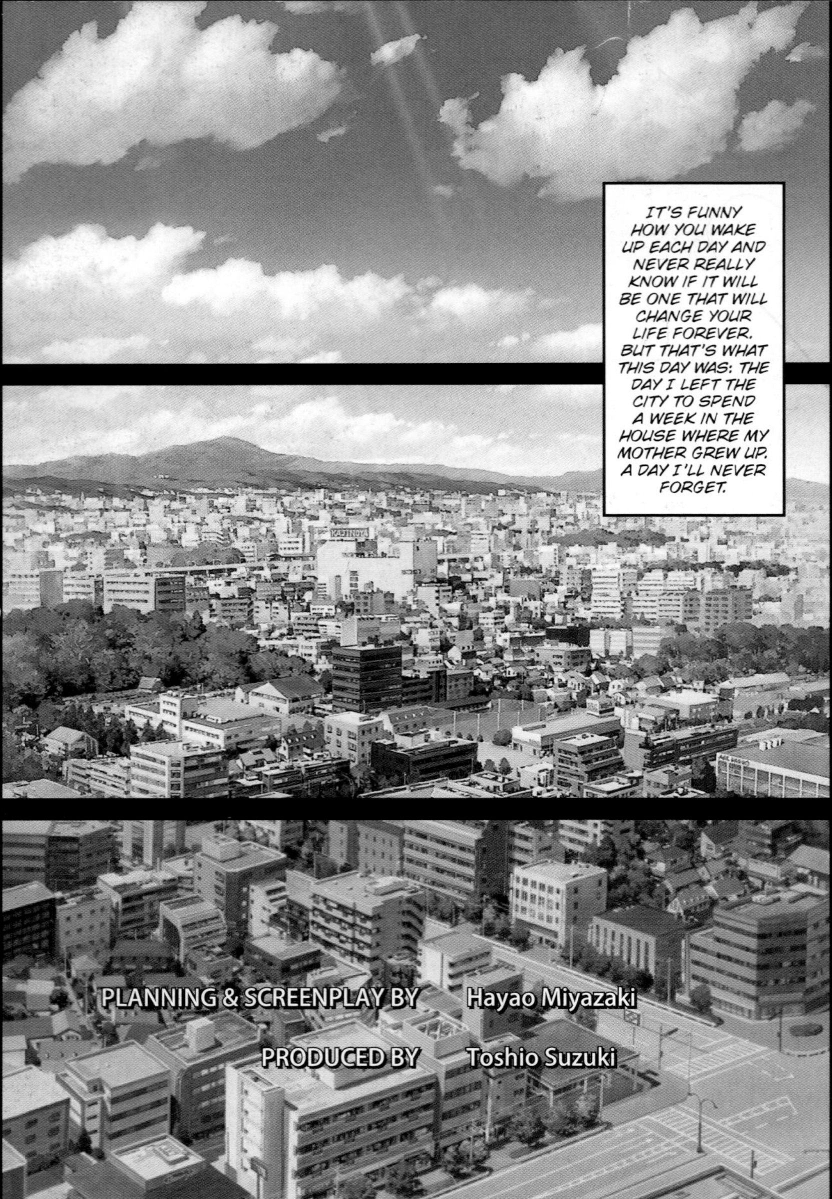
IT'S FUNNY HOW YOU WAKE UP EACH DAY AND NEVER REALLY KNOW IF IT WILL BE ONE THAT WILL CHANGE YOUR LIFE FOREVER. BUT THAT'S WHAT THIS DAY WAS: THE DAY I LEFT THE CITY TO SPEND A WEEK IN THE HOUSE WHERE MY MOTHER GREW UP. A DAY I'LL NEVER FORGET.
PLANNING & SCREENPLAY BY Hayao Miyazaki
PRODUCED BY Toshio Suzuki

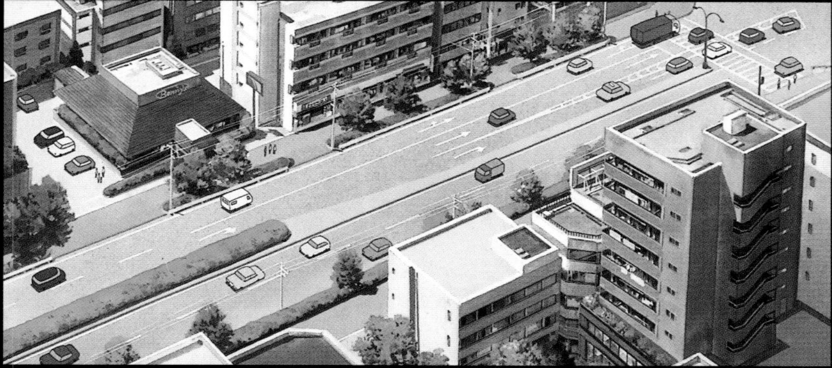

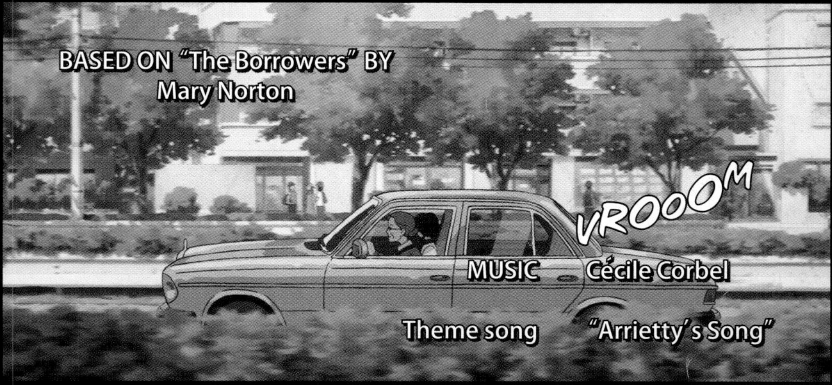
BASED ON "The Borrowers" BY
Mary Norton
VROOOM
MUSIC Cécile Corbel
Theme song "Arrietty's Song"

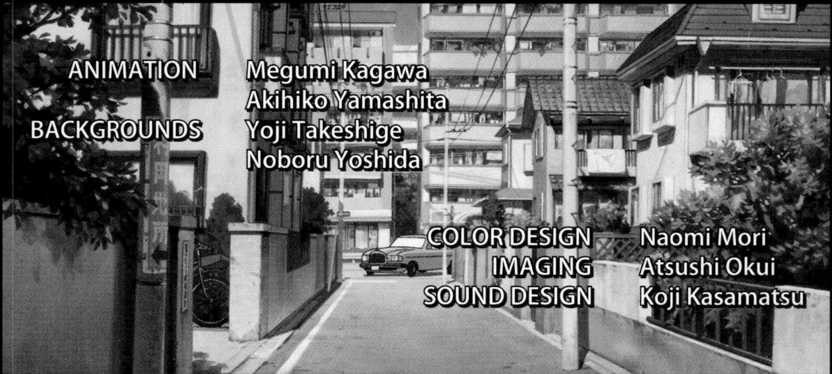
ANIMATION Megumi Kagawa
Akihiko Yamashita
BACKGROUNDS Yoji Takeshige
Noboru Yoshida
COLOR DESIGN Naomi Mori
IMAGING Atsushi Okui
SOUND DESIGN Koji Kasamatsu

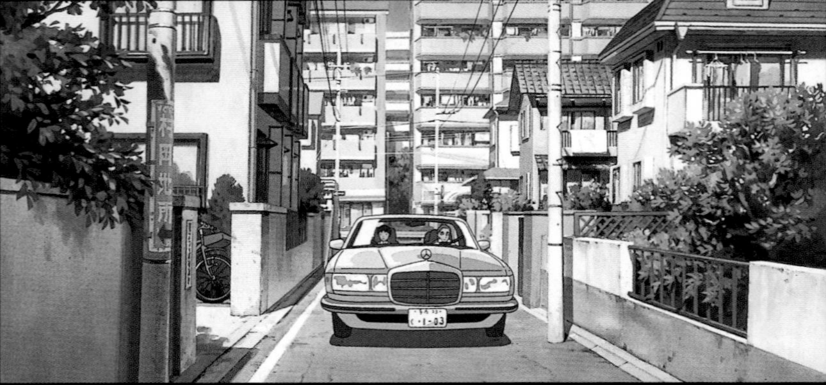

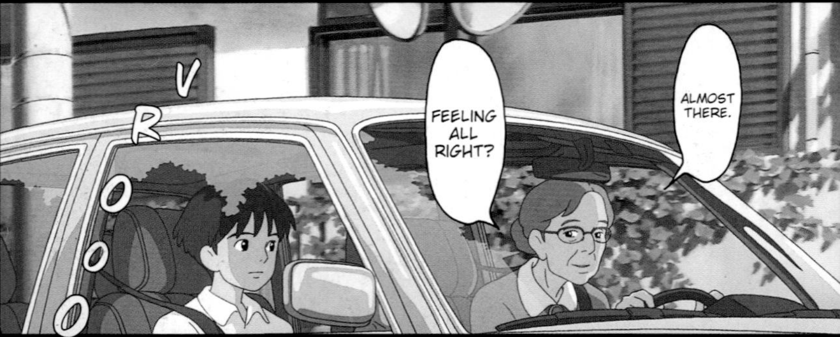
ALMOST THERE.
FEELING ALL RIGHT?
VROOOOM

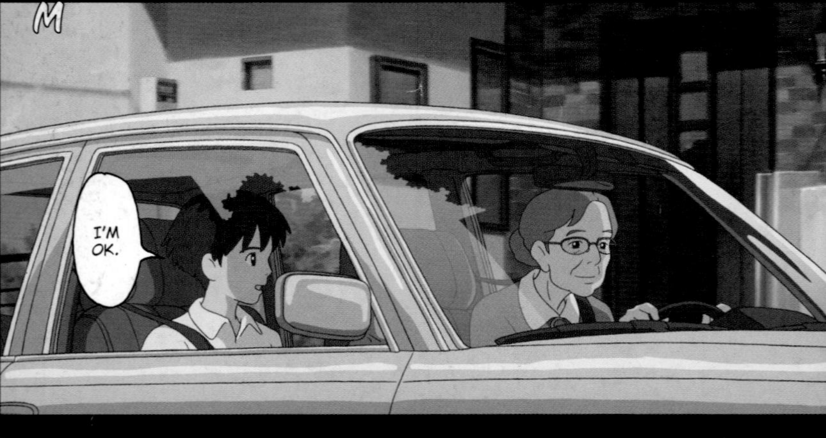
I'M OK.

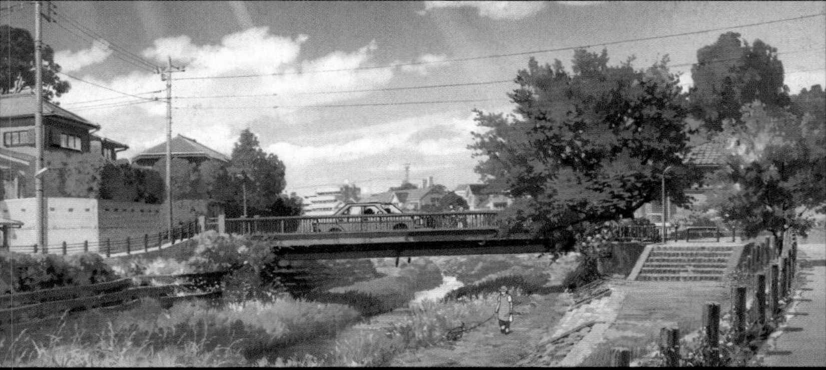

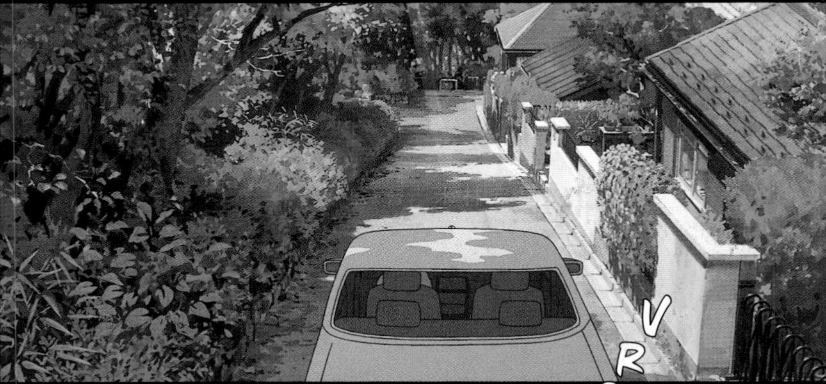

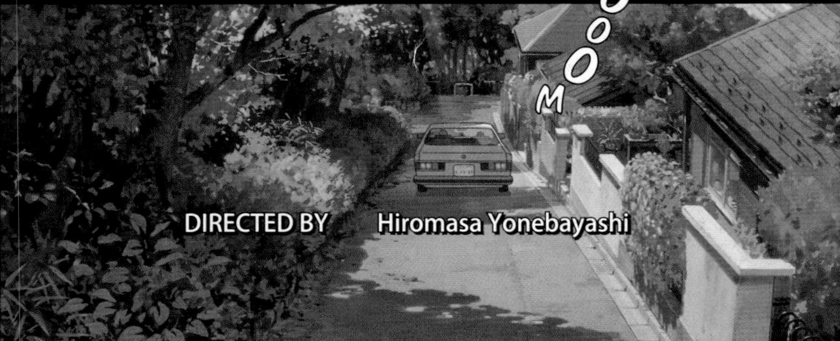
VROOOOM
DIRECTED BY Hiromasa Yonebayashi

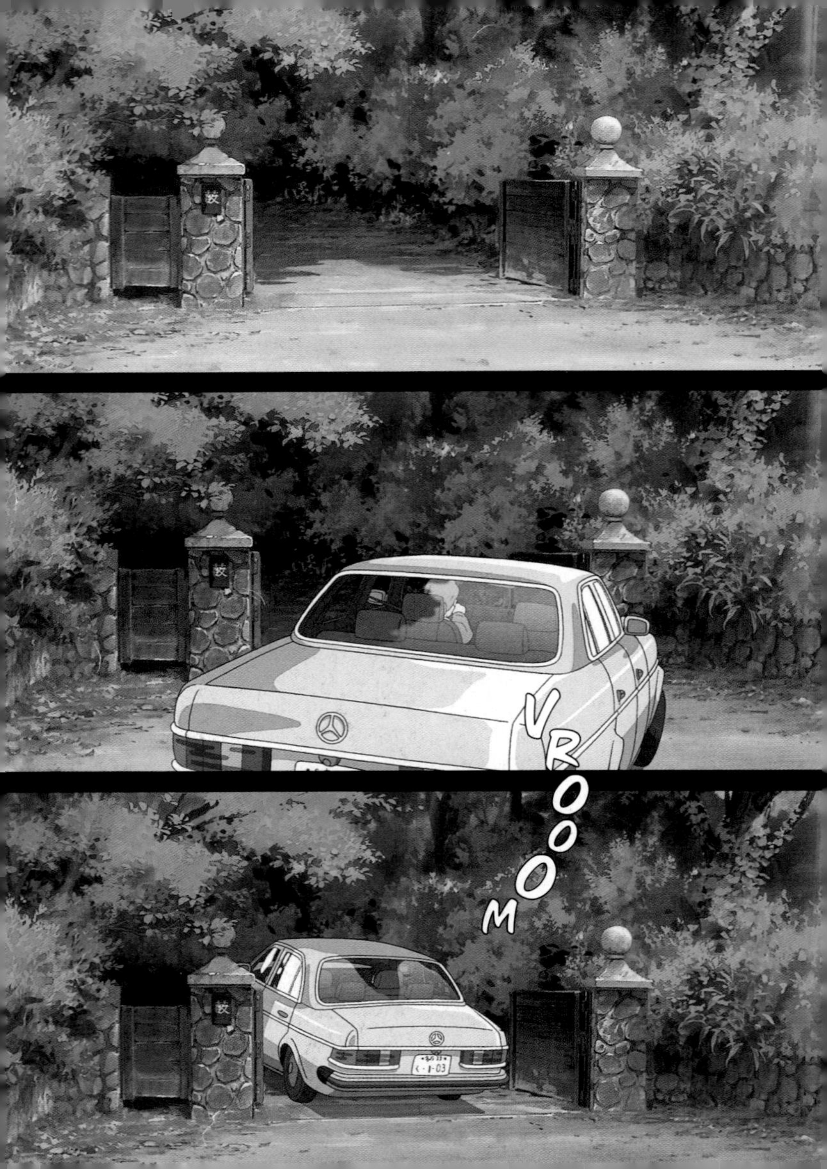
VROOOM

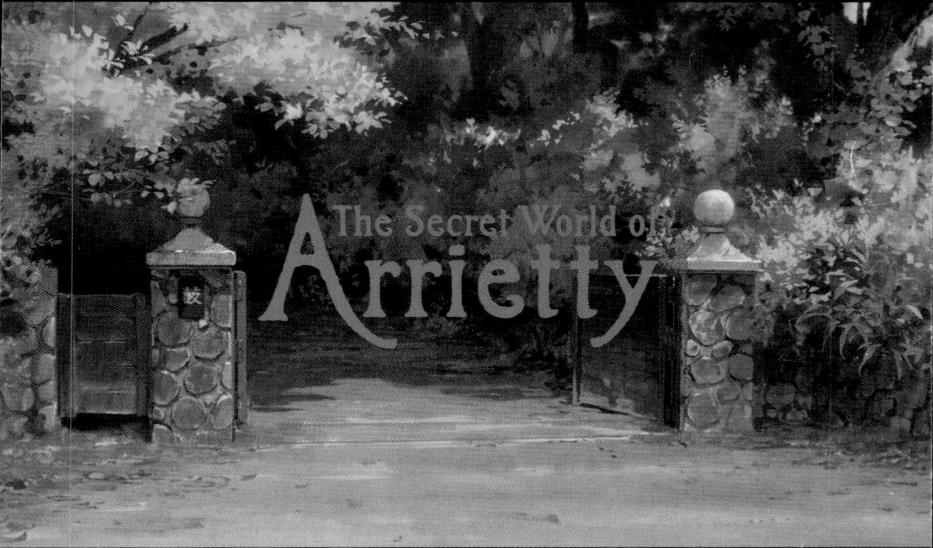
The Secret World of
Arrietty

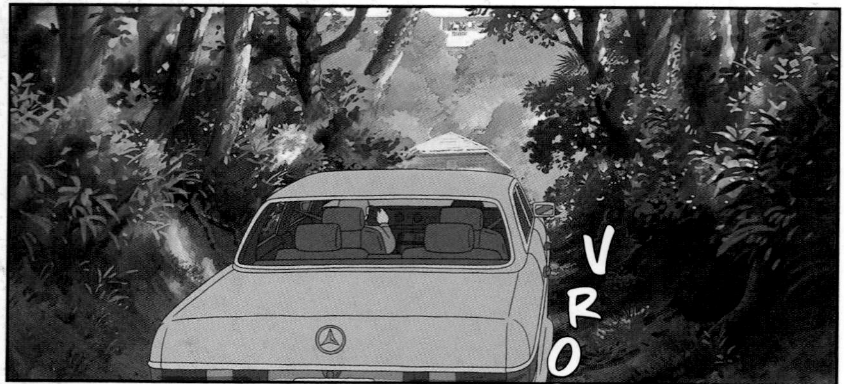
VROOOOM
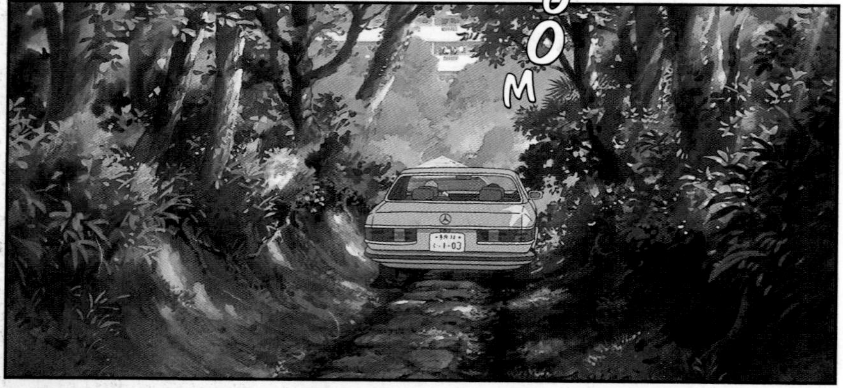
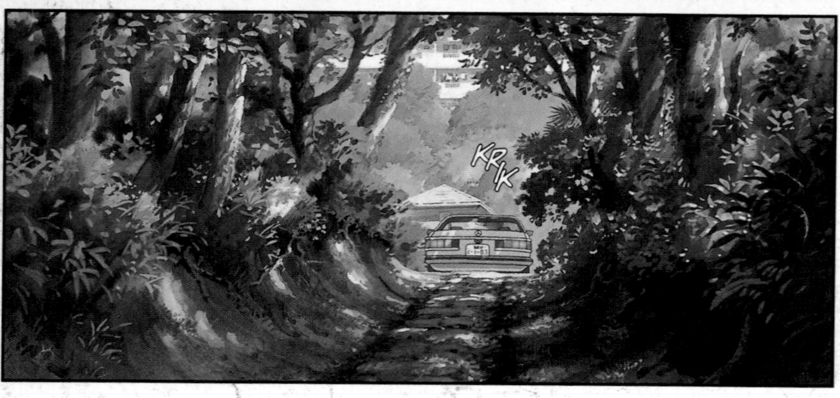
KRIK

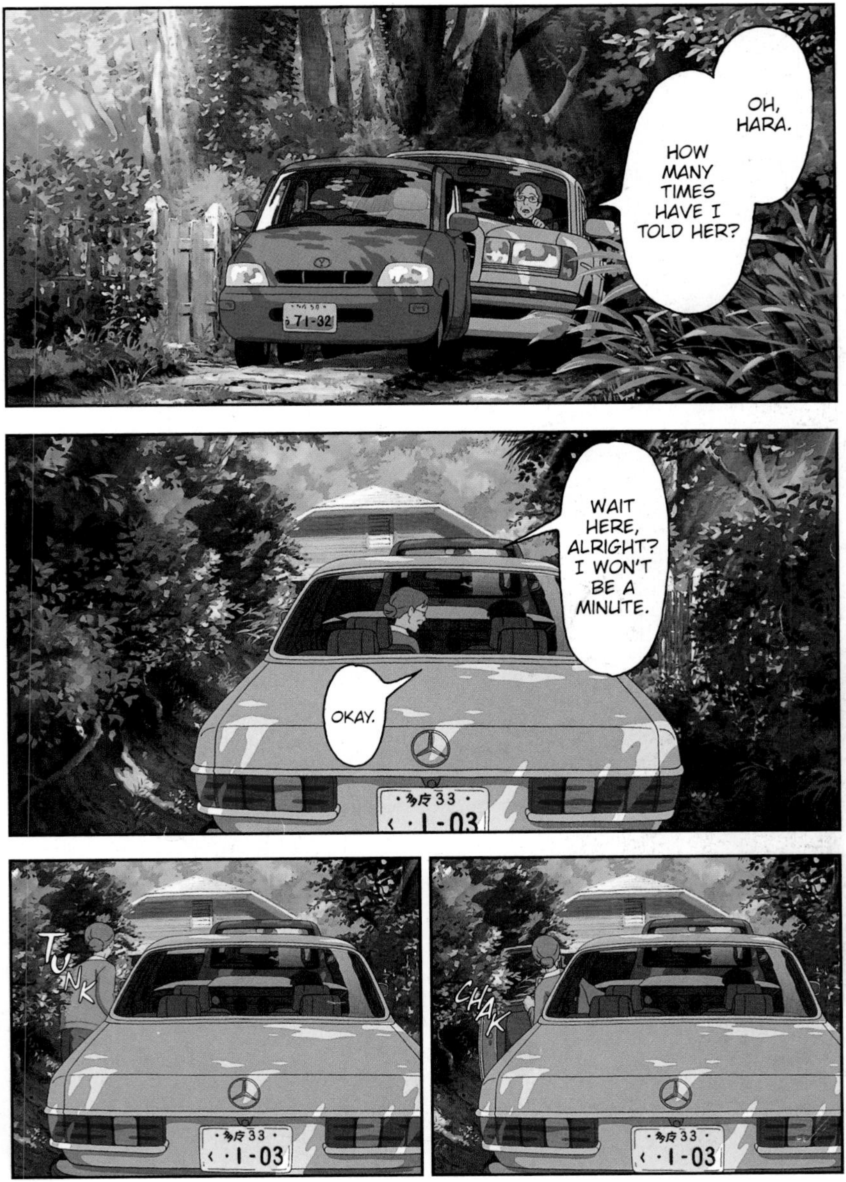
OH, HARA.
HOW MANY TIMES HAVE I TOLD HER?
WAIT HERE, ALRIGHT? I WON'T BE A MINUTE.
OKAY.
CHAK
TUNK

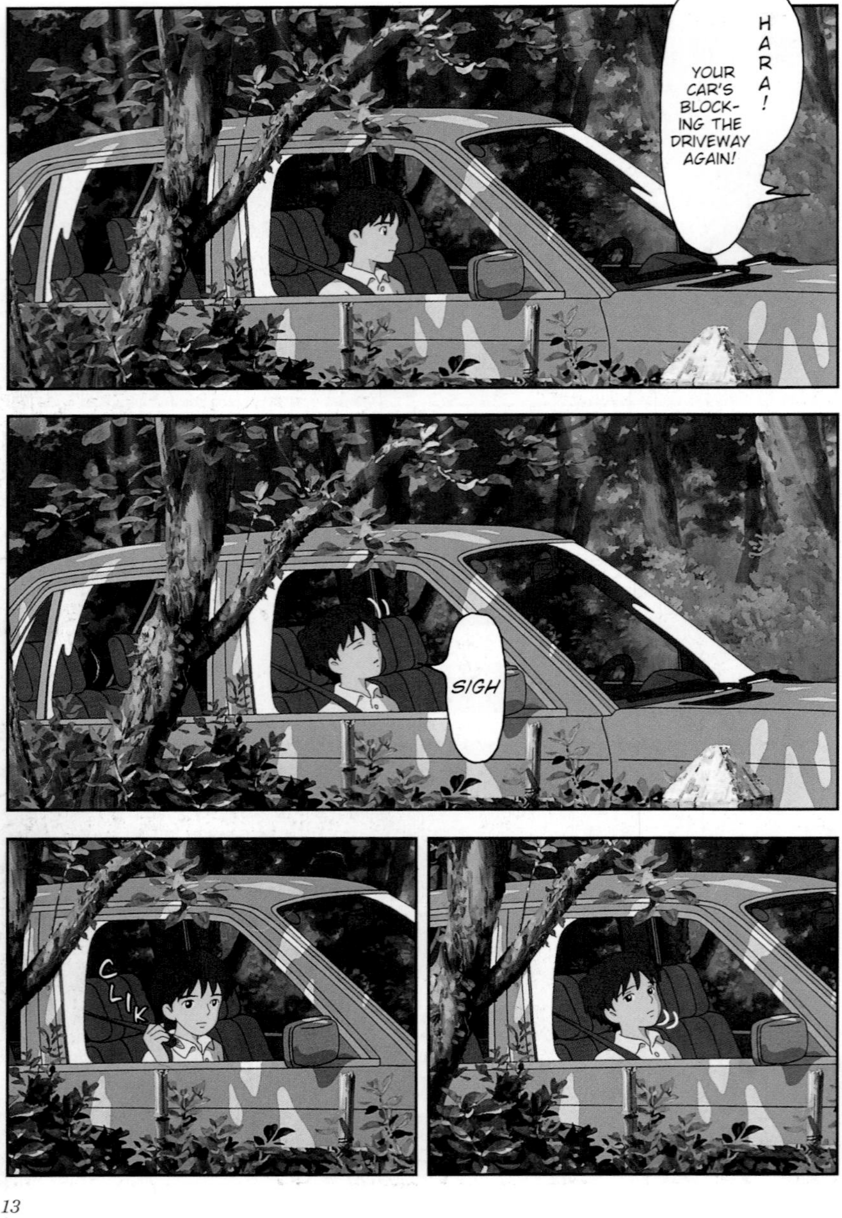
HARA!
YOUR CAR'S BLOCK-ING THE DRIVEWAY AGAIN!
SIGH
CLIK

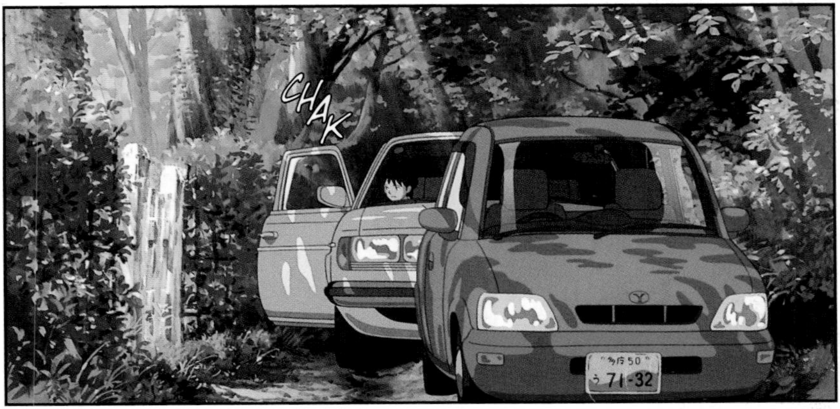
CHAK

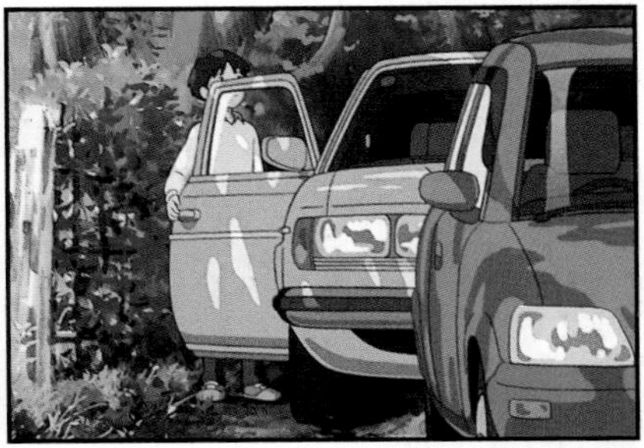

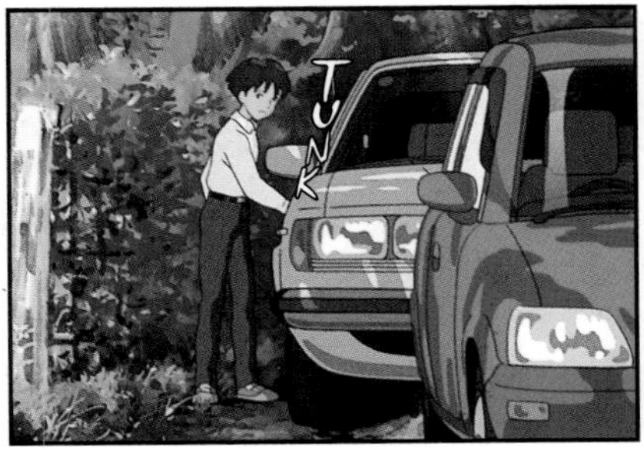
TUNK

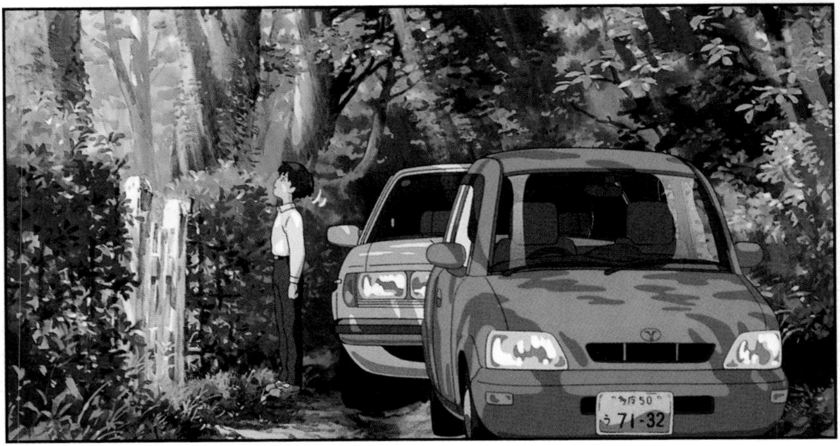

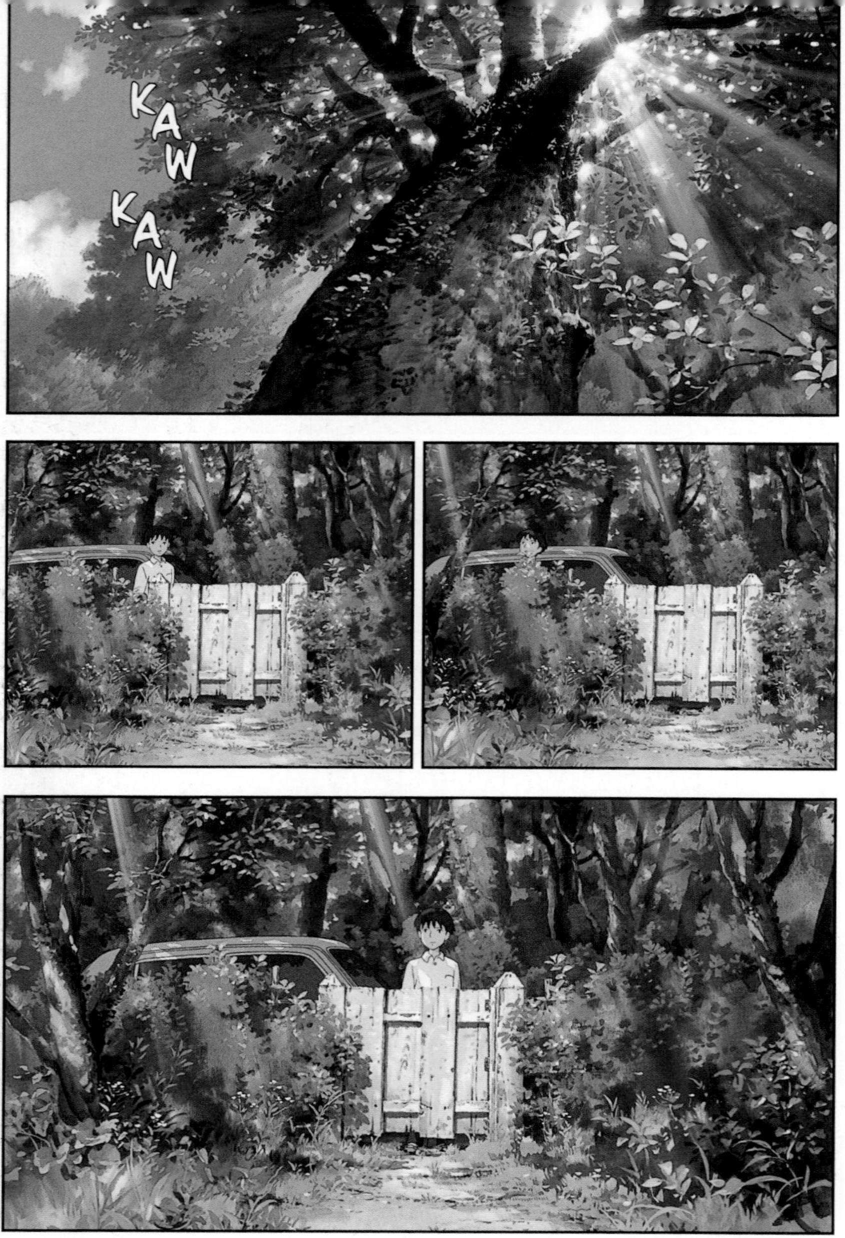
KAW KAW
KAW KAW

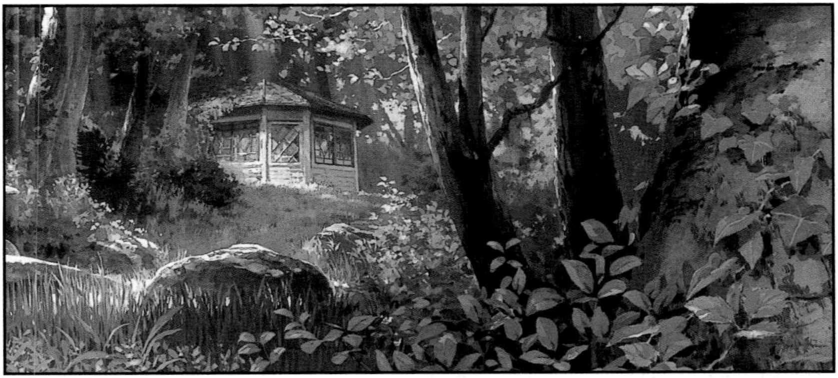
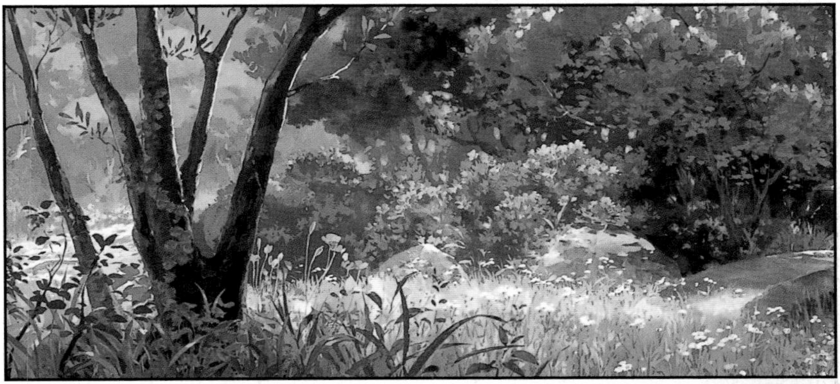
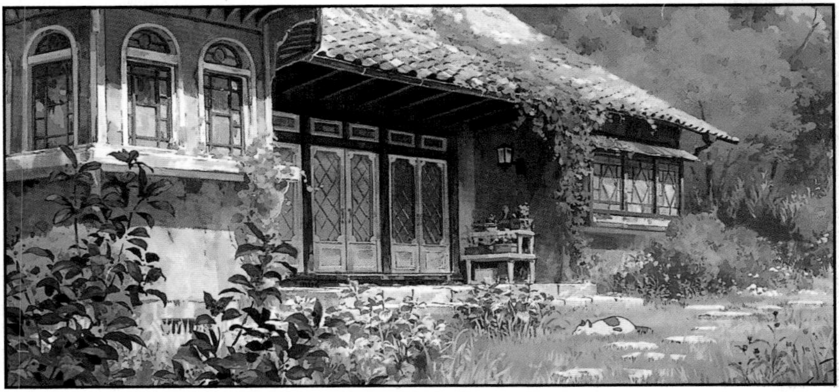

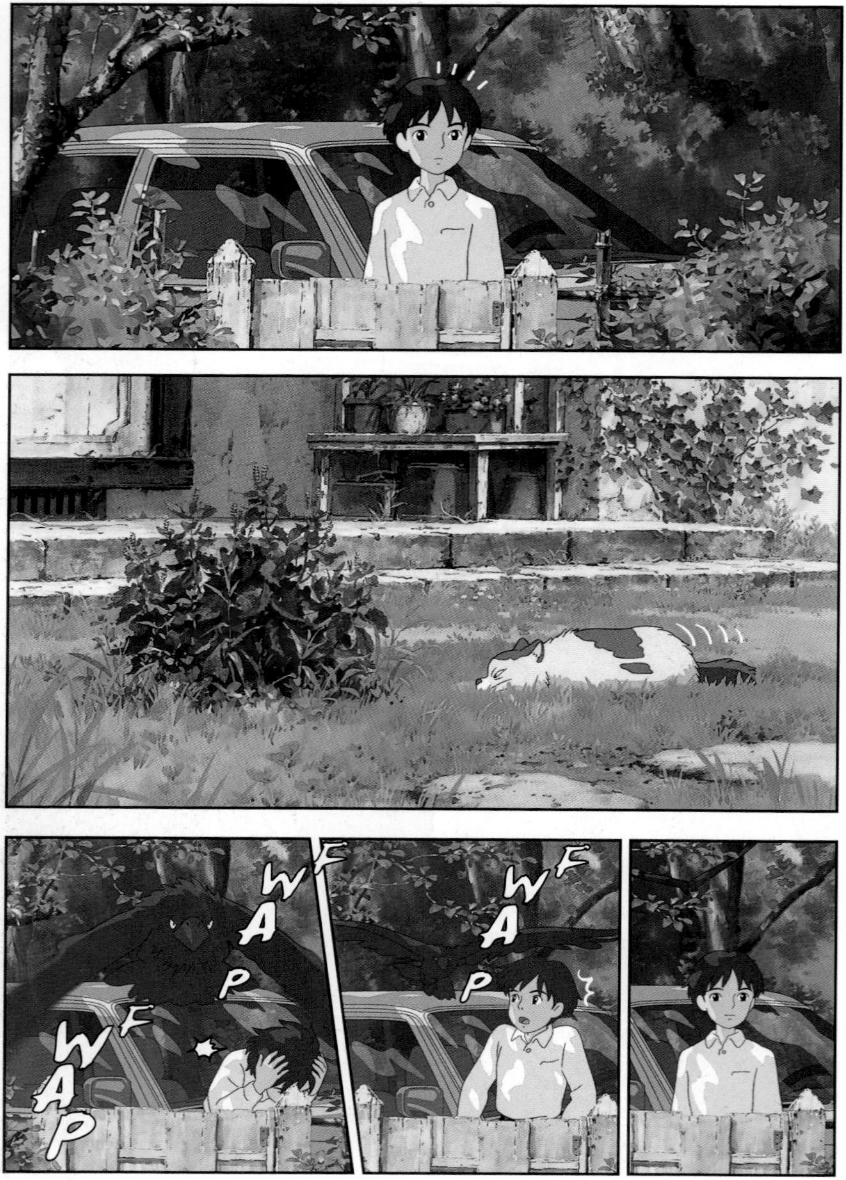
WFAP
WFAP
WFAP

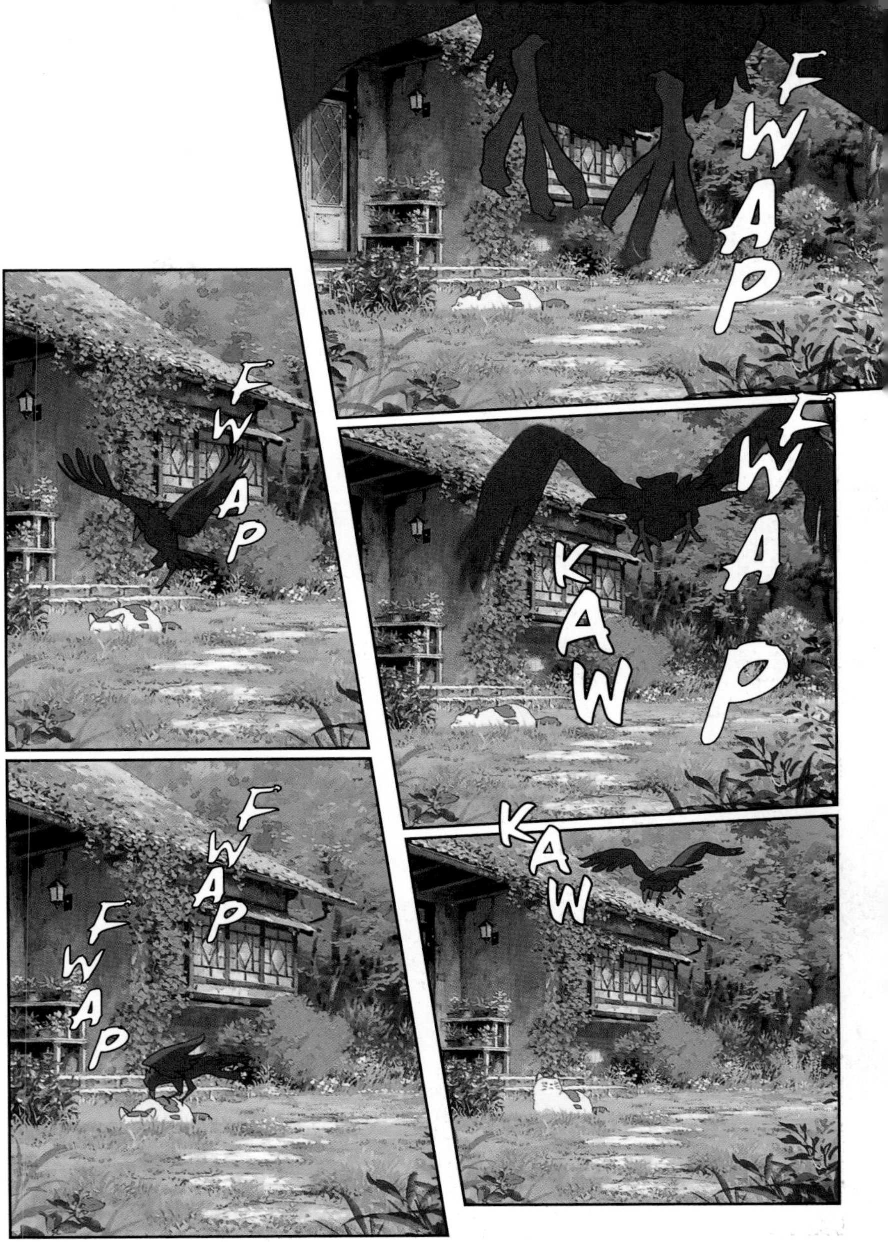
FWAP
FWAP
KAW
FWAP
KAW
FWAP
FWAP

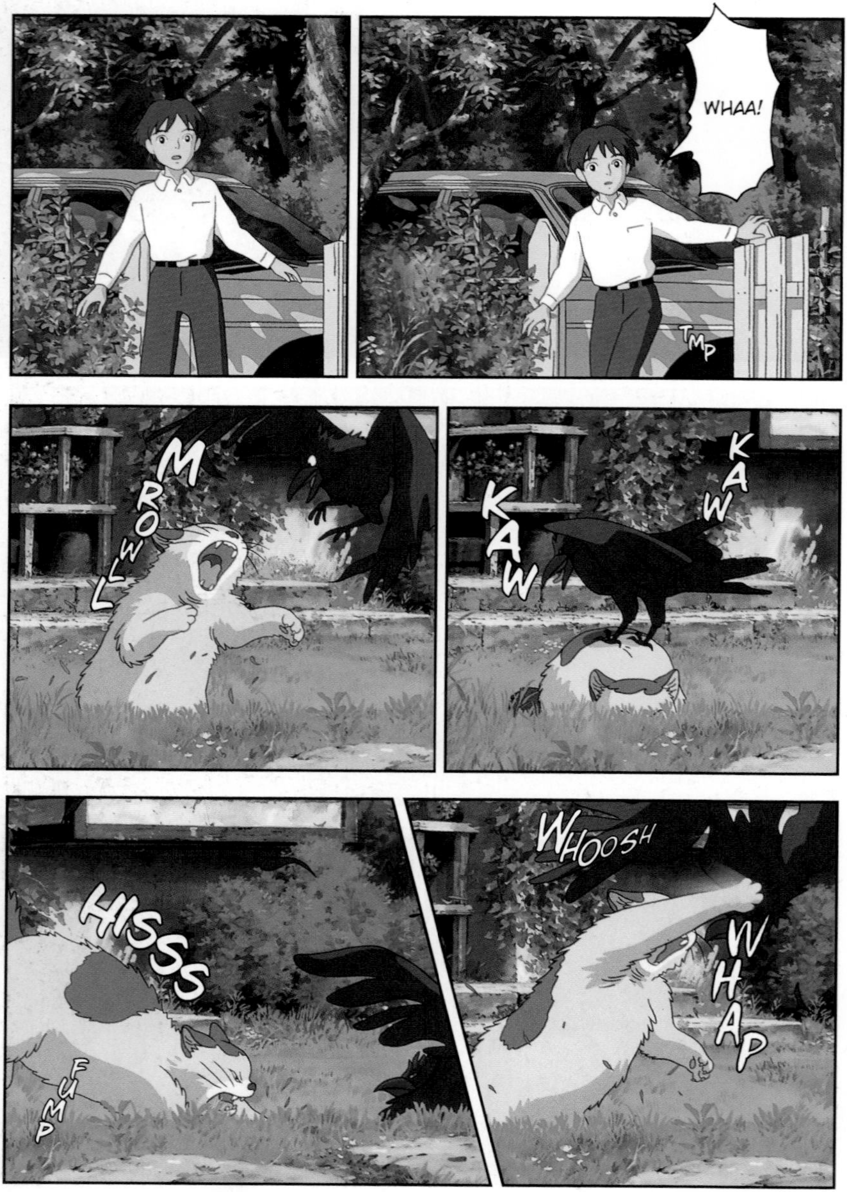
WHAA!
TMP
MROWLL
KAW
KAW
HISSS
FUMP
WHOOSH
WHAP

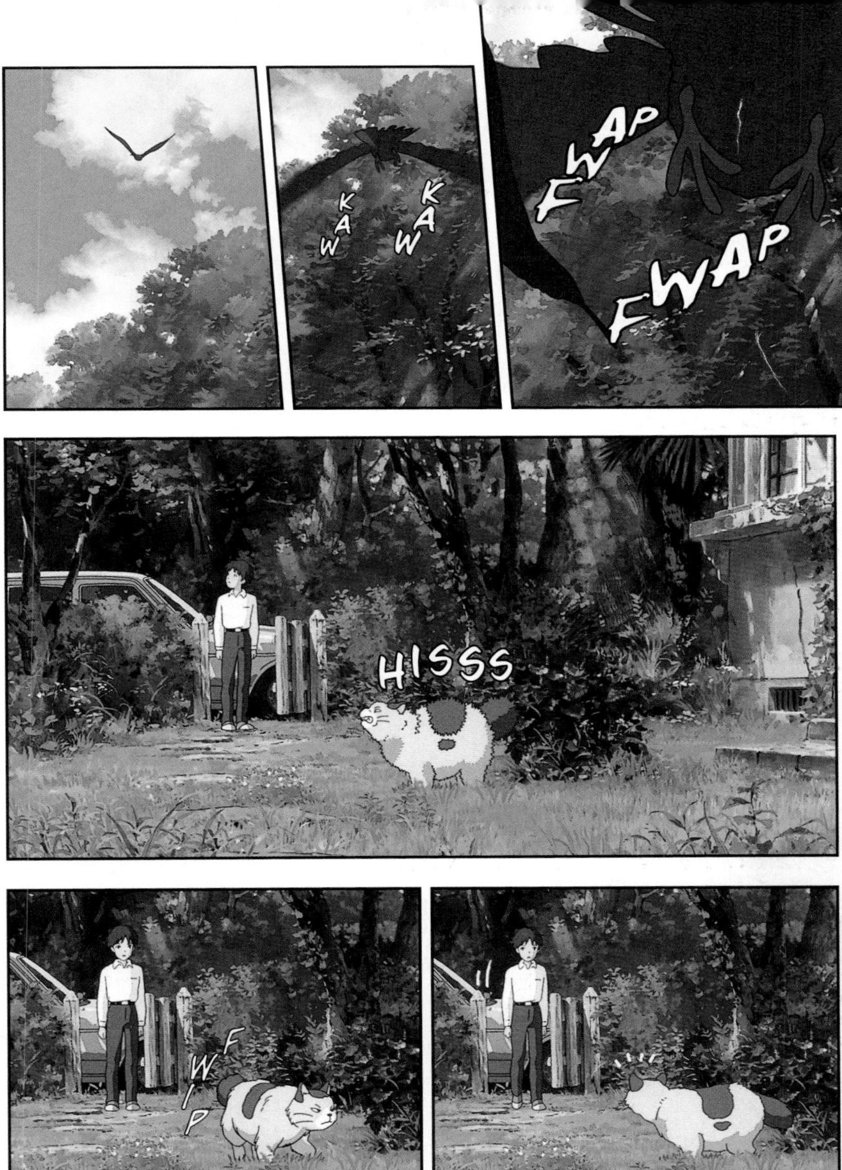
FWAP
FWAP
KAW
KAW
HISSS
FWIP

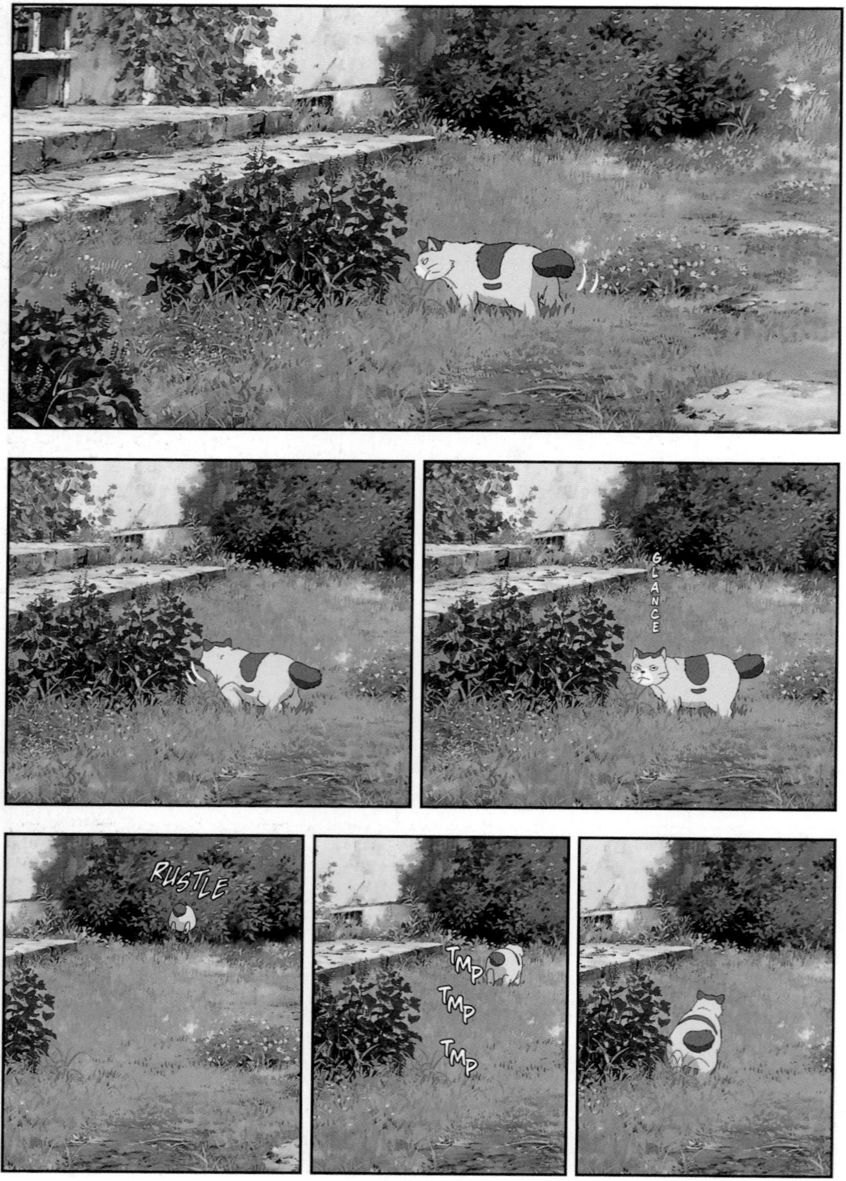
GLANCE
TMP
TMP
TMP
RUSTLE

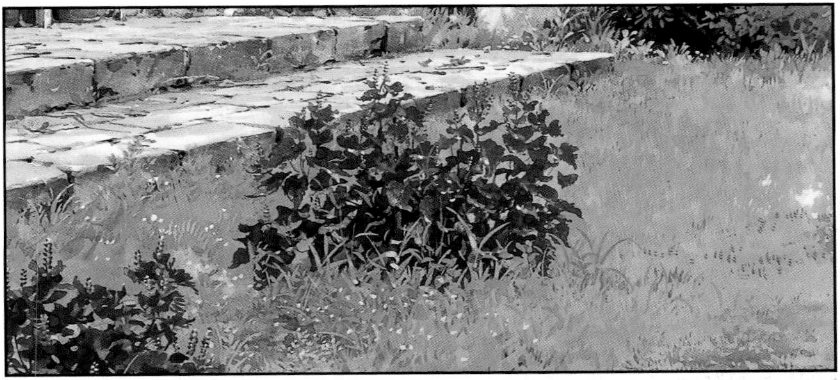
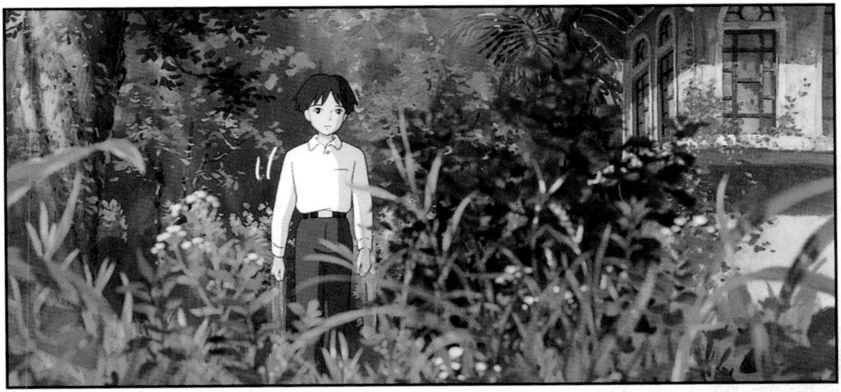
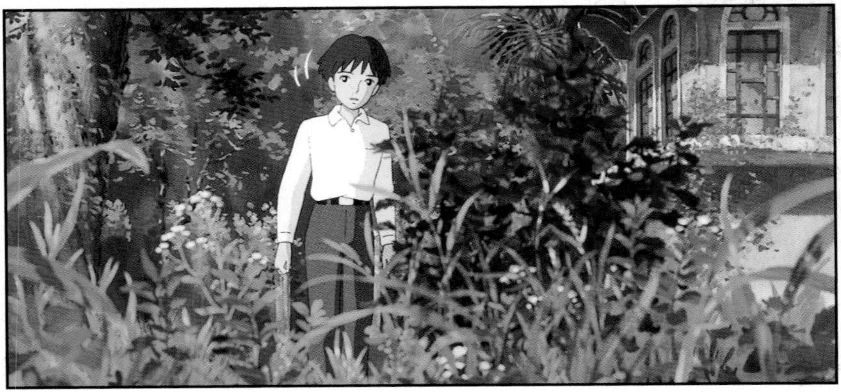

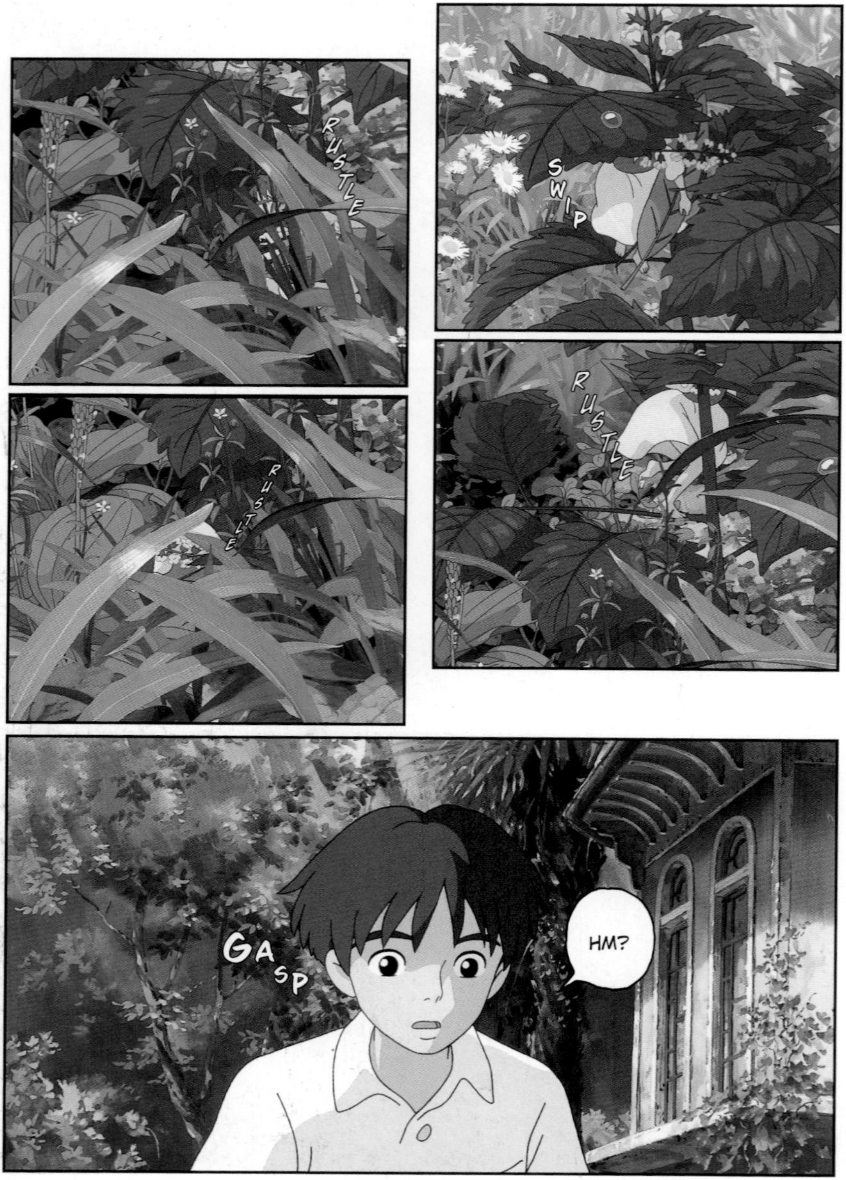
SWIP
RUSTLE
RUSTLE
RUSTLE
HM?
GASP

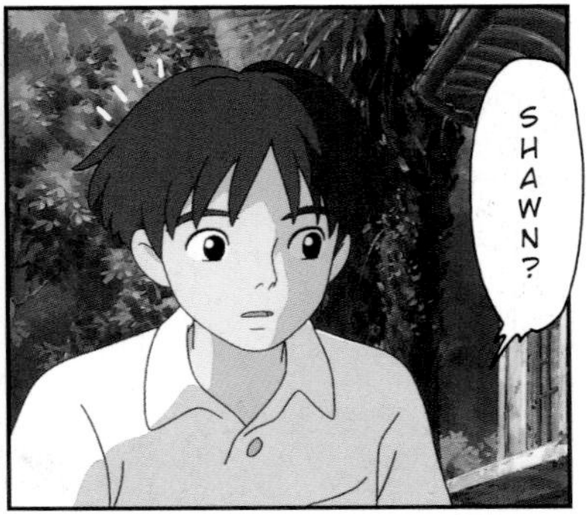
SHAWN?
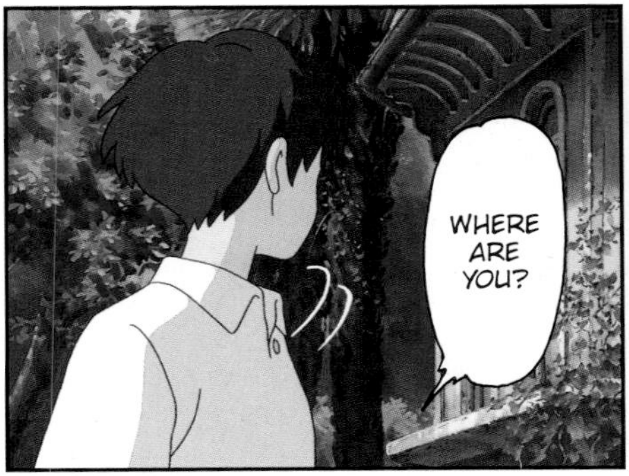
WHERE ARE YOU?
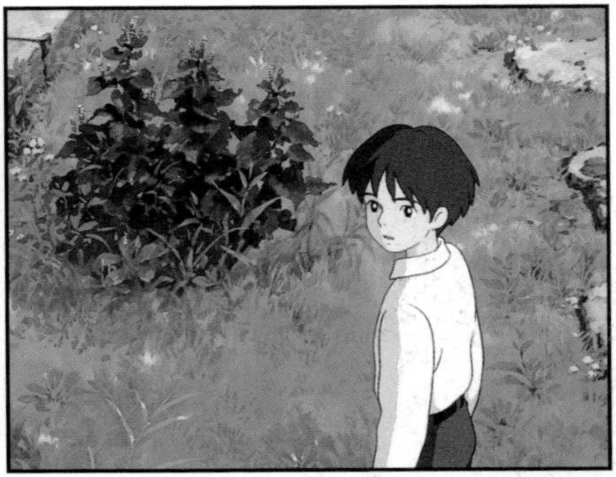
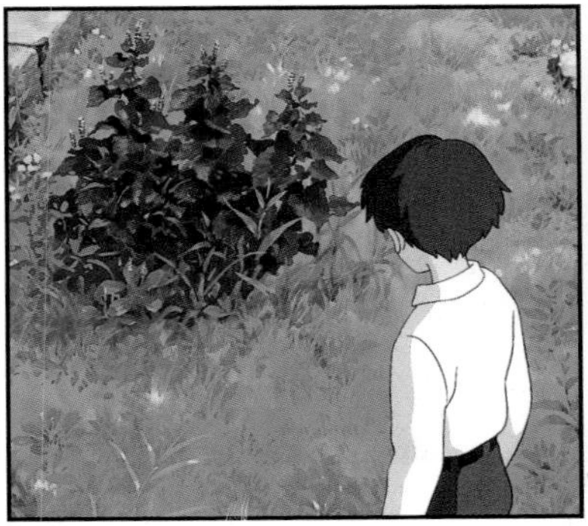
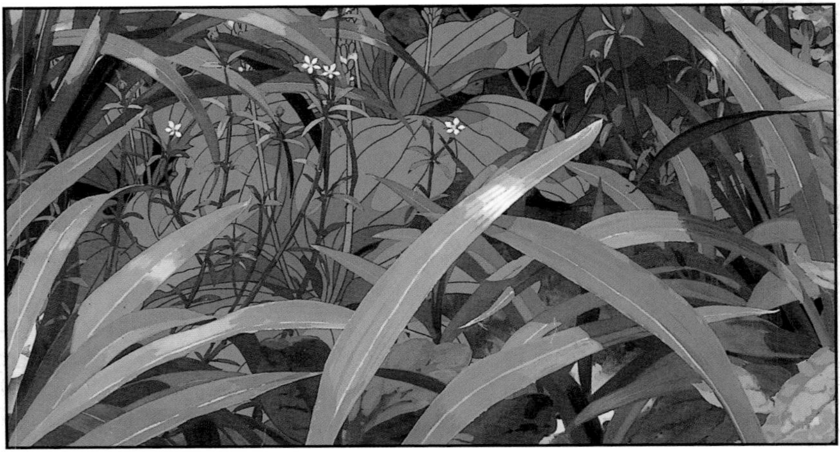

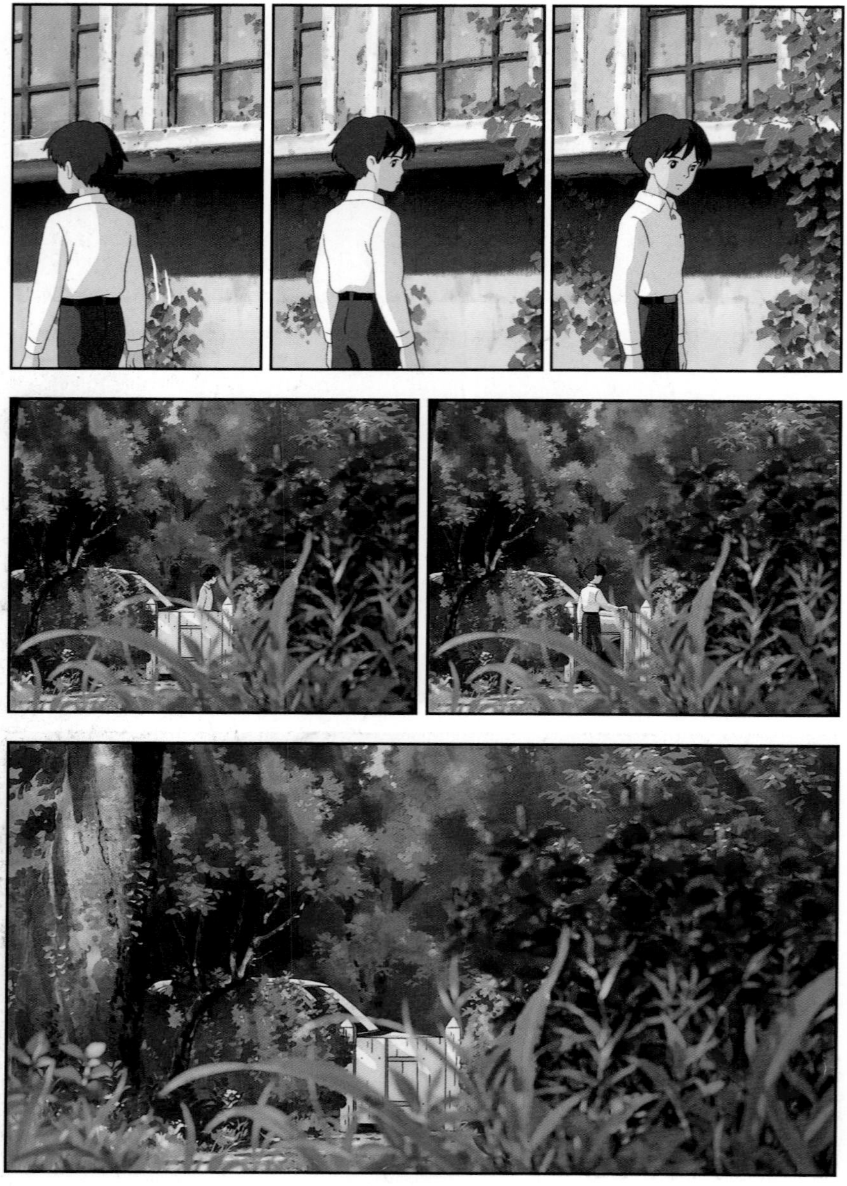

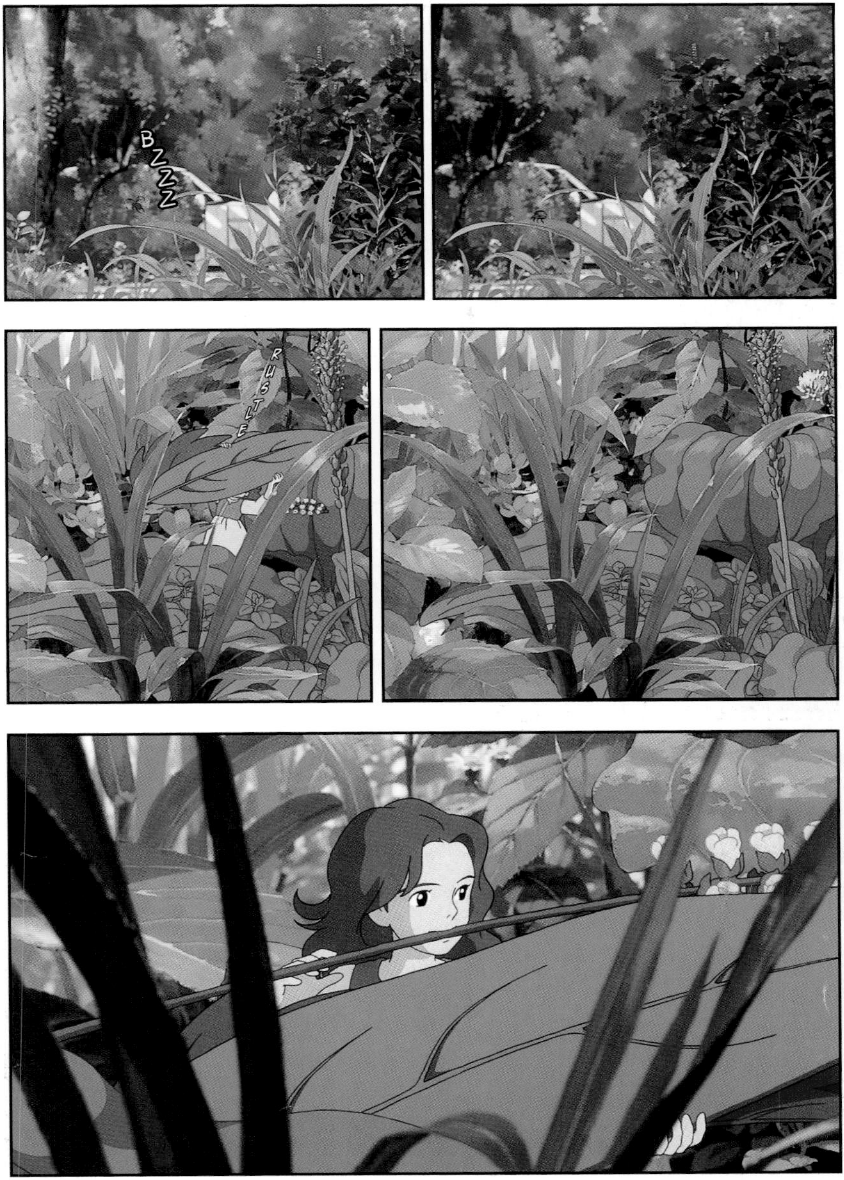
BZZZ
RUSTLE

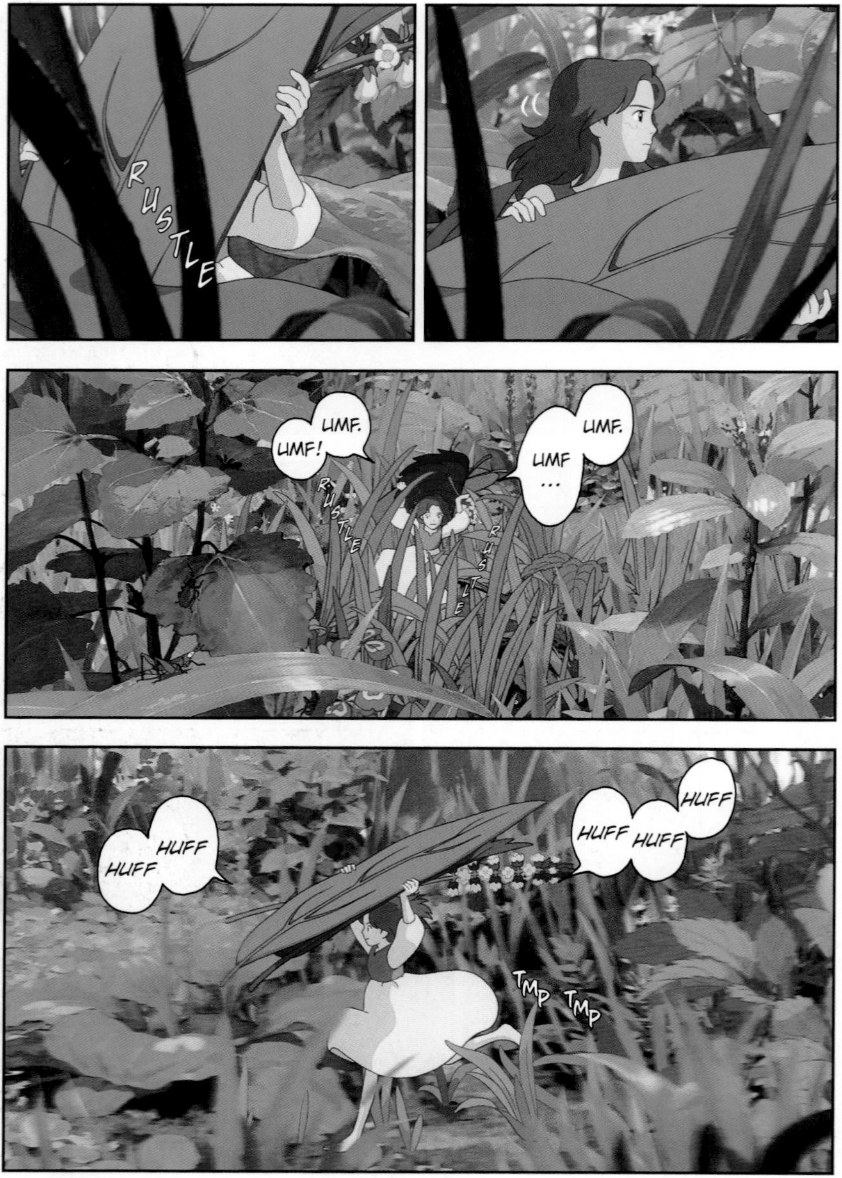
RUSTLE
UMF. UMF ...
RUSTLE
UMF. UMF!
RUSTLE
HUFF HUFF HUFF
HUFF HUFF
TMP TMP

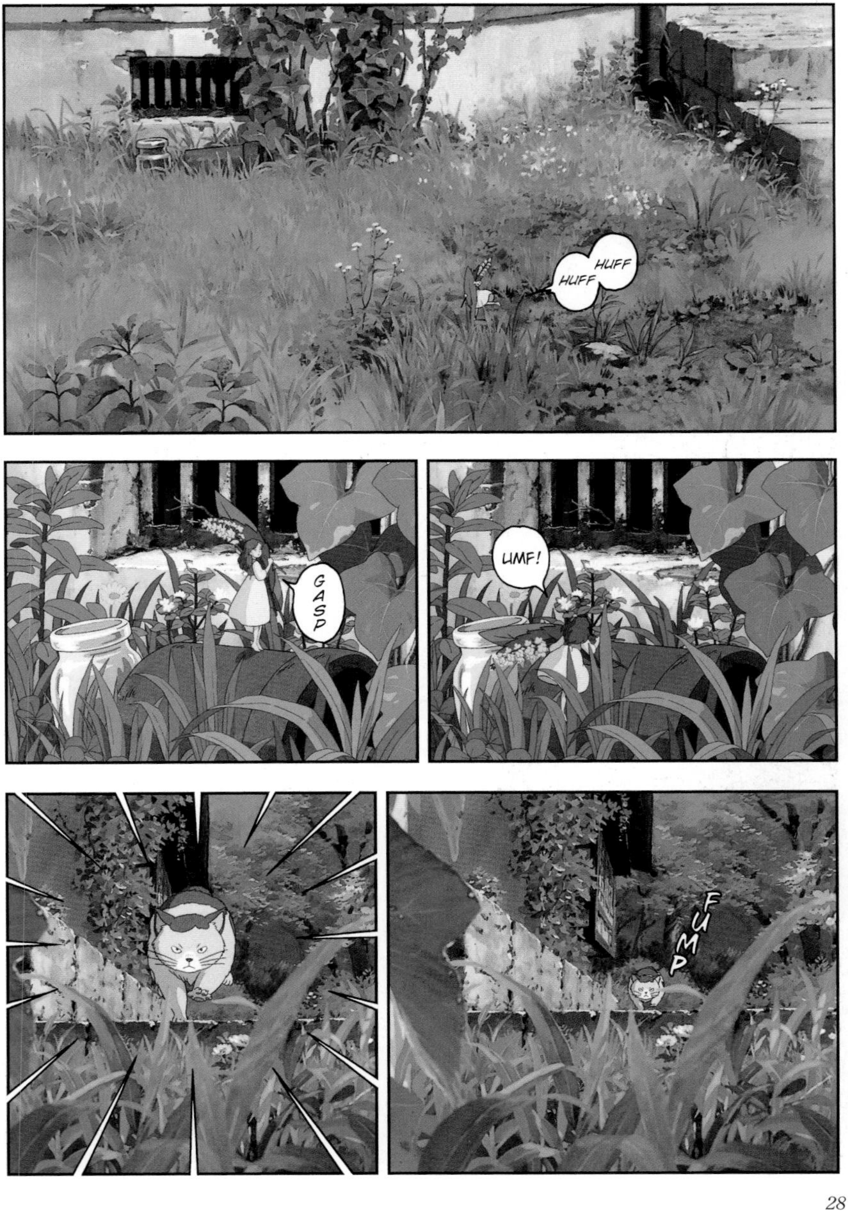
HUFF HUFF
UMF!
GASP
FUMP

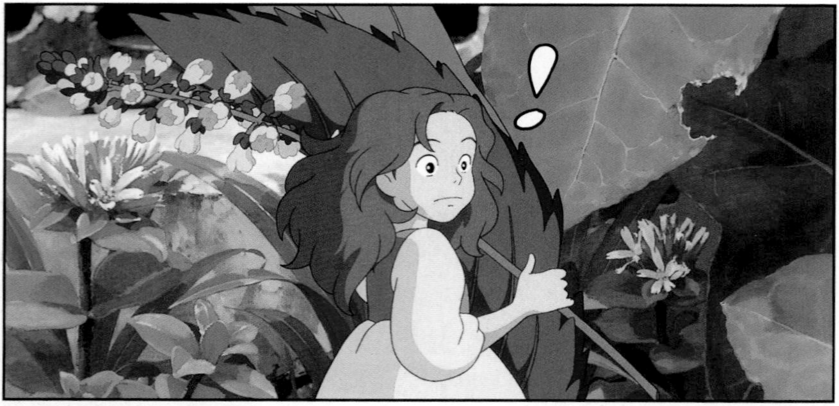
!

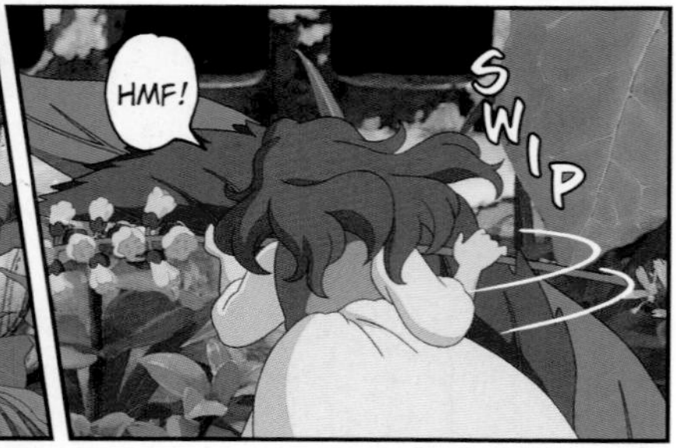
HMF!
SWIP

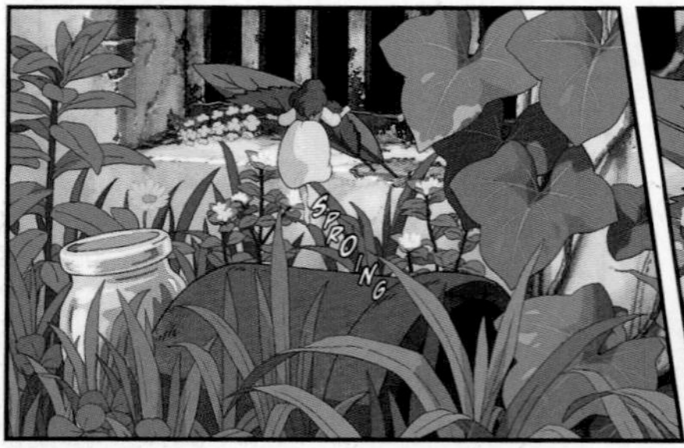
SPROING

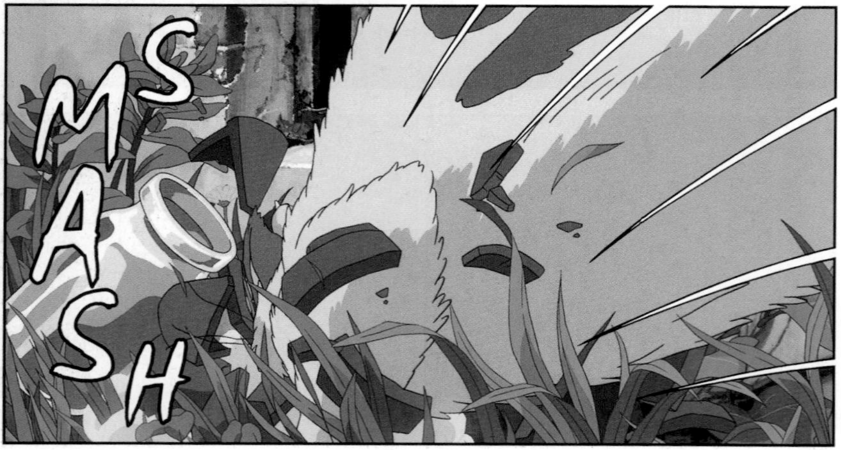
SMASH

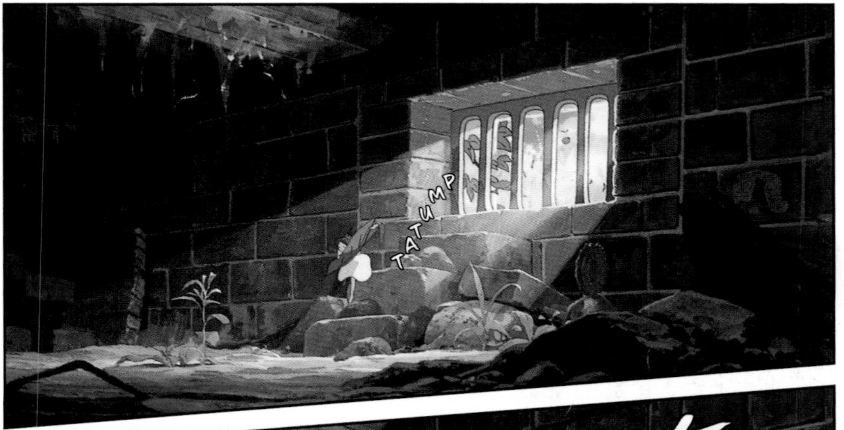
TATUMP

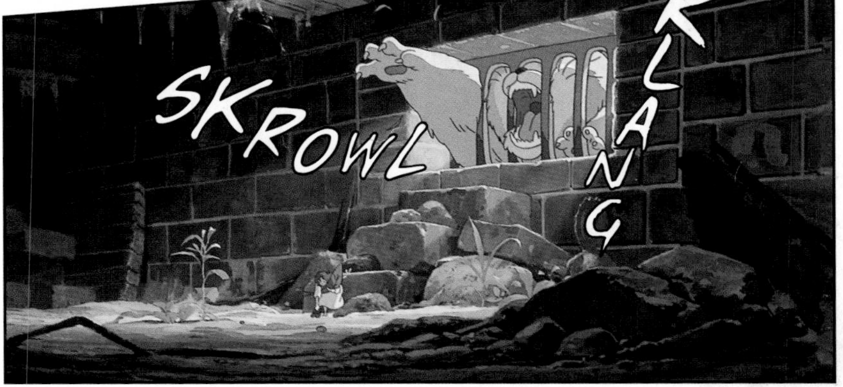
SKROWL
KLANG

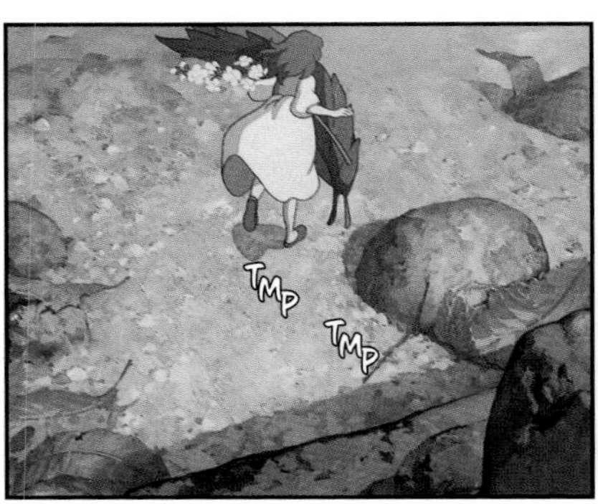
TMP TMP

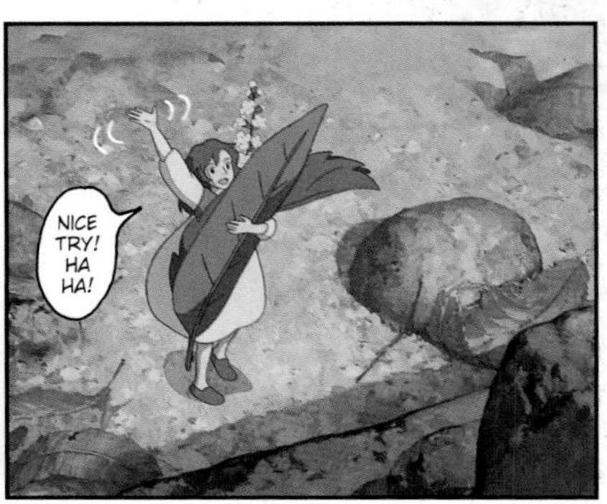
NICE TRY! HA HA!

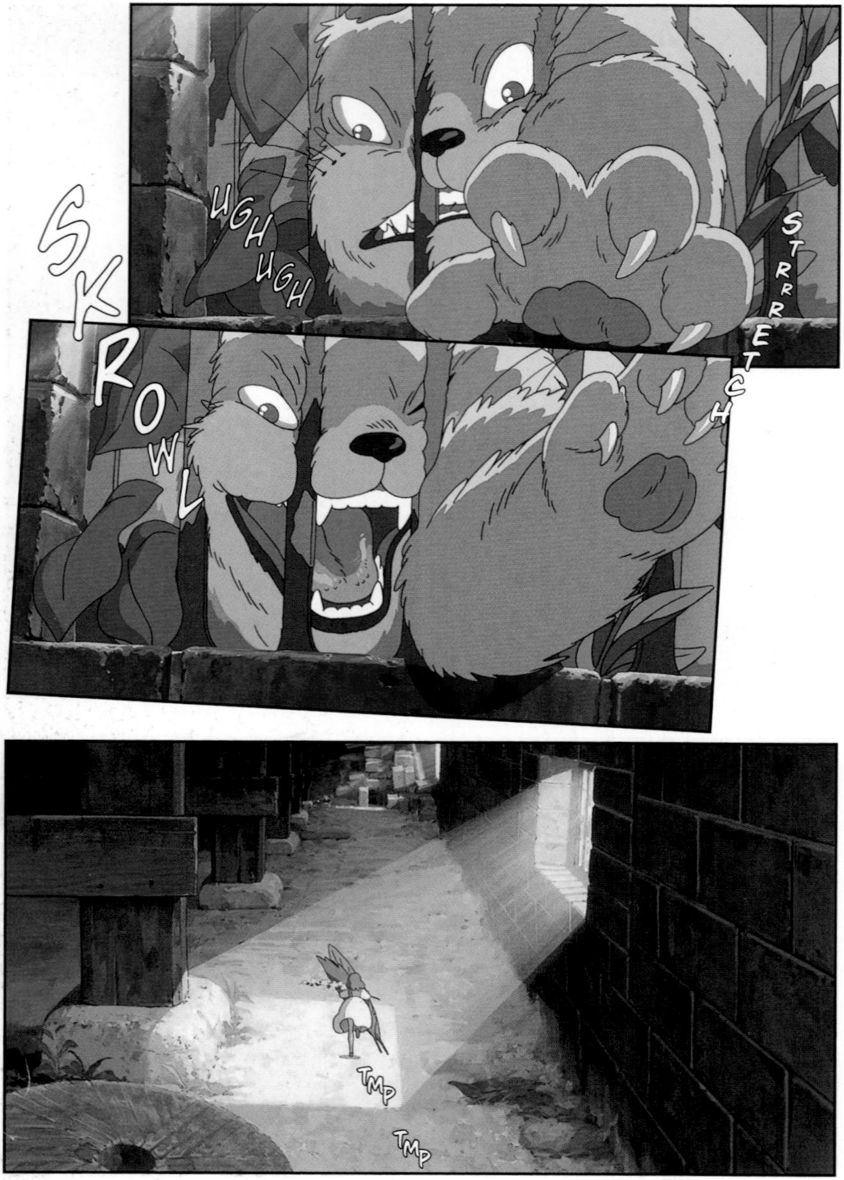
STRRRETCH
UGH UGH UGH
SKROWL
TMP
TMP

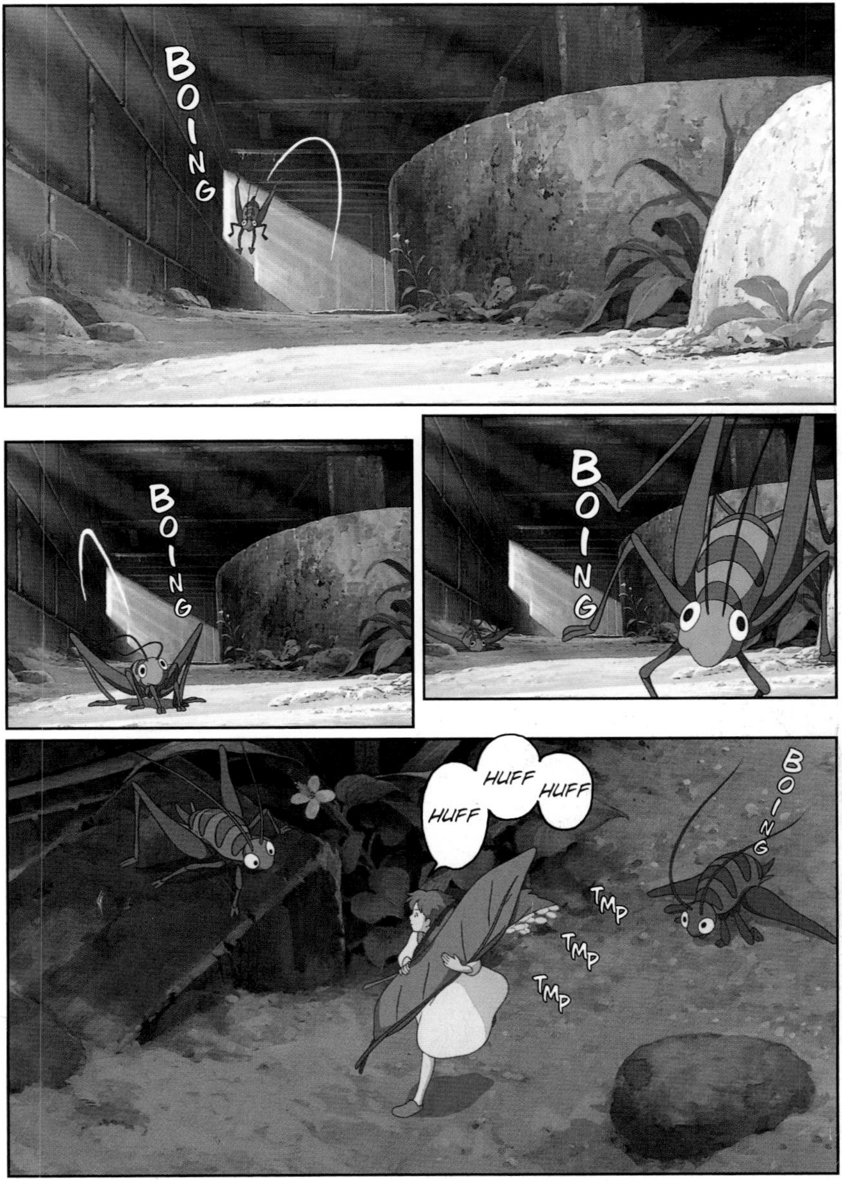
BOING
BOING
BOING
BOING
HUFF HUFF HUFF
TMP TMP TMP

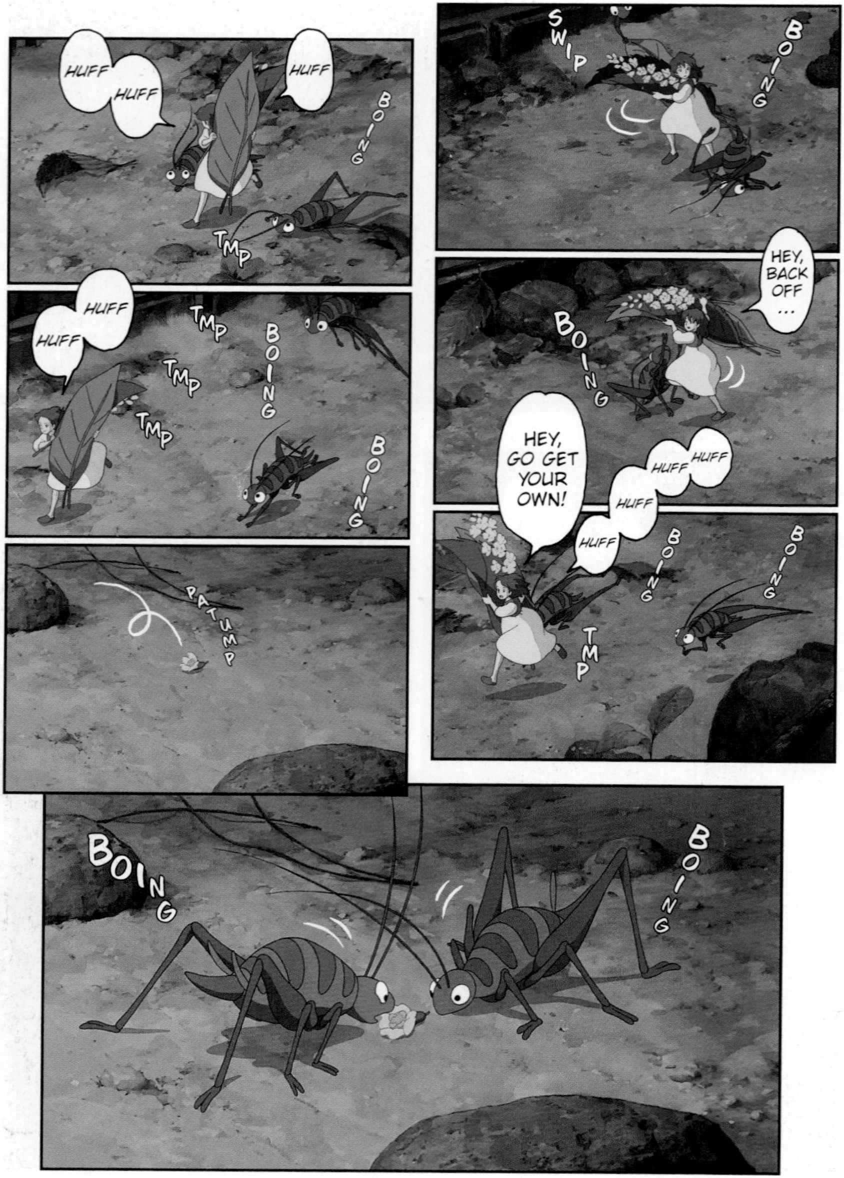
SWIP
BOING
HUFF
HUFF
HUFF
BOING
TMP
HEY, BACK OFF...
BOING
HUFF
HUFF
TMP
BOING
TMP
TMP
BOING
HEY, GO GET YOUR OWN!
HUFF
HUFF
HUFF
HUFF
BOING
BOING
TMP
PATUMP
BOING
BOING

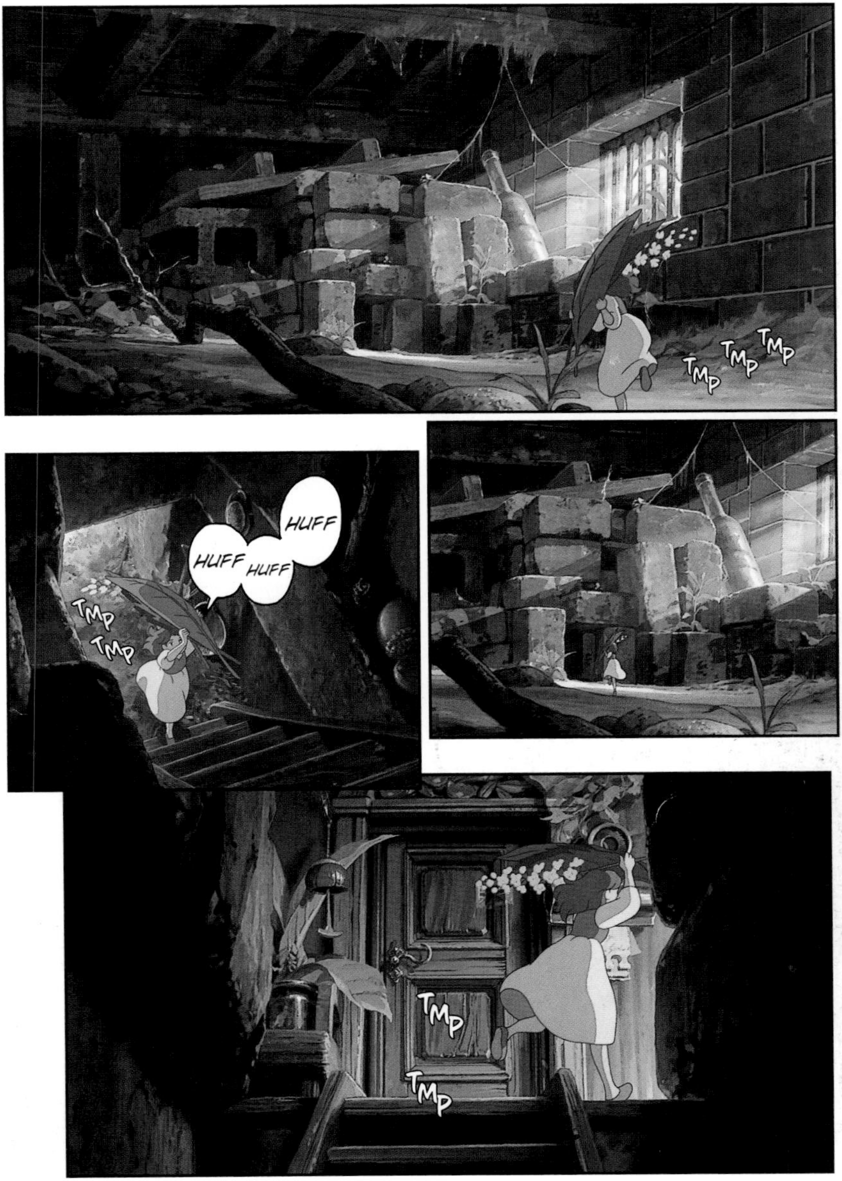
TMP
TMP
TMP
HUFF
HUFF
HUFF
TMP
TMP
TMP
TMP

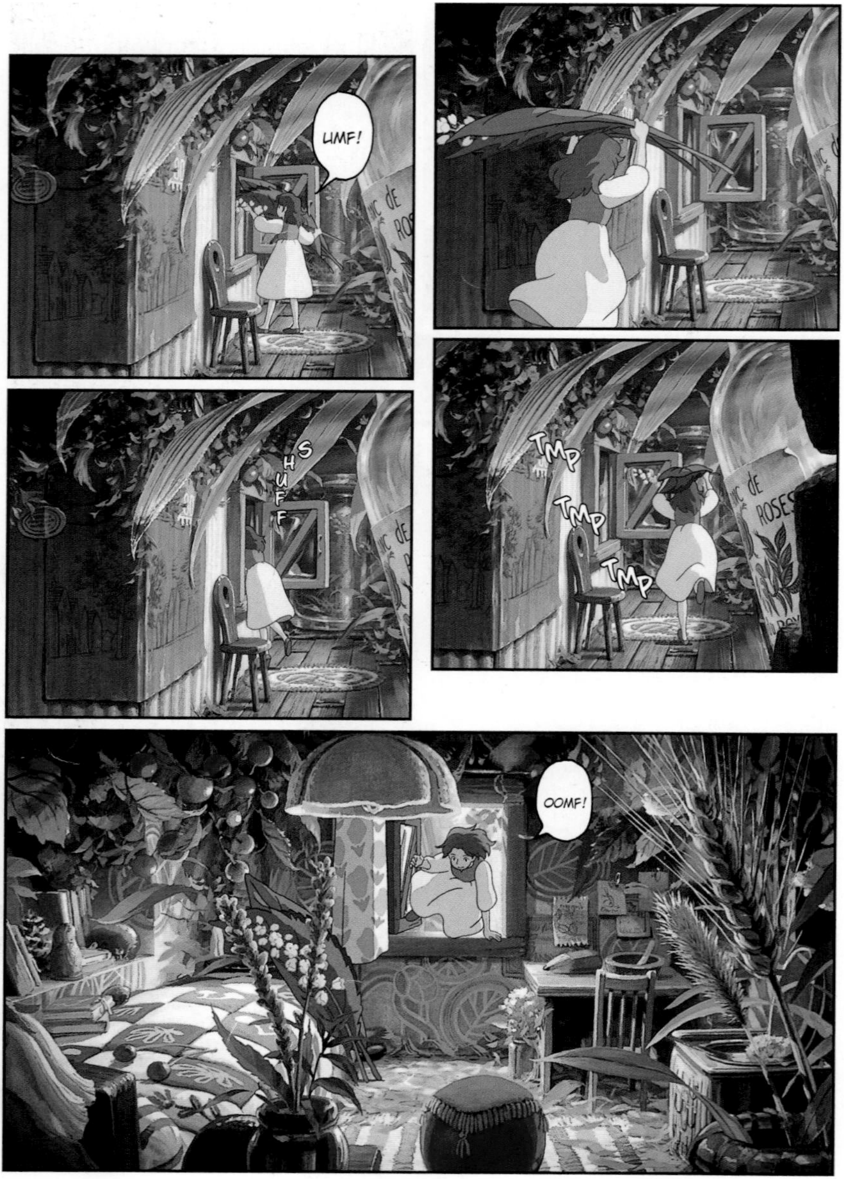
UMF!
TMP
TMP
TMP
SHUFF
OOMF!

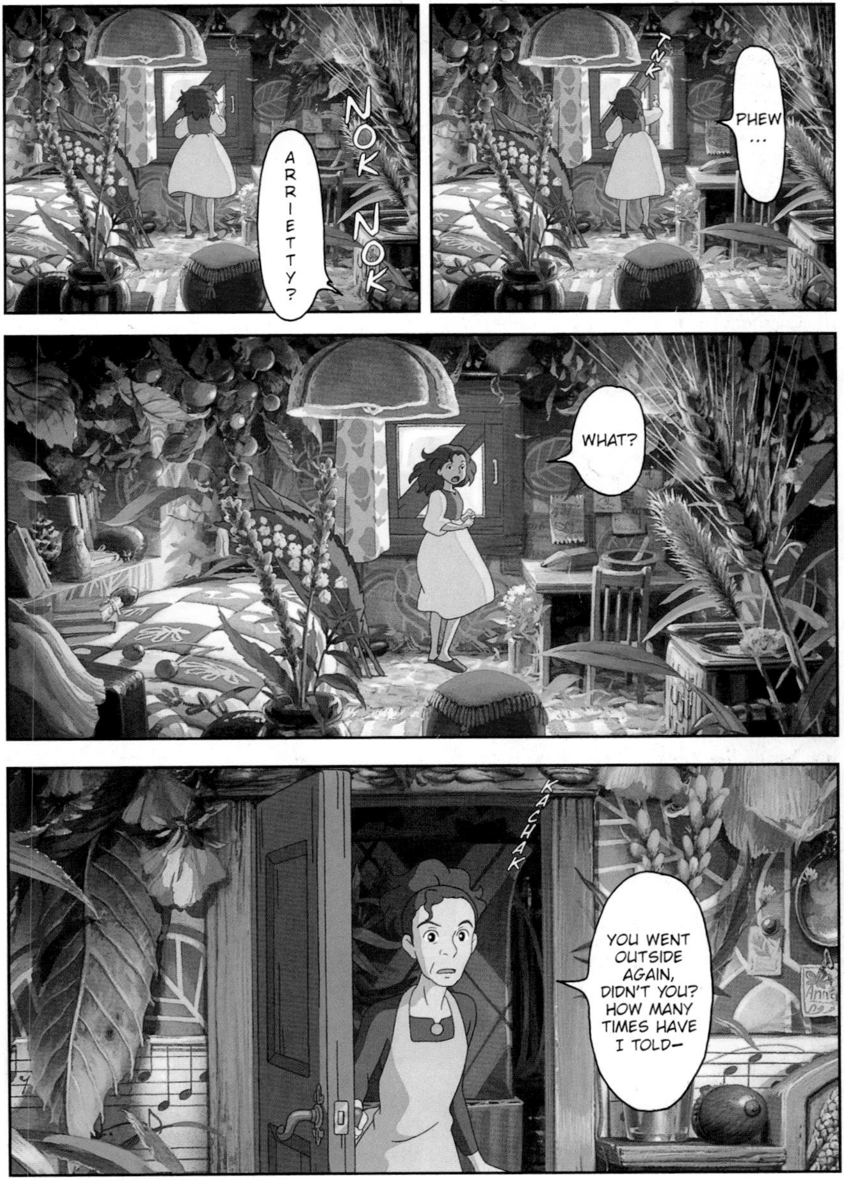
TNK
PHEW...
NOK NOK
ARRIETTY?
WHAT?
KACHAK
YOU WENT OUTSIDE AGAIN, DIDN'T YOU? HOW MANY TIMES HAVE I TOLD—

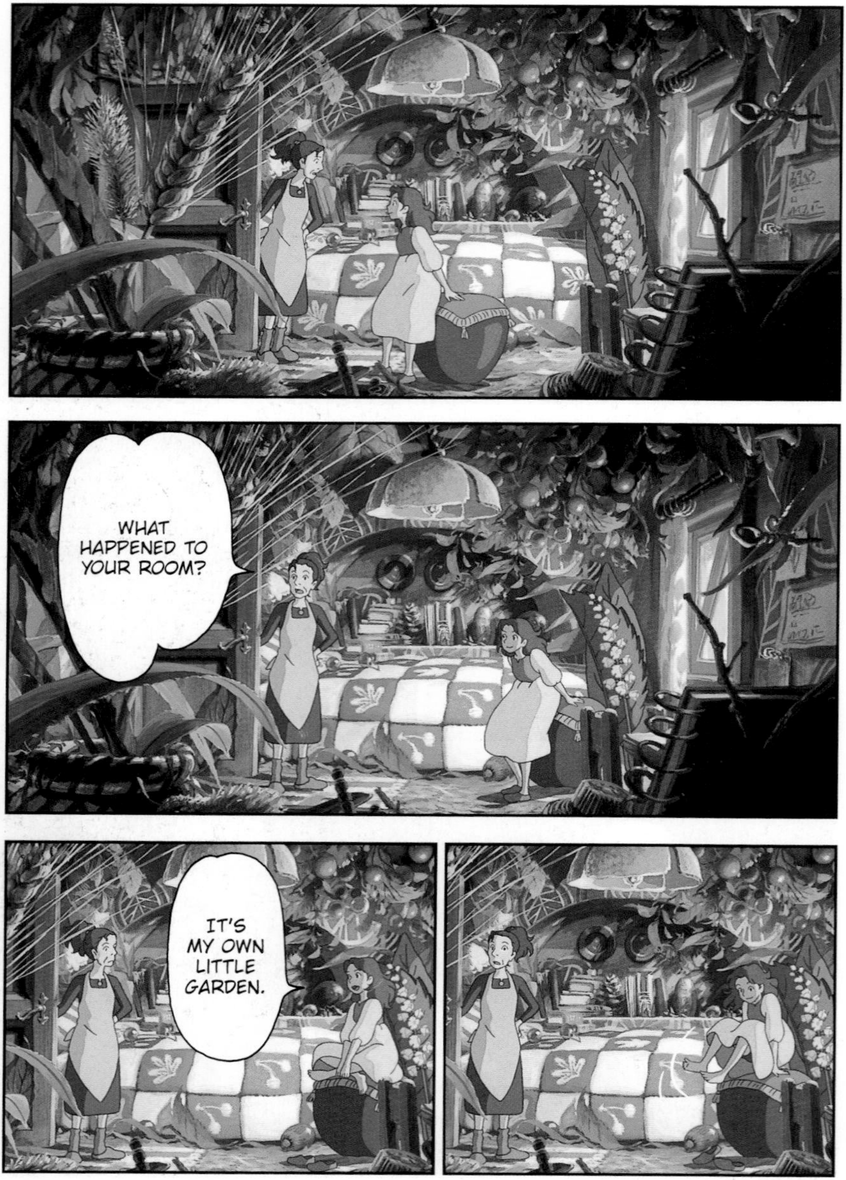
WHAT HAPPENED TO YOUR ROOM?
IT'S MY OWN LITTLE GARDEN.

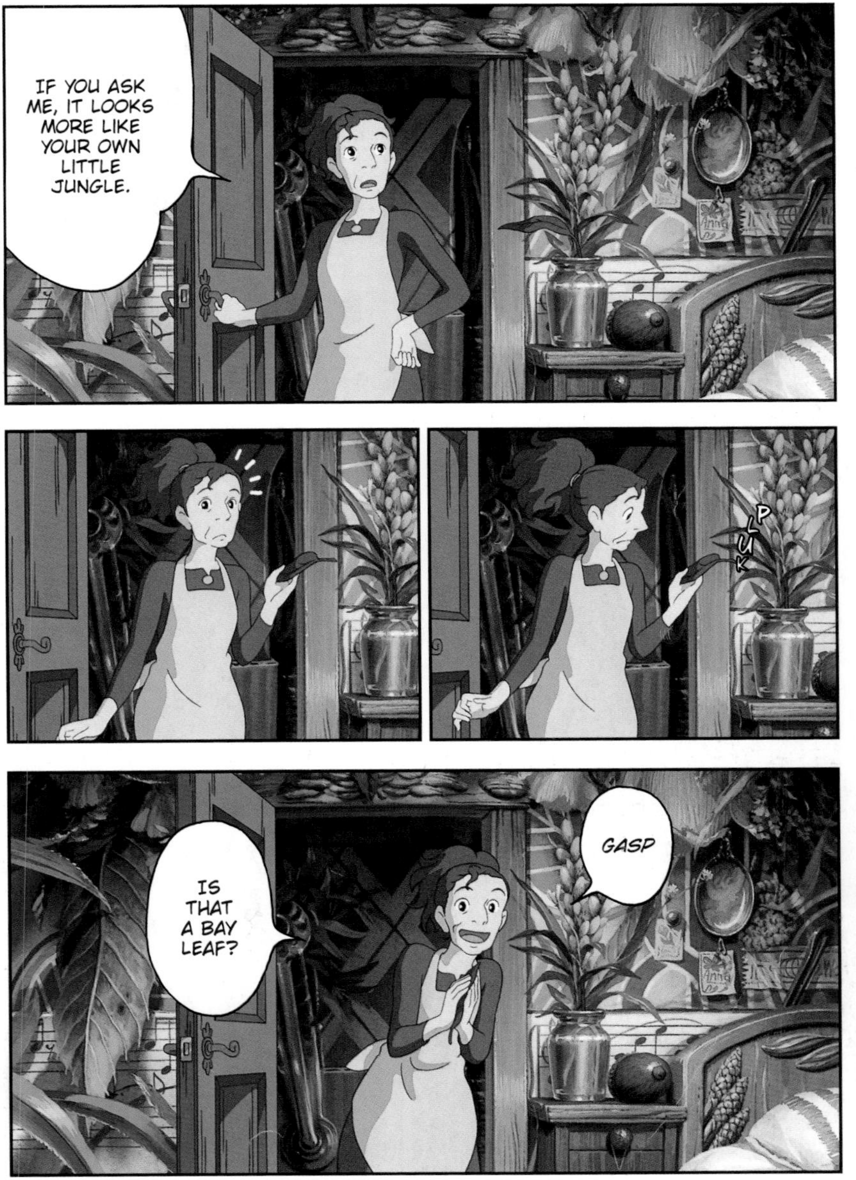
IF YOU ASK ME, IT LOOKS MORE LIKE YOUR OWN LITTLE JUNGLE.
PLUK
GASP
IS THAT A BAY LEAF?

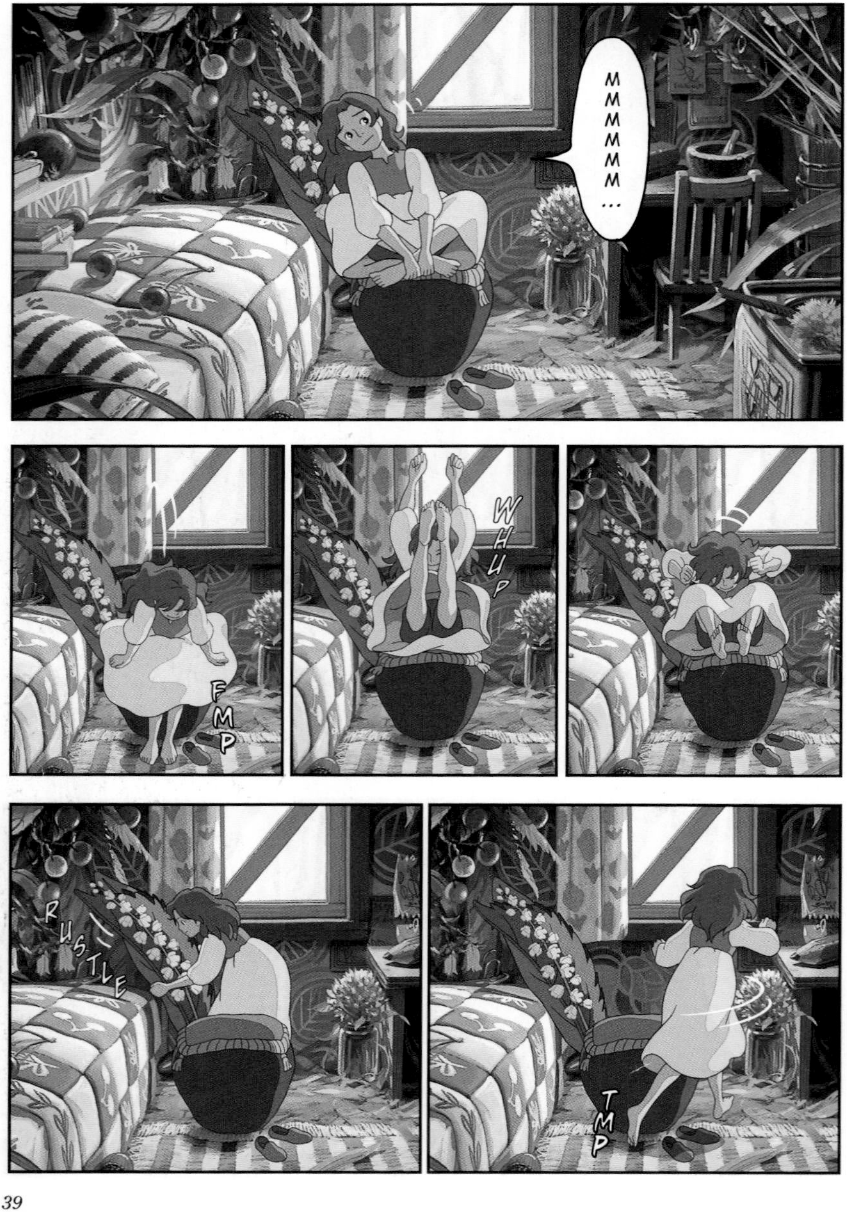

MMMMMM...
WHUP
FMP
TMP
RUSTLE

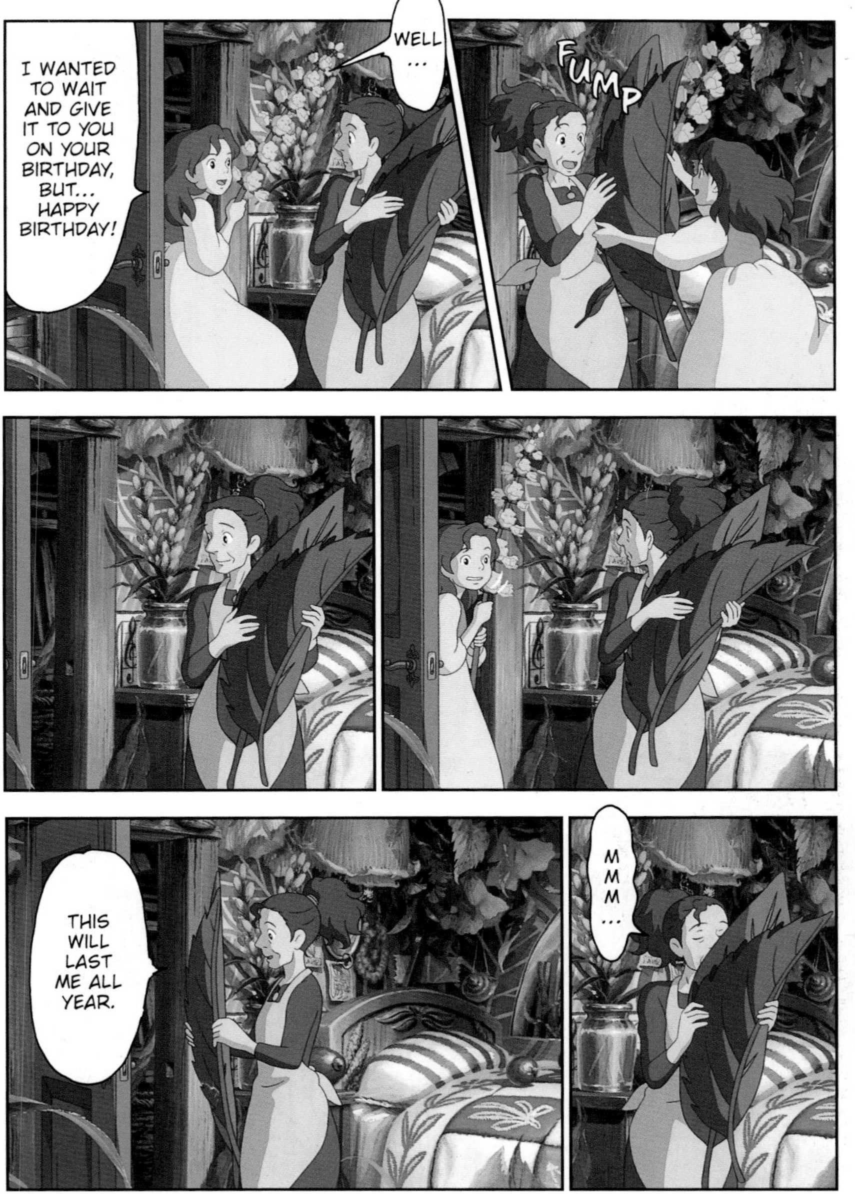
I WANTED TO WAIT AND GIVE IT TO YOU ON YOUR BIRTHDAY, BUT... HAPPY BIRTHDAY!
WELL ...
FUMP
THIS WILL LAST ME ALL YEAR.
MMM ...

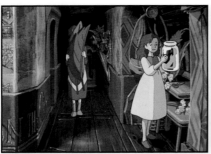
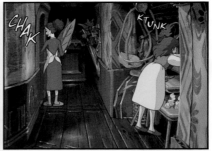

CHAK

KTUNK

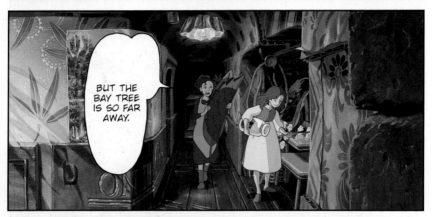

BUT THE BAY TREE IS SO FAR AWAY.

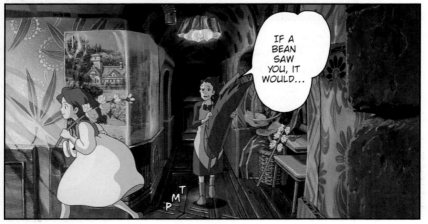

IF A BEAN SAW YOU, IT WOULD...

P
M
T

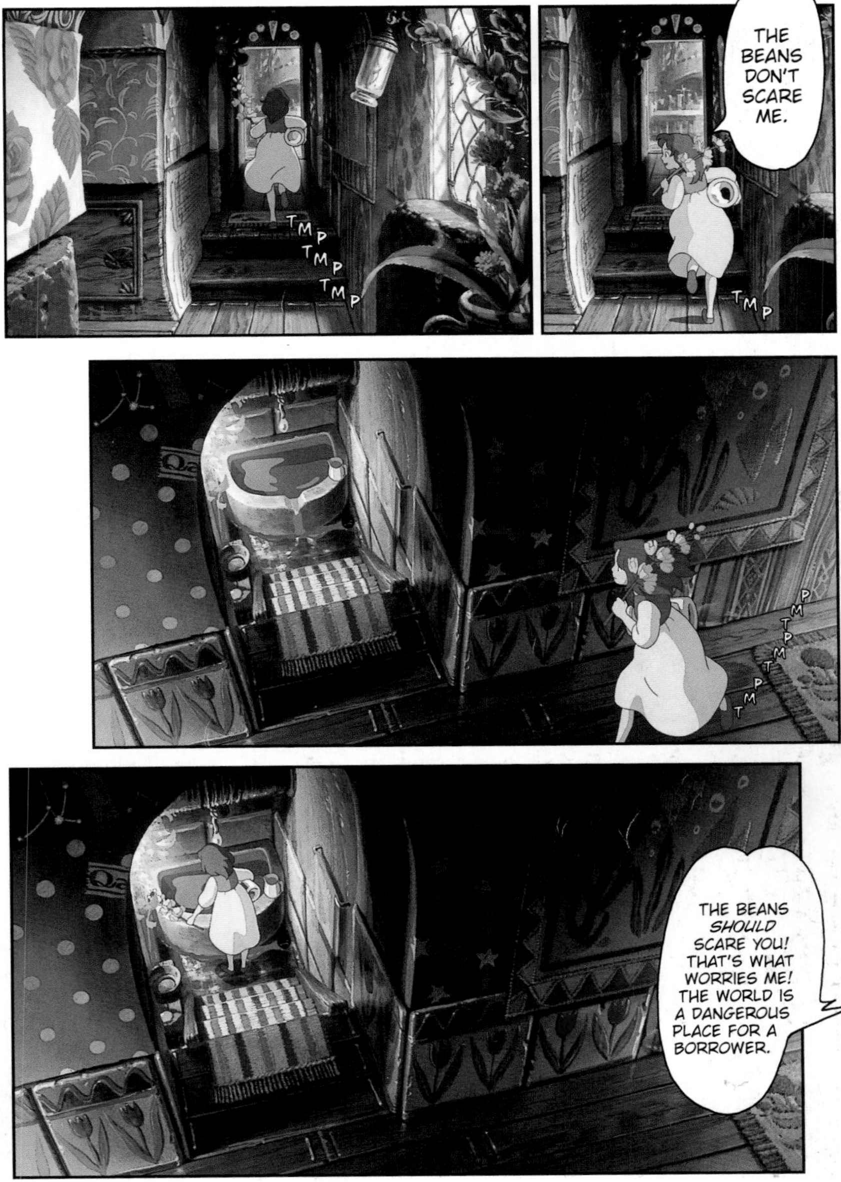
THE BEANS DON'T SCARE ME.
TMP
TMP
TMP
TMP
TMP
TMP
TMP
THE BEANS *SHOULD* SCARE YOU! THAT'S WHAT WORRIES ME! THE WORLD IS A DANGEROUS PLACE FOR A BORROWER.

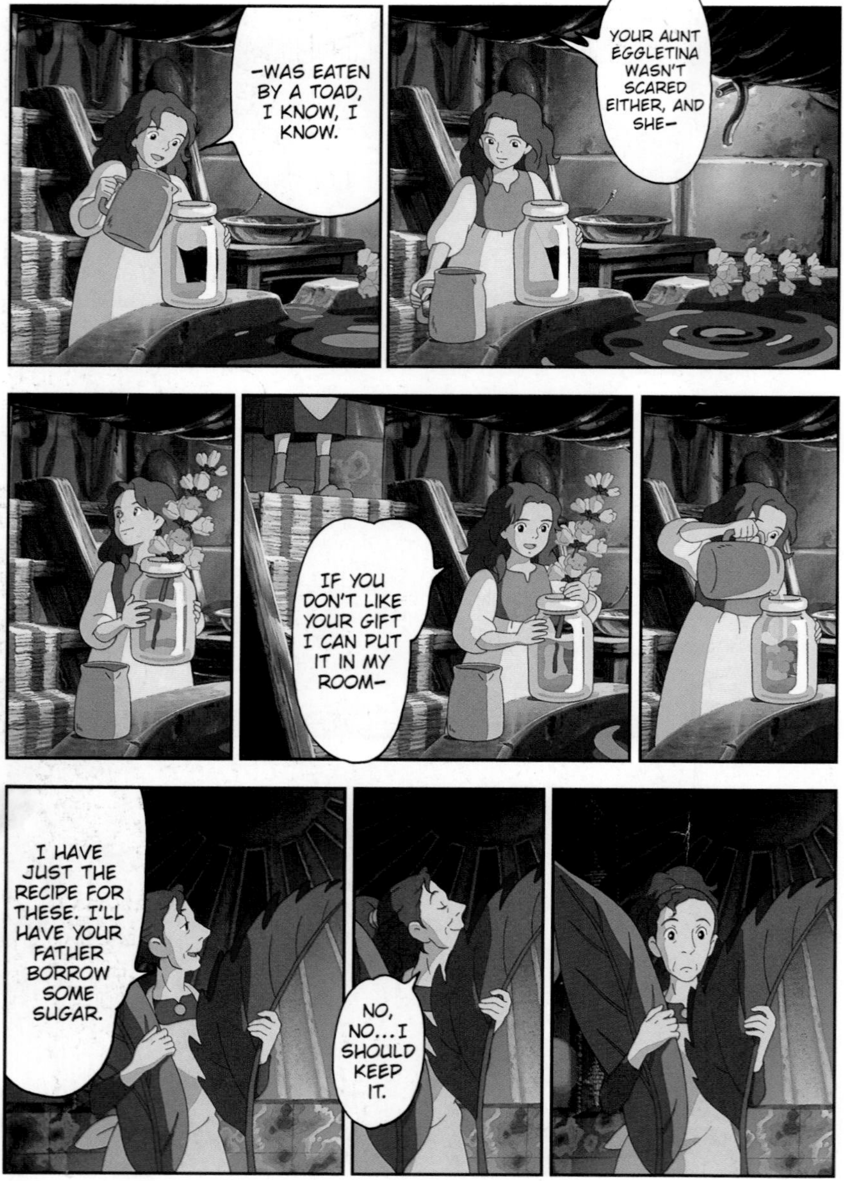
YOUR AUNT EGGLETINA WASN'T SCARED EITHER, AND SHE–
–WAS EATEN BY A TOAD, I KNOW, I KNOW.
IF YOU DON'T LIKE YOUR GIFT I CAN PUT IT IN MY ROOM–
NO, NO... I SHOULD KEEP IT.
I HAVE JUST THE RECIPE FOR THESE. I'LL HAVE YOUR FATHER BORROW SOME SUGAR.

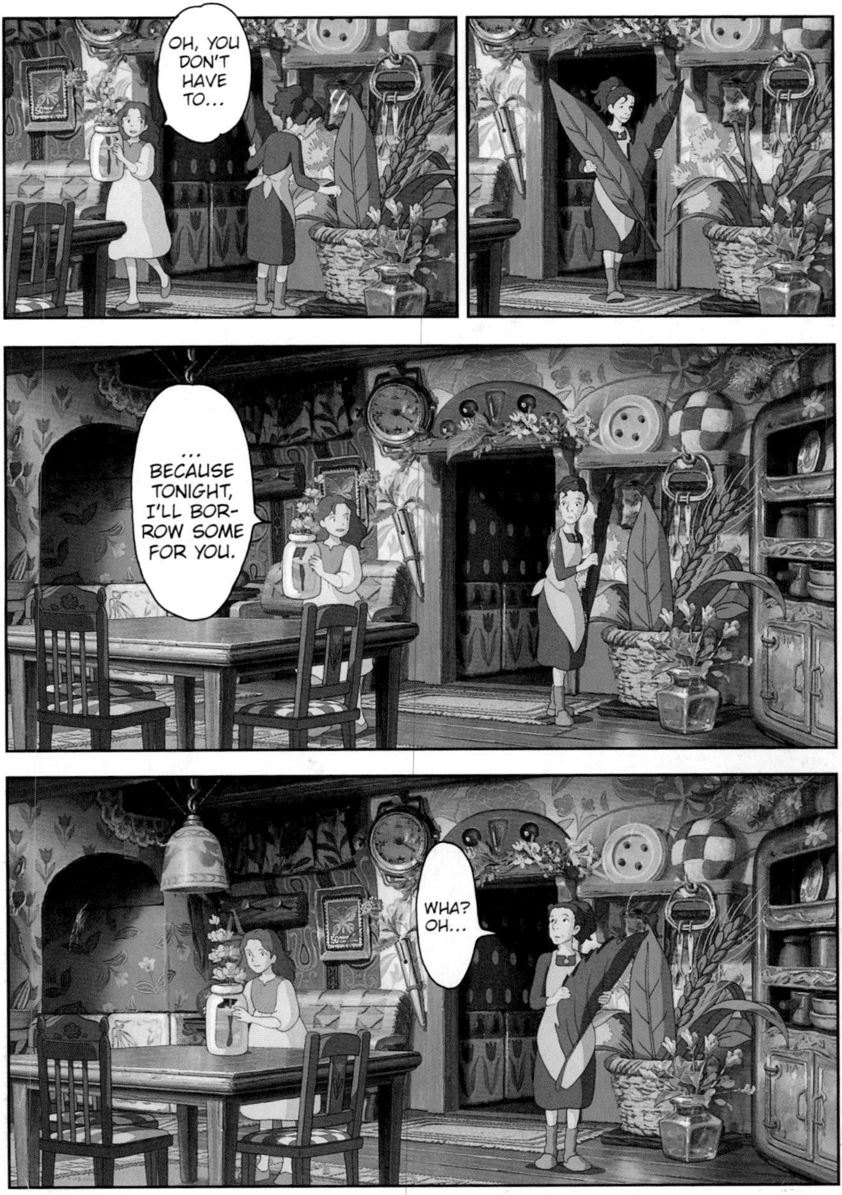
OH, YOU DON'T HAVE TO...
...BECAUSE TONIGHT, I'LL BOR-ROW SOME FOR YOU.
WHA? OH...

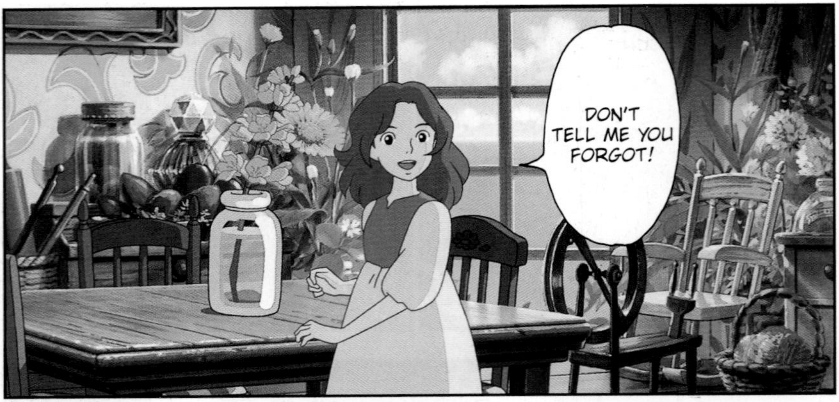
DON'T TELL ME YOU FORGOT!

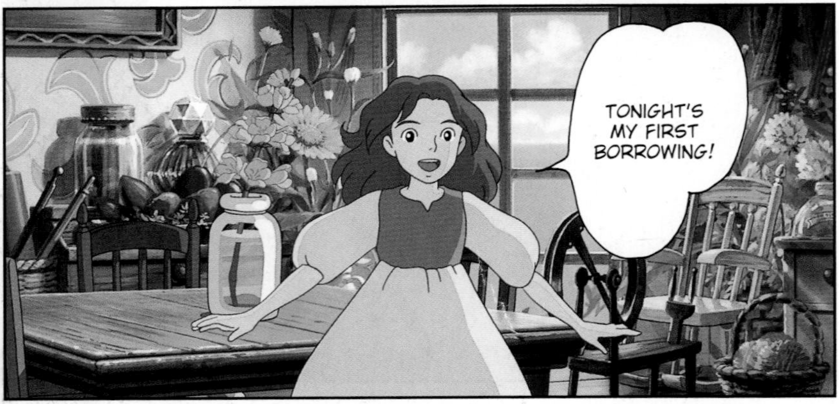
TONIGHT'S MY FIRST BORROWING!

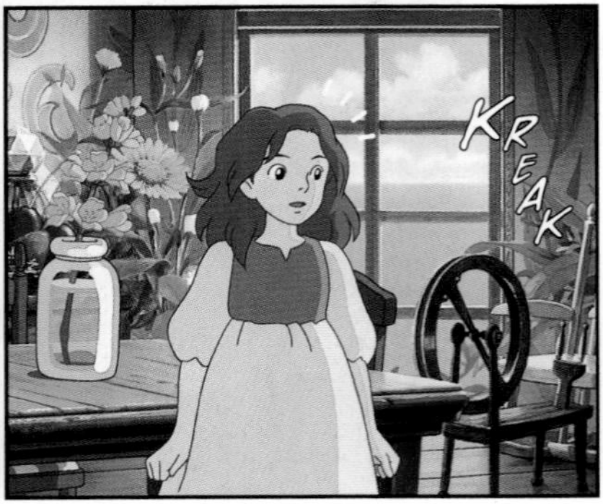
KREAK

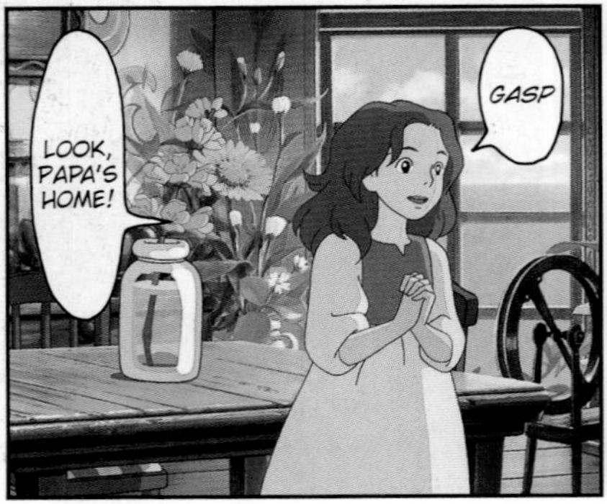
GASP
LOOK, PAPA'S HOME!

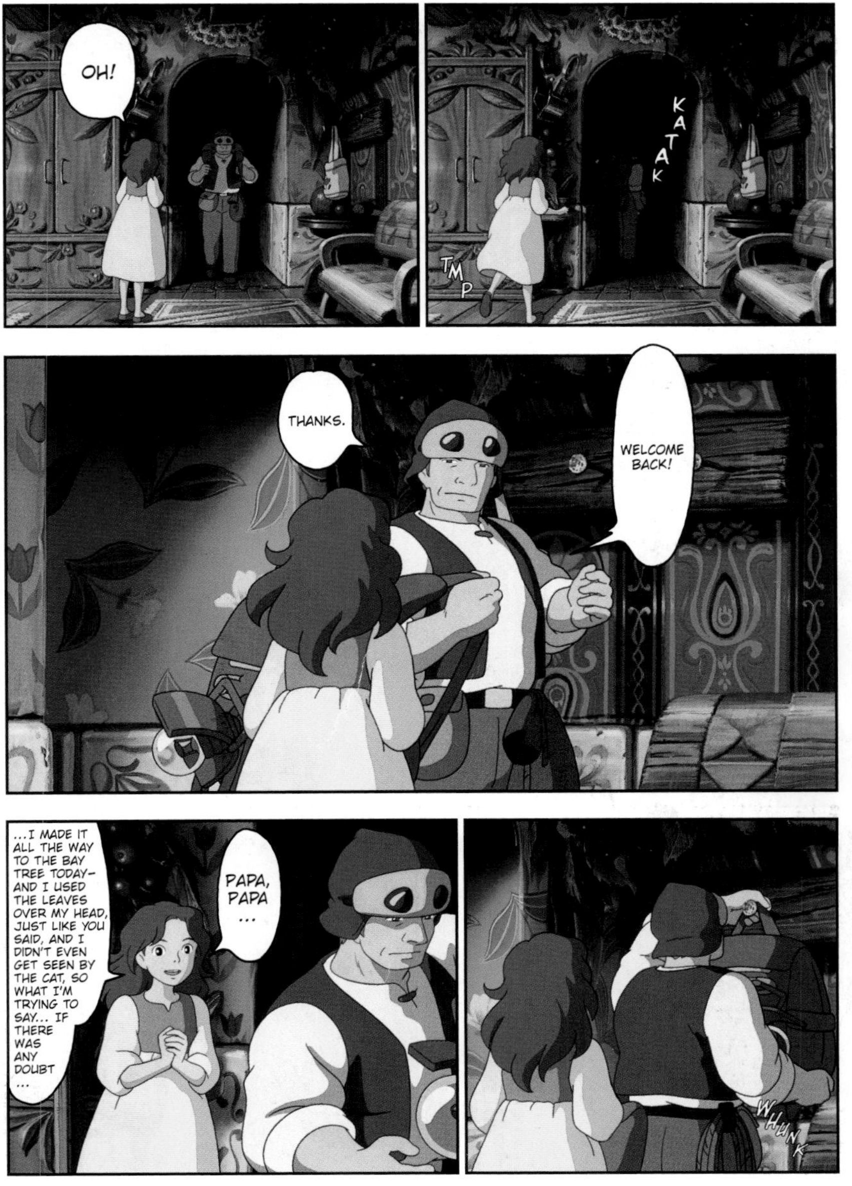
TMP
KATAK
OH!
WELCOME BACK!
THANKS.
WHUNK
PAPA, PAPA ...
...I MADE IT ALL THE WAY TO THE BAY TREE TODAY–AND I USED THE LEAVES OVER MY HEAD, JUST LIKE YOU SAID, AND I DIDN'T EVEN GET SEEN BY THE CAT, SO WHAT I'M TRYING TO SAY... IF THERE WAS ANY DOUBT ...

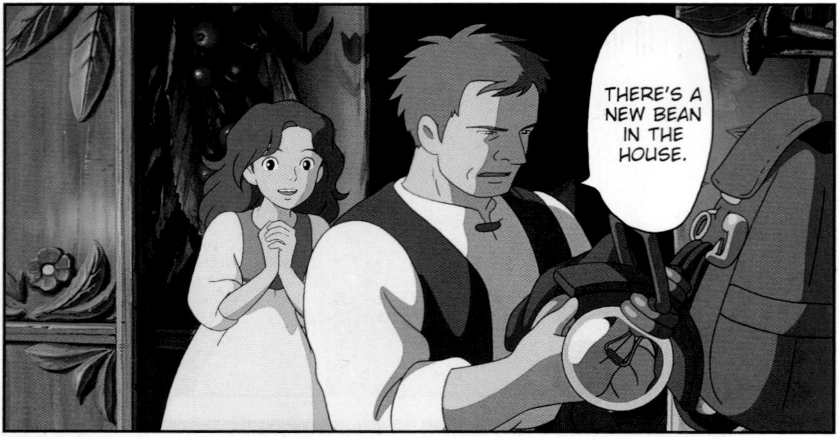
THERE'S A NEW BEAN IN THE HOUSE.

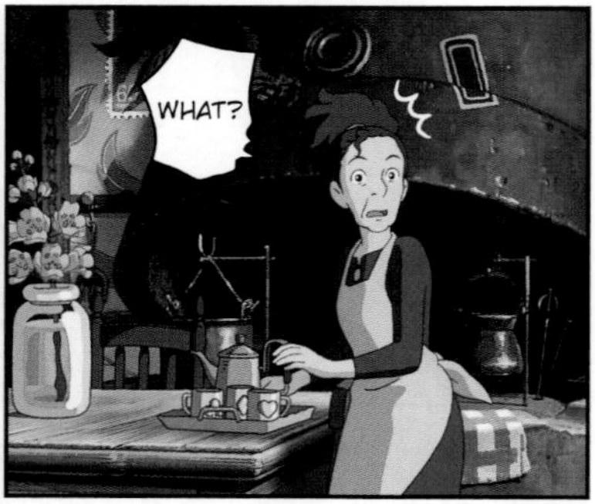
WHAT?

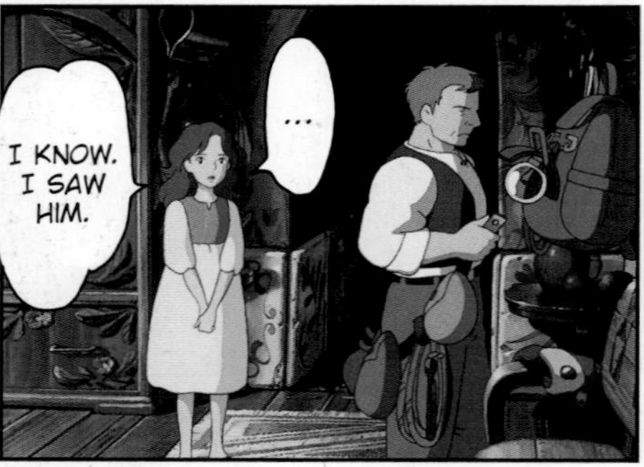
...
I KNOW. I SAW HIM.

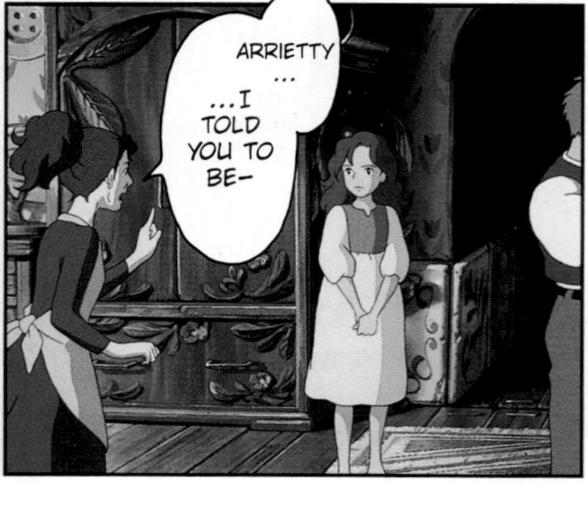
ARRIETTY ...
...I TOLD YOU TO BE–

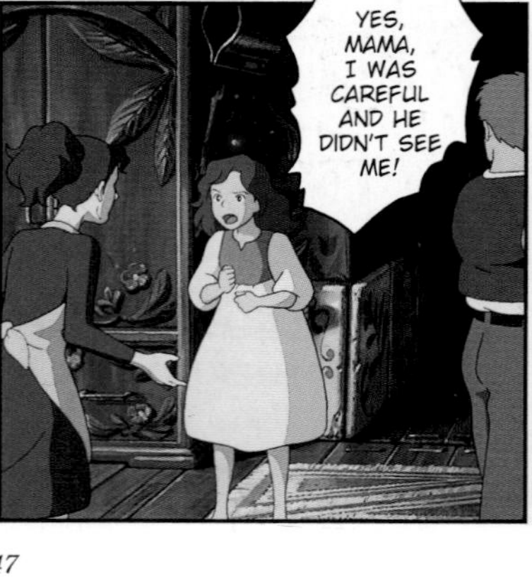
YES, MAMA, I WAS CAREFUL AND HE DIDN'T SEE ME!

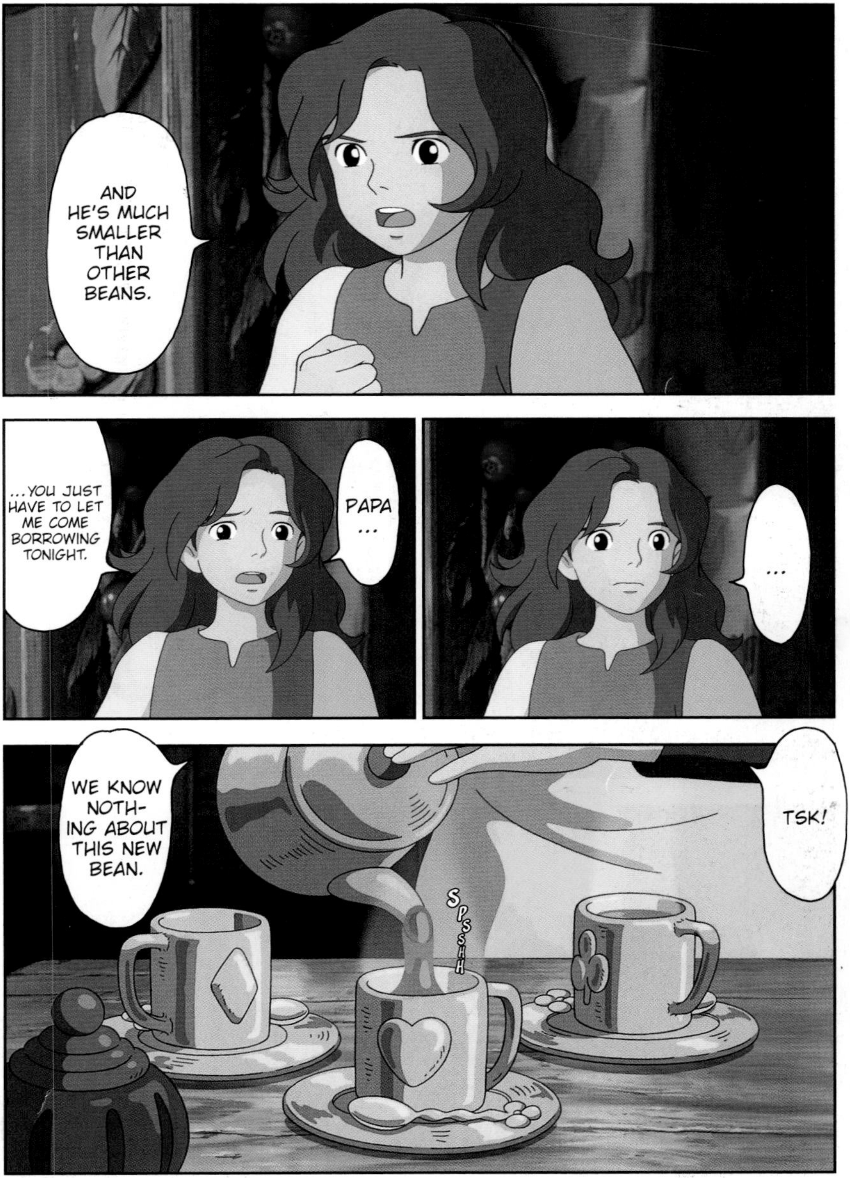
AND HE'S MUCH SMALLER THAN OTHER BEANS.
...
PAPA ...
...YOU JUST HAVE TO LET ME COME BORROWING TONIGHT.
TSK!
WE KNOW NOTH-ING ABOUT THIS NEW BEAN.
SPSSHH

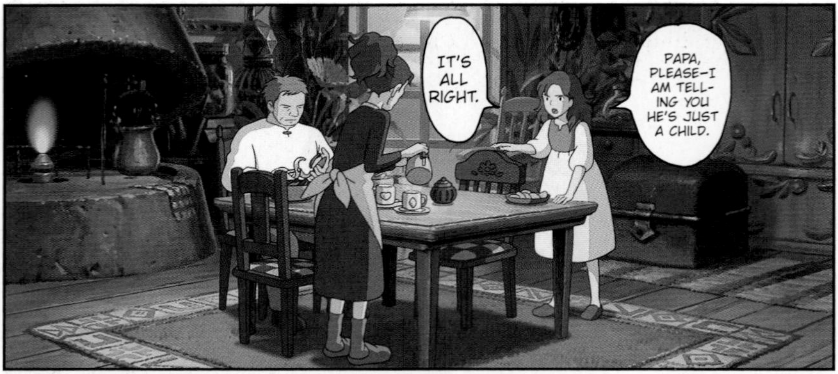
PAPA, PLEASE—I AM TELL-ING YOU HE'S JUST A CHILD.
IT'S ALL RIGHT.

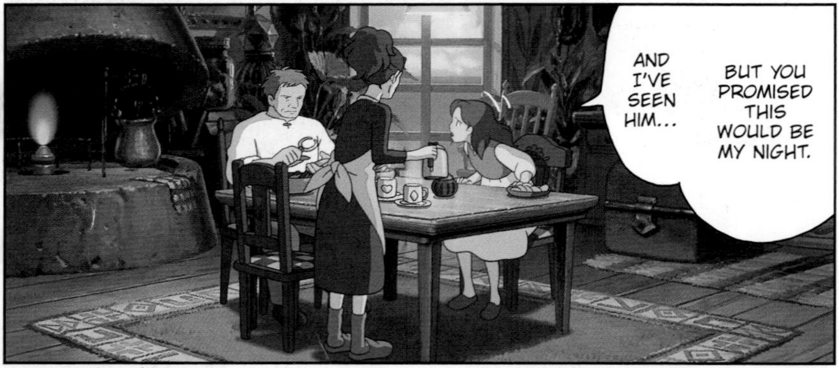
BUT YOU PROMISED THIS WOULD BE MY NIGHT.
AND I'VE SEEN HIM...

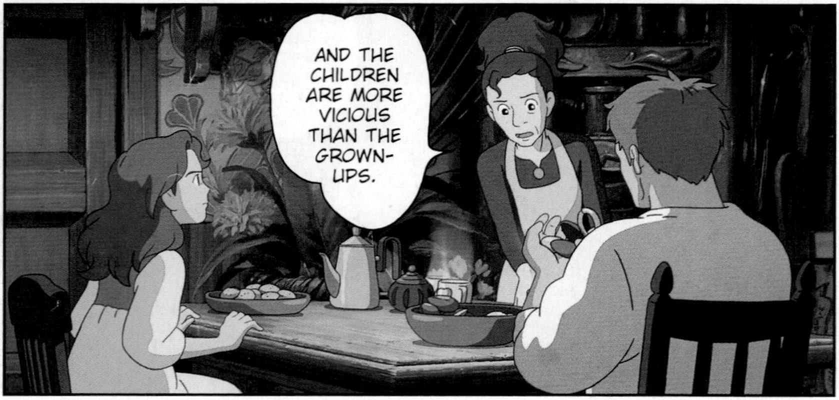
AND THE CHILDREN ARE MORE VICIOUS THAN THE GROWN-UPS.

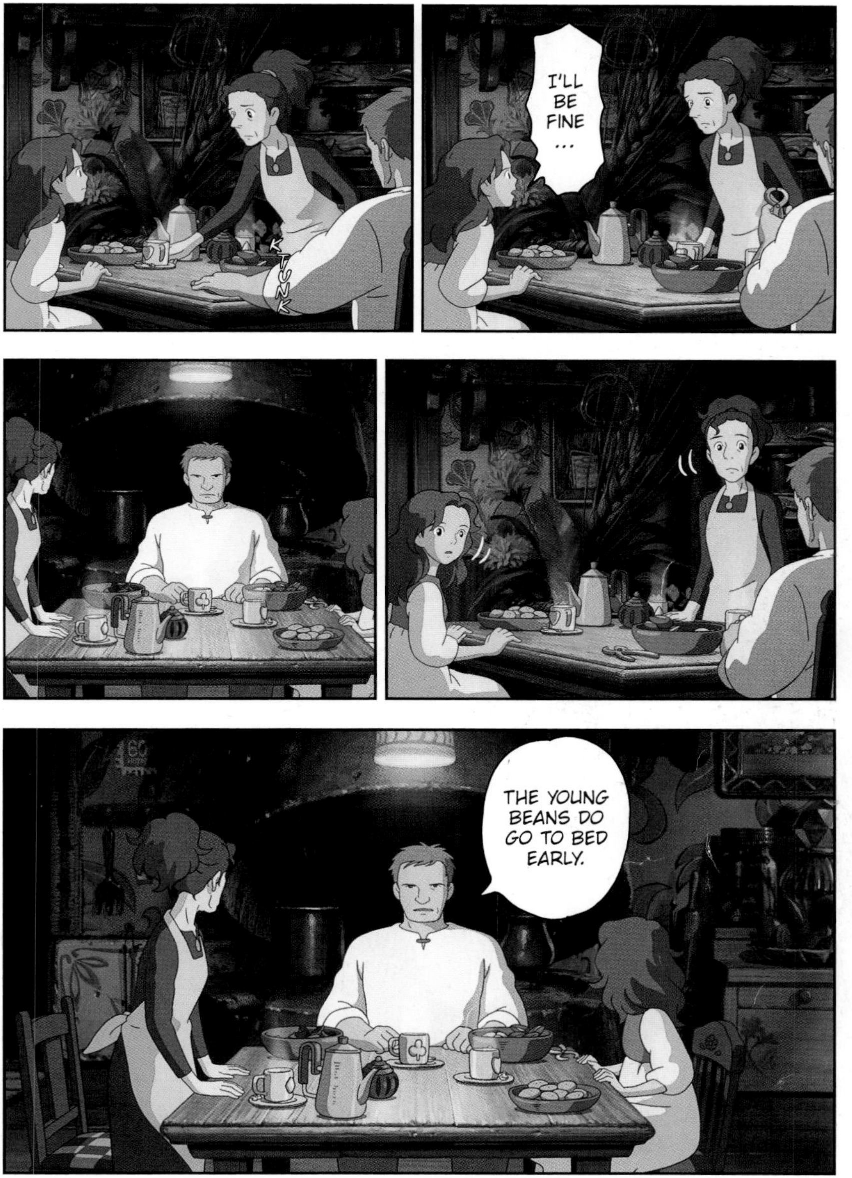
I'LL BE FINE ...
KTUNK
THE YOUNG BEANS DO GO TO BED EARLY.

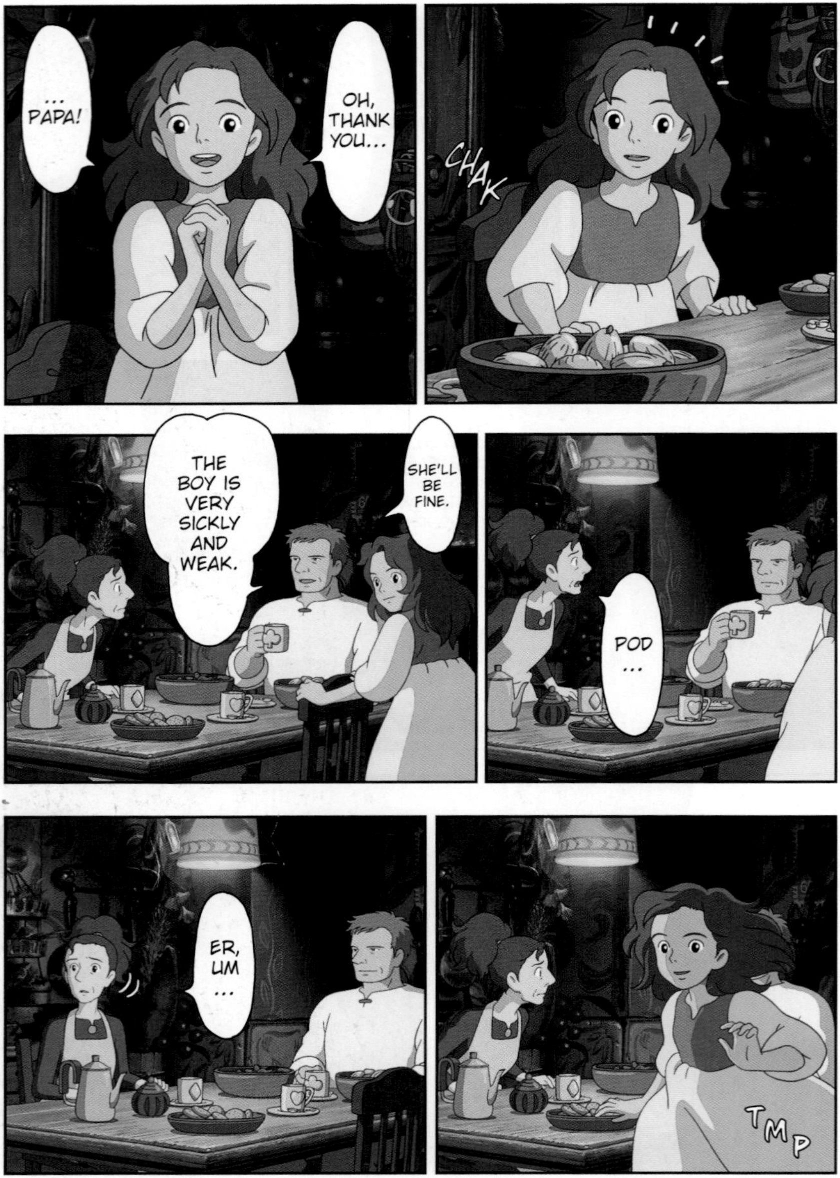
OH, THANK YOU...
... PAPA!
CHAK
THE BOY IS VERY SICKLY AND WEAK.
SHE'LL BE FINE.
POD ...
ER, UM ...
TMP

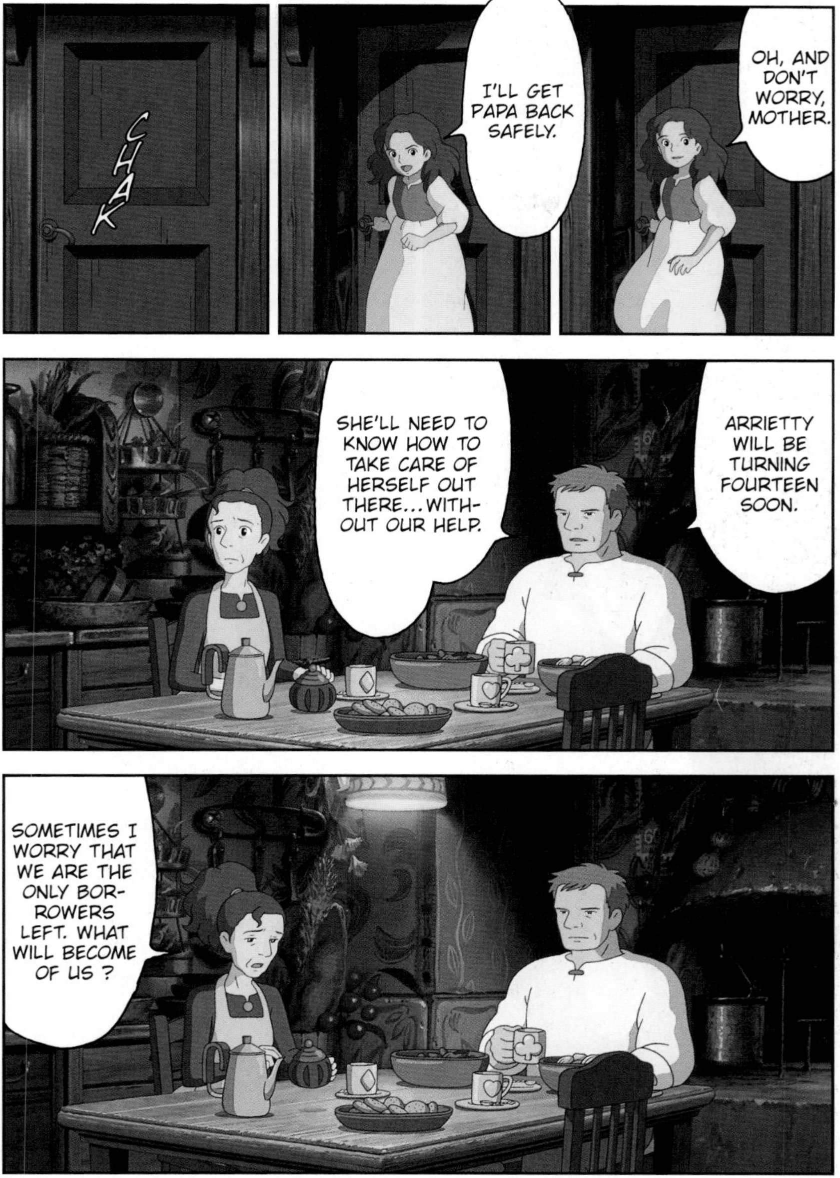
OH, AND DON'T WORRY, MOTHER.
I'LL GET PAPA BACK SAFELY.
CHAK
ARRIETTY WILL BE TURNING FOURTEEN SOON.
SHE'LL NEED TO KNOW HOW TO TAKE CARE OF HERSELF OUT THERE...WITH-OUT OUR HELP.
SOMETIMES I WORRY THAT WE ARE THE ONLY BOR-ROWERS LEFT. WHAT WILL BECOME OF US ?

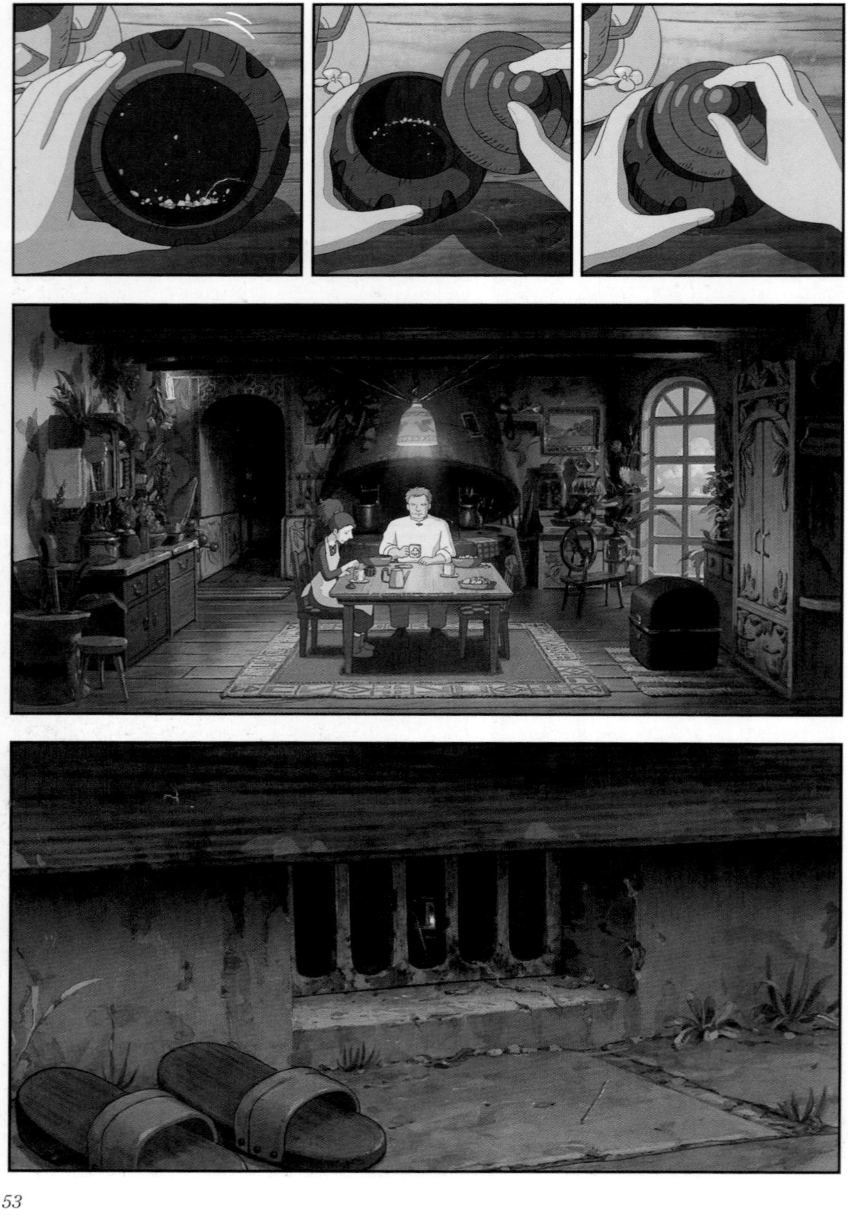

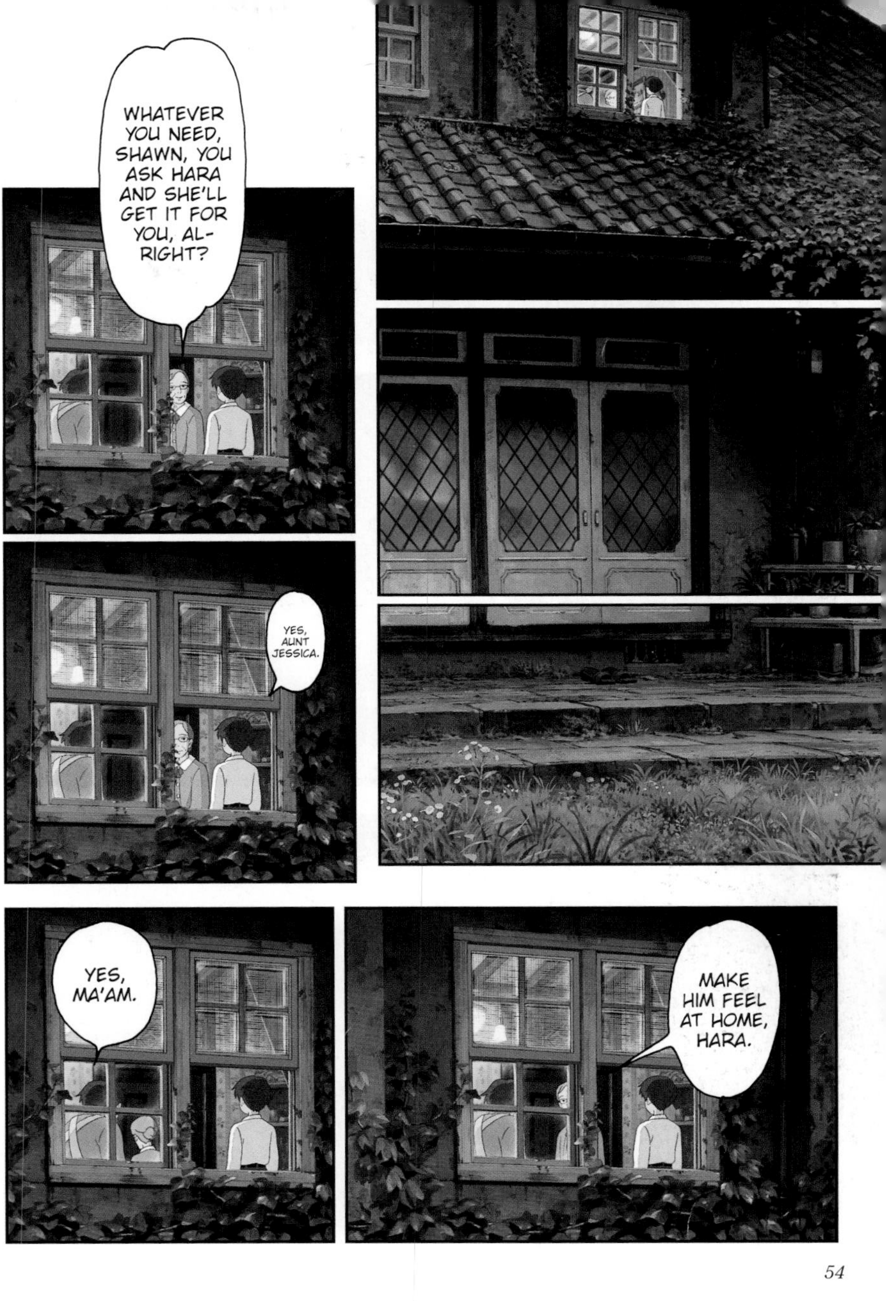
WHATEVER YOU NEED, SHAWN, YOU ASK HARA AND SHE'LL GET IT FOR YOU, AL-RIGHT?
YES, AUNT JESSICA.
MAKE HIM FEEL AT HOME, HARA.
YES, MA'AM.

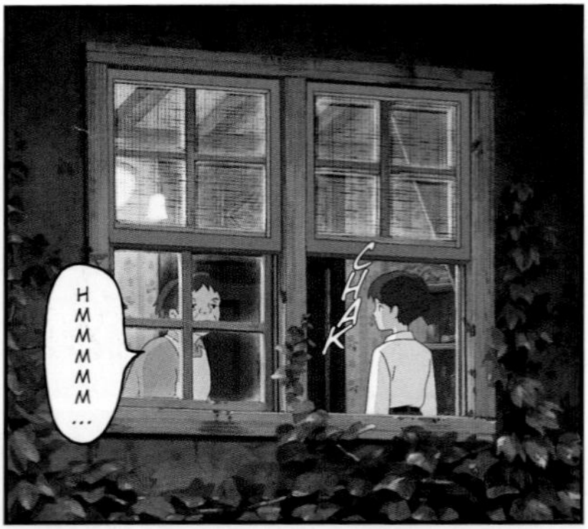
HMMMMM...
CHAK
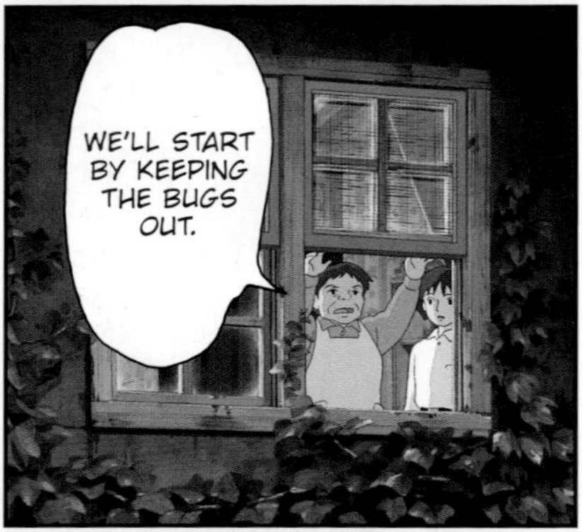
WE'LL START BY KEEPING THE BUGS OUT.
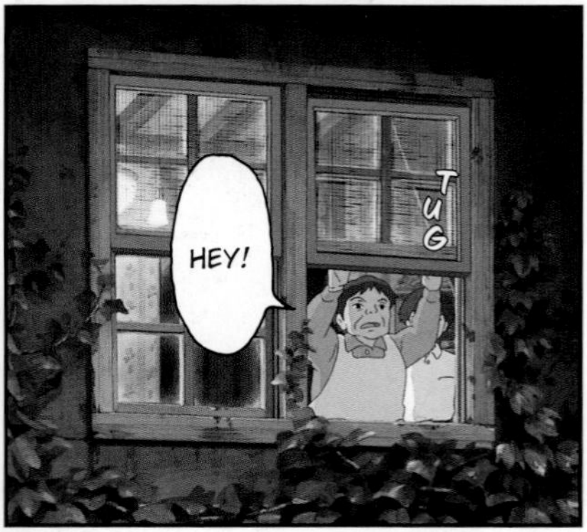
HEY!
TUG
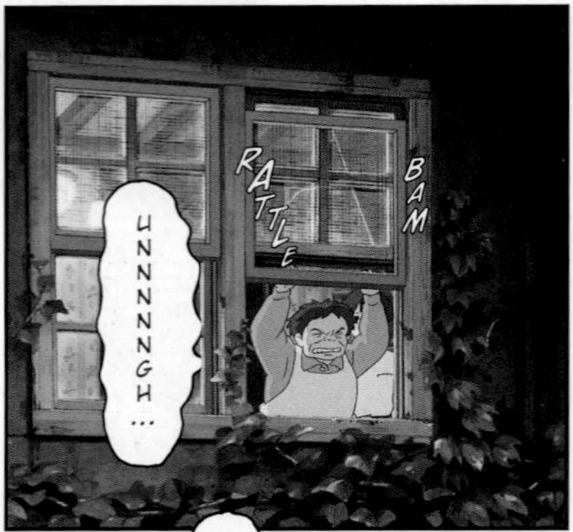
UNNNNNGH...
RATTLE
BAM
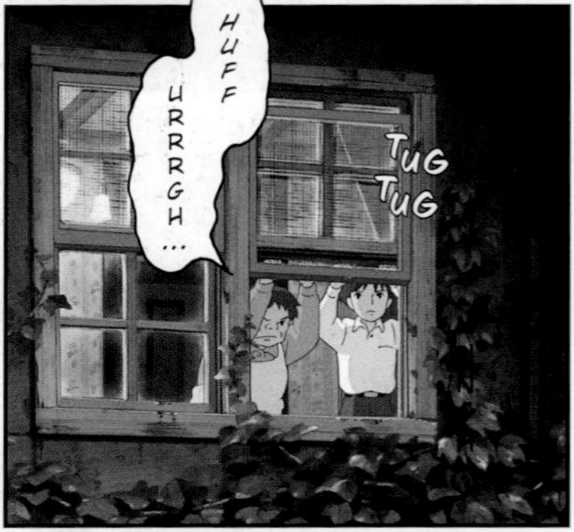
HUFF
URRRGH...
TUG TUG
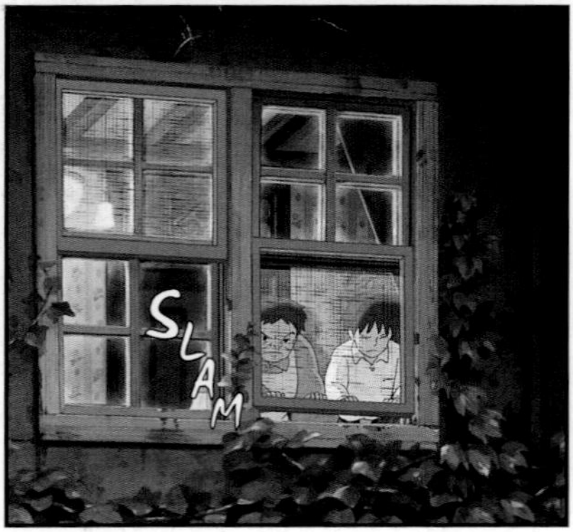
SLAM

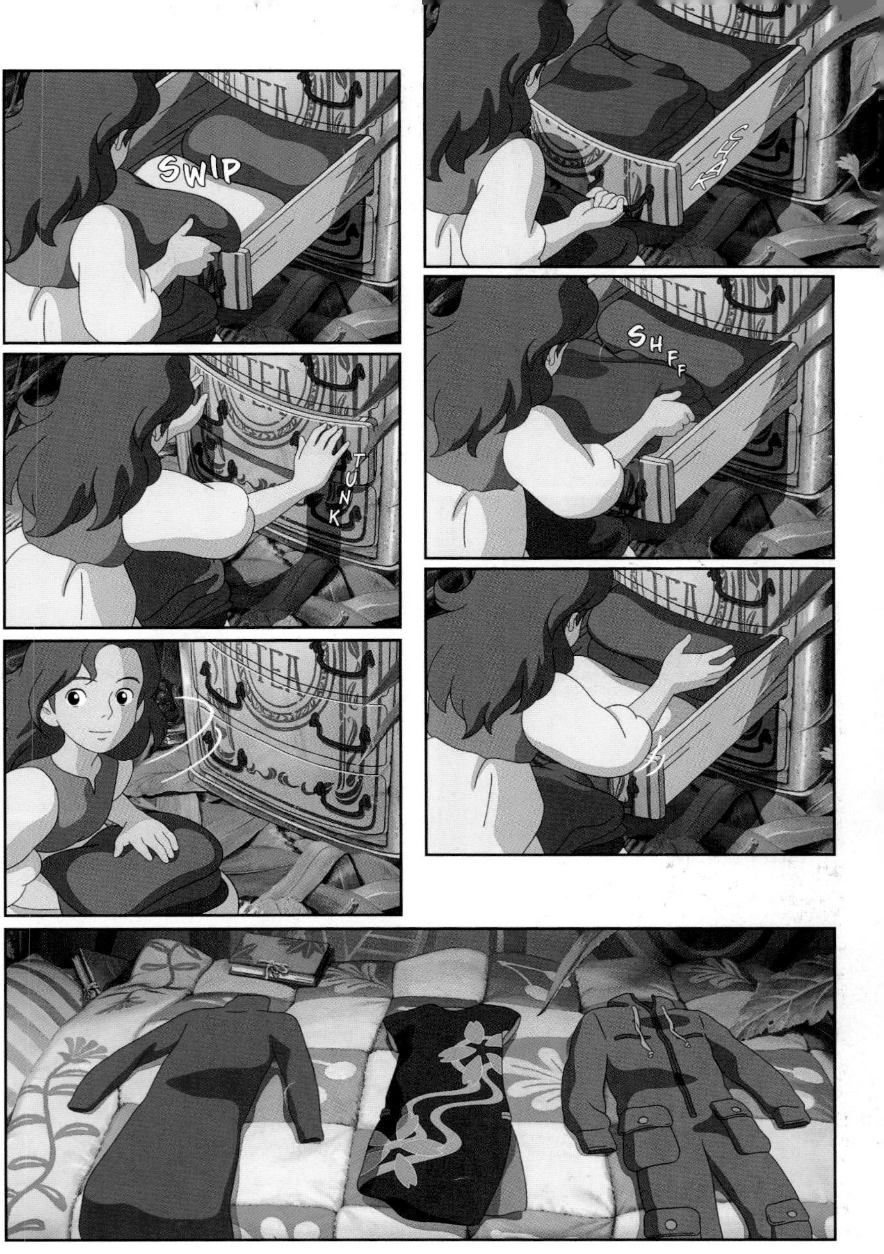
CHAK
SWIP
SHFF
TUNK

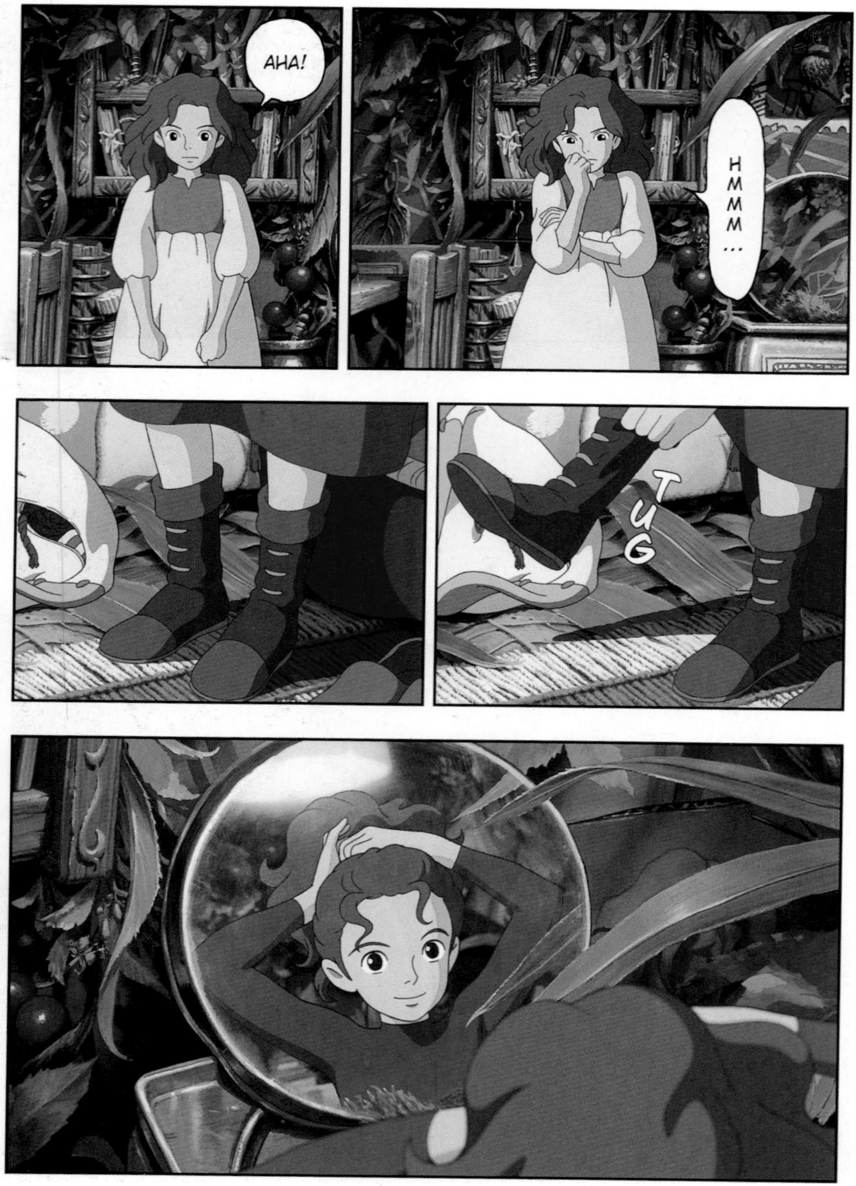
HMMM...
AHA!
TUG

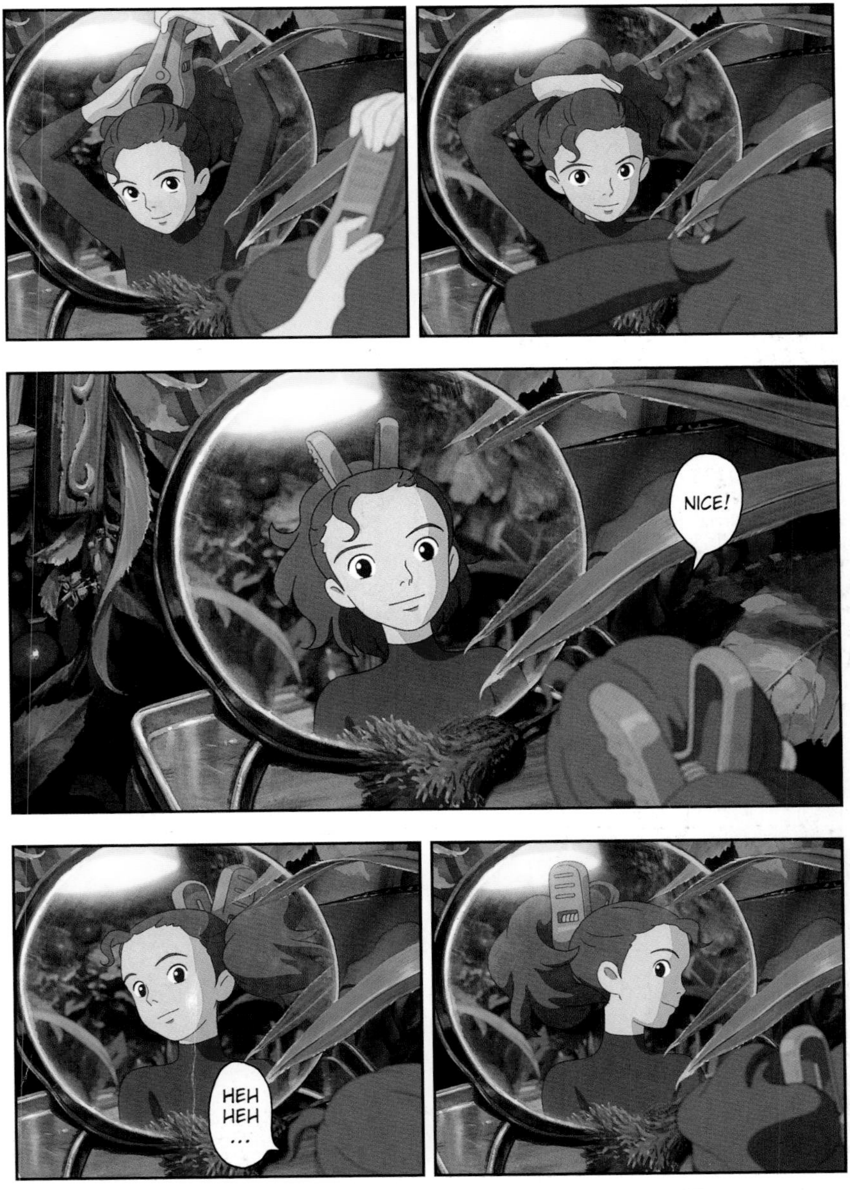
NICE!
HEH HEH ...

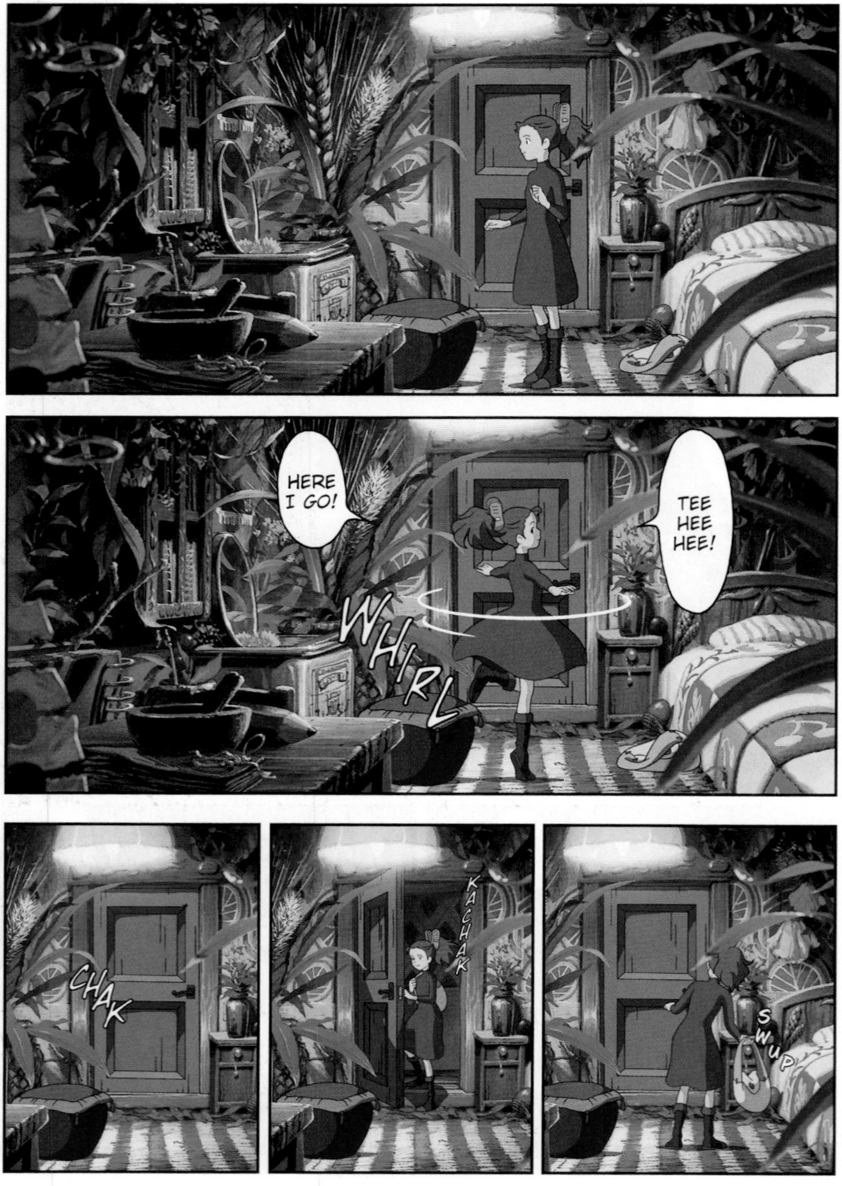
HERE I GO!
TEE HEE HEE!
WHIRL
CHAK
KACHAK
SWUP

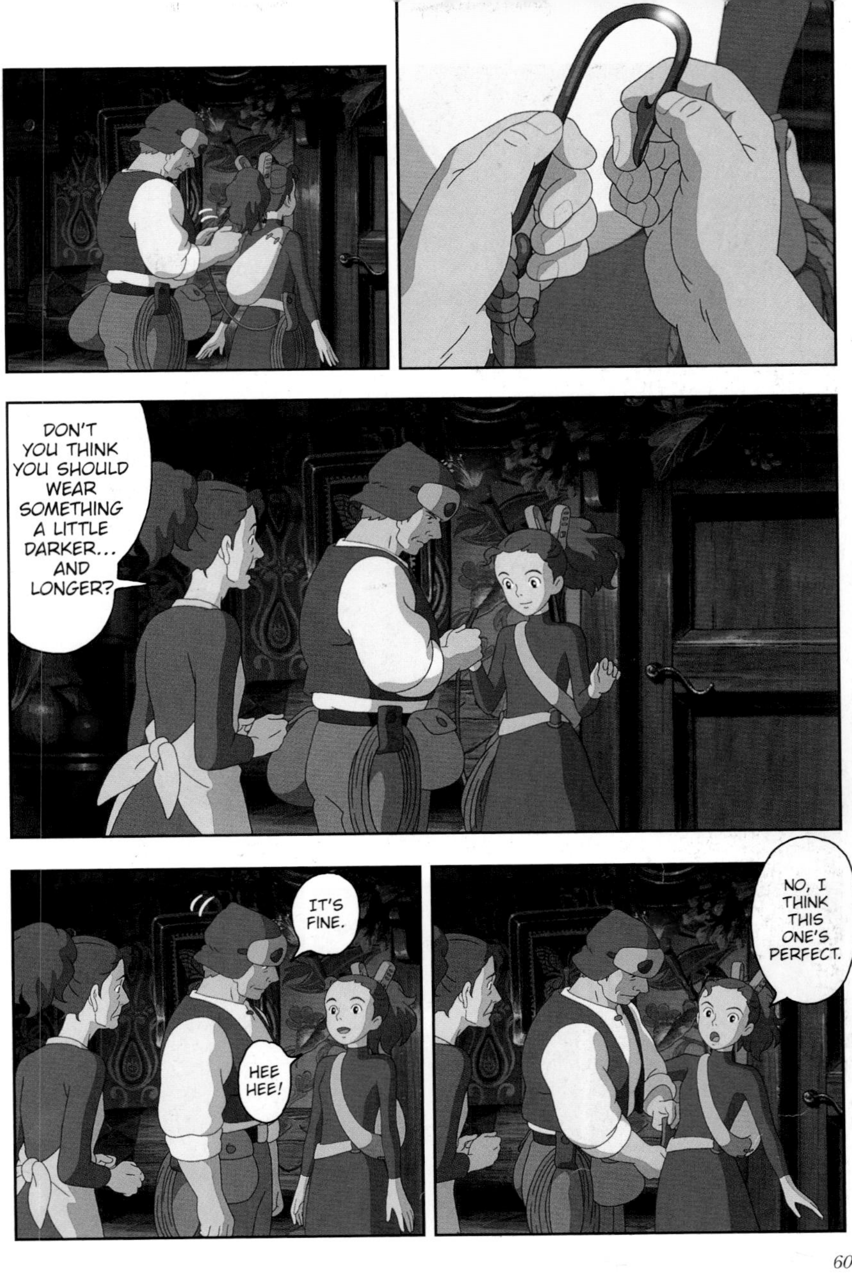
DON'T YOU THINK YOU SHOULD WEAR SOMETHING A LITTLE DARKER... AND LONGER?
IT'S FINE.
HEE HEE!
NO, I THINK THIS ONE'S PERFECT.

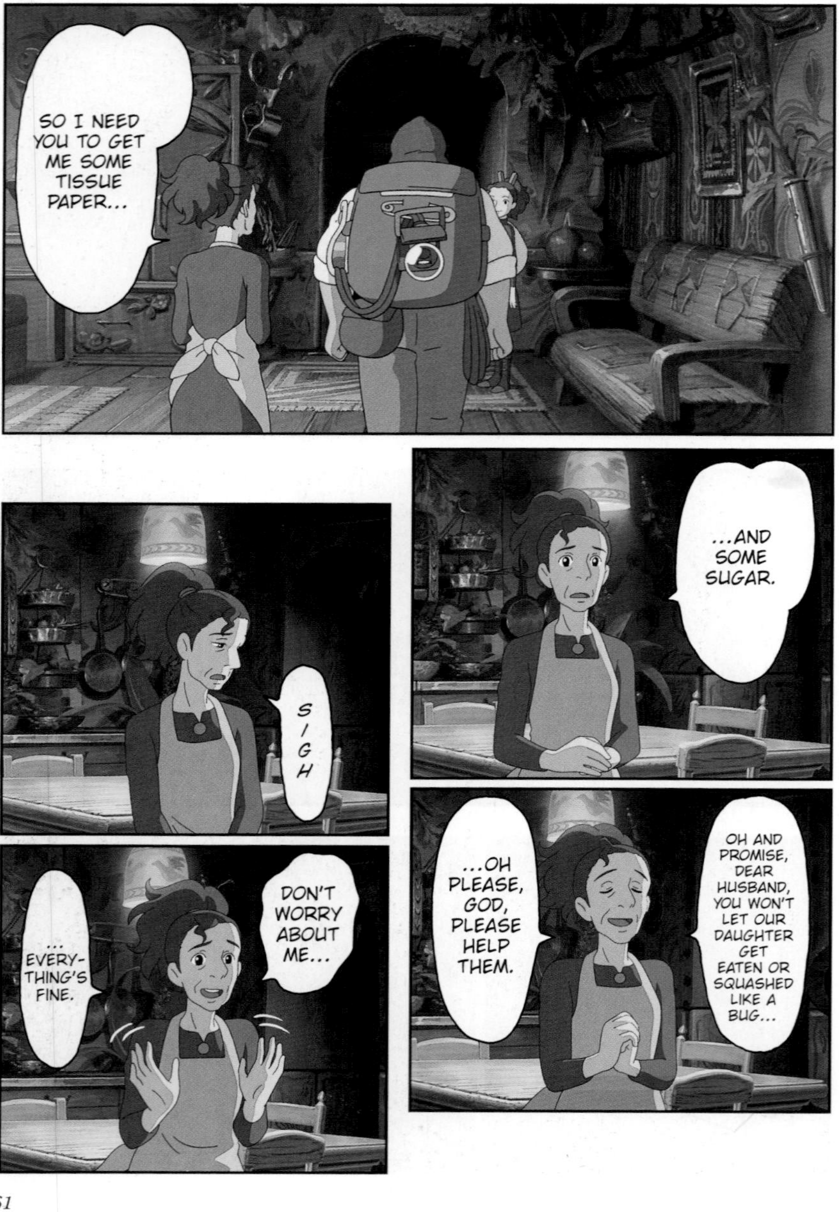
SO I NEED YOU TO GET ME SOME TISSUE PAPER...
...AND SOME SUGAR.
SIGH
OH AND PROMISE, DEAR HUSBAND, YOU WON'T LET OUR DAUGHTER GET EATEN OR SQUASHED LIKE A BUG...
...OH PLEASE, GOD, PLEASE HELP THEM.
DON'T WORRY ABOUT ME...
...EVERYTHING'S FINE.

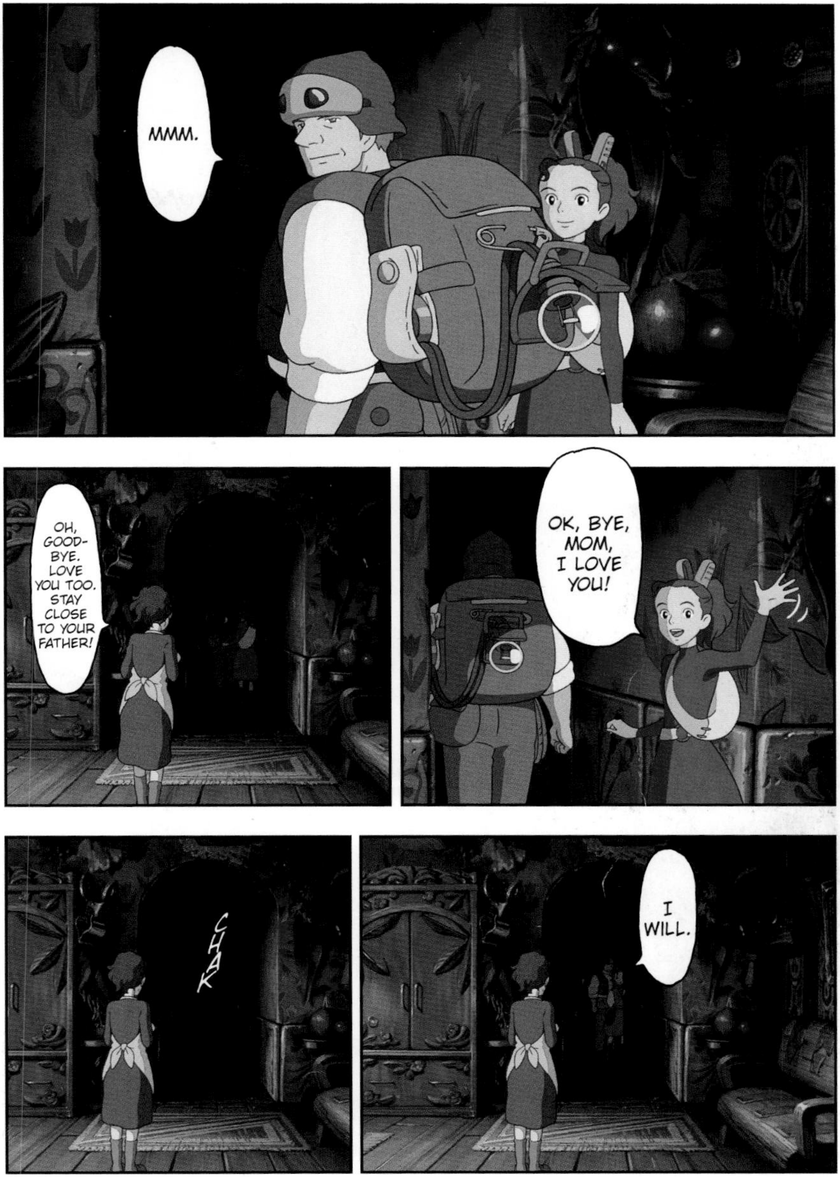
MMM.
OK, BYE, MOM, I LOVE YOU!
OH, GOOD-BYE. LOVE YOU TOO. STAY CLOSE TO YOUR FATHER!
I WILL.
CHAK

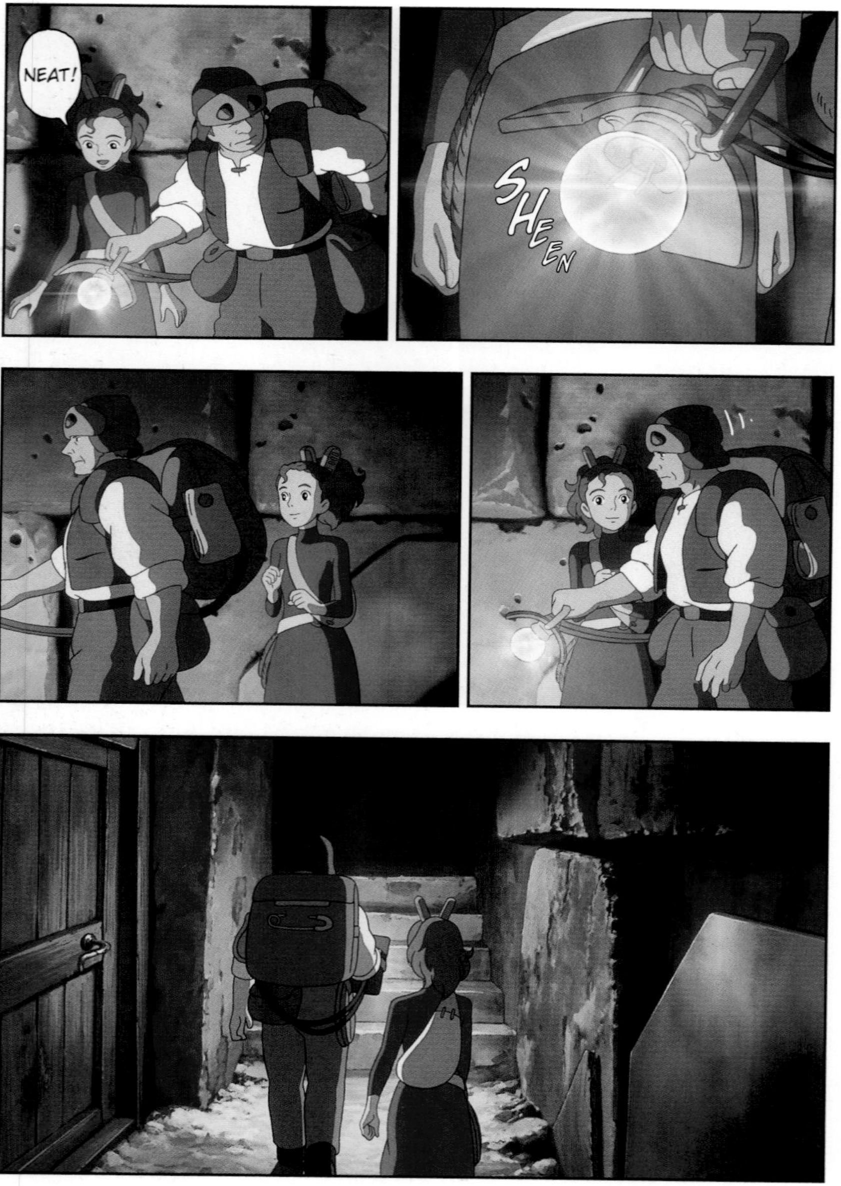
SHEEN
NEAT!

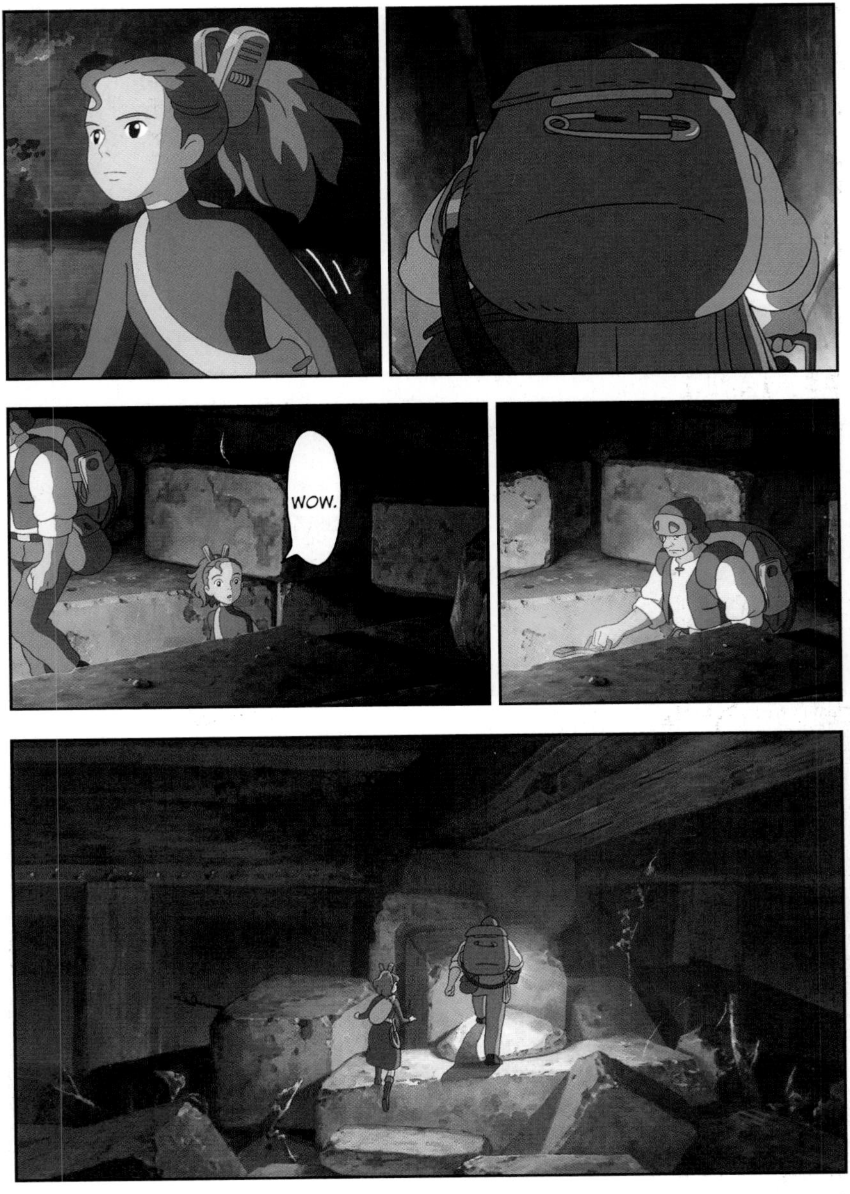
WOW.

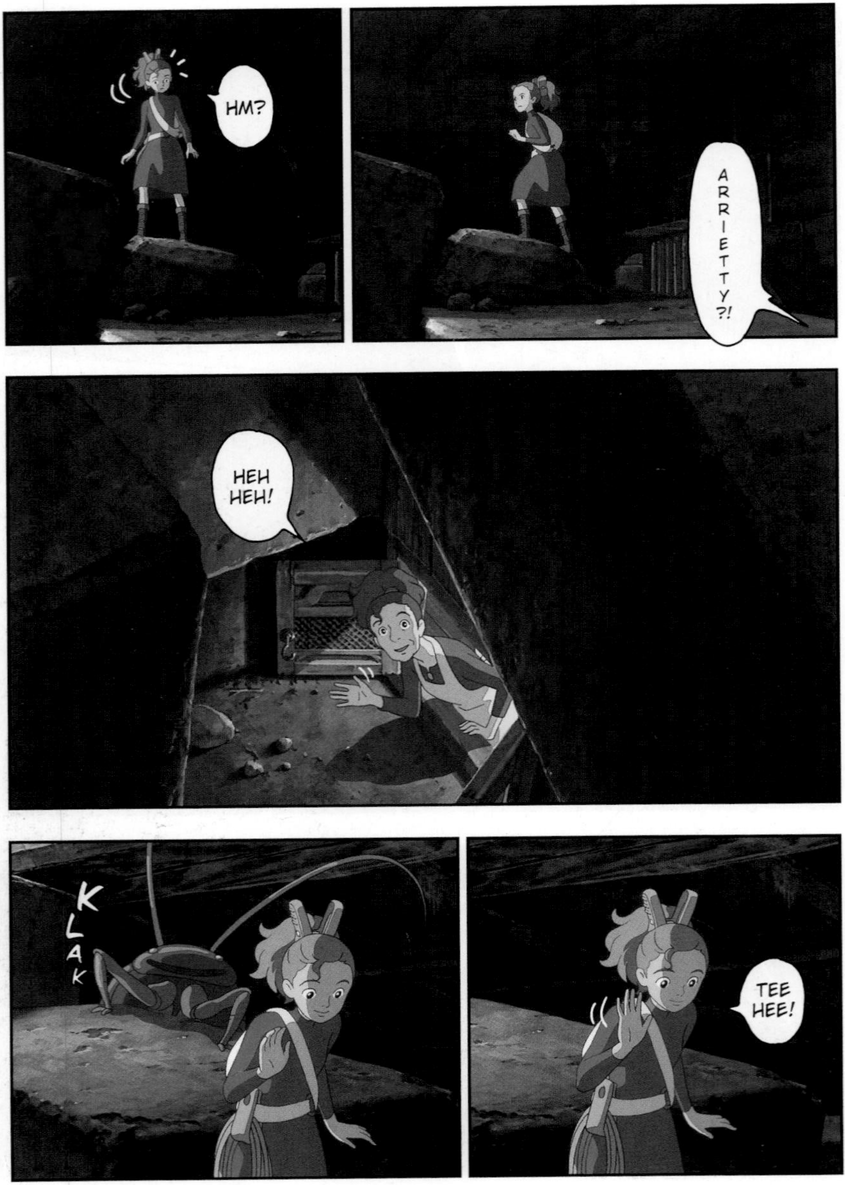
HM?
ARRIETTY?!
HEH HEH!
KLAK
TEE HEE!

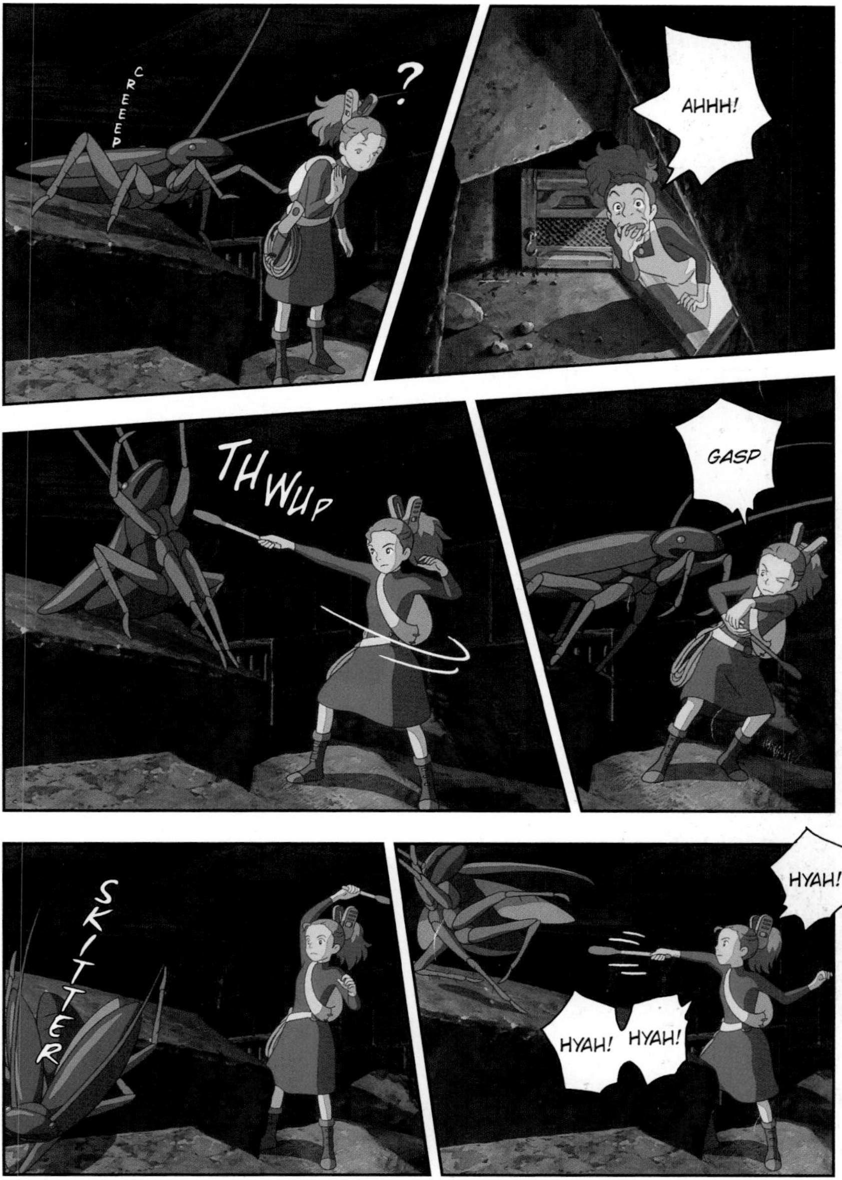
AHHH!
CREEEP
?
GASP
THWUP
HYAH!
HYAH! HYAH!
SKITTER

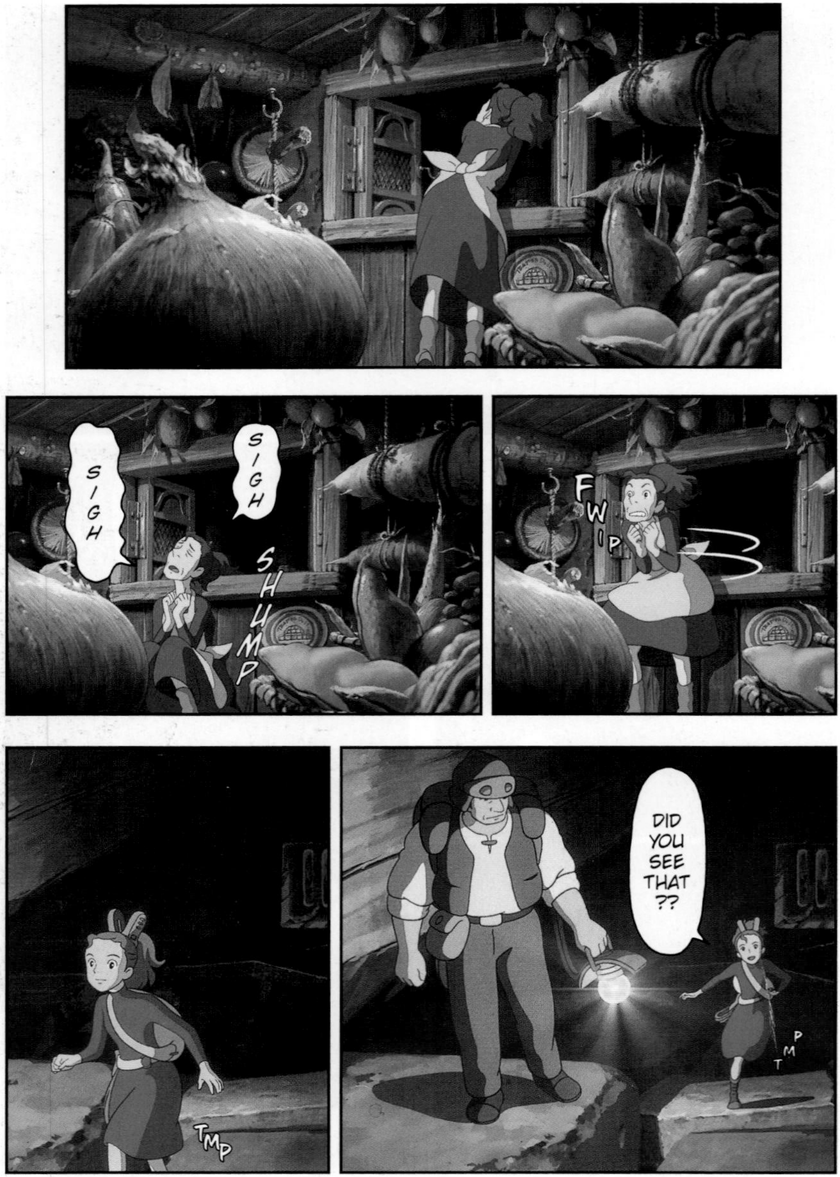
SIGH
SIGH
SHUMP
FWIP
TMP
DID YOU SEE THAT??
TMP

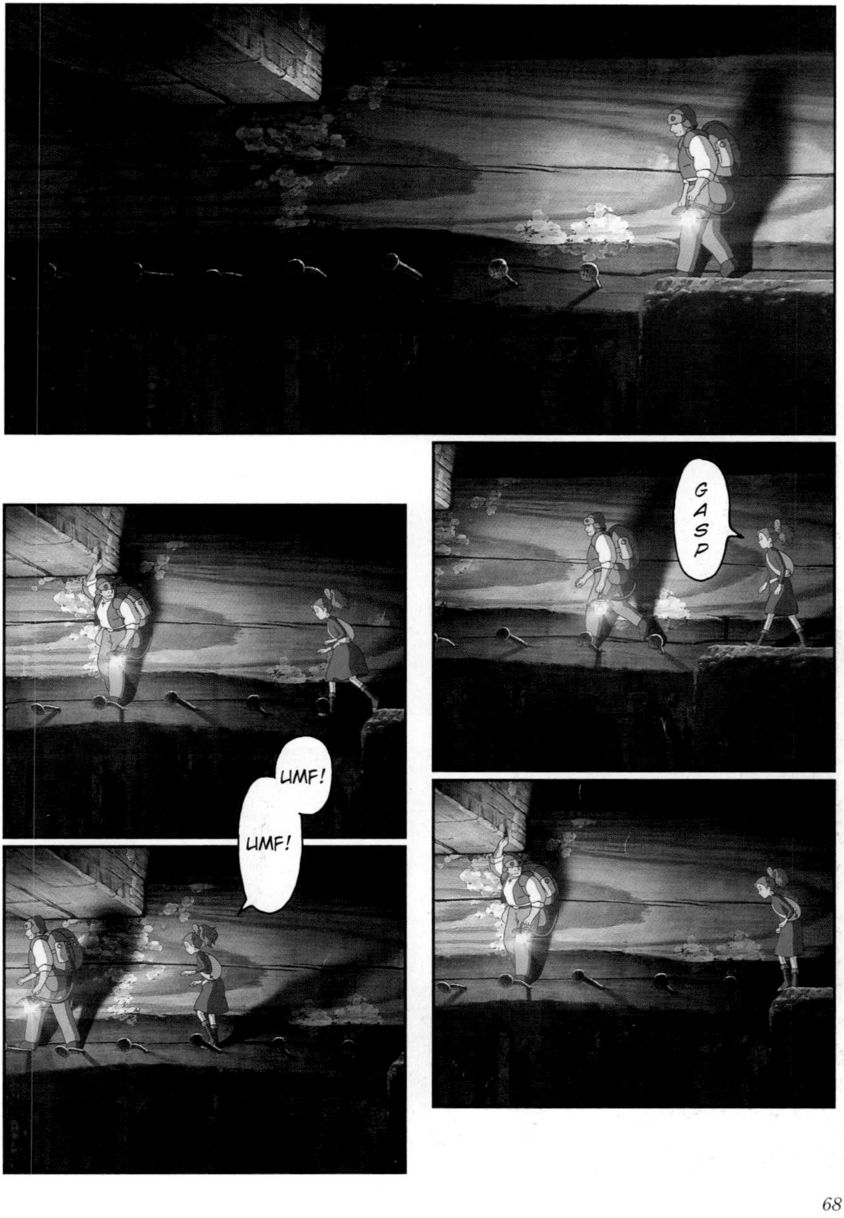
GASP
UMF!
UMF!

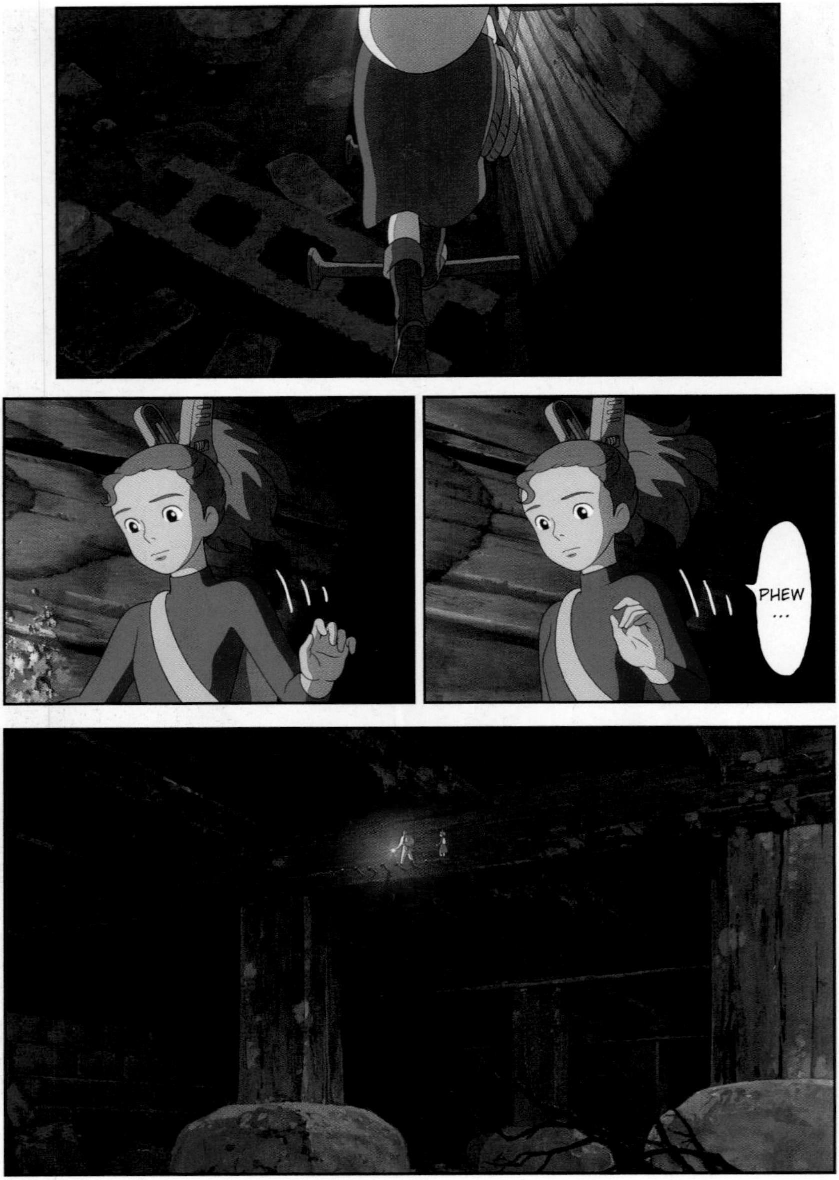
PHEW ...

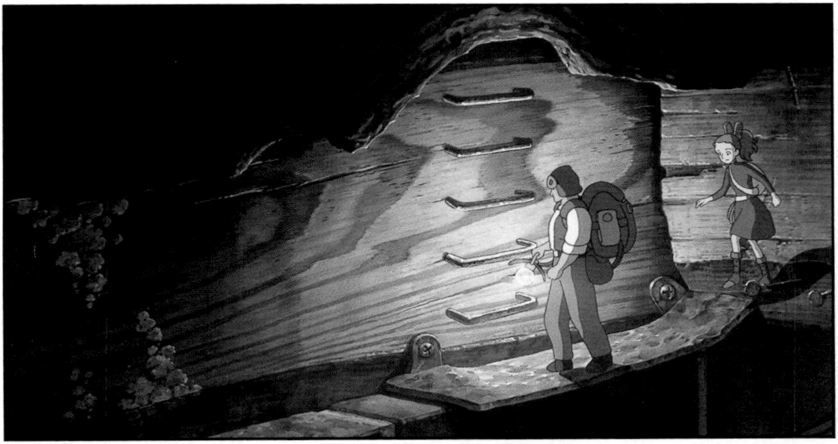

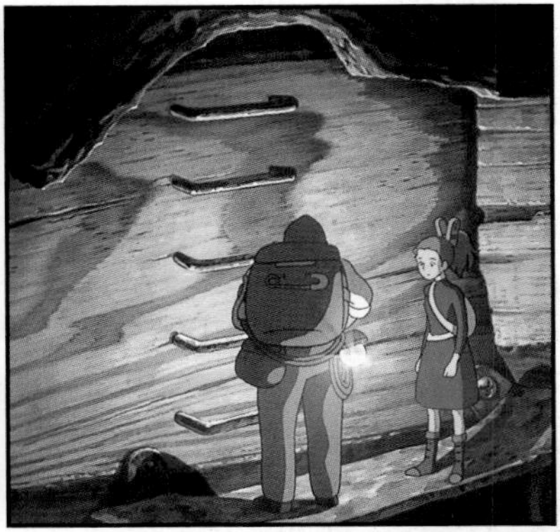

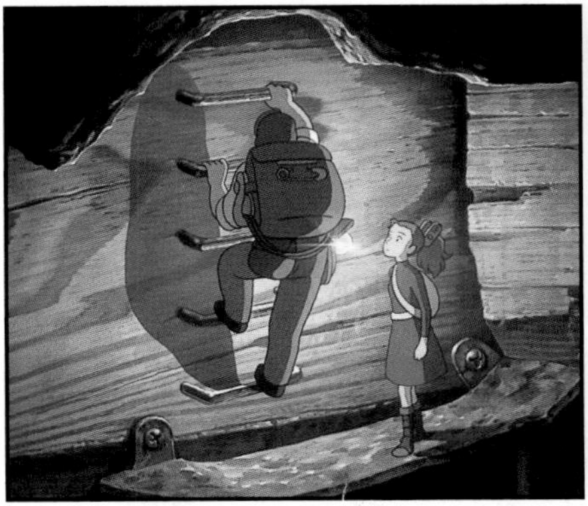

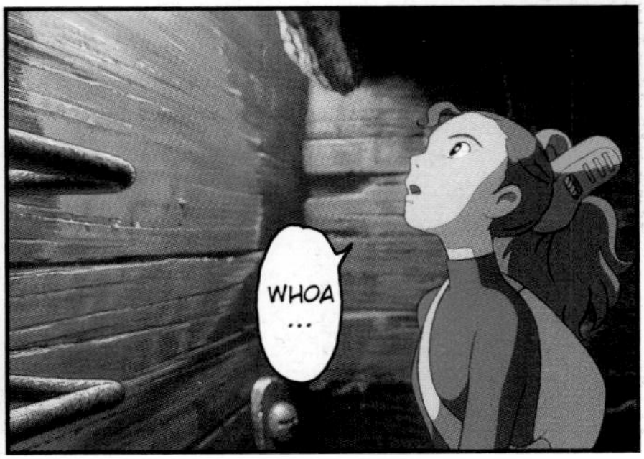
WHOA ...

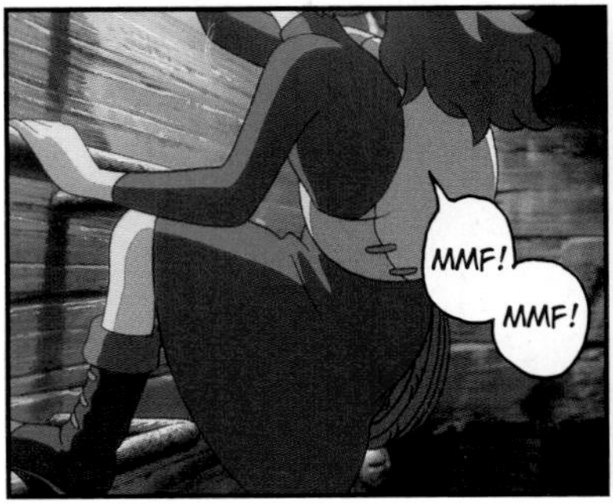
MMF!
MMF!

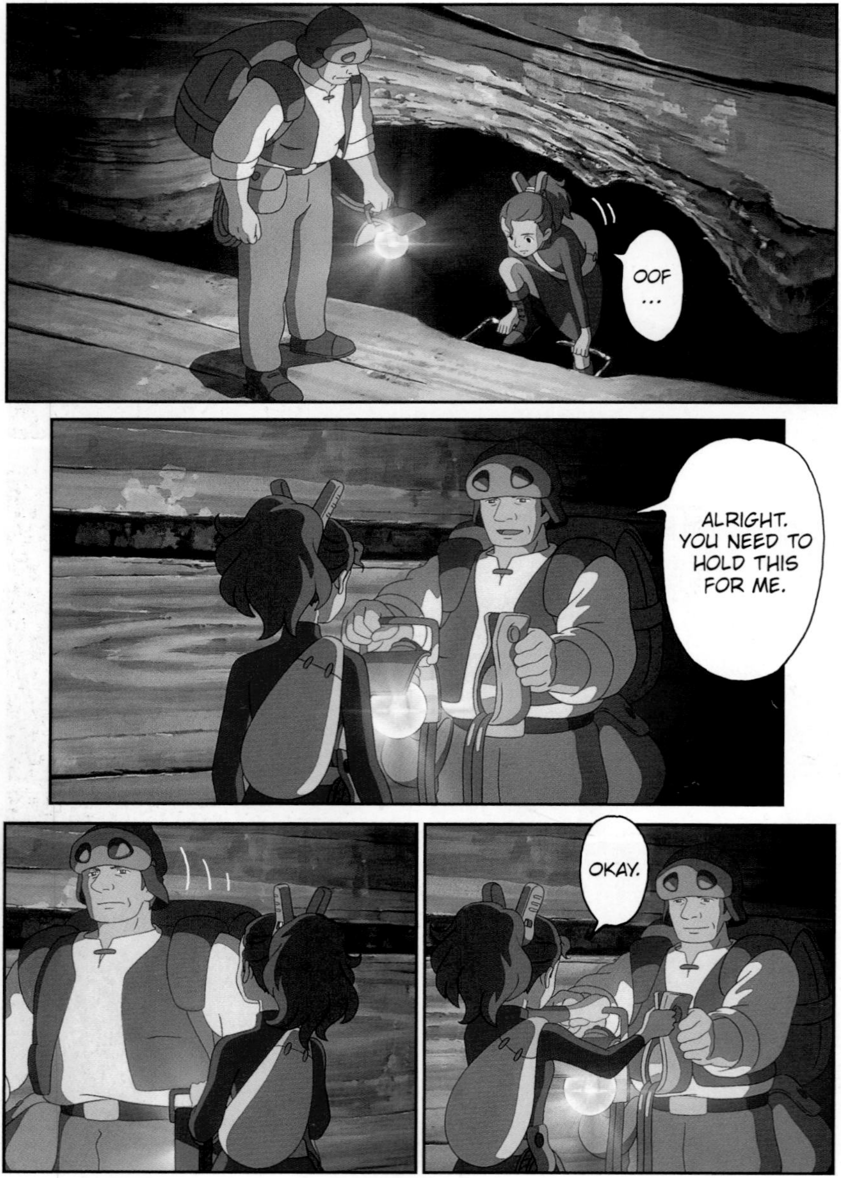
OOF ...
ALRIGHT. YOU NEED TO HOLD THIS FOR ME.
OKAY.

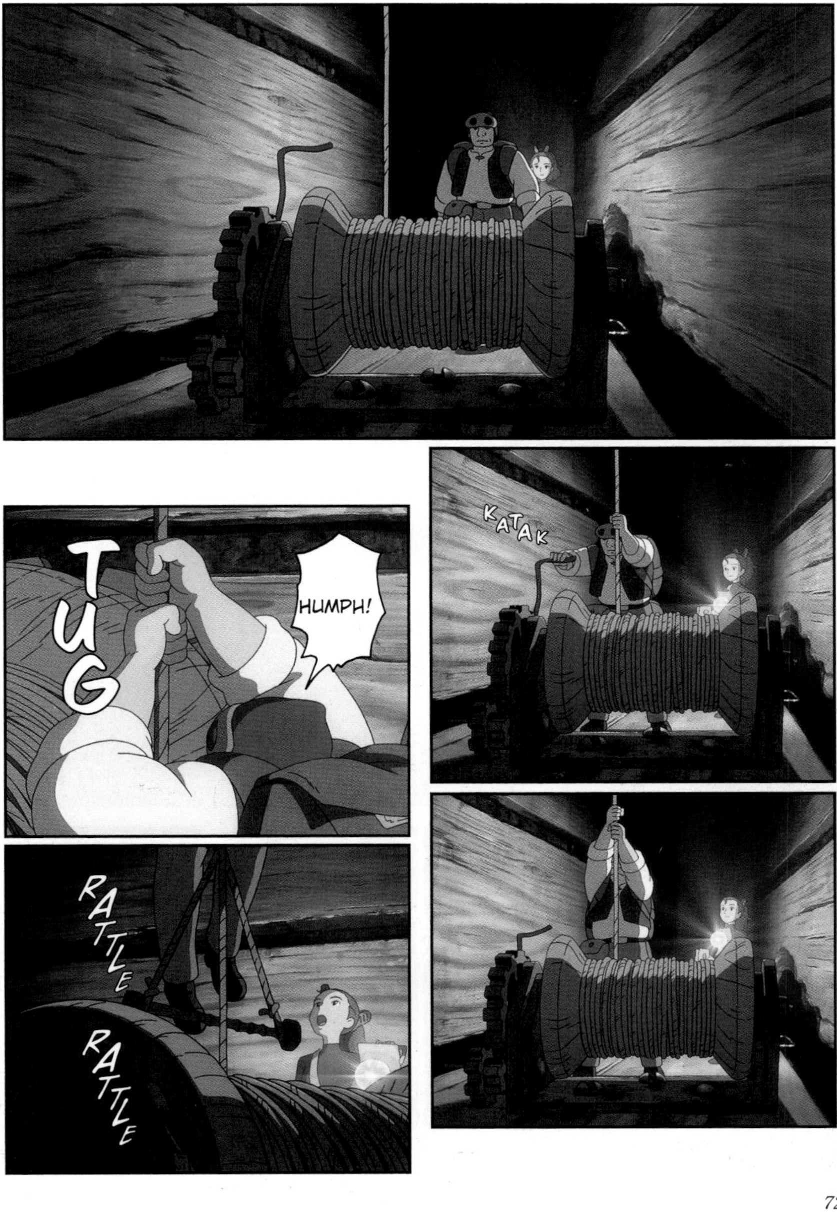
KATAK
HUMPH!
TUG
RATTLE RATTLE

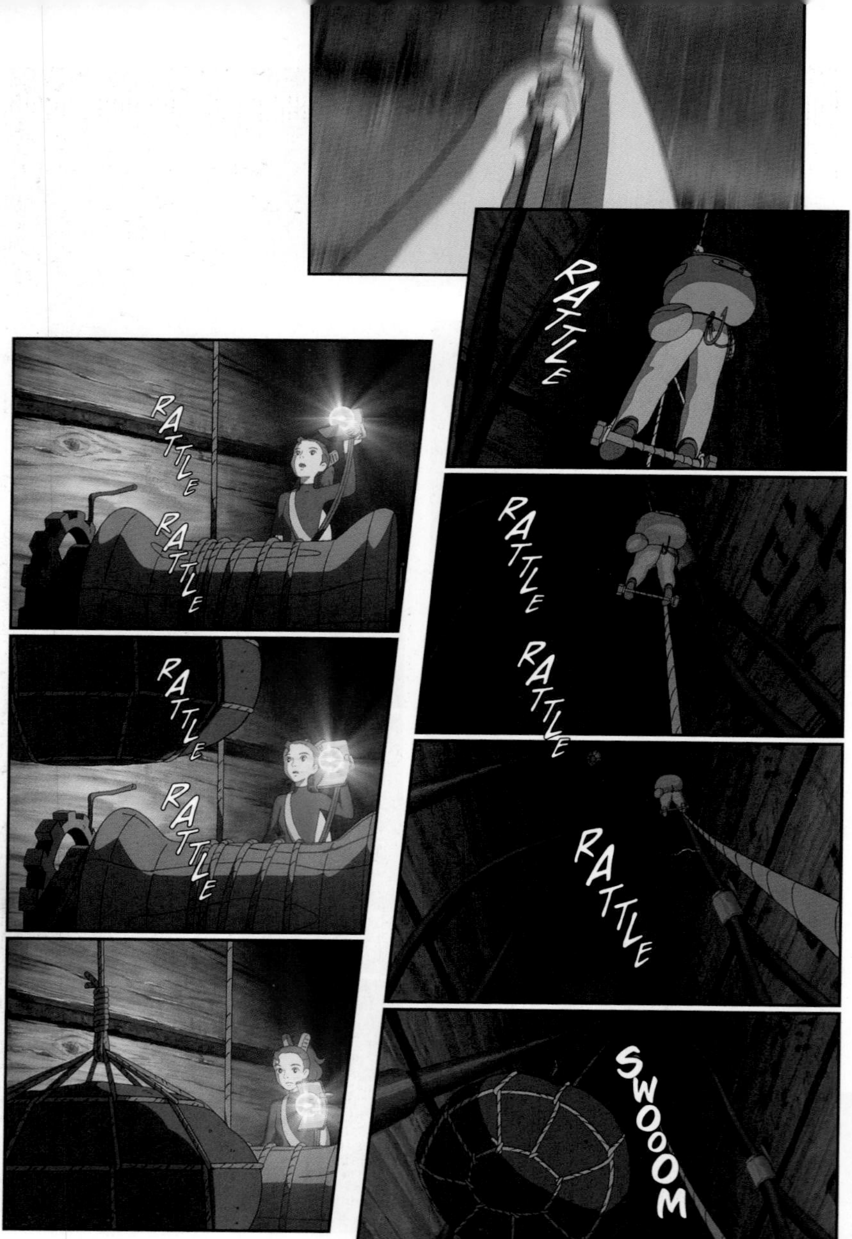
RATTLE
RATTLE
RATTLE
RATTLE
SWOOOM
RATTLE
RATTLE
RATTLE
RATTLE

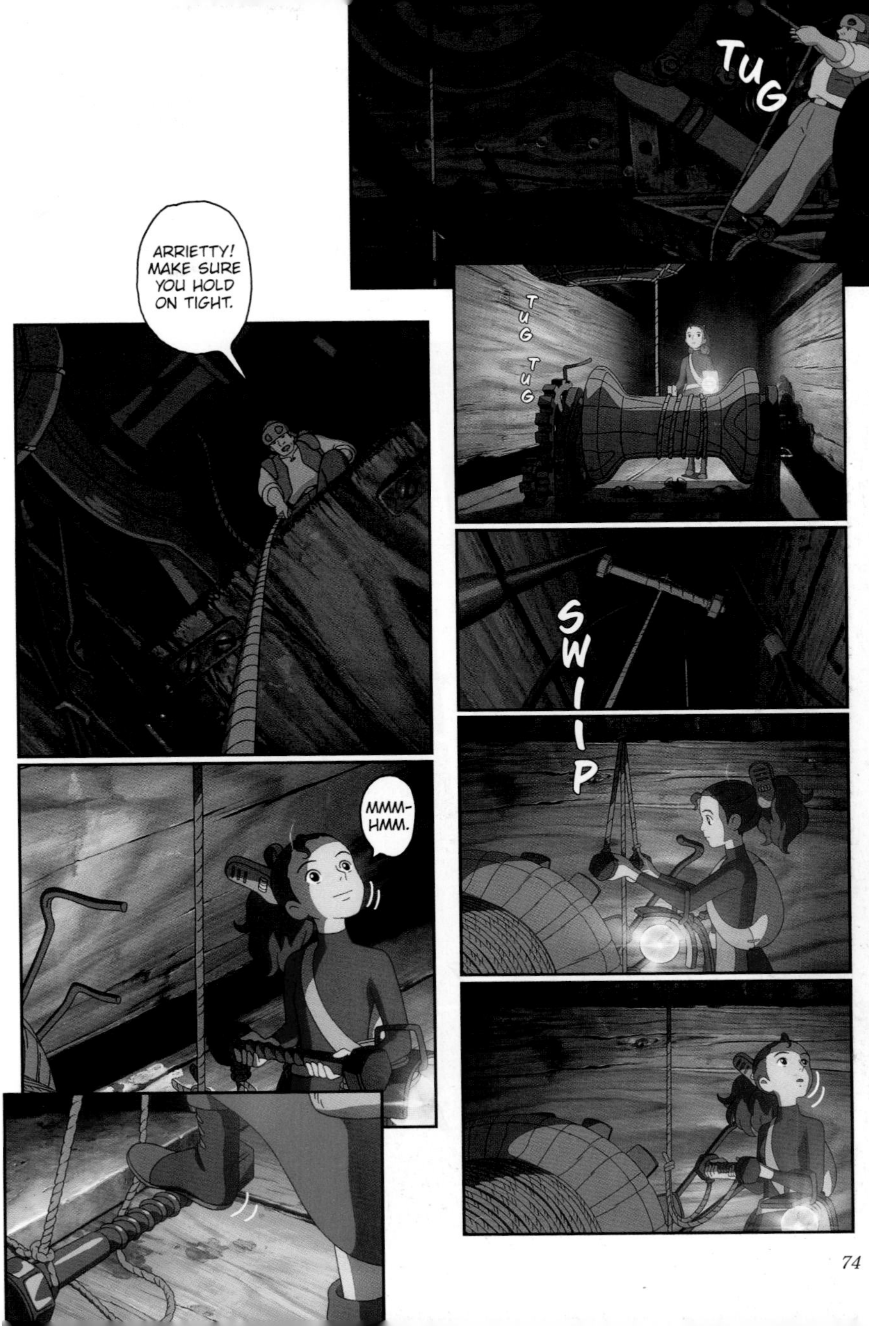
TUG
TUG TUG TUG
SWIIP
ARRIETTY! MAKE SURE YOU HOLD ON TIGHT.
MMM-HMM.

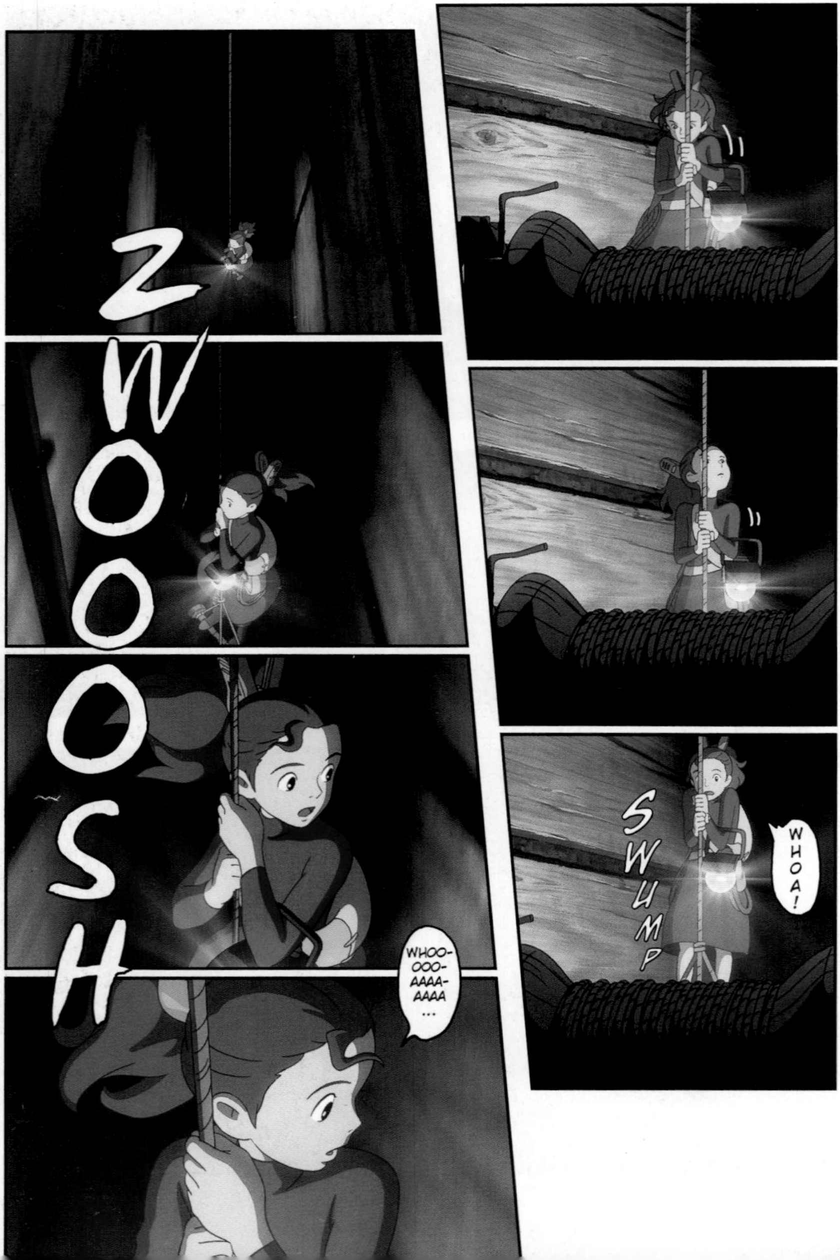
SWUMP
WHOA!
ZWOOOOSH
WHOO-OOO-AAAA-AAAA...

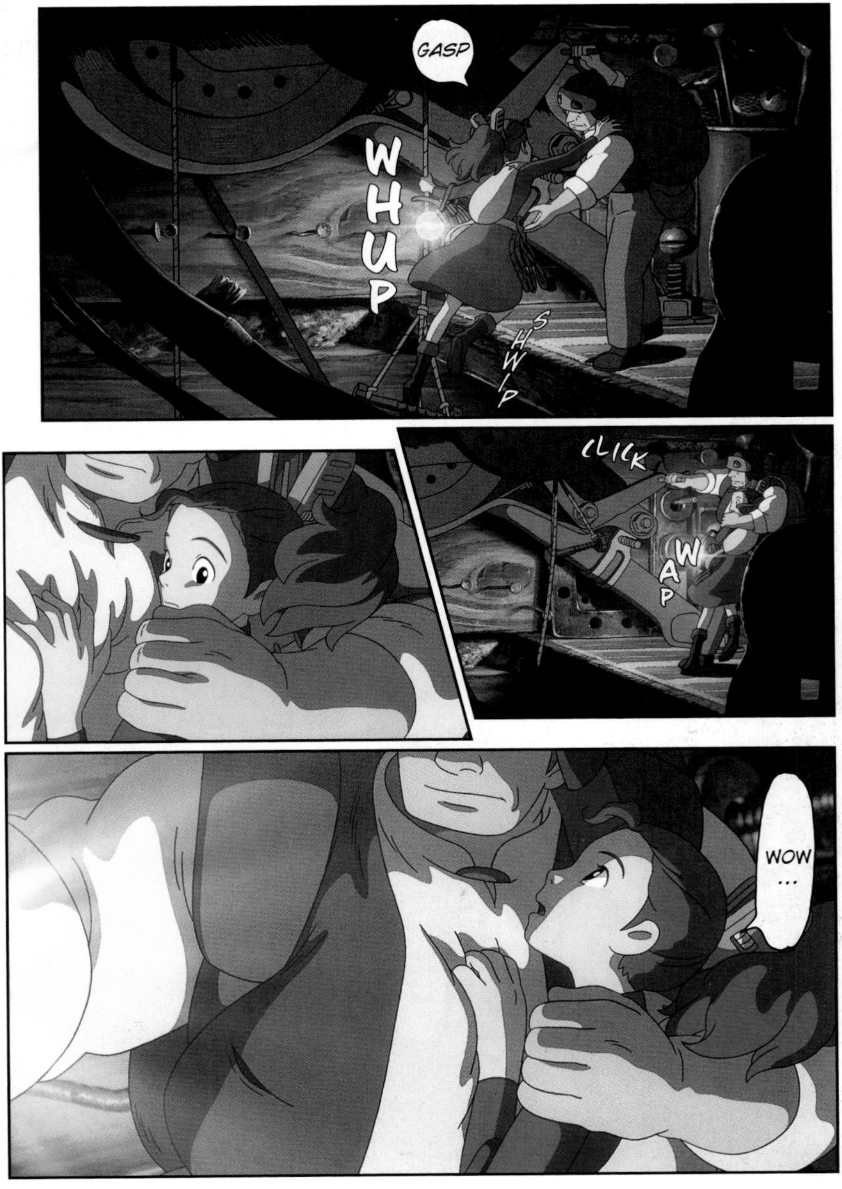
GASP
WHUP
SHWIP
CLICK
WAP
WOW ...

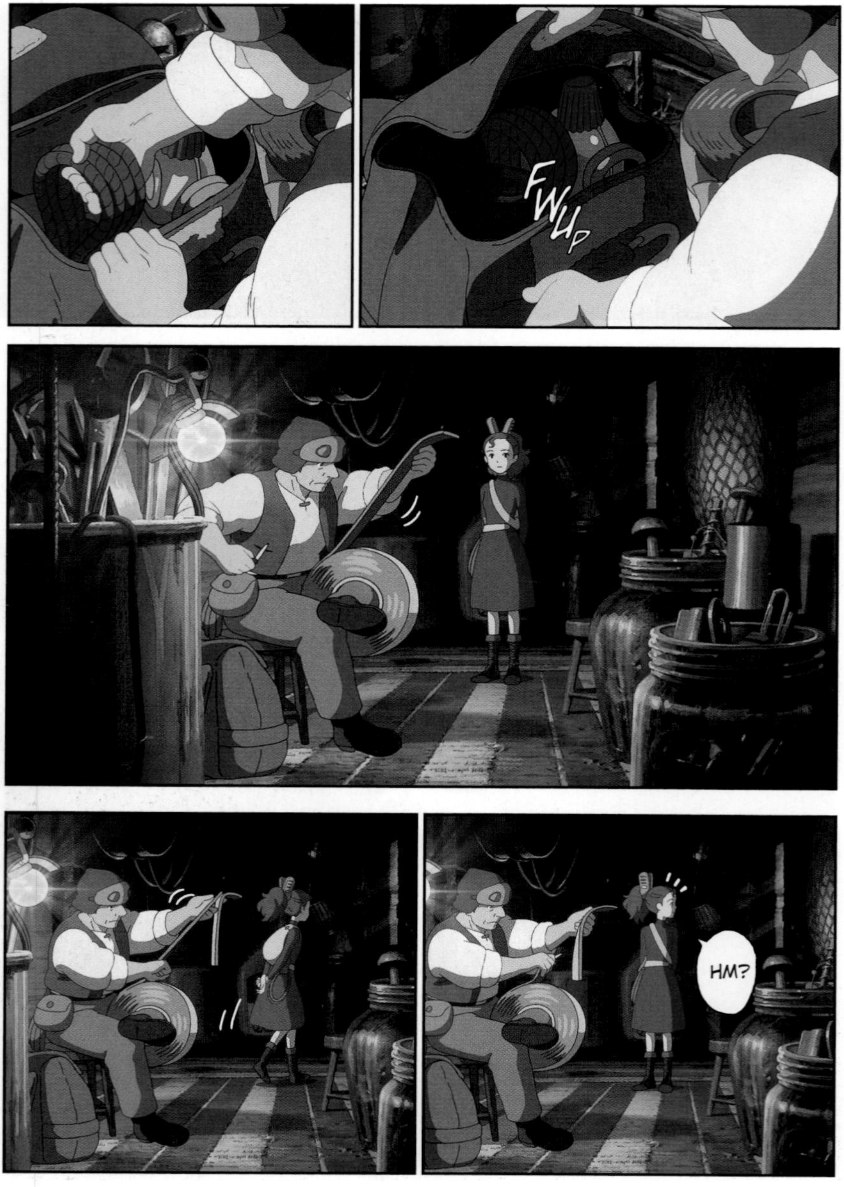
FWUP
HM?

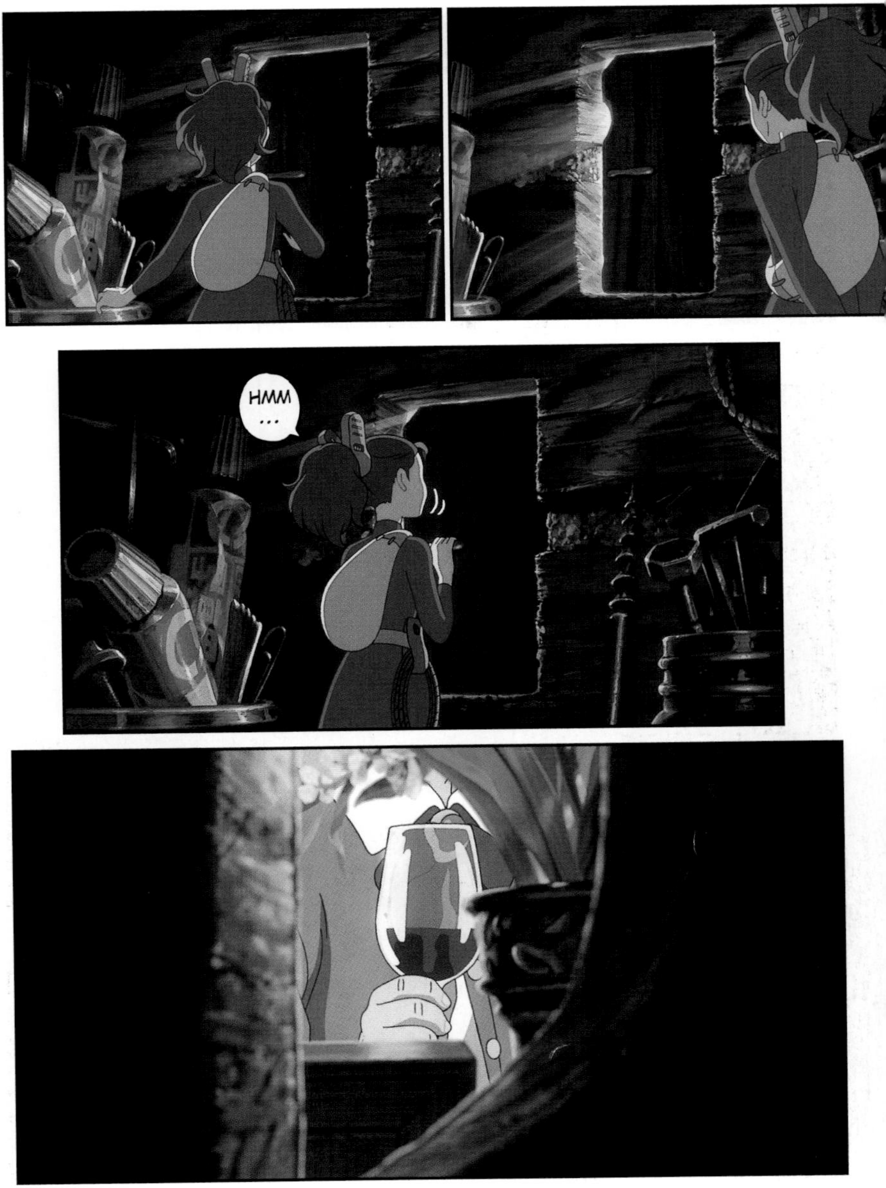
HMM
...

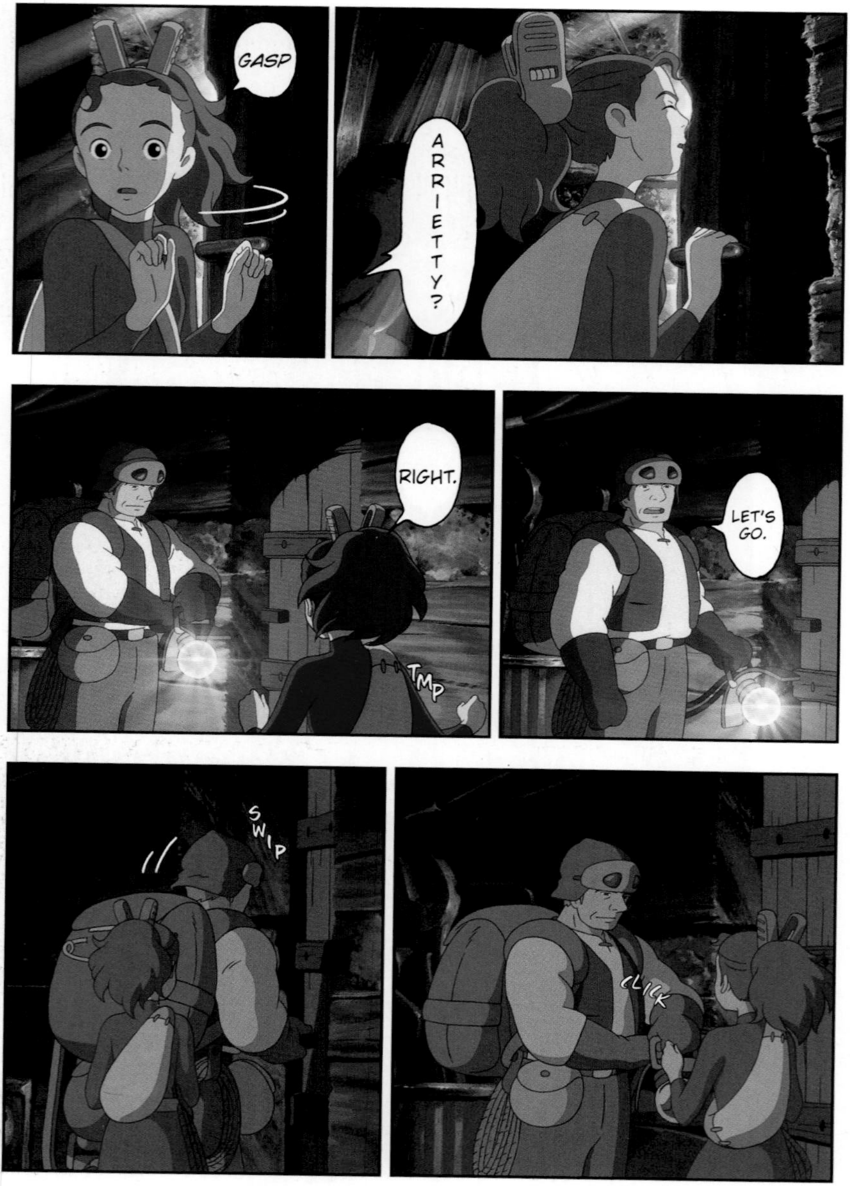
ARRIETTY?
GASP
LET'S GO.
RIGHT.
TMP
CLICK
SWIP

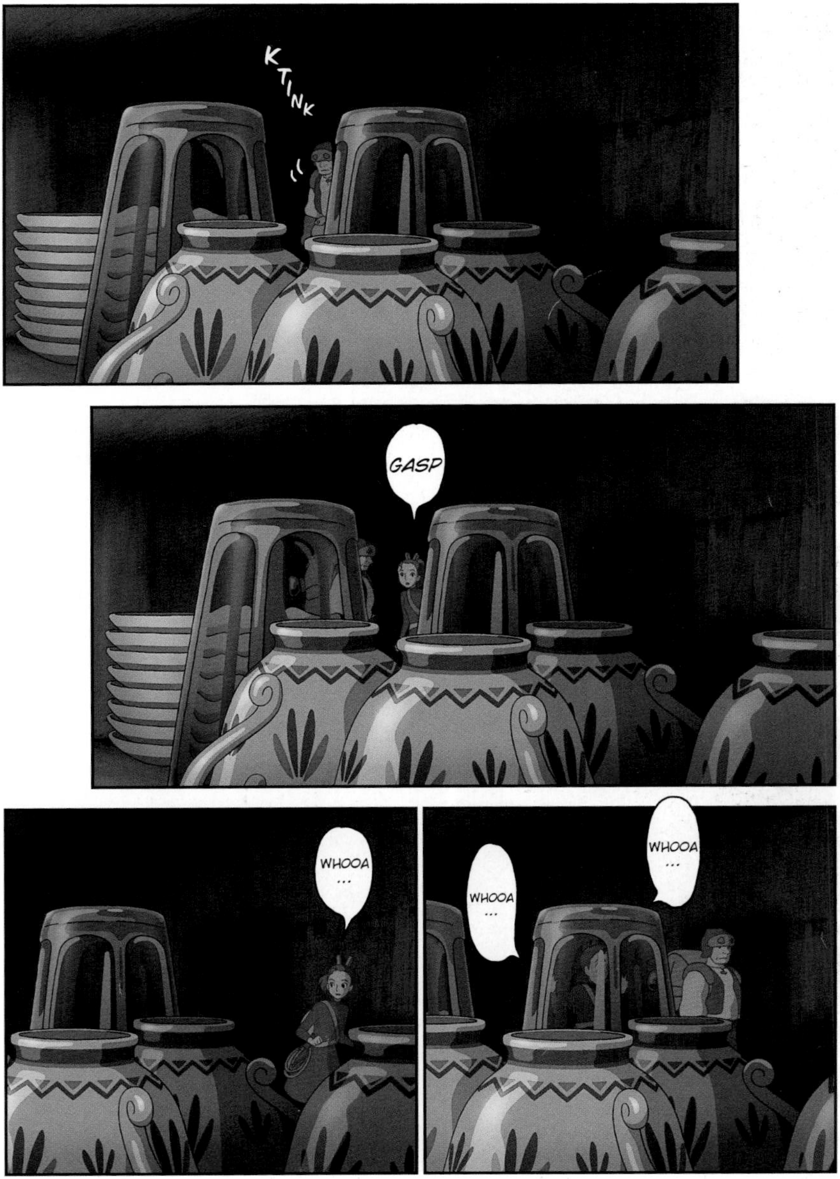
KTINK
GASP
WHOOA ...
WHOOA ...
WHOOA ...

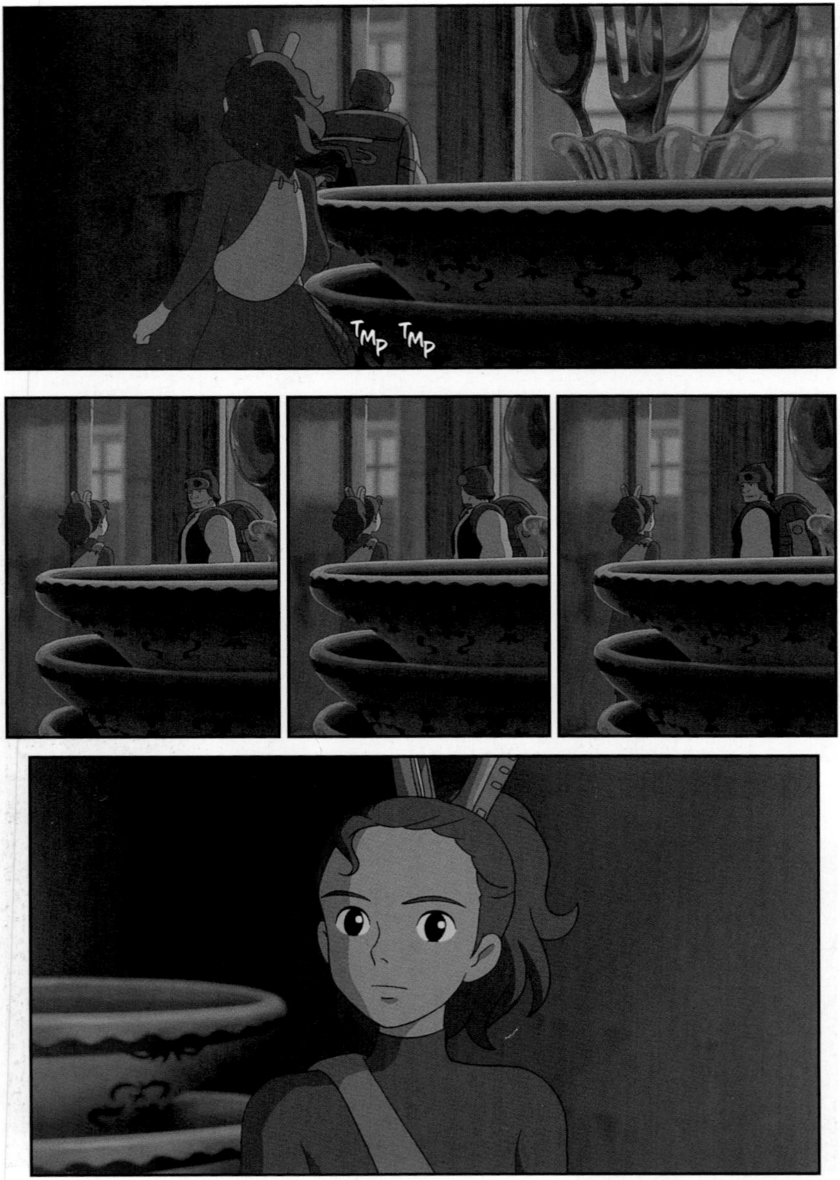
TMP TMP

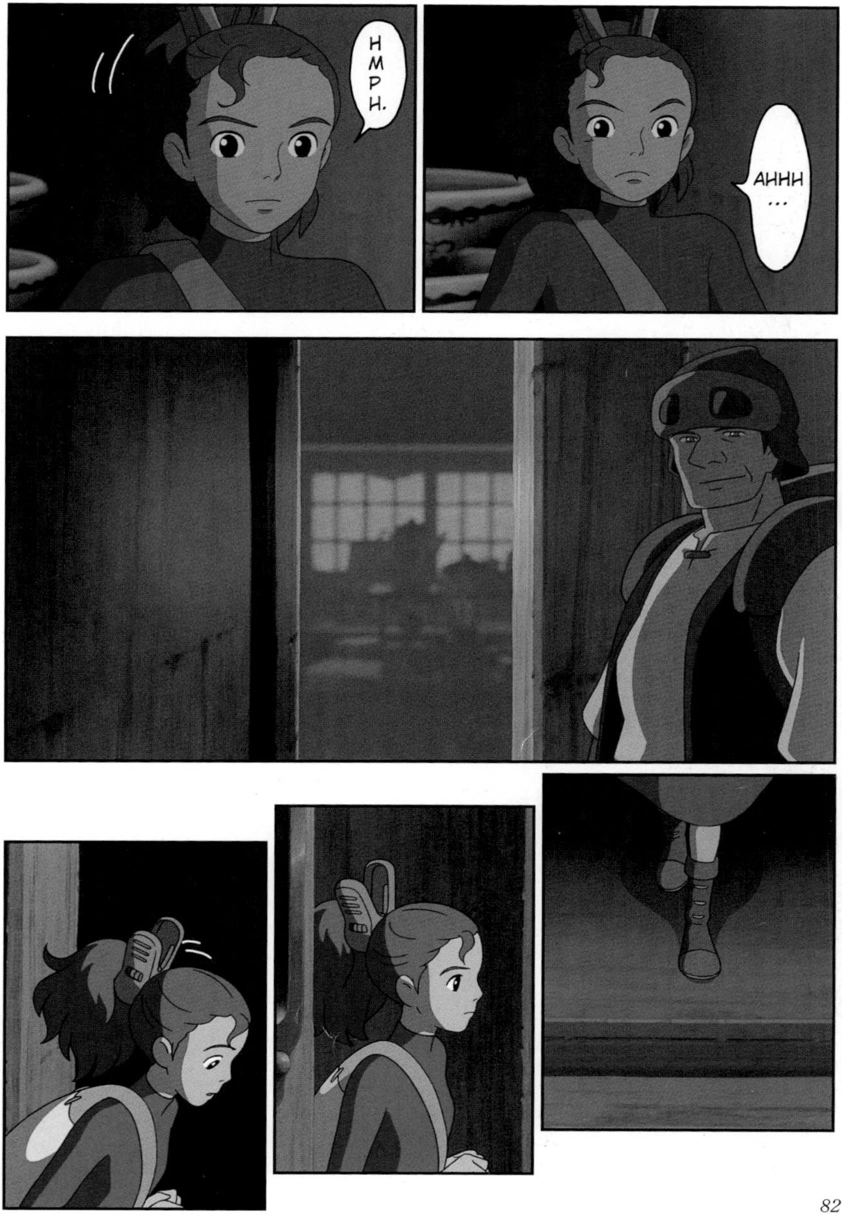
AHHH ...
HMPH.

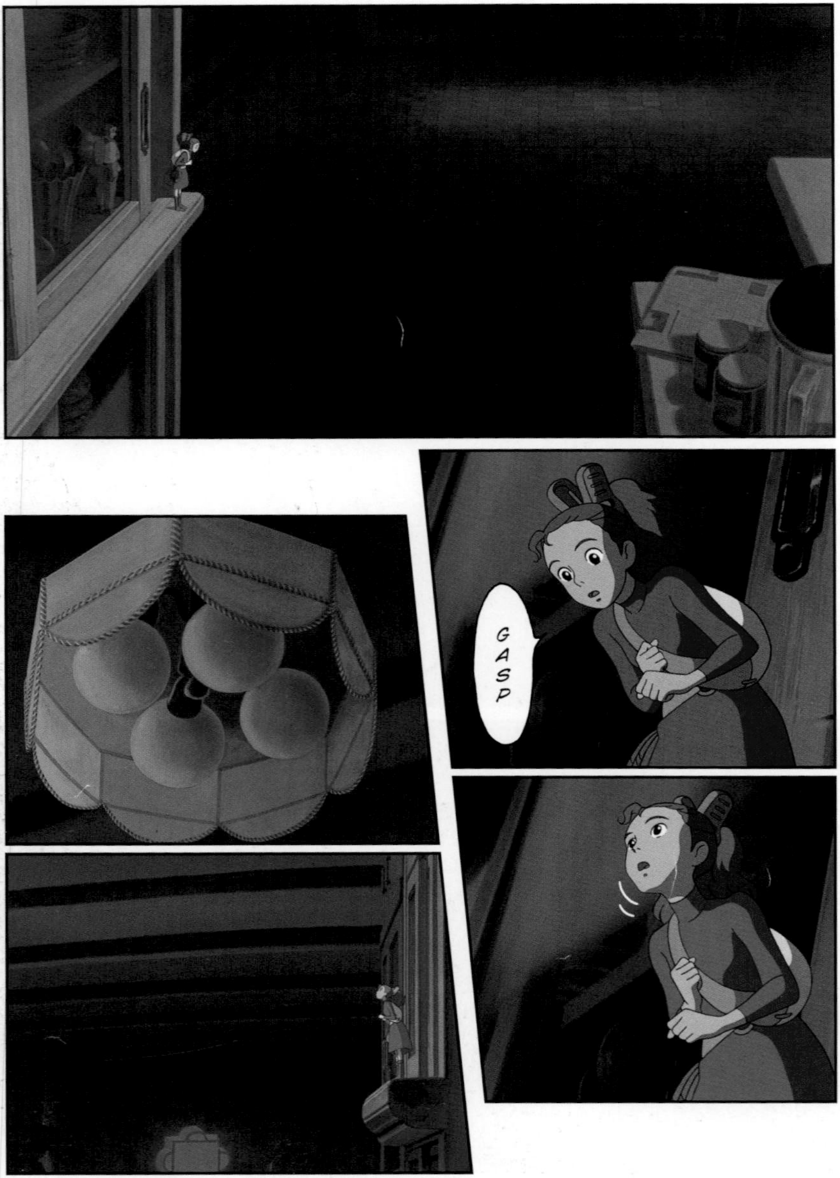
GASP

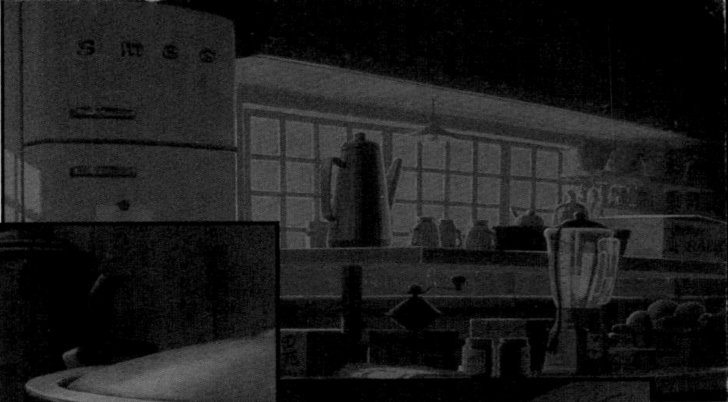
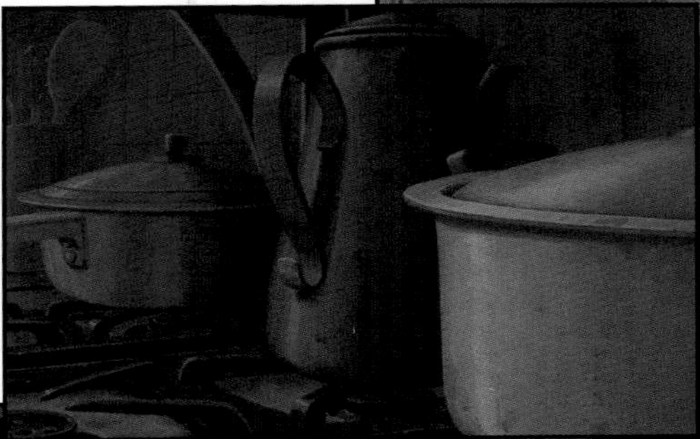
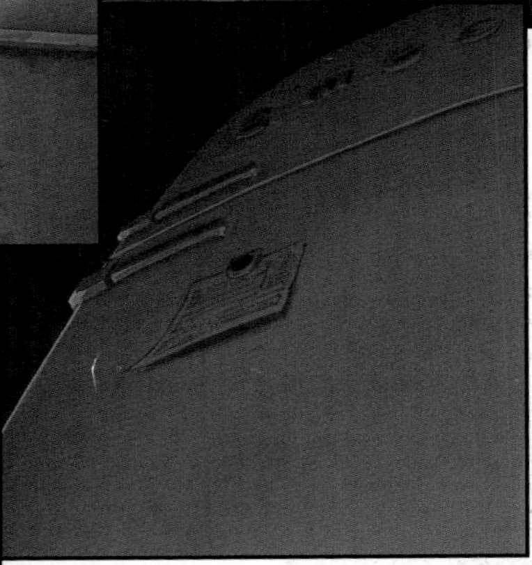
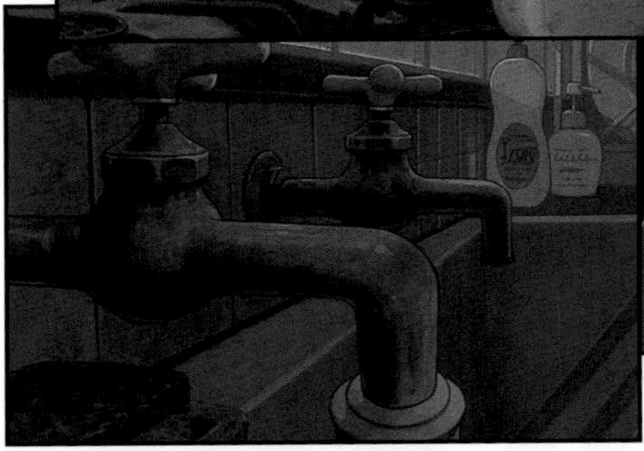
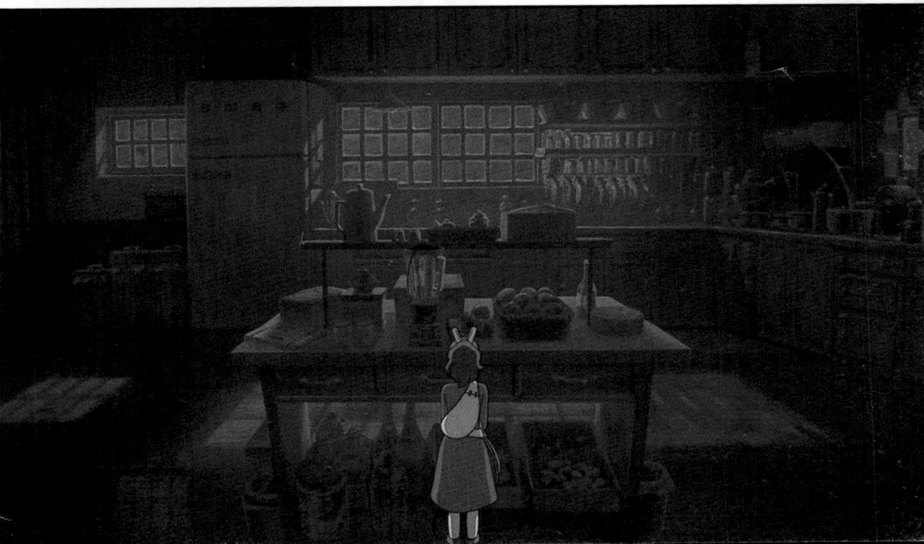

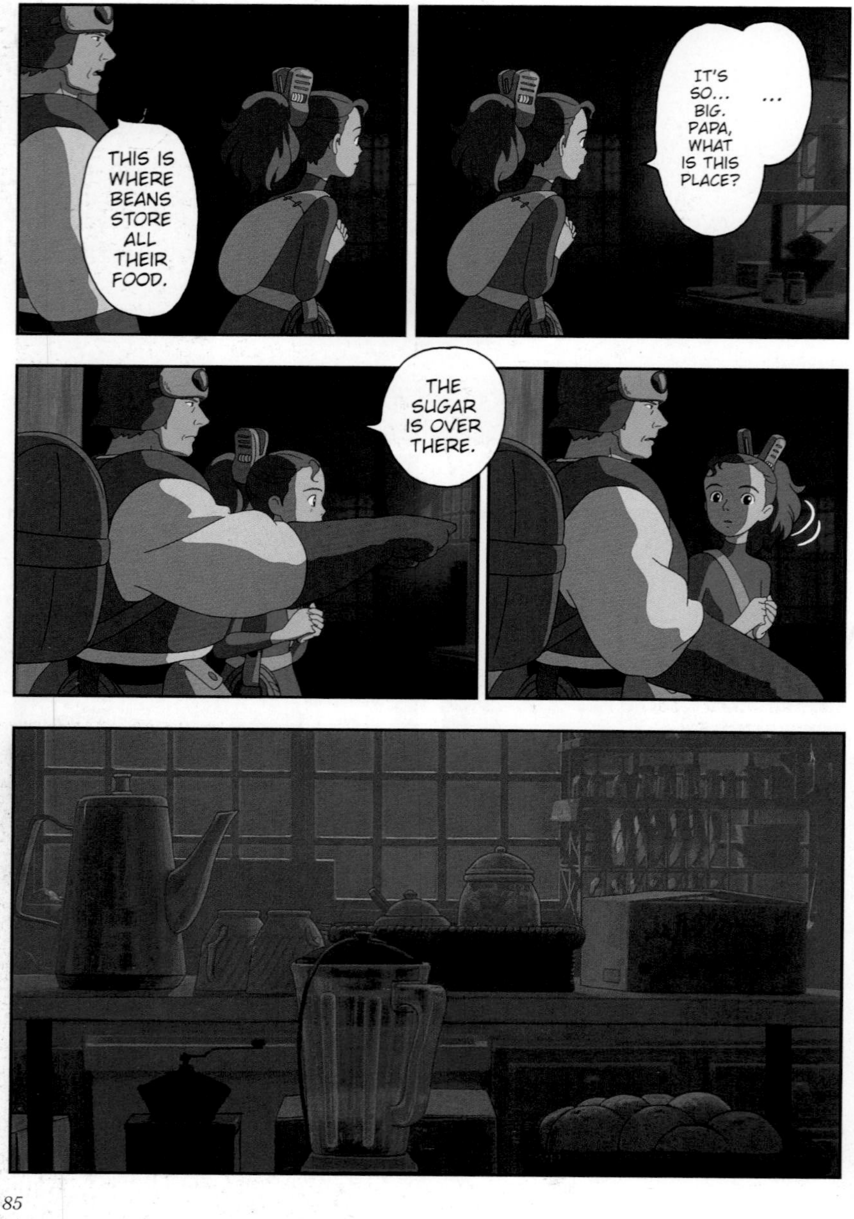
...
IT'S SO... BIG. PAPA, WHAT IS THIS PLACE?
THIS IS WHERE BEANS STORE ALL THEIR FOOD.
THE SUGAR IS OVER THERE.

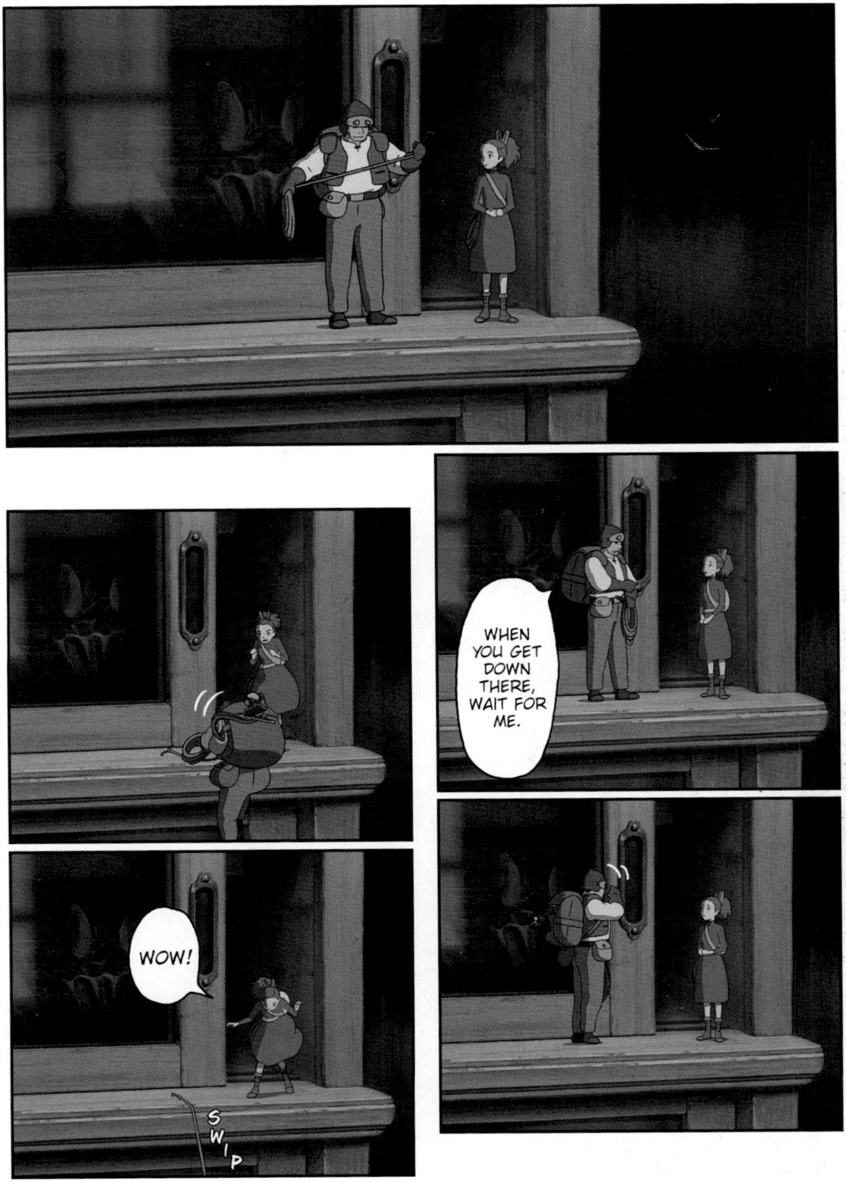
WHEN YOU GET DOWN THERE, WAIT FOR ME.
WOW!
SWIP

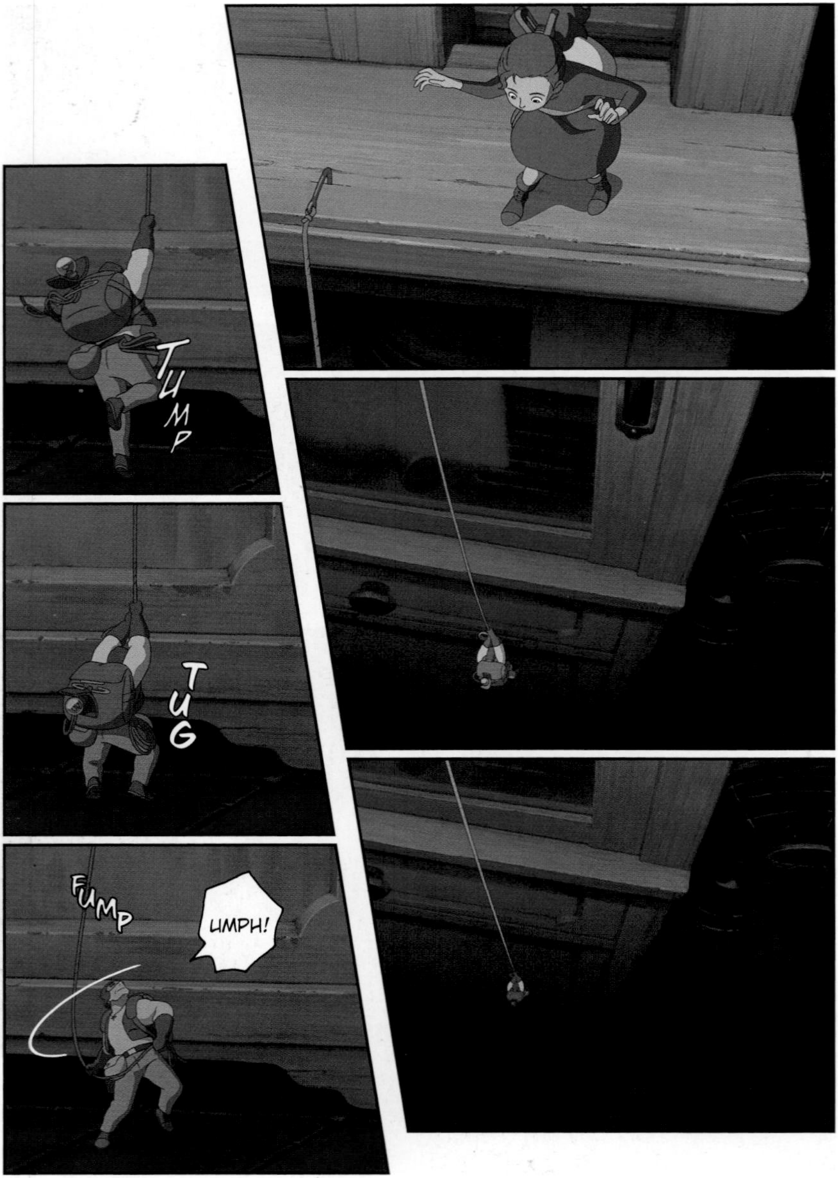
TUMP
TUG
FUMP
UMPH!

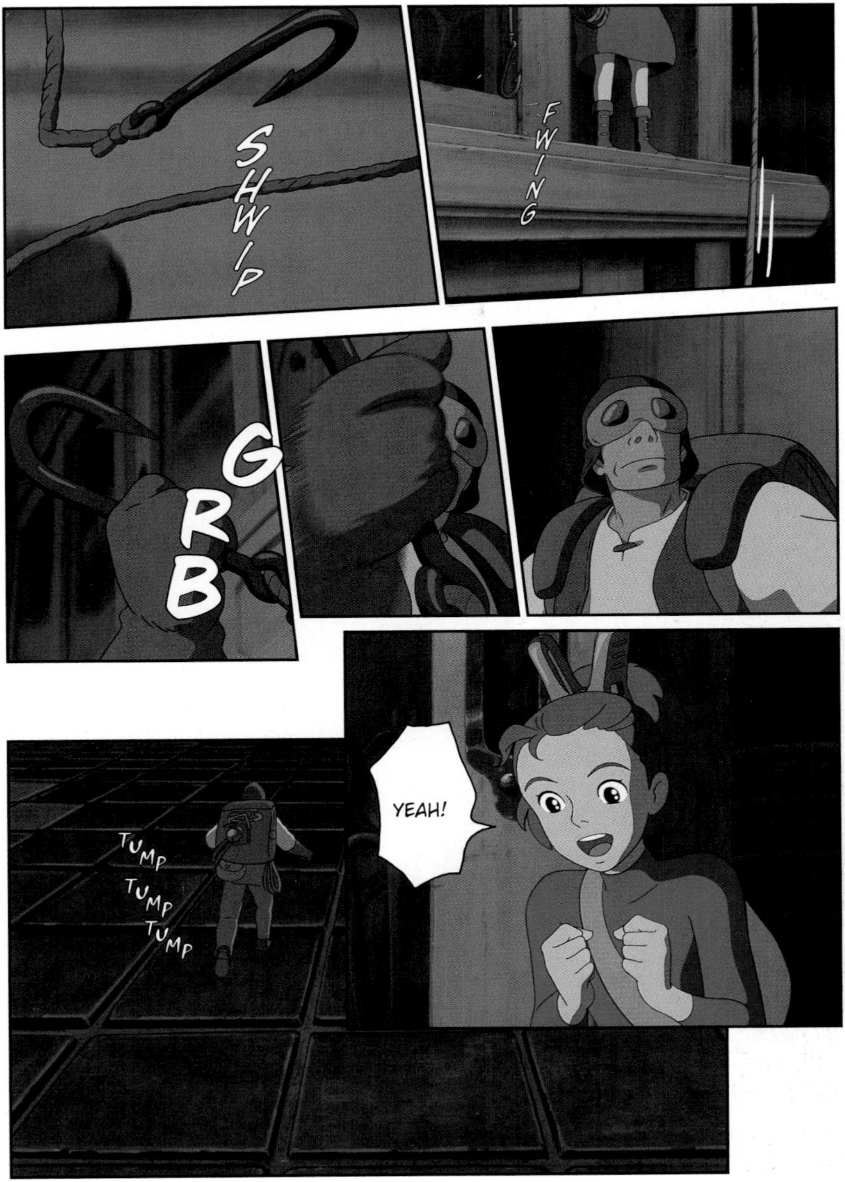
SHWIP
FWING
GRB
YEAH!
TUMP
TUMP
TUMP

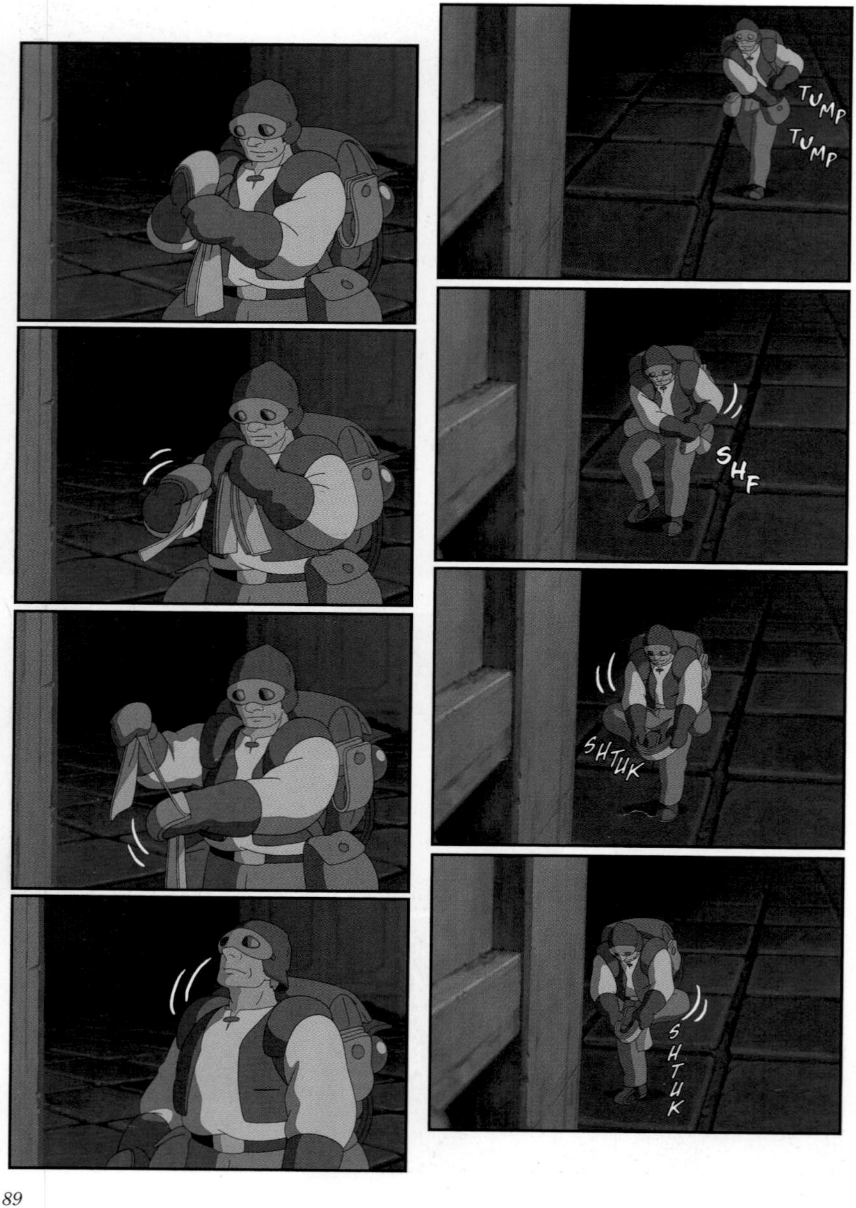
TUMP
TUMP
SHF
SHTUK
SHTUK

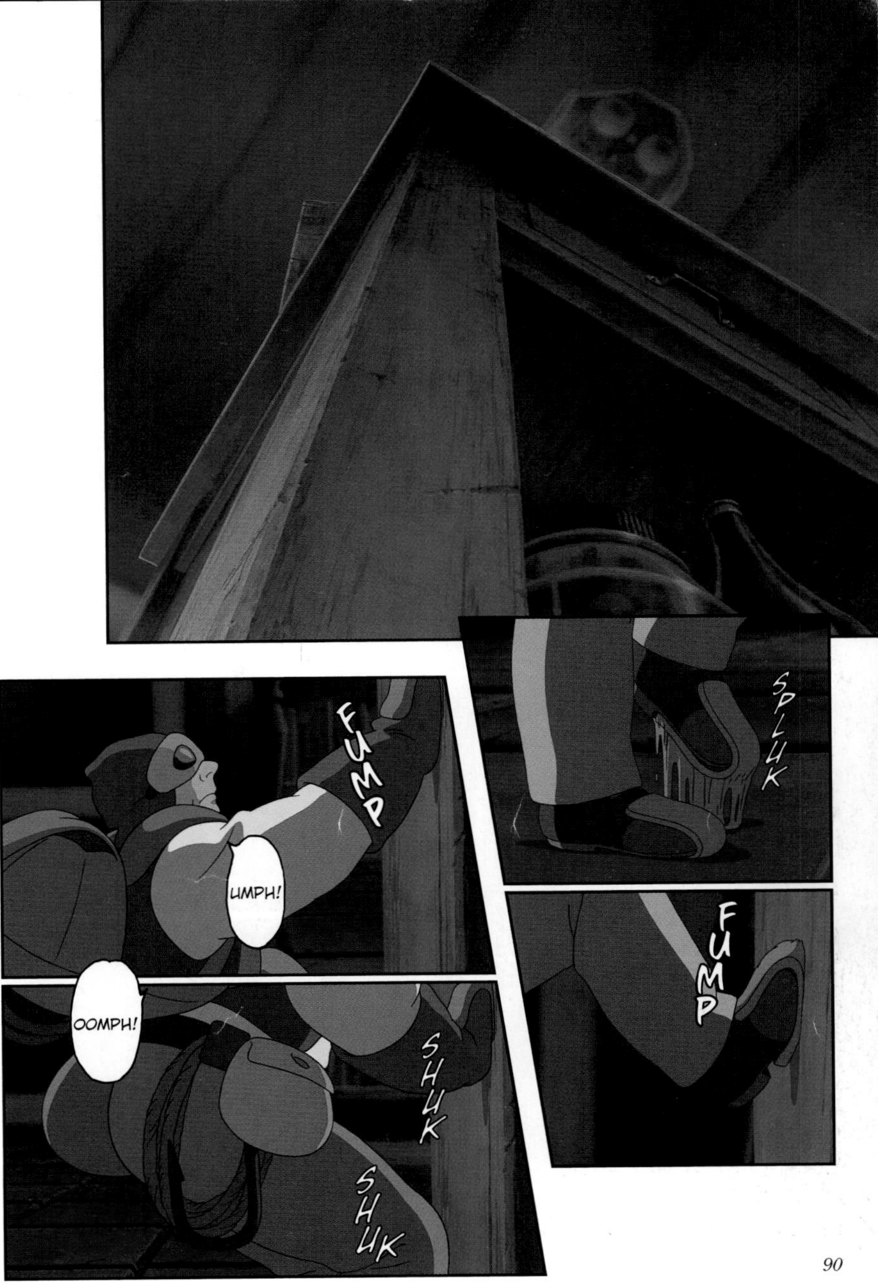
SPLUK
FUMP
FUMP
UMPH!
OOMPH!
SHUK
SHUK

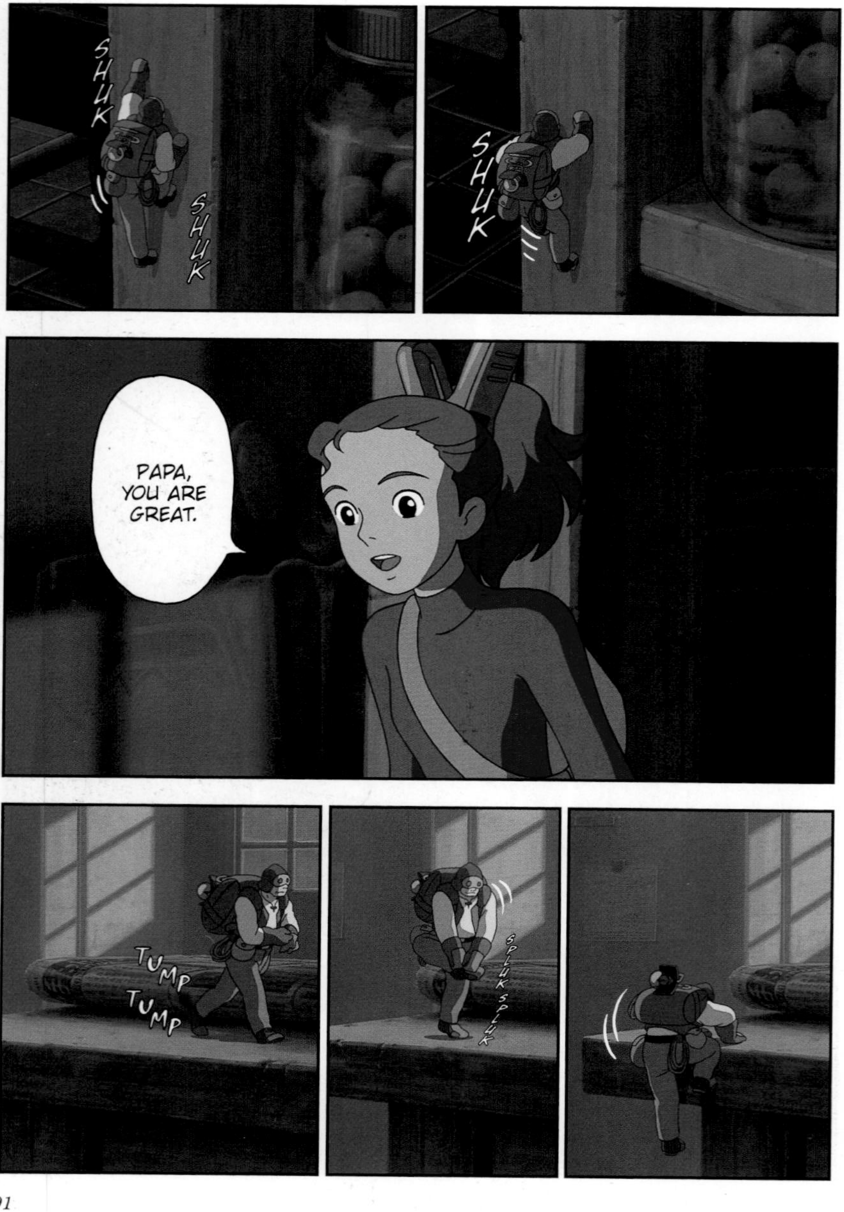
SHUK
SHUK
SHUK
PAPA, YOU ARE GREAT.
SPLUK SPLUK
TUMP TUMP

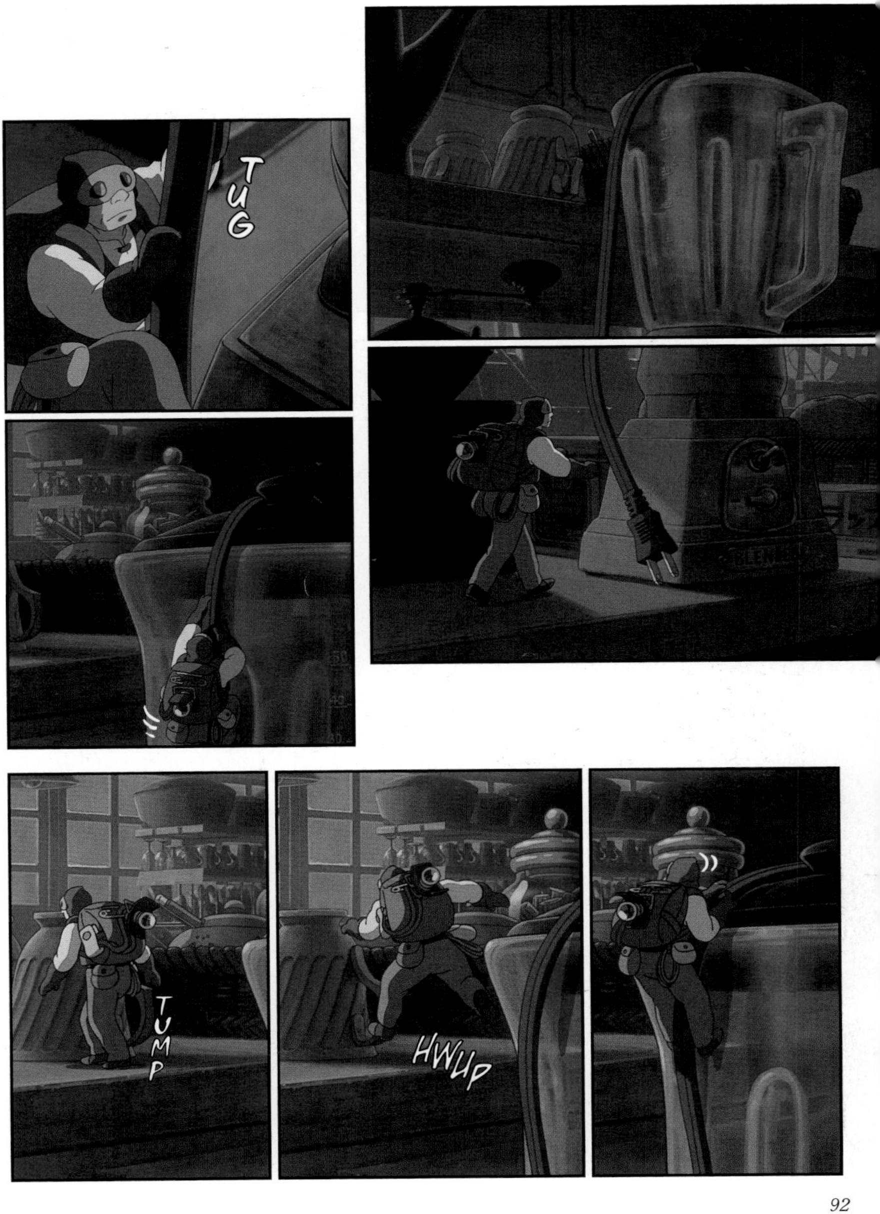
TUG
TUMP
HWUP

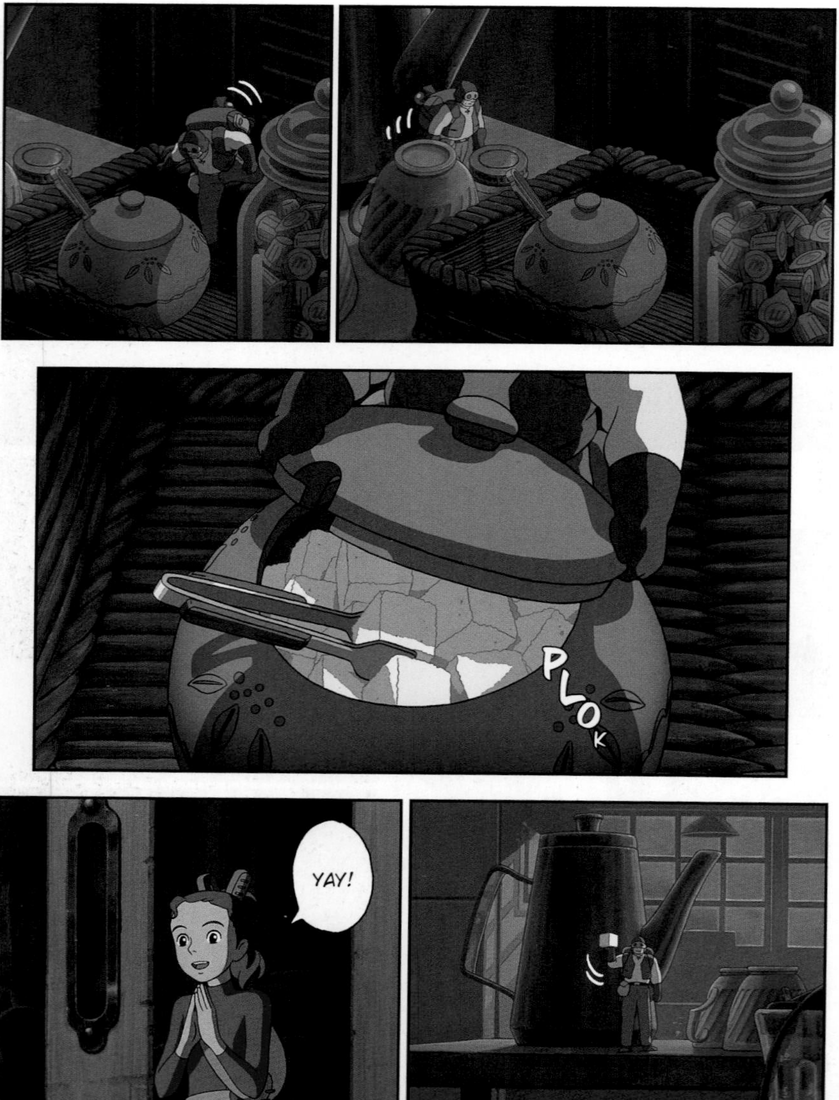
PLOK
YAY!

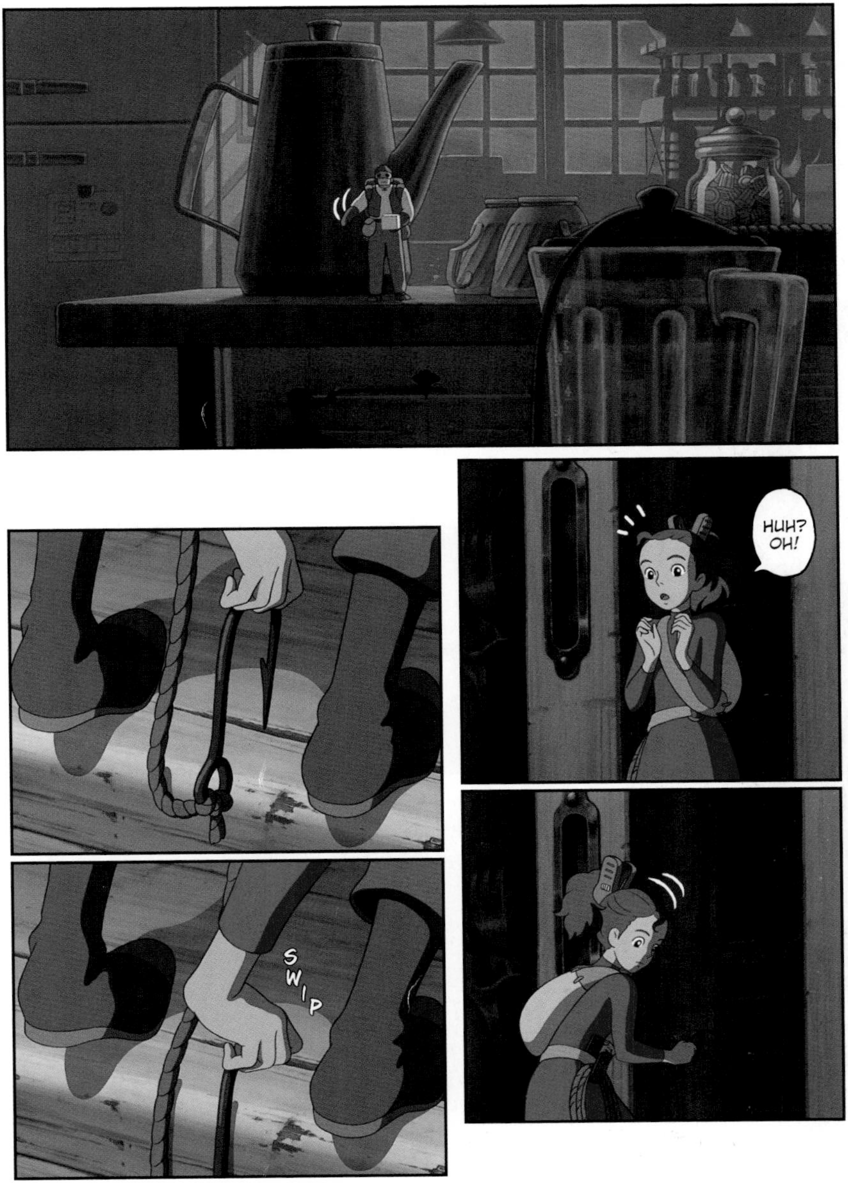
HUH? OH!
SWIP

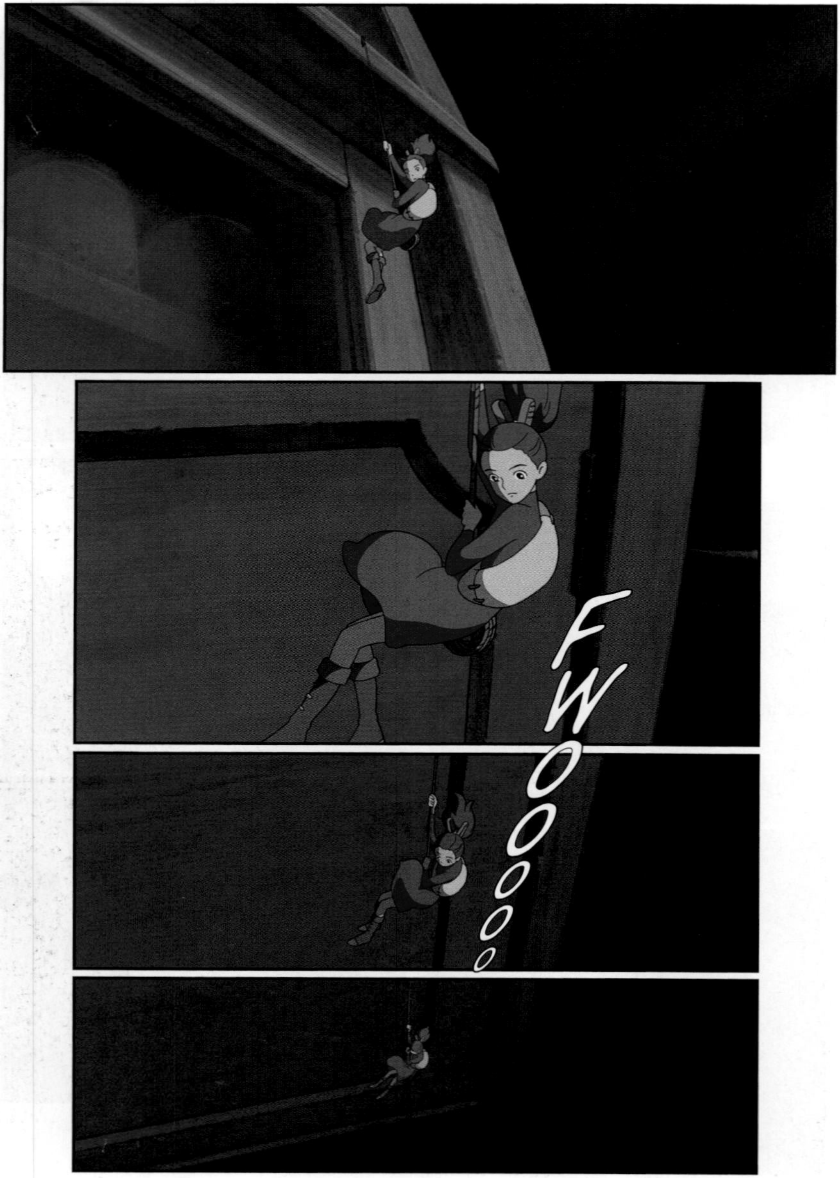
FWOOOOO

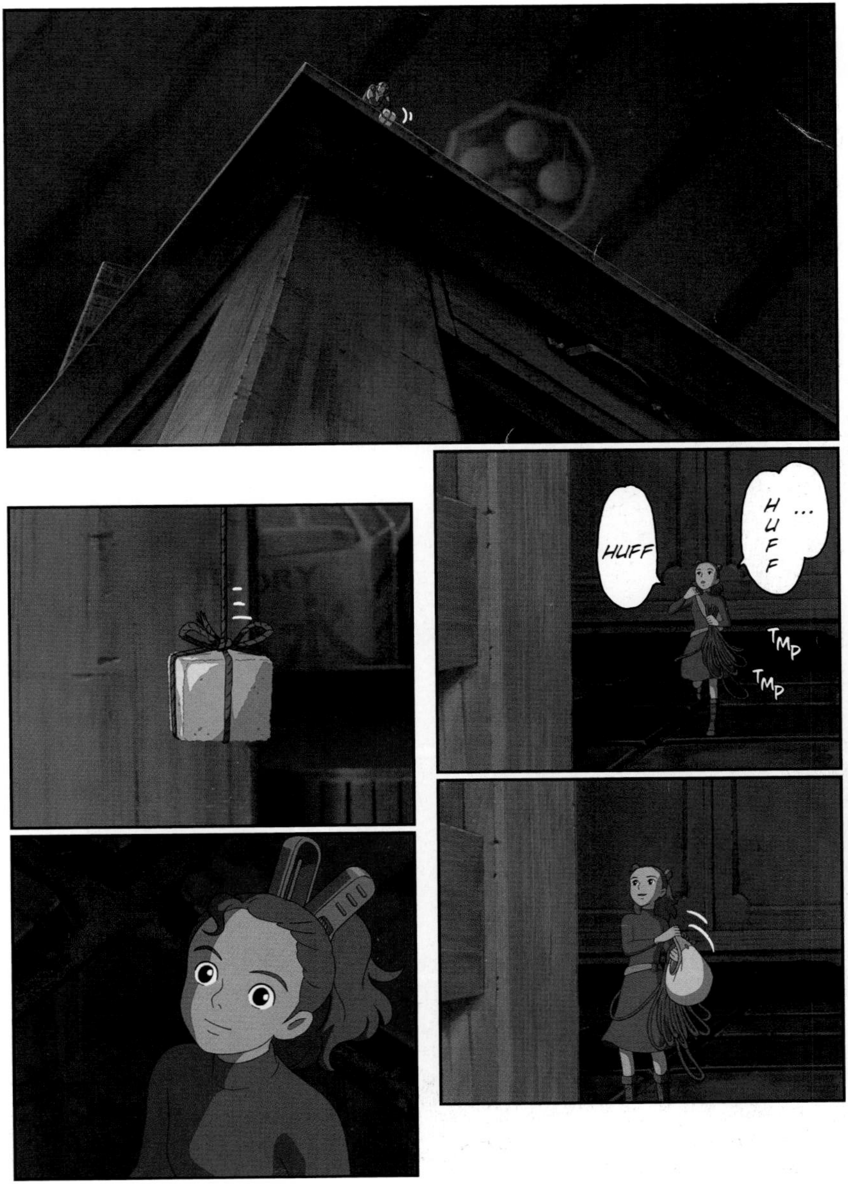
HUFF...
HUFF
TMP
TMP

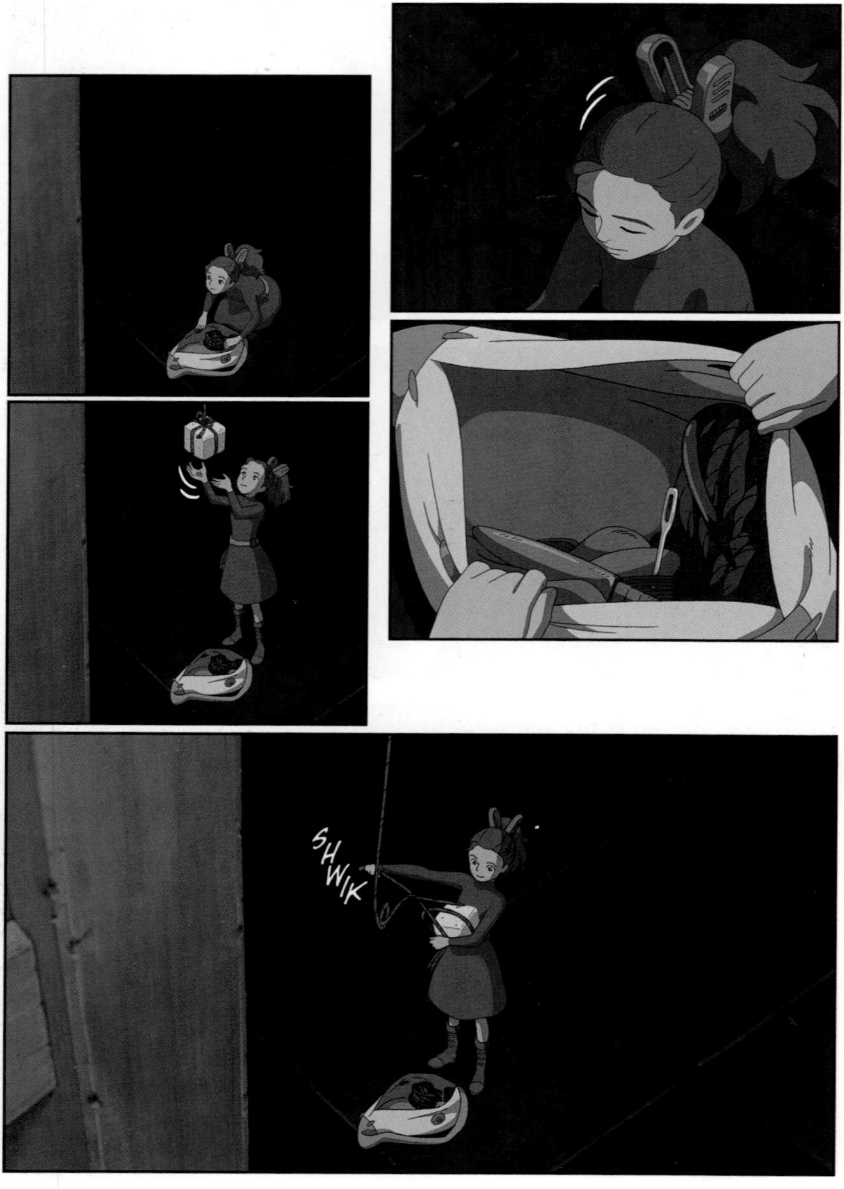
SHWIK

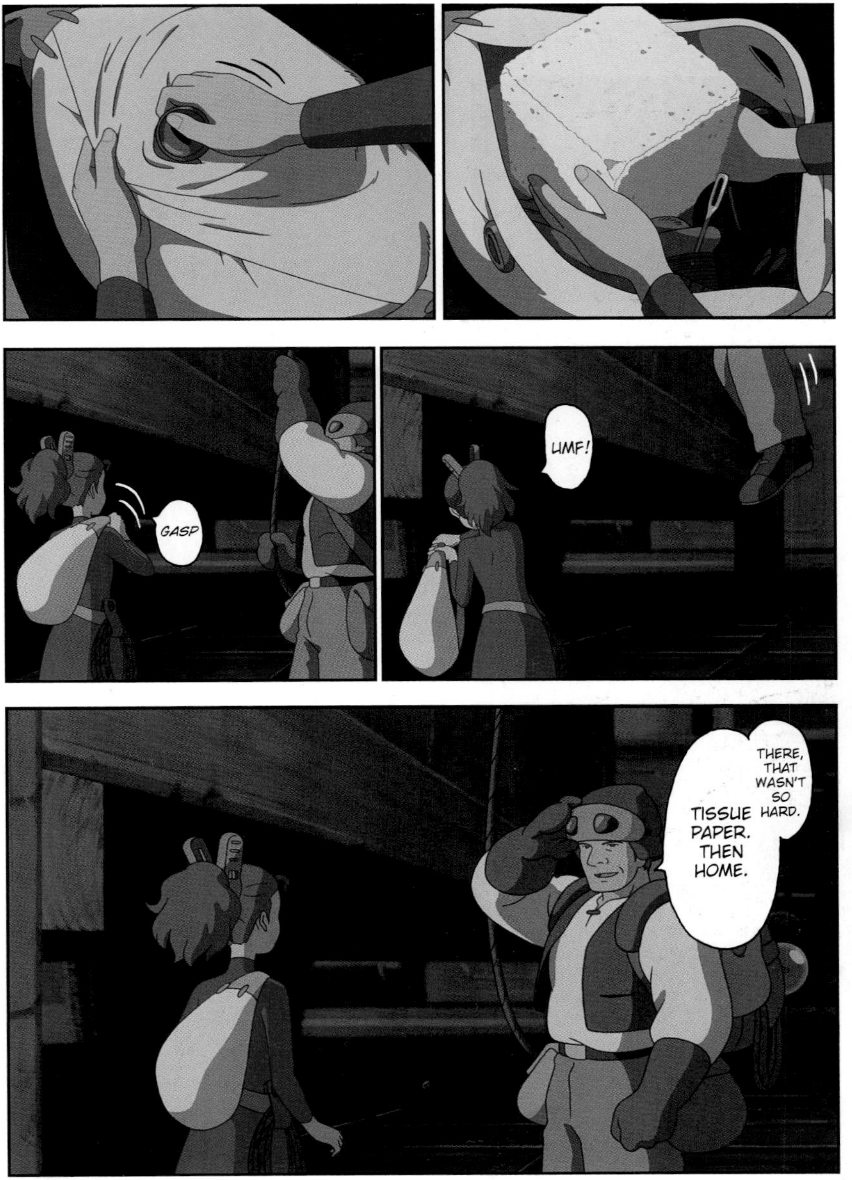
GASP
UMF!
THERE, THAT WASN'T SO HARD.
TISSUE PAPER. THEN HOME.

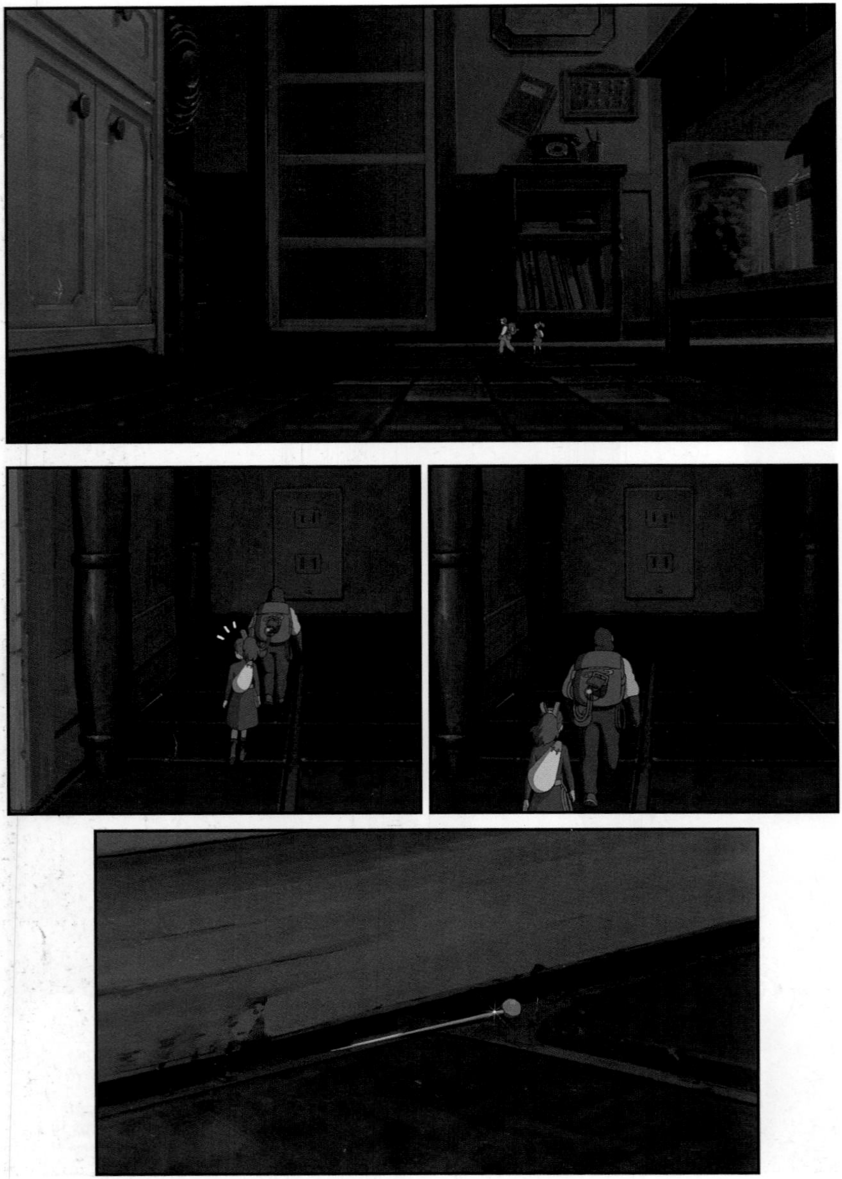

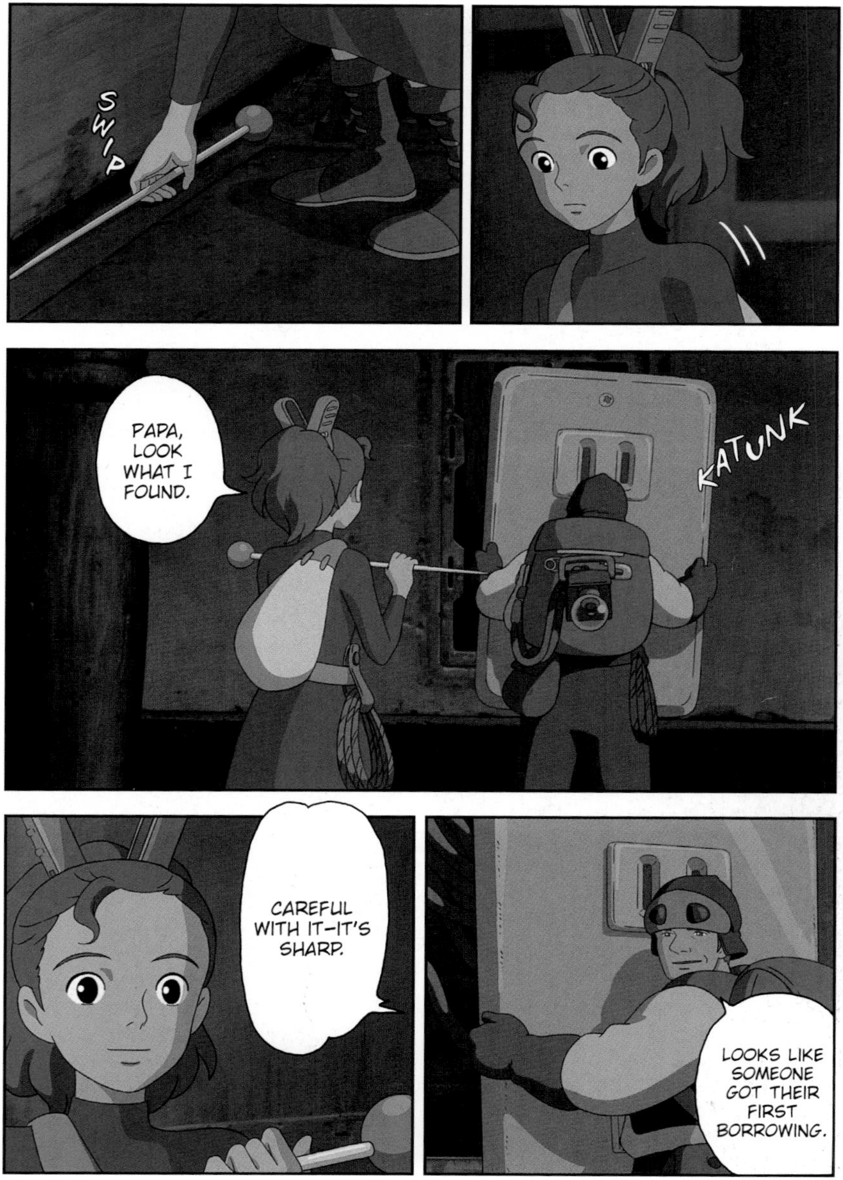
SWIP
PAPA, LOOK WHAT I FOUND.
KATUNK
CAREFUL WITH IT—IT'S SHARP.
LOOKS LIKE SOMEONE GOT THEIR FIRST BORROWING.

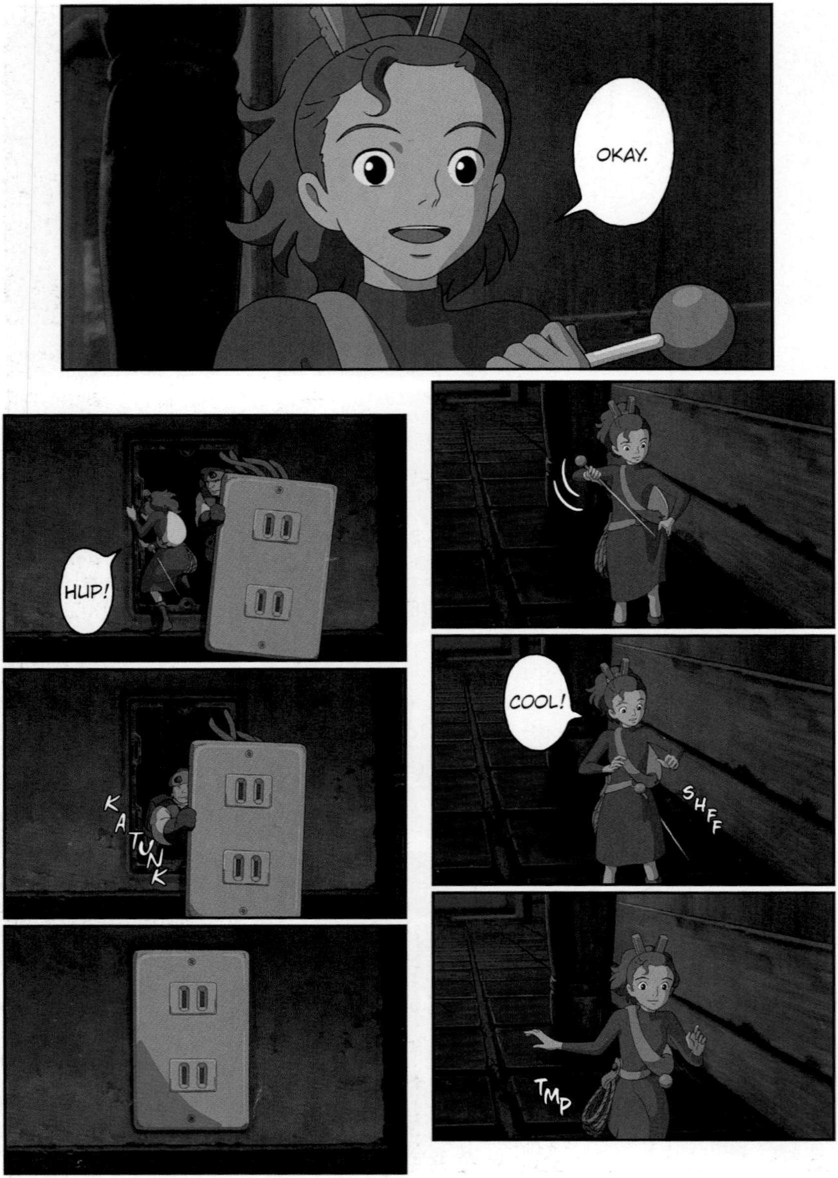
OKAY.
COOL!
SHFF
TMP
HUP!
KATUNK

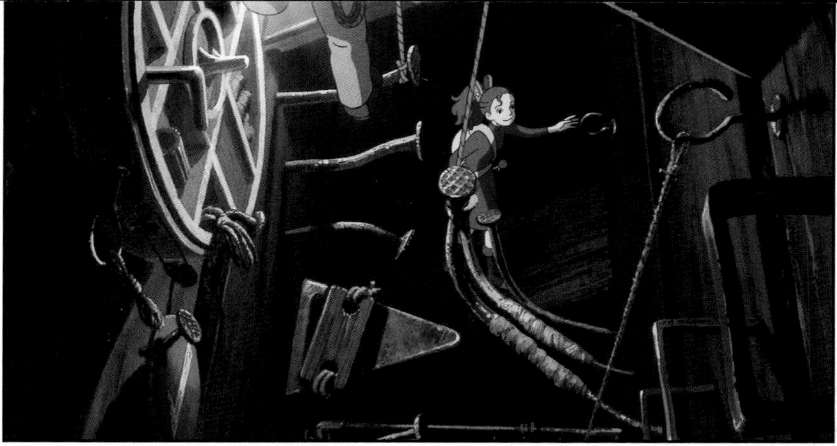
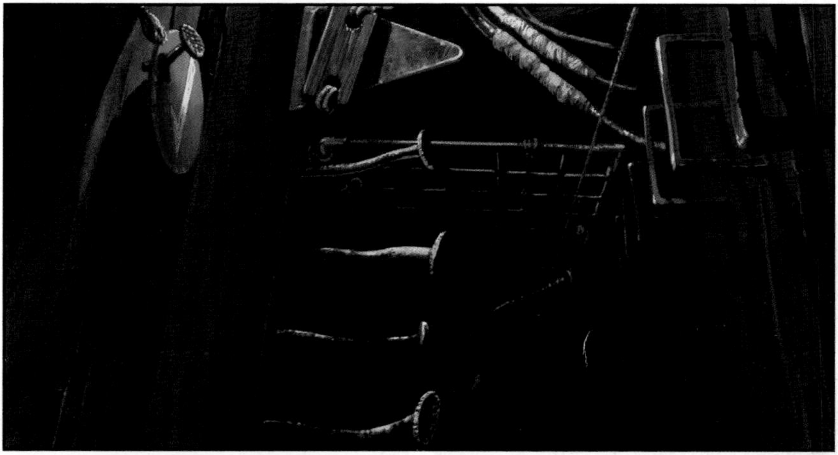
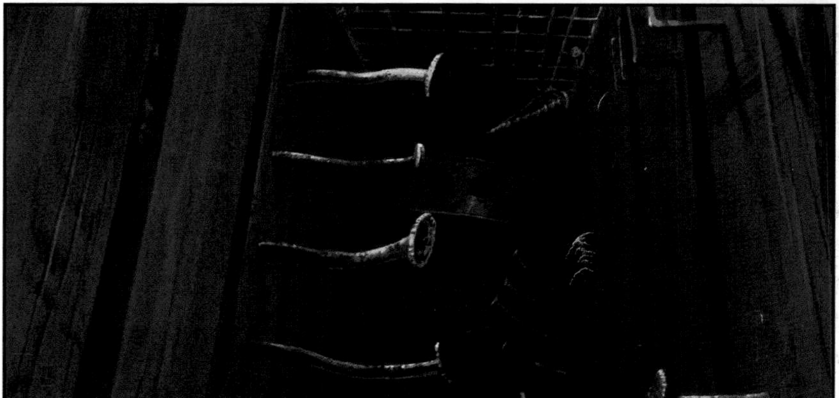

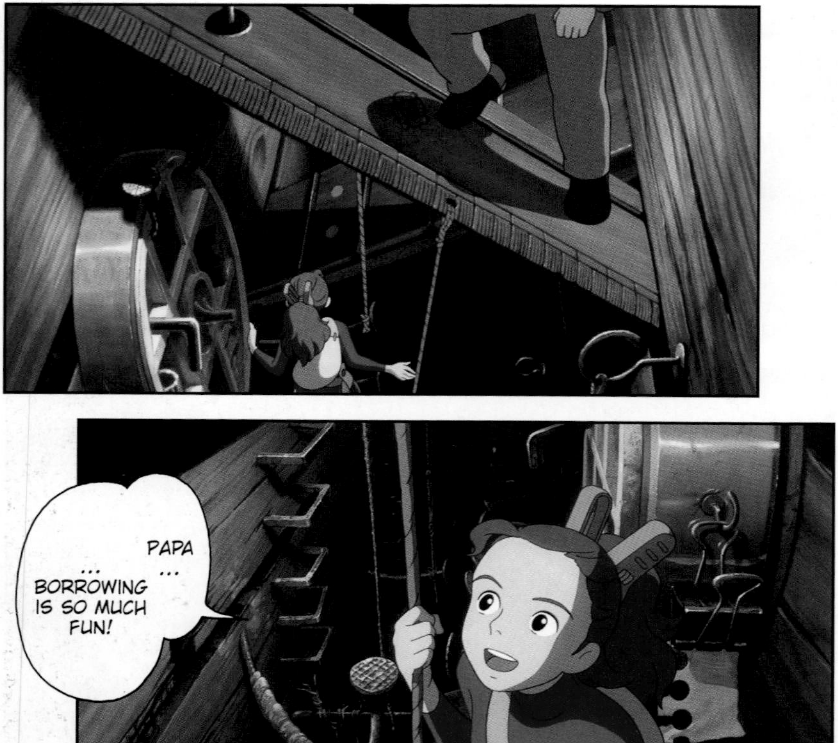
PAPA ... ... BORROWING IS SO MUCH FUN!
WHUP

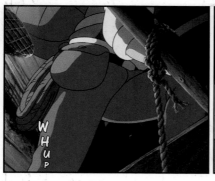

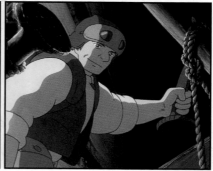

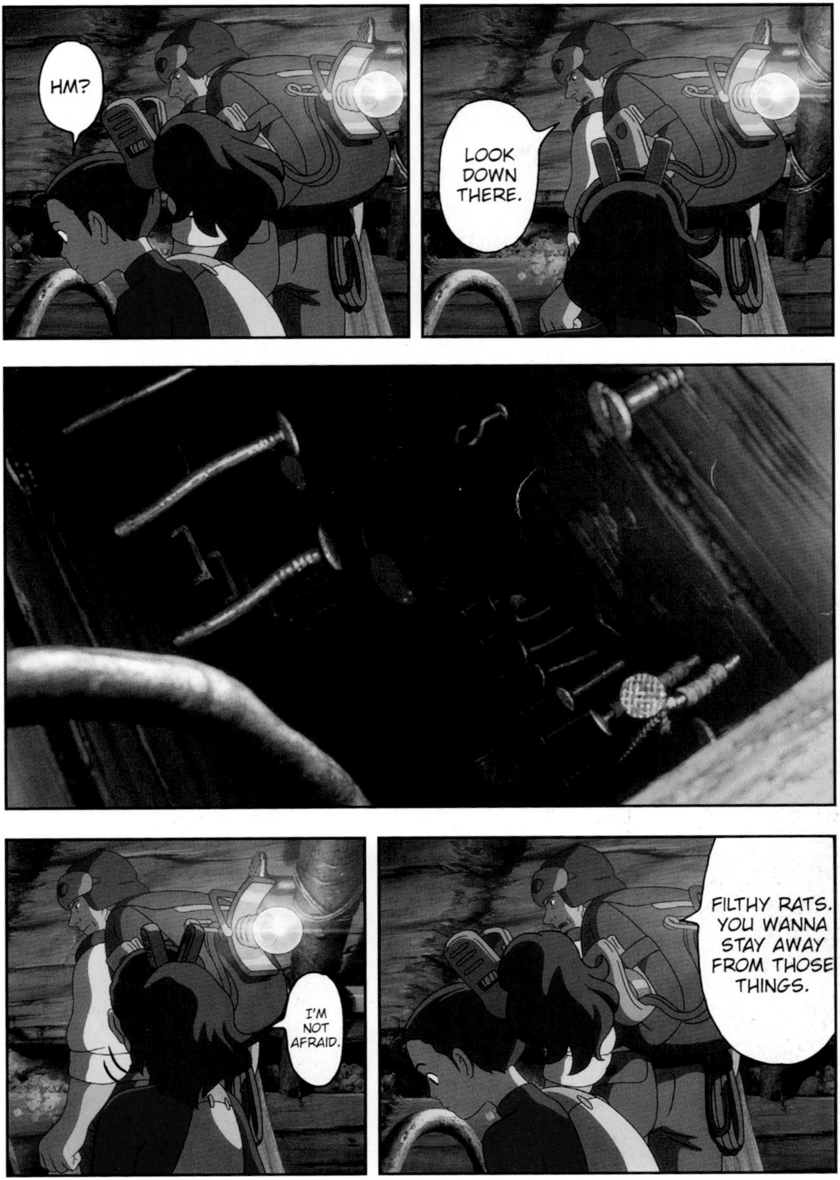
LOOK DOWN THERE.
HM?
FILTHY RATS. YOU WANNA STAY AWAY FROM THOSE THINGS.
I'M NOT AFRAID.

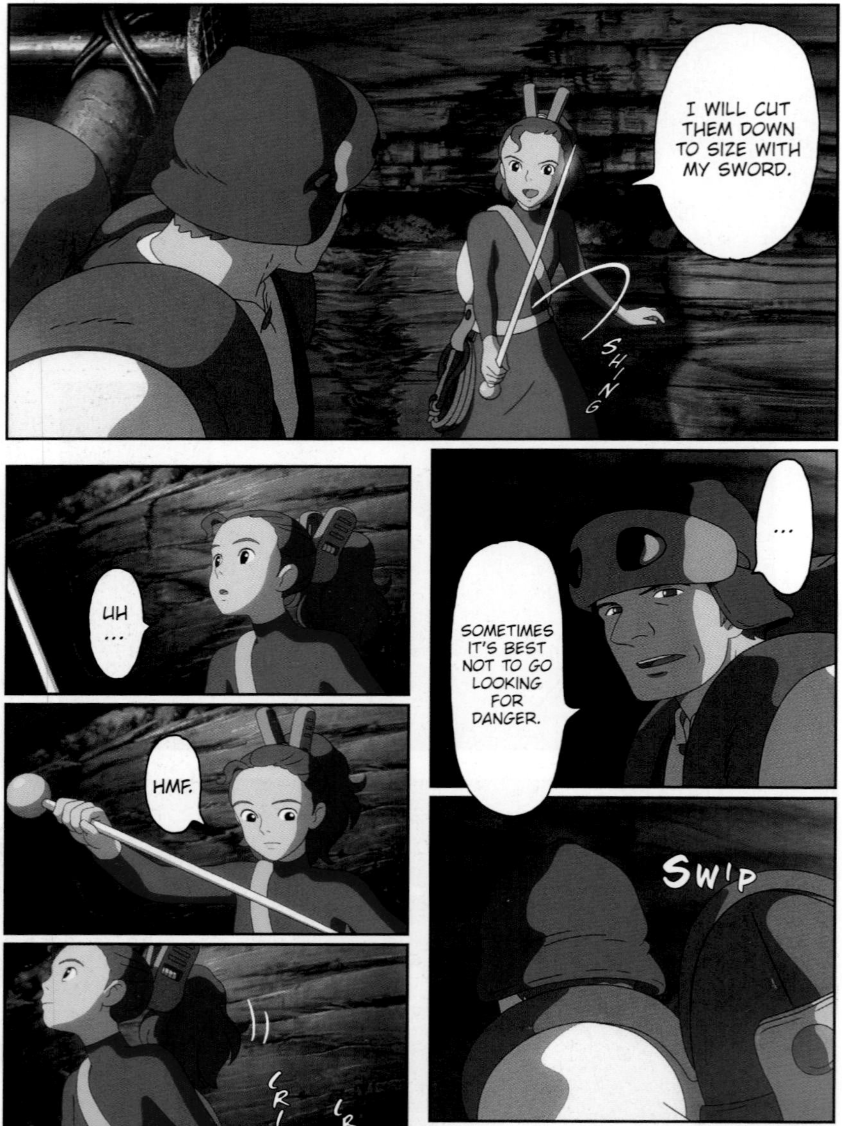
I WILL CUT THEM DOWN TO SIZE WITH MY SWORD.
SHING
...
SOMETIMES IT'S BEST NOT TO GO LOOKING FOR DANGER.
SWIP
UH ...
HMF.
CRIK
CRIK

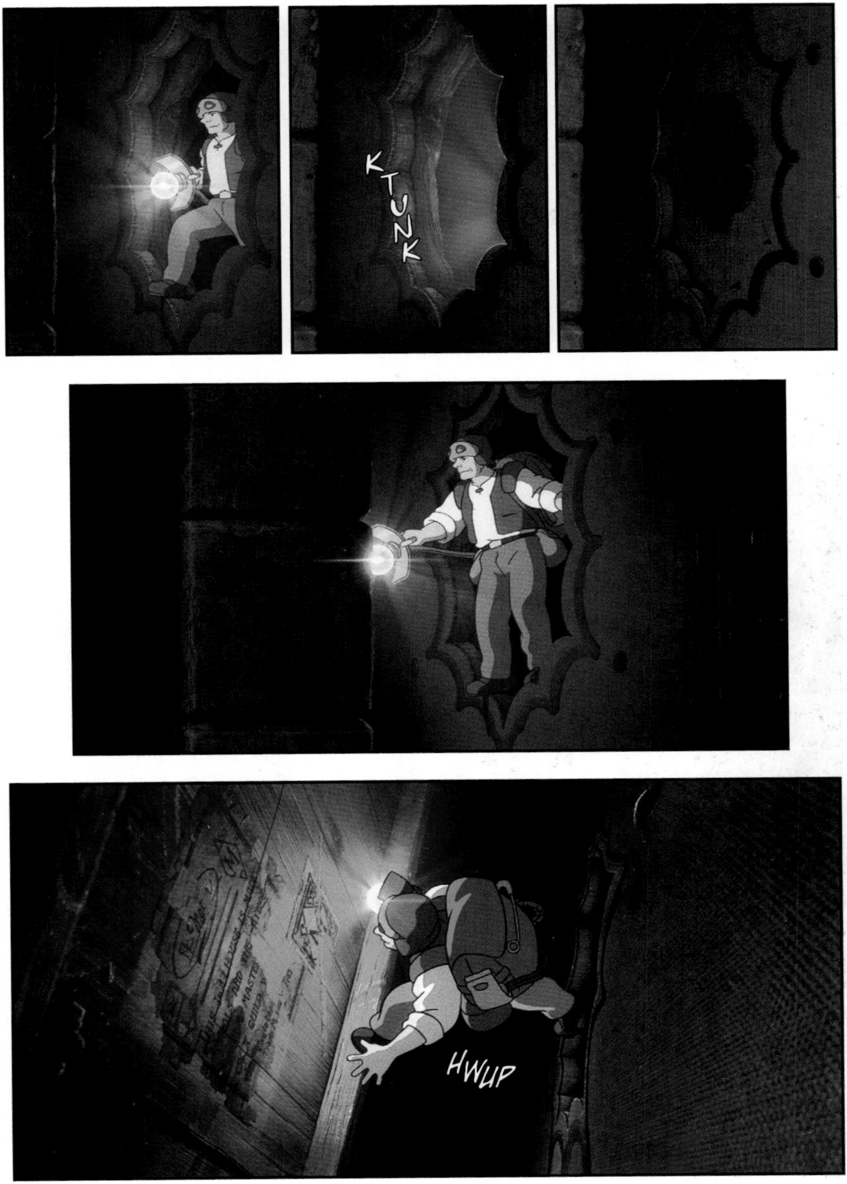
KTUNK
HWUP

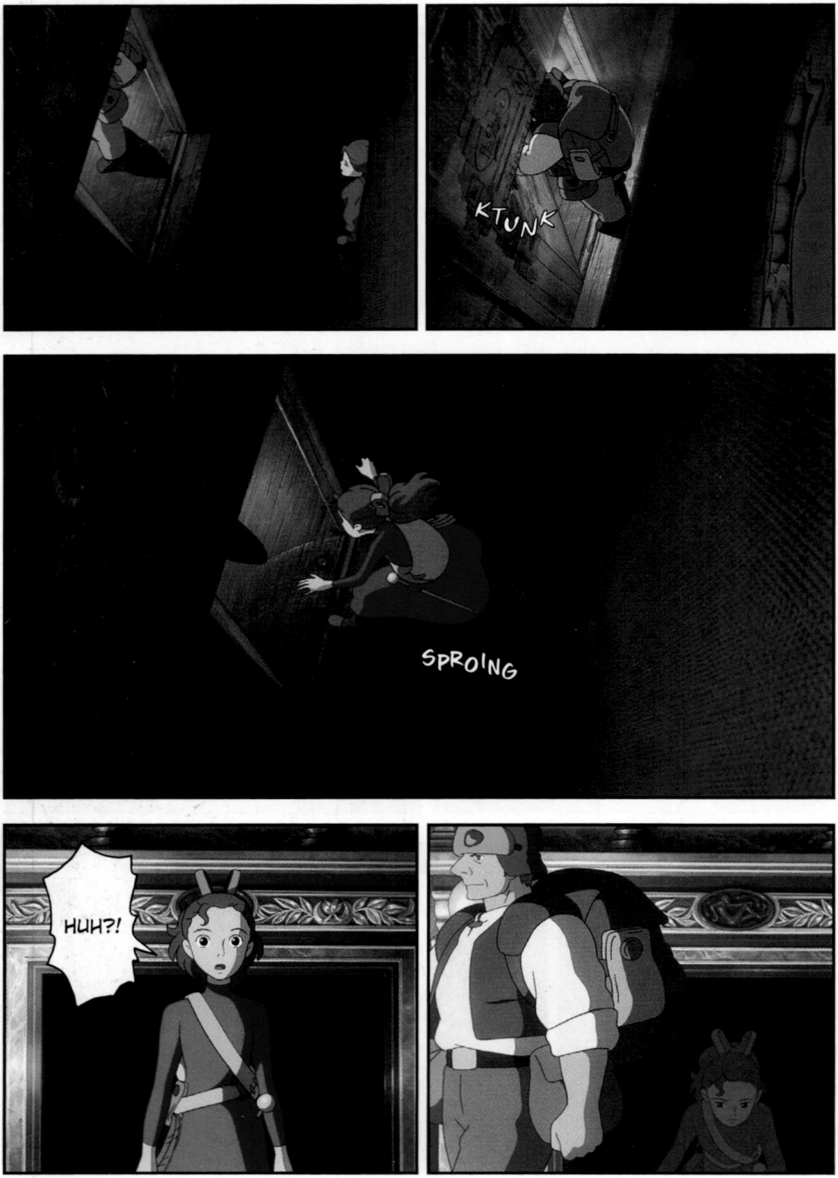
KTUNK
SPROING
HUH?!

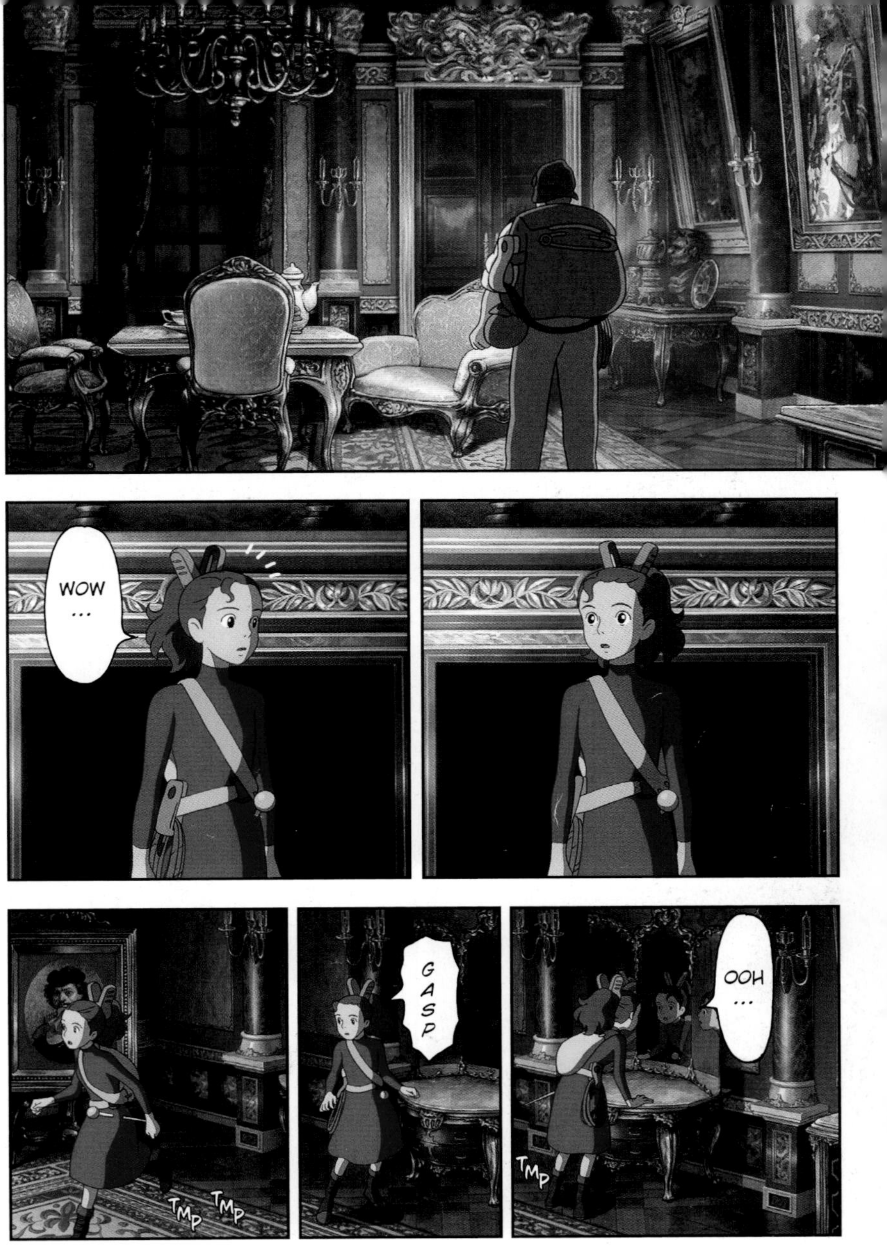
WOW ...
OOH ...
TMP
GASP
TMP TMP

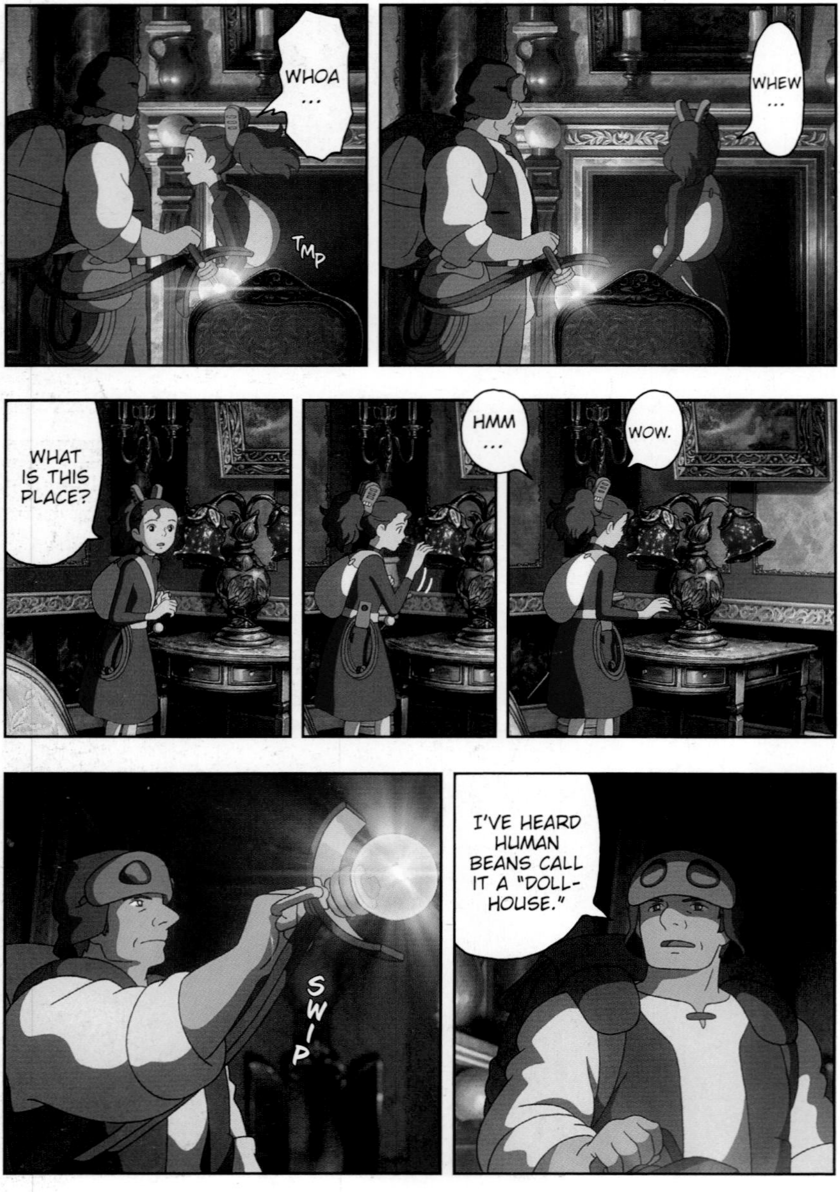
WHOA ...
TMP
WHEW ...
WHAT IS THIS PLACE?
HMM ...
WOW.
SWIP
I'VE HEARD HUMAN BEANS CALL IT A "DOLL-HOUSE."

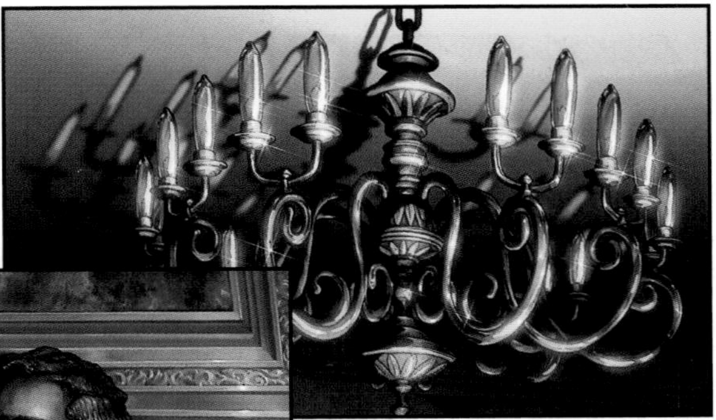

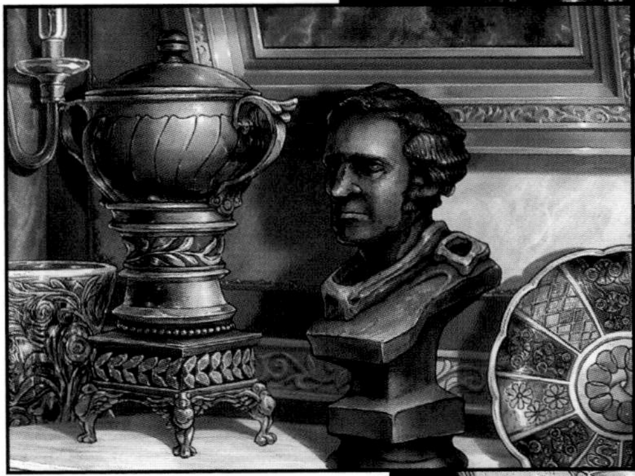

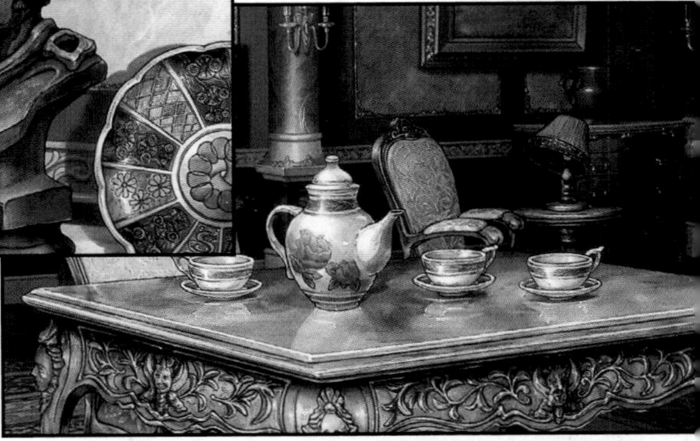

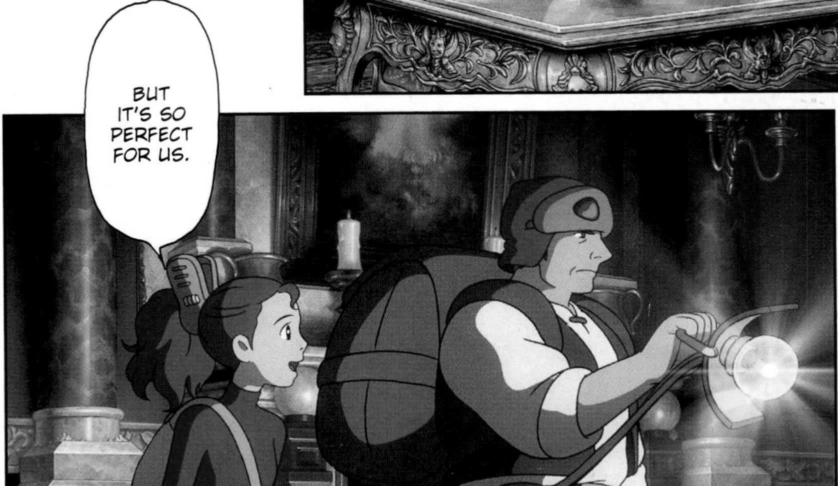
BUT IT'S SO PERFECT FOR US.

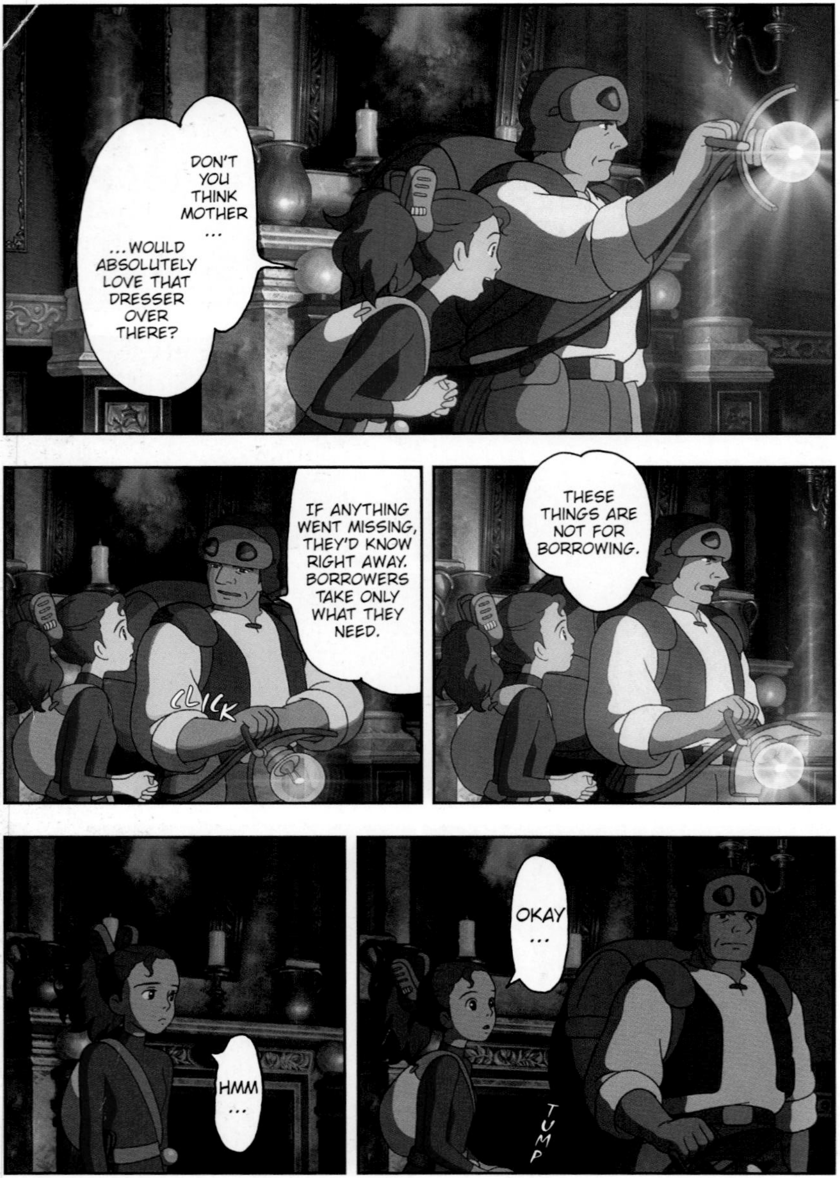
DON'T YOU THINK MOTHER ... ...WOULD ABSOLUTELY LOVE THAT DRESSER OVER THERE?
THESE THINGS ARE NOT FOR BORROWING.
IF ANYTHING WENT MISSING, THEY'D KNOW RIGHT AWAY. BORROWERS TAKE ONLY WHAT THEY NEED.
CLICK
OKAY ...
TUMP
HMM ...

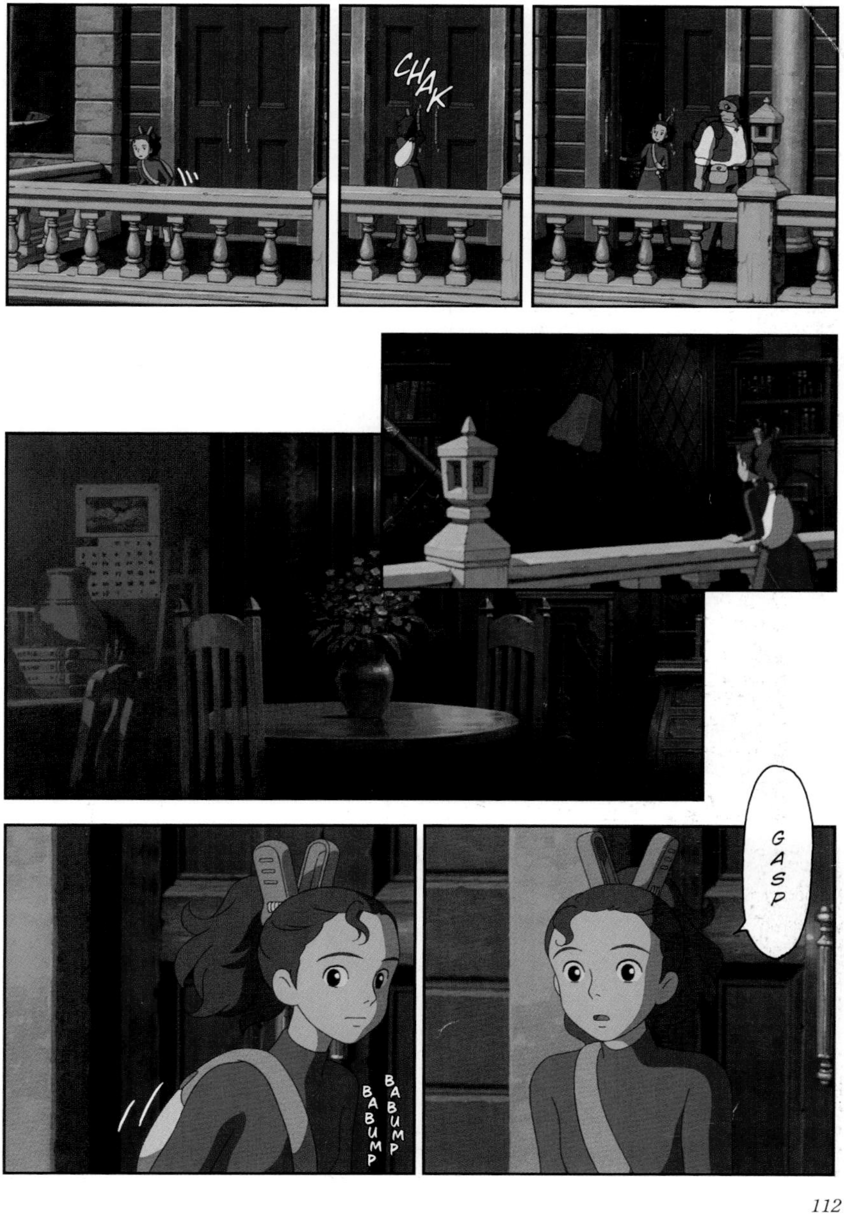
CHAK
GASP
BABUMP
BABUMP

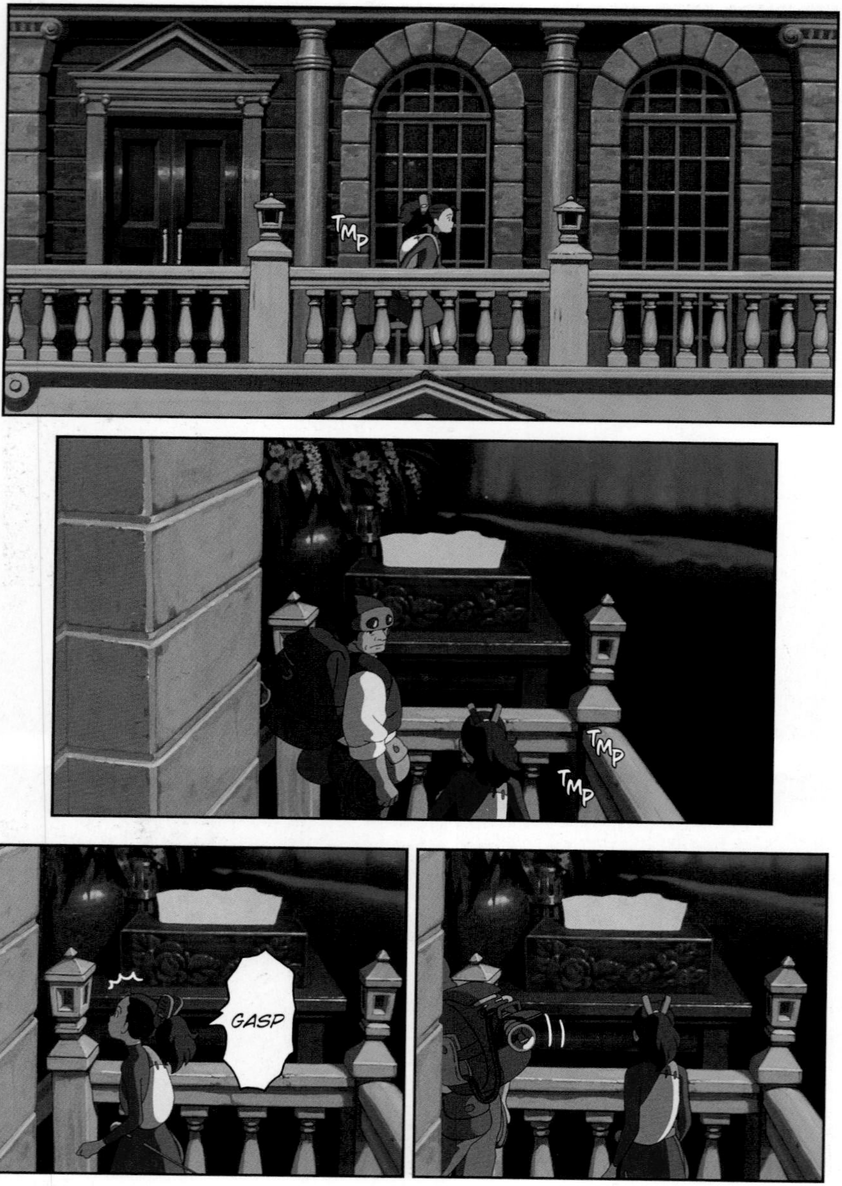
TMP
TMP
TMP
GASP

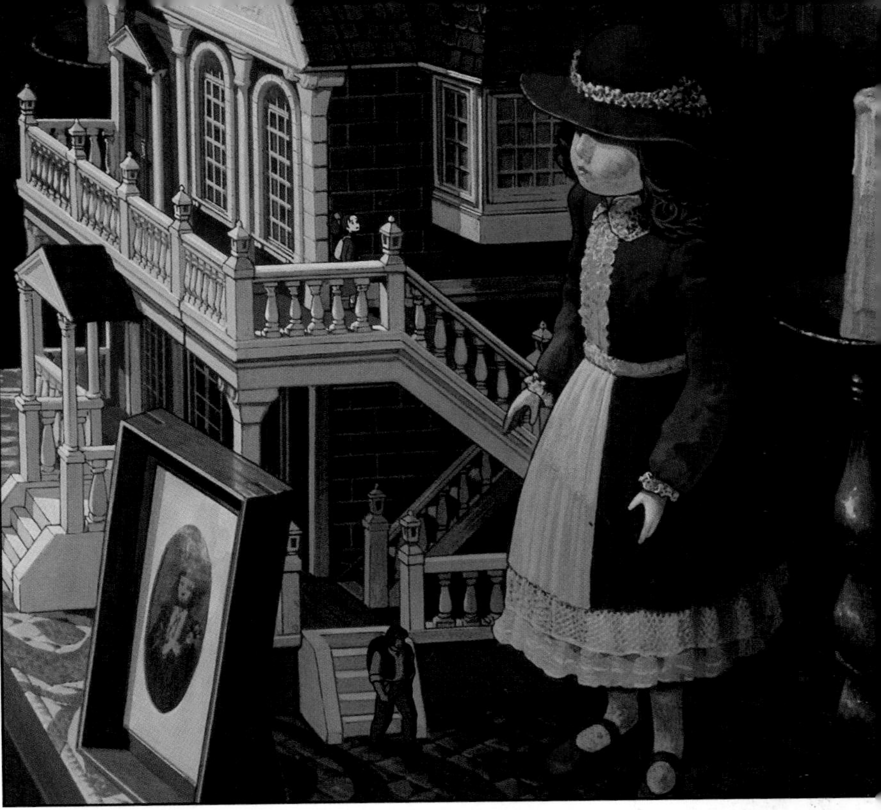

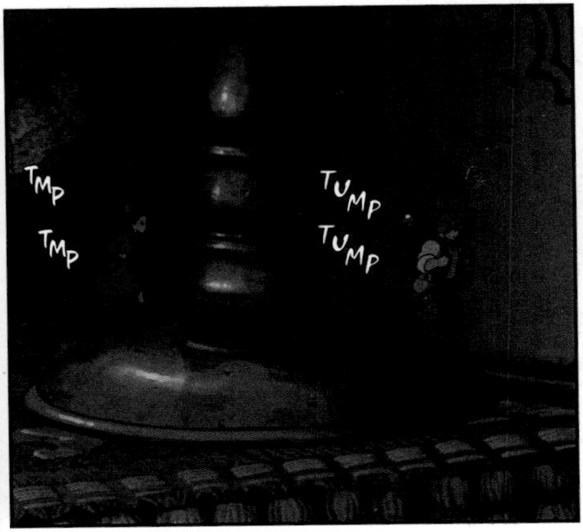
TUMP
TUMP
TMP
TMP

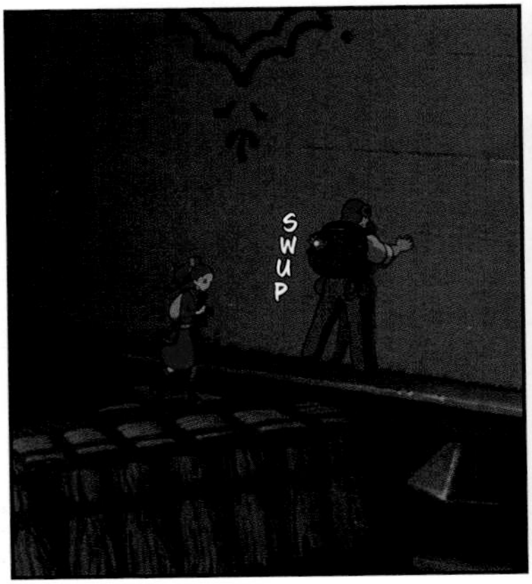
SWUP

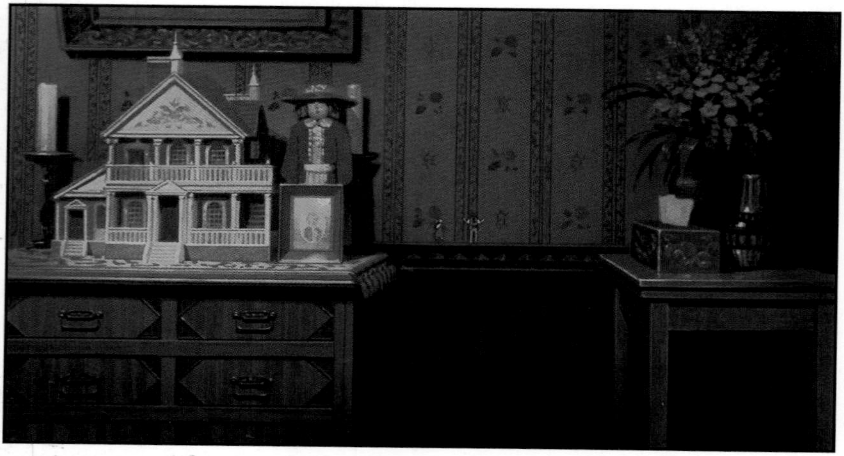

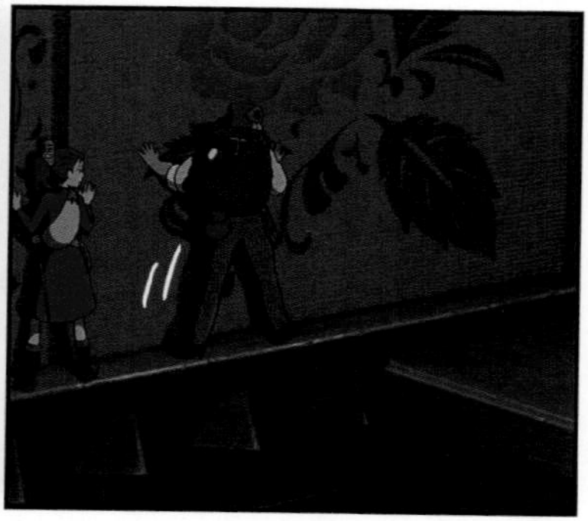

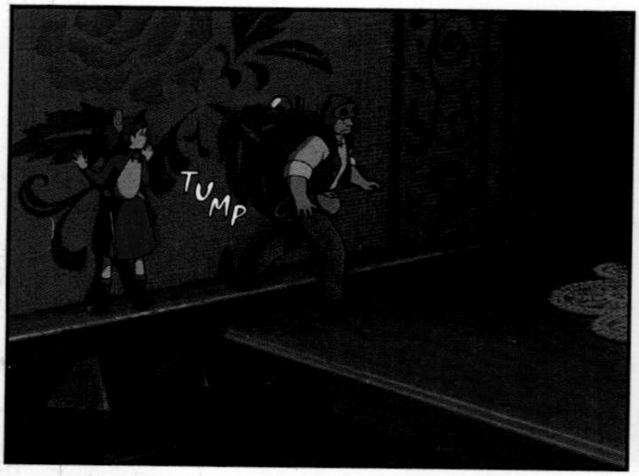
TUMP

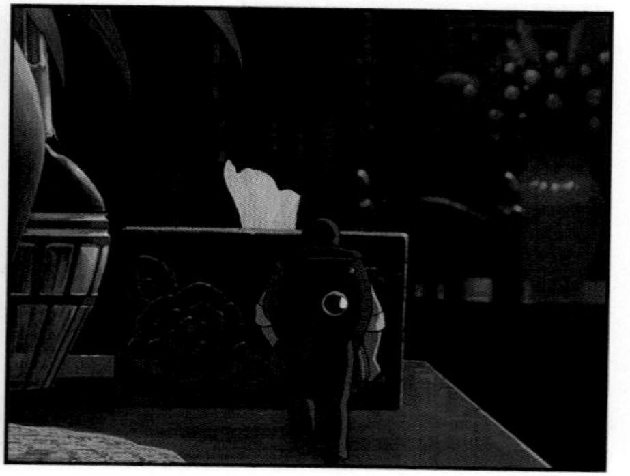

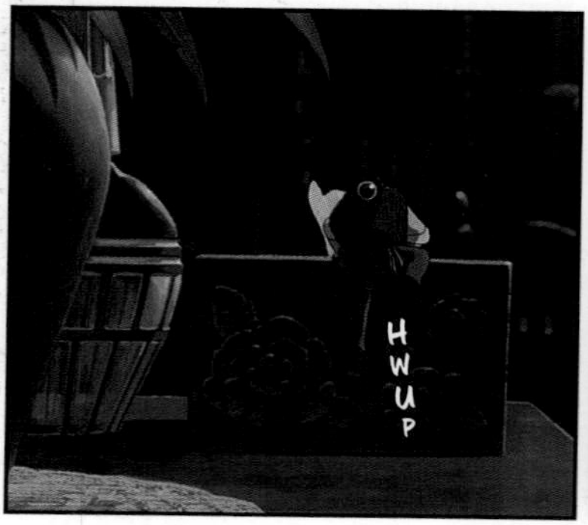
HWUP

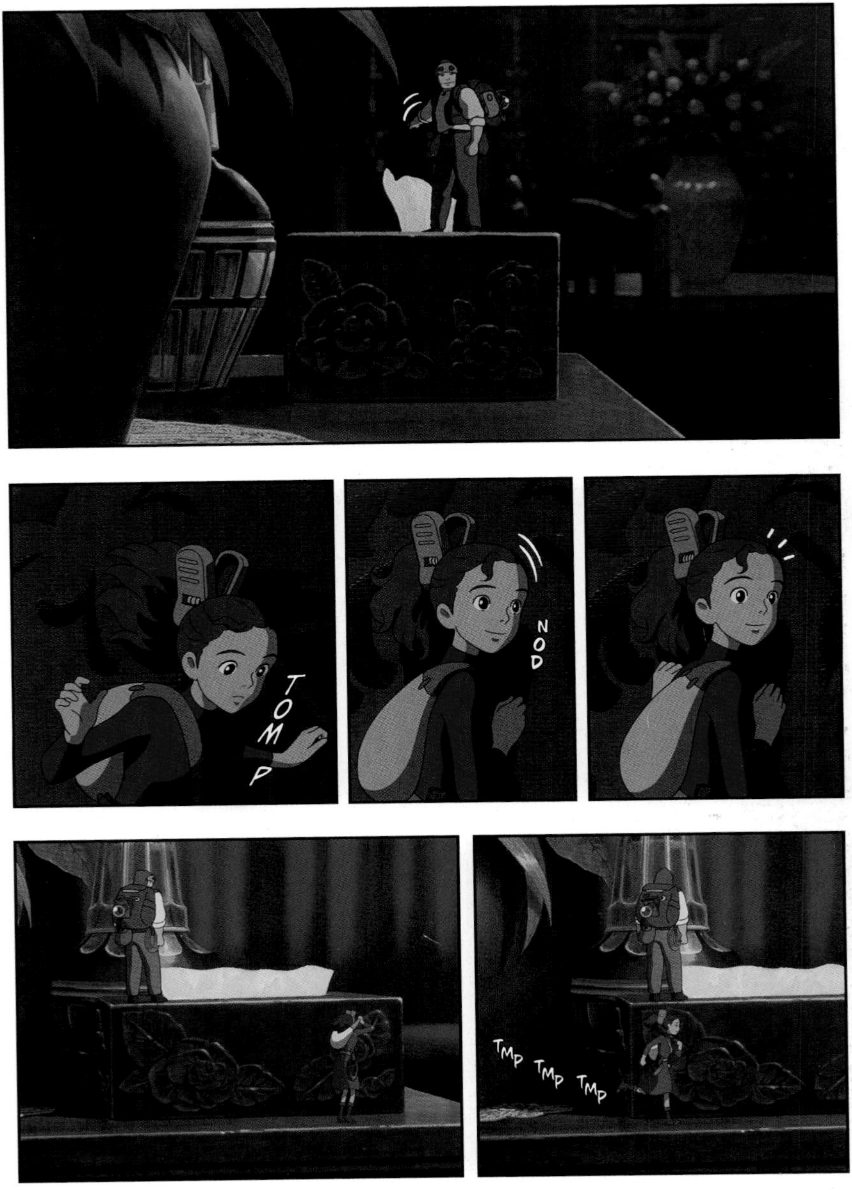
TOMP
NOD
TMP TMP TMP

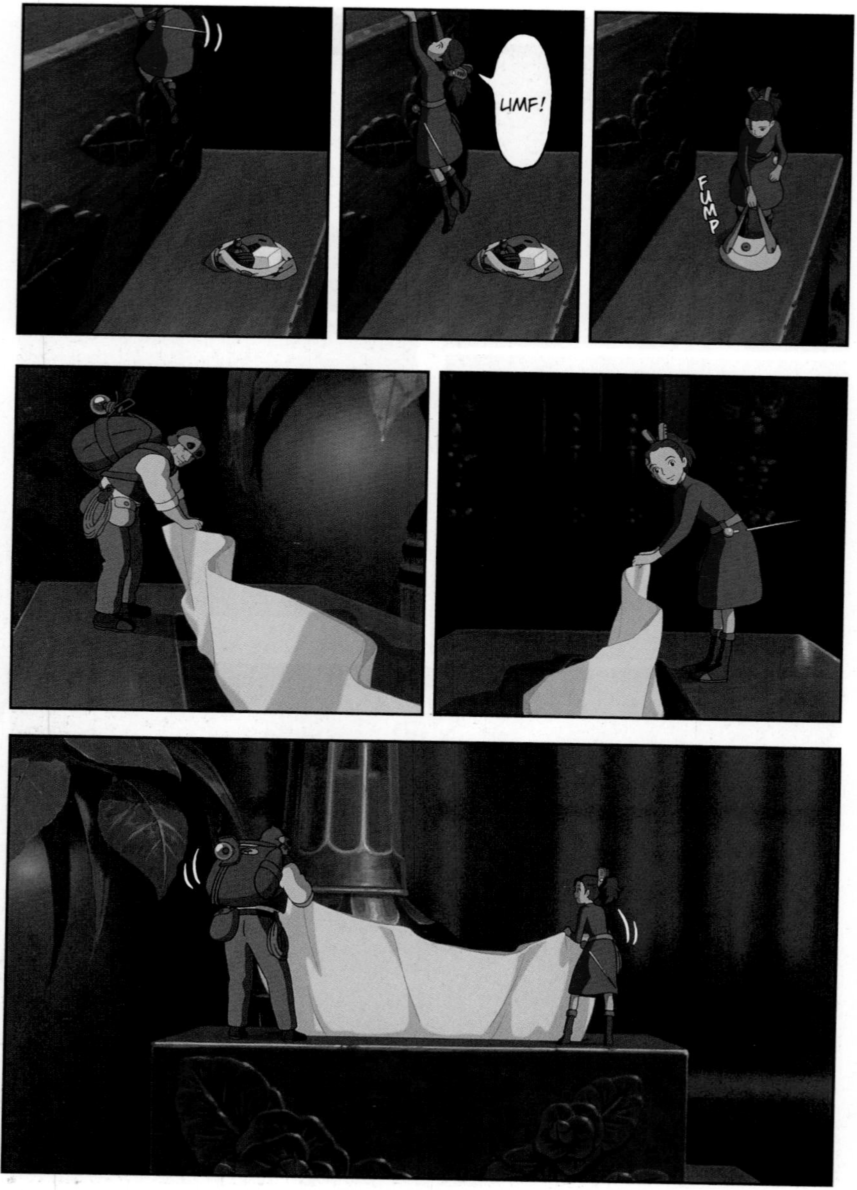
UMF!
FUMP

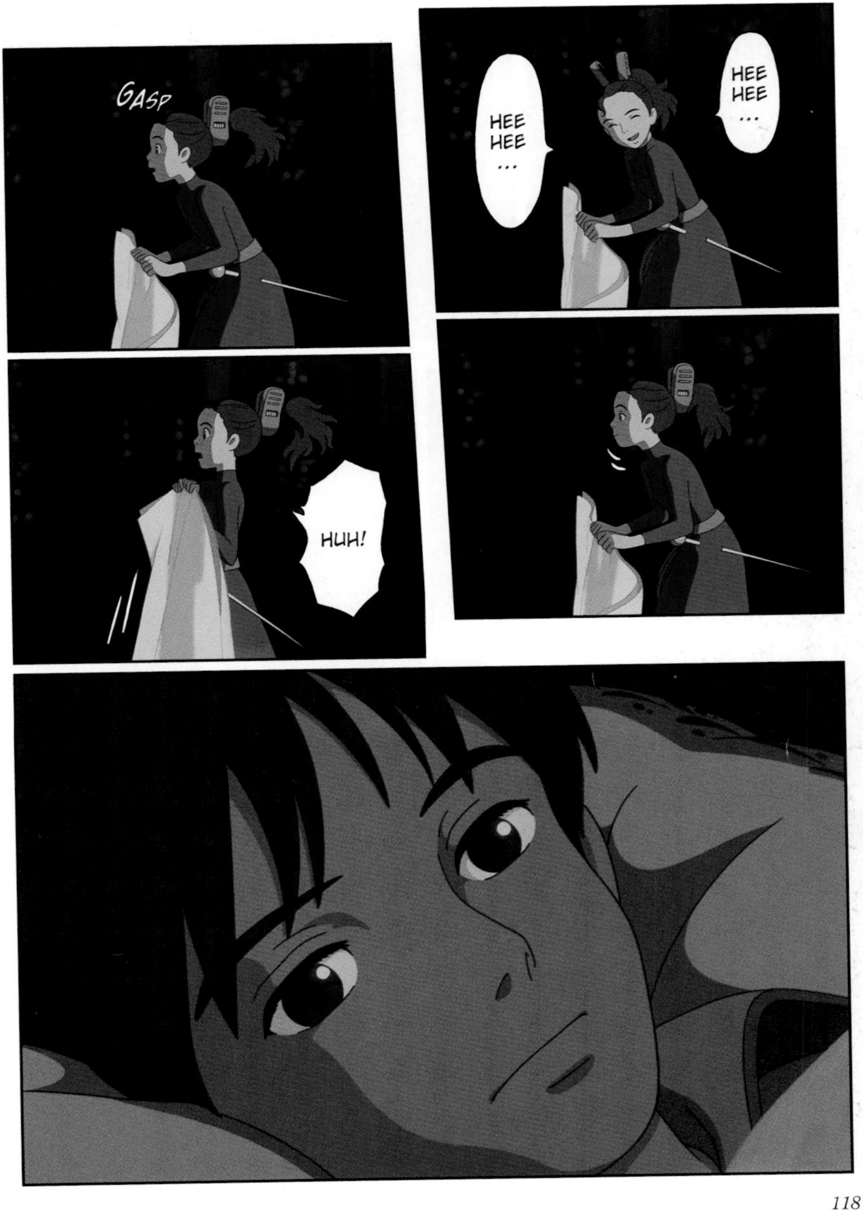
HEE HEE ...
HEE HEE ...
GASP
HUH!

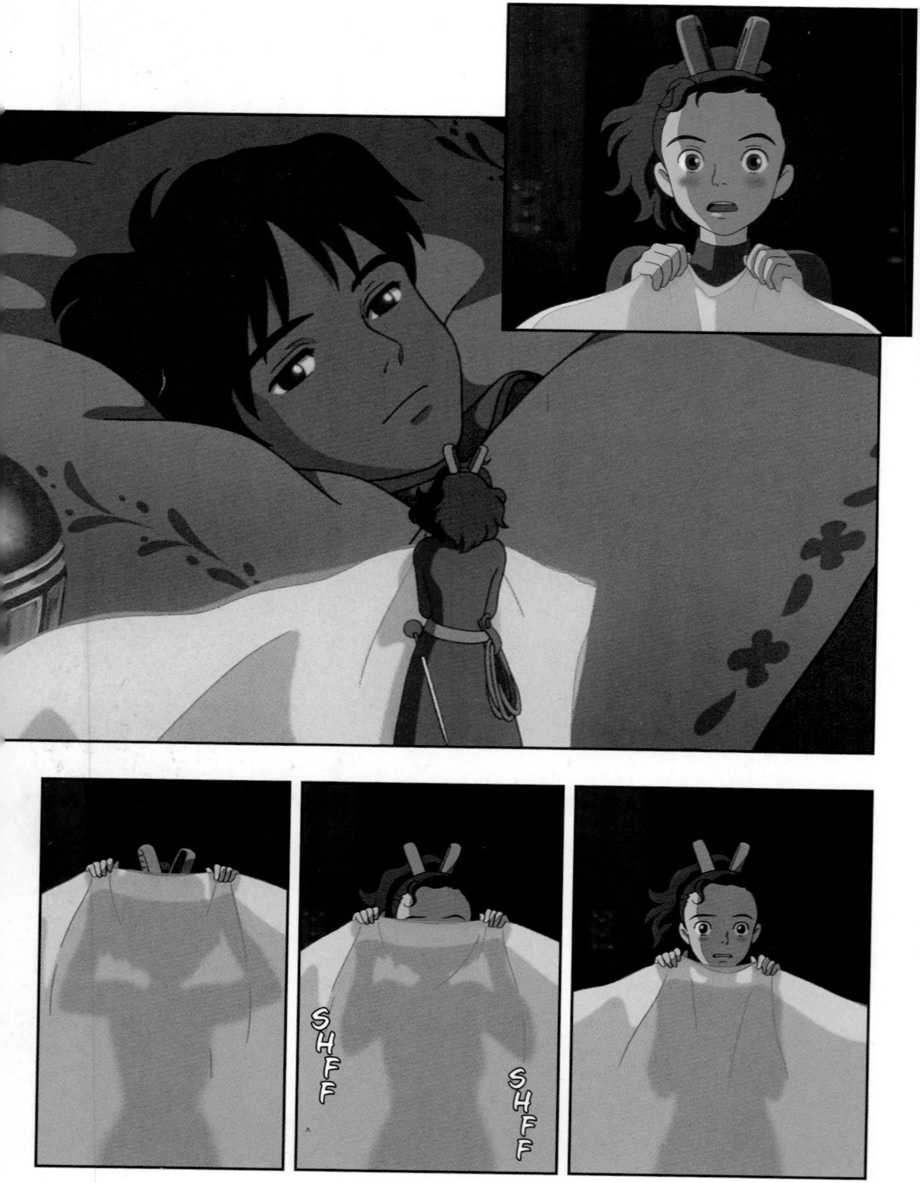
SHFF
SHFF

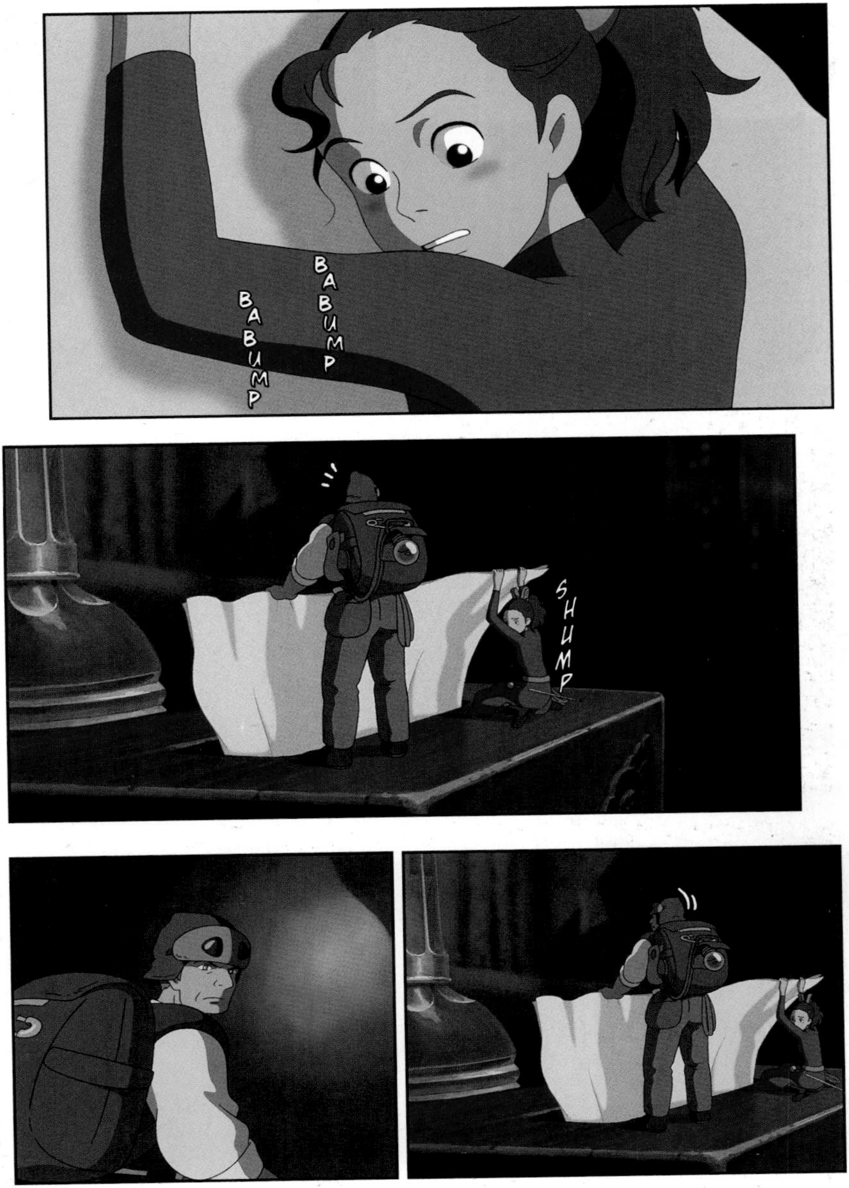
BABUMP
BABUMP
SHUMP

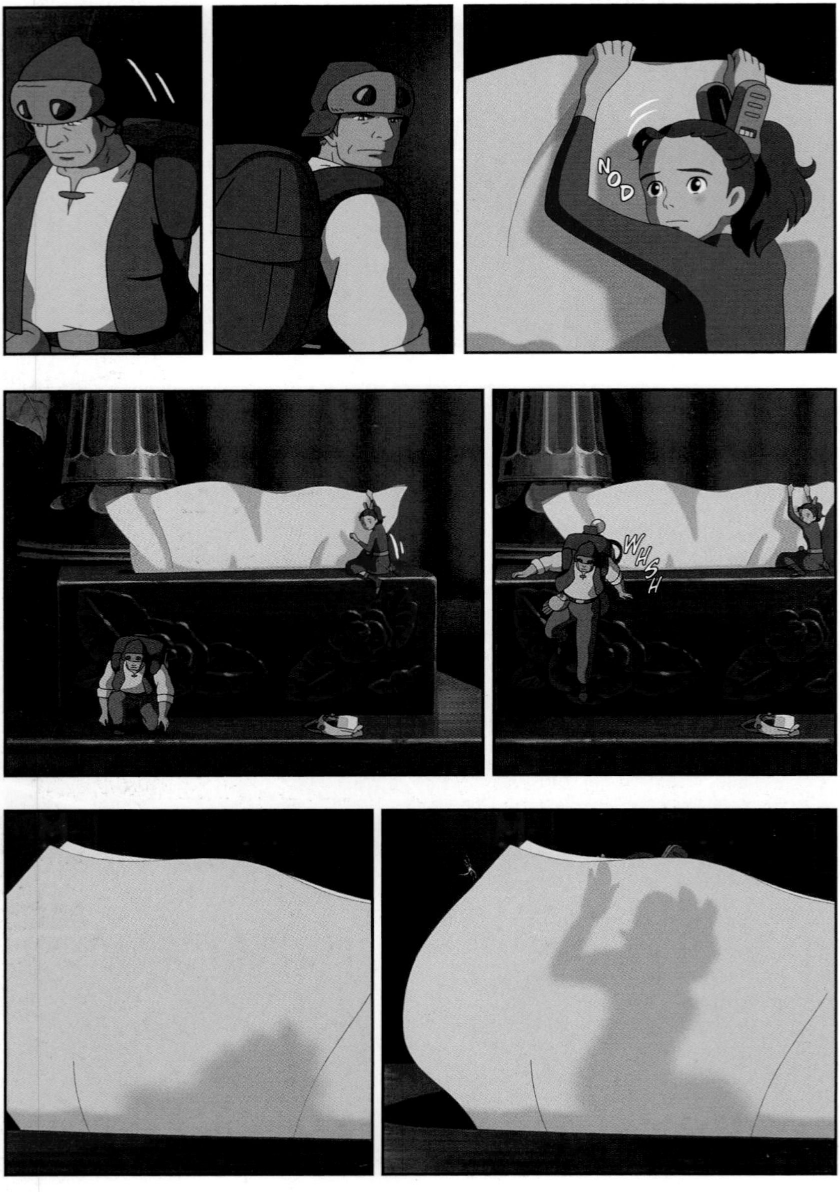
NOD
WHSH

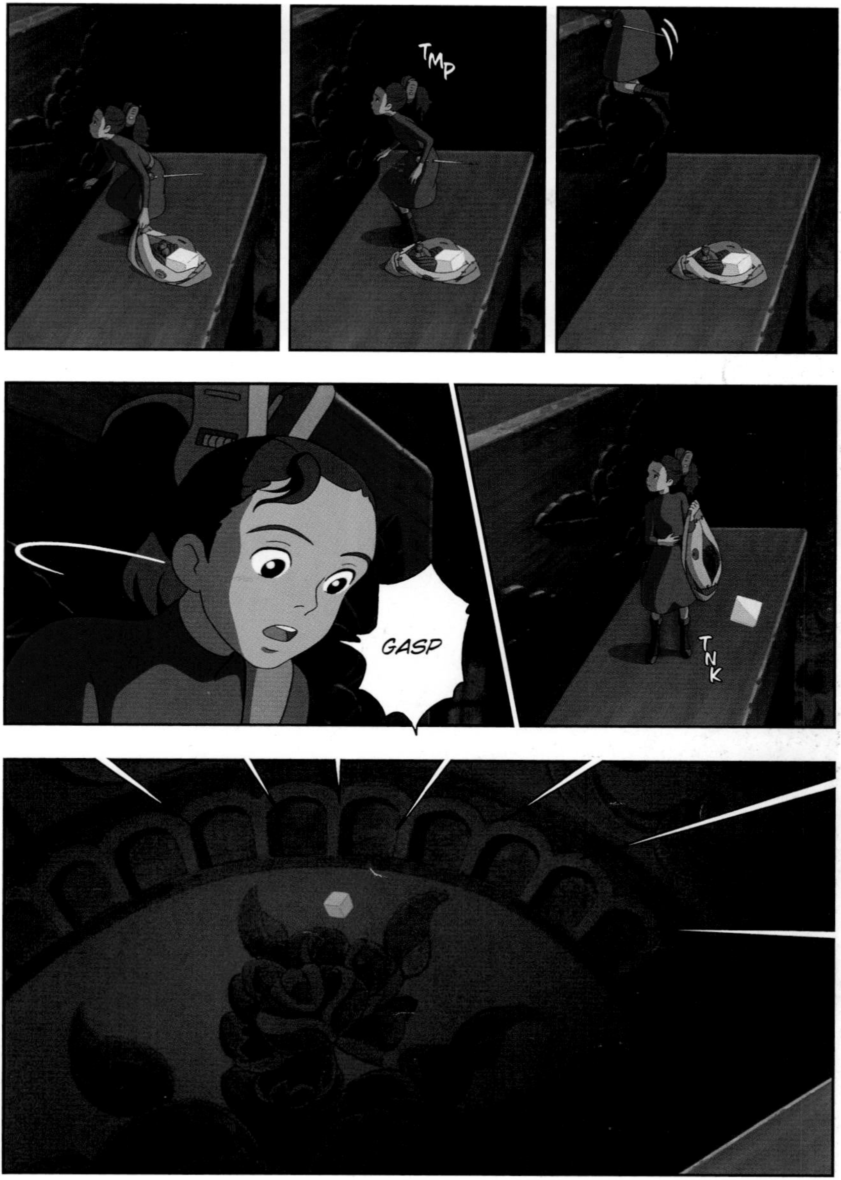
TMP
TNK
GASP

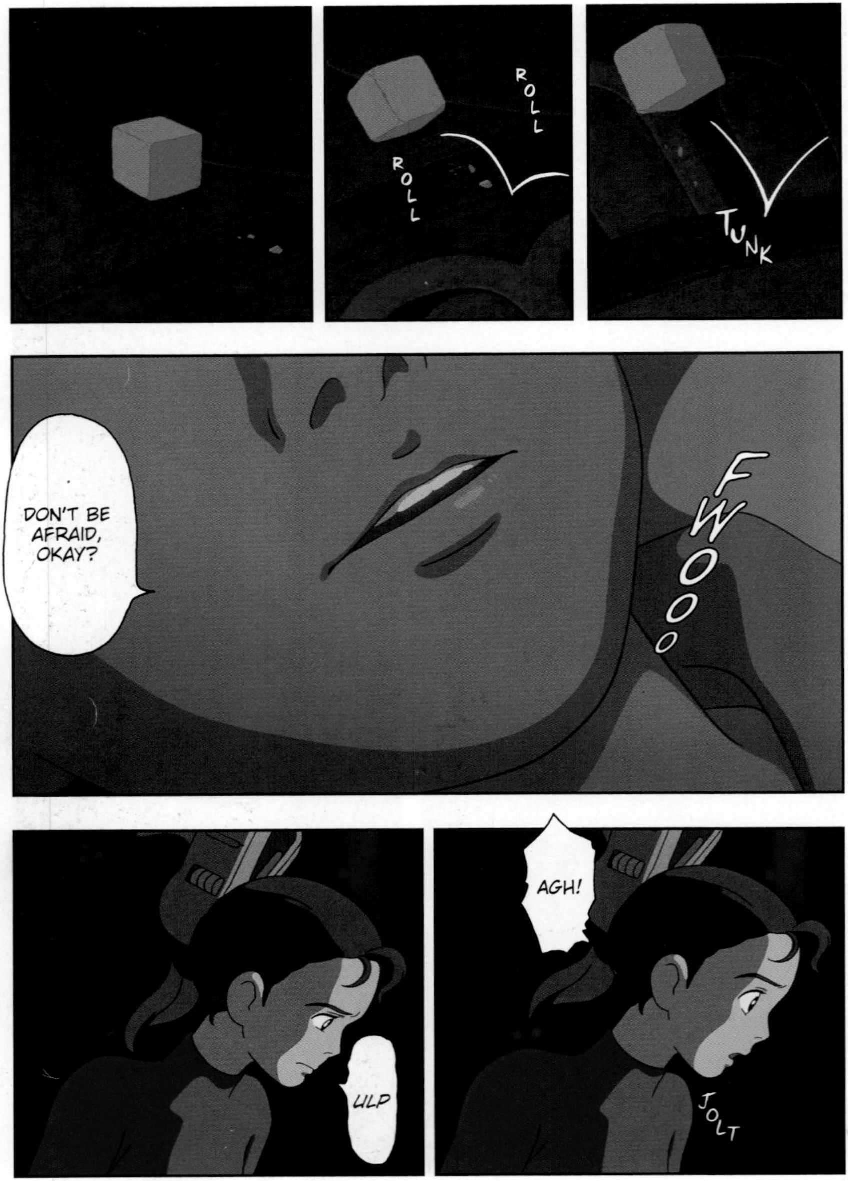
ROLL
ROLL
TUNK
DON'T BE AFRAID, OKAY?
FWOOOO
ULP
AGH!
JOLT

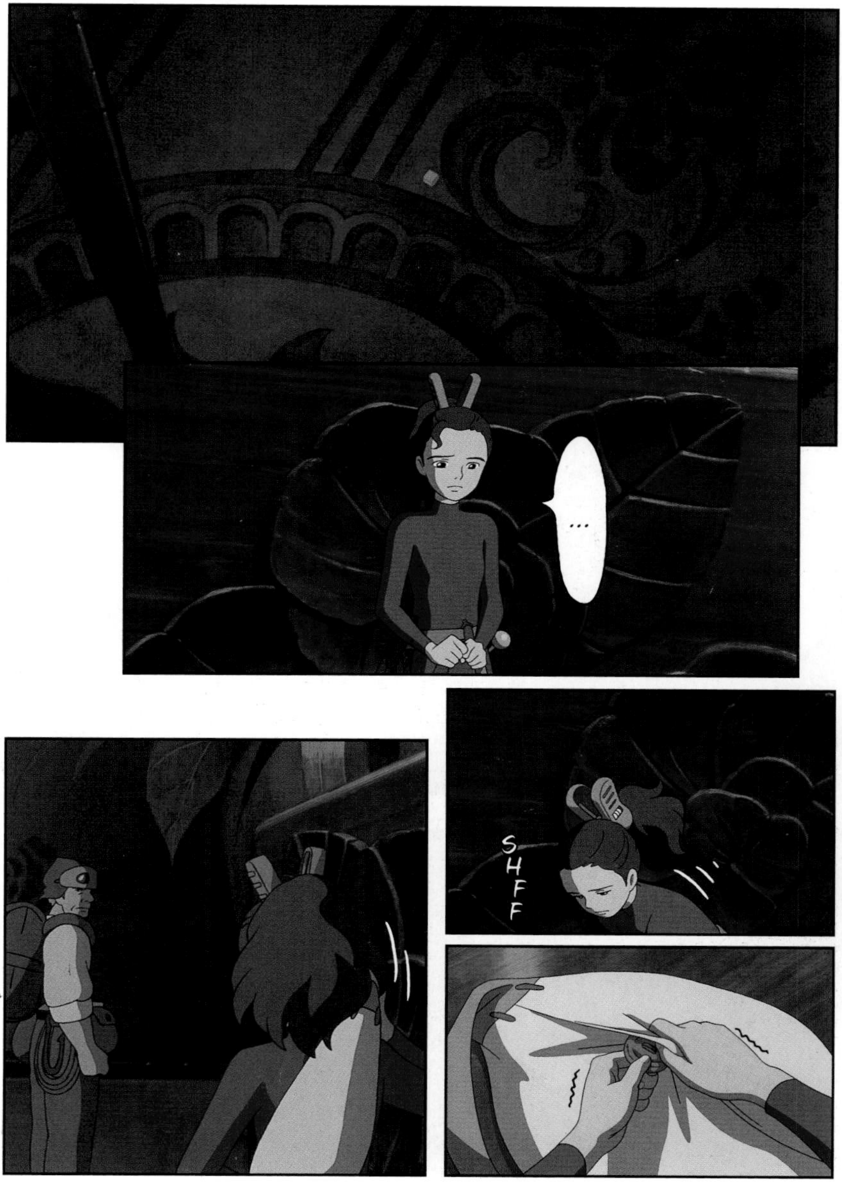
...
SHFF

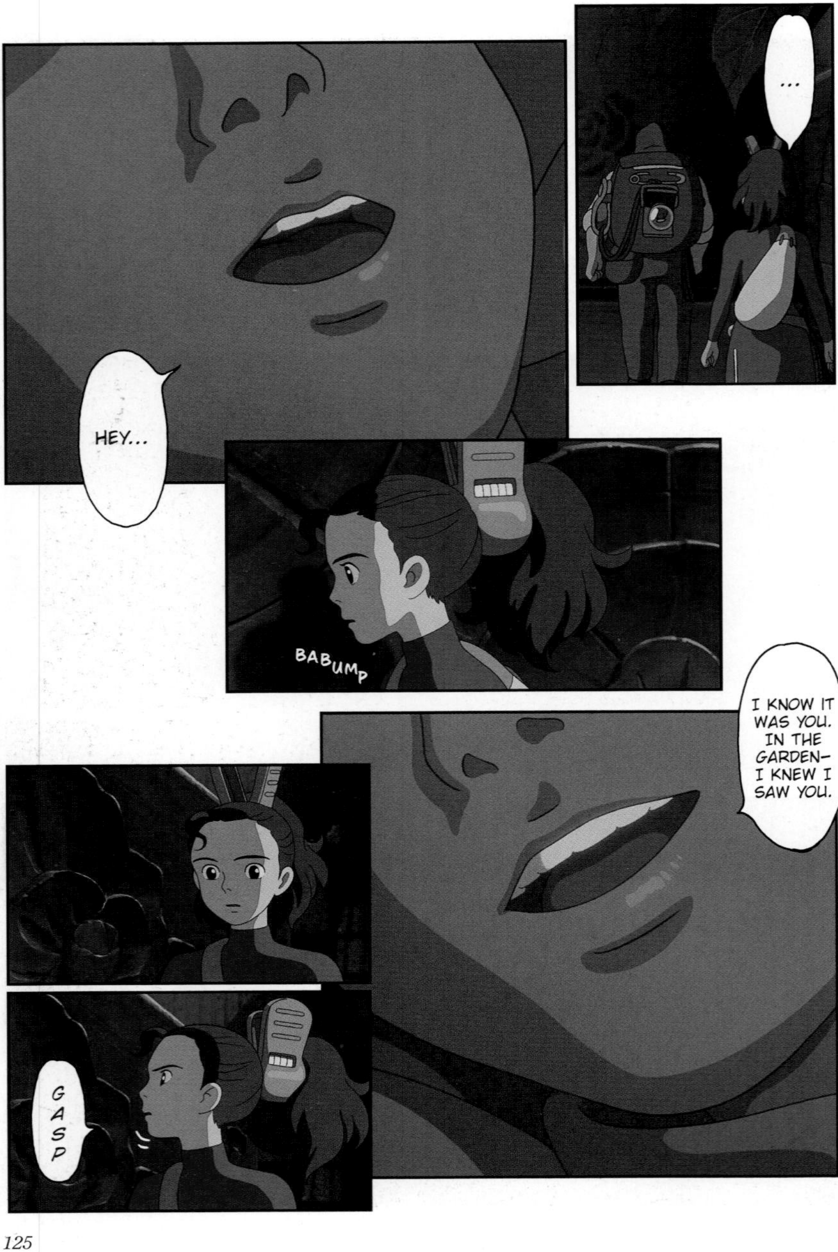
...
HEY...
BABUMP
I KNOW IT WAS YOU. IN THE GARDEN— I KNEW I SAW YOU.
GASP

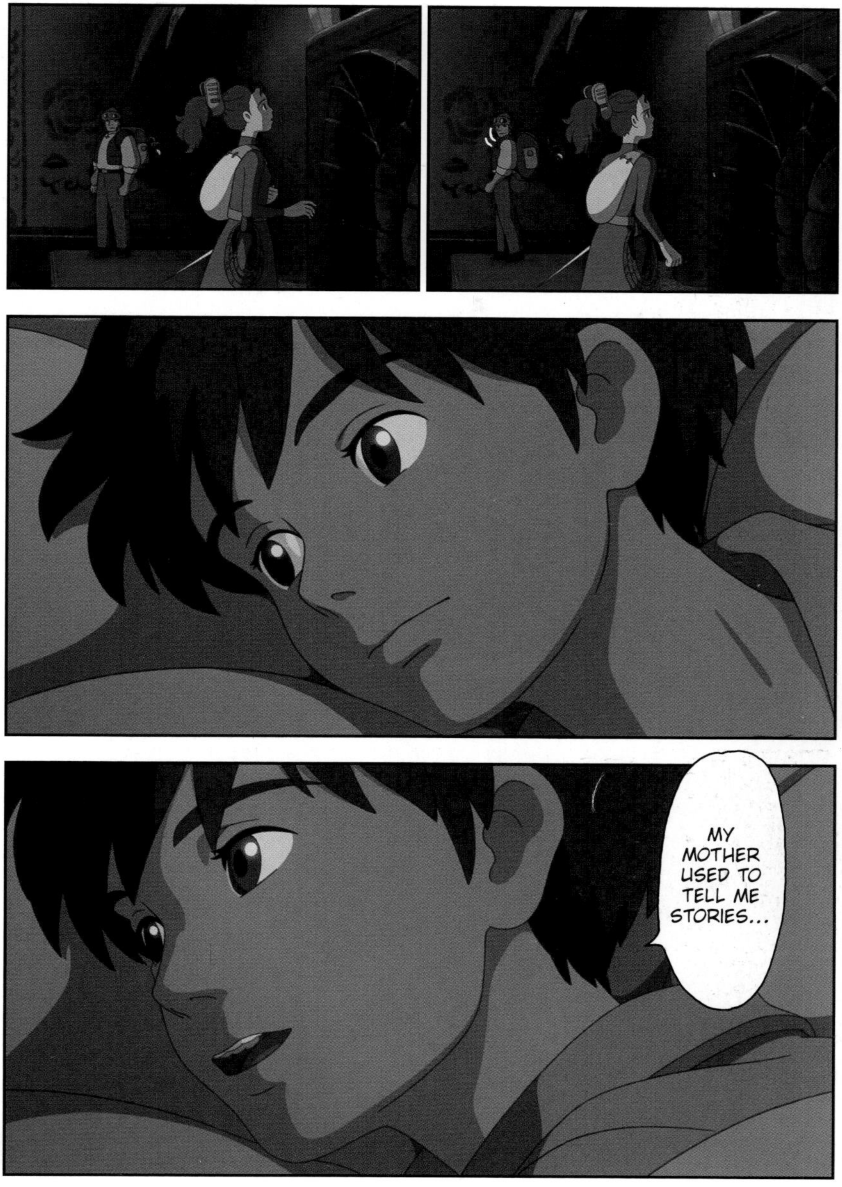
MY MOTHER USED TO TELL ME STORIES...

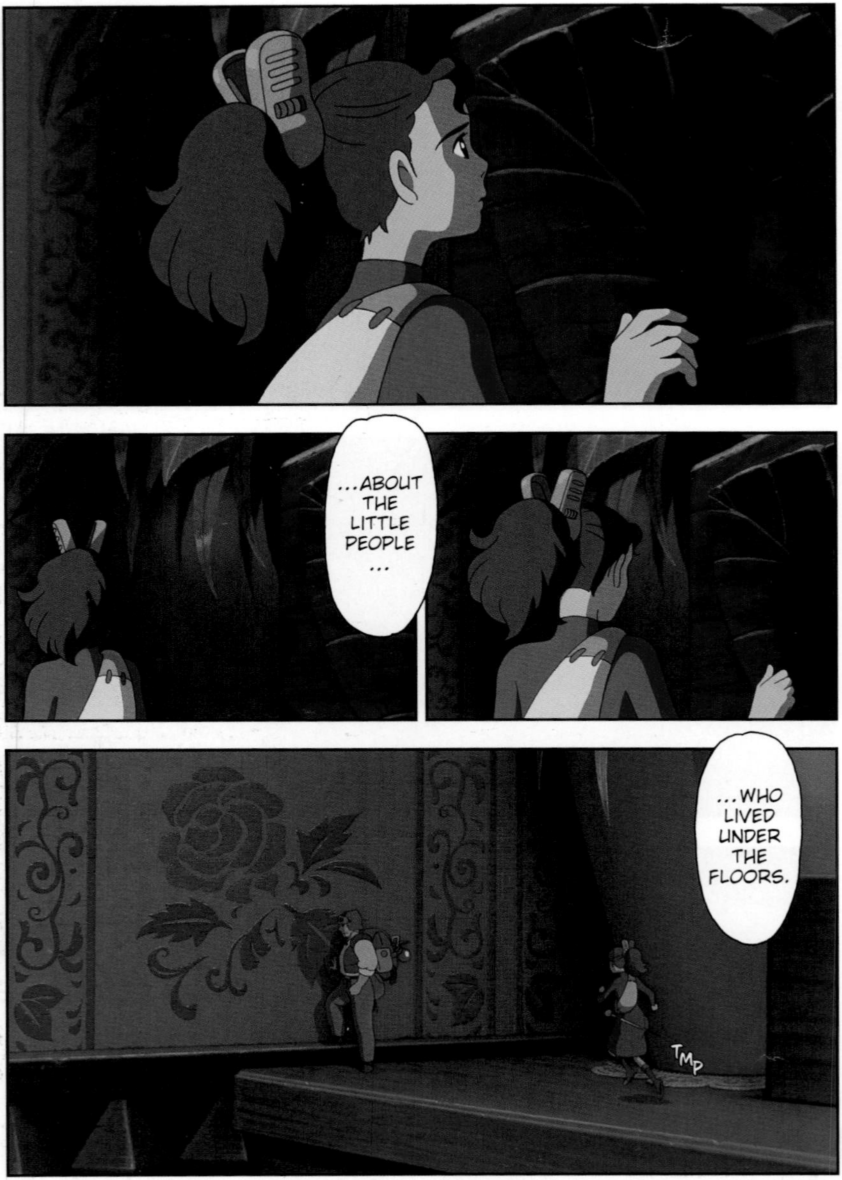
...ABOUT THE LITTLE PEOPLE...
...WHO LIVED UNDER THE FLOORS.
TMP

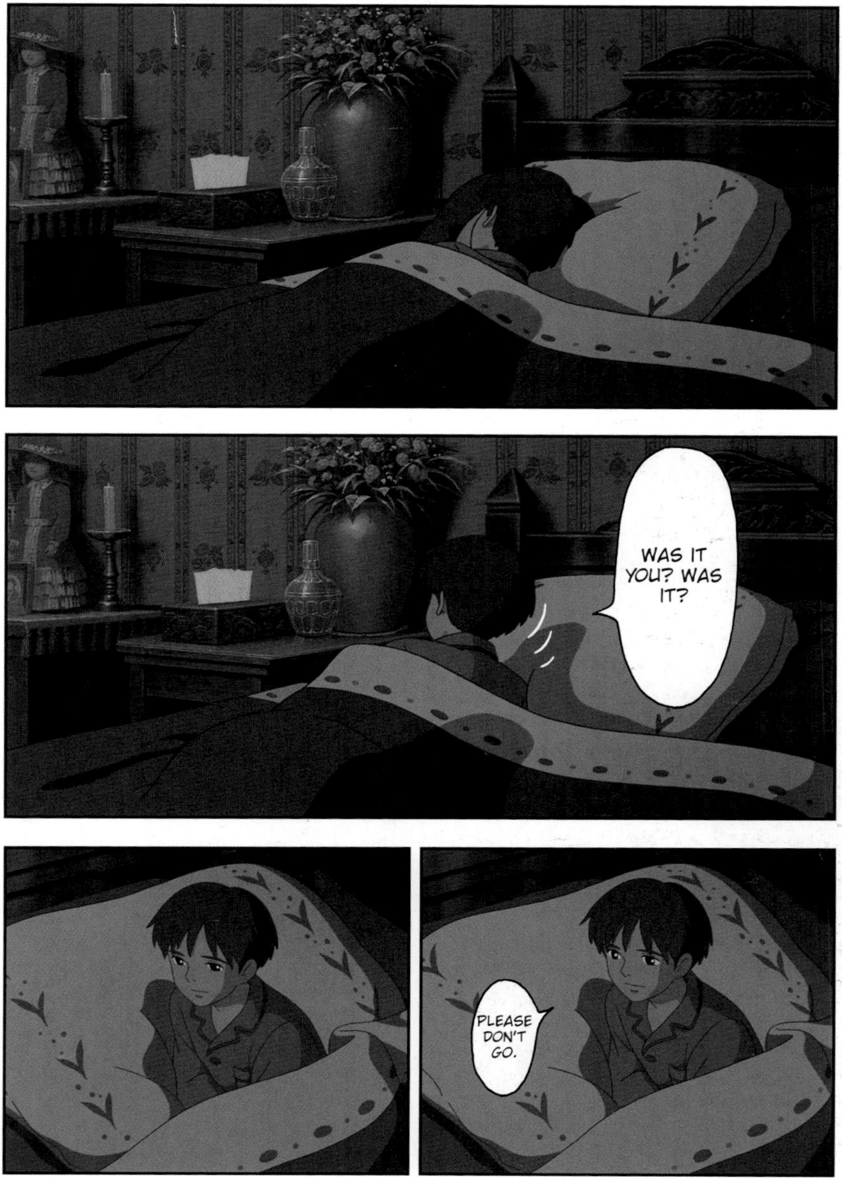
WAS IT YOU? WAS IT?
PLEASE DON'T GO.

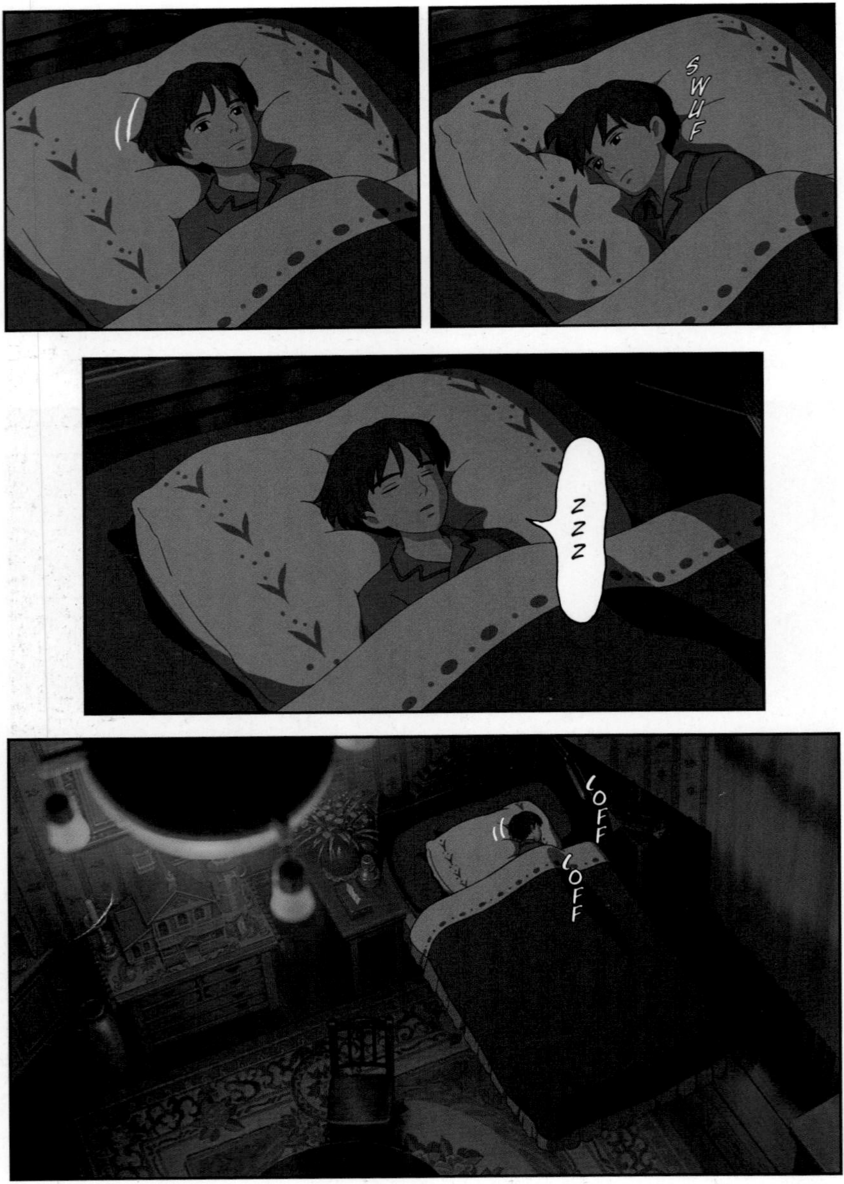
SWUF
Z Z Z
COFF
COFF

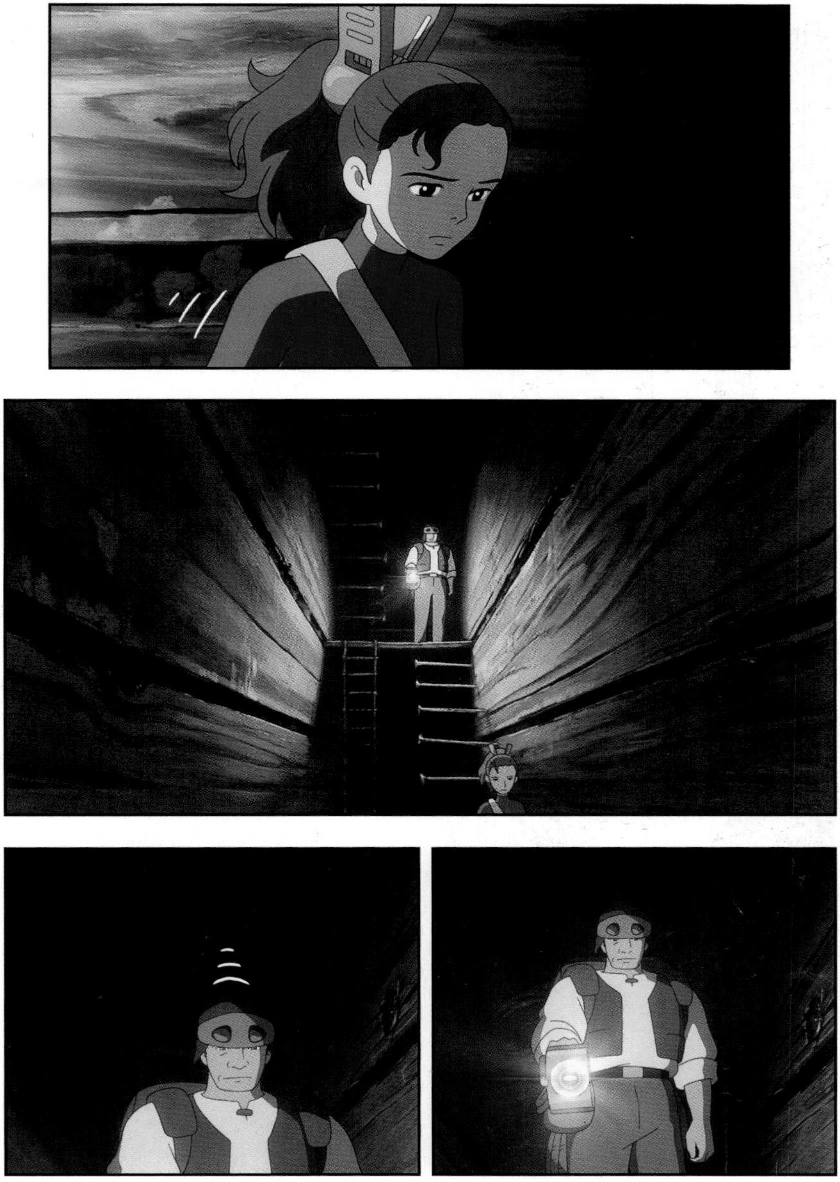

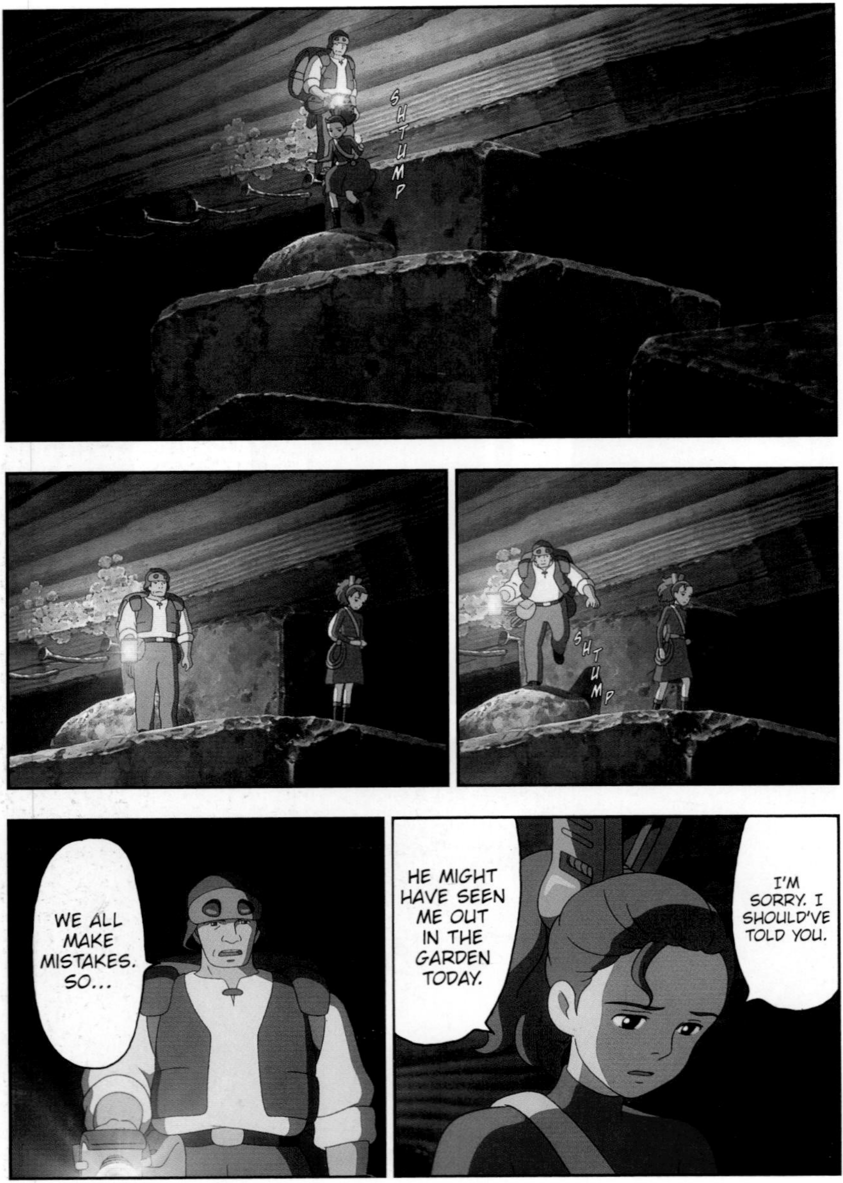
SHTUMP
SHTUMP
I'M SORRY. I SHOULD'VE TOLD YOU.
HE MIGHT HAVE SEEN ME OUT IN THE GARDEN TODAY.
WE ALL MAKE MISTAKES. SO...

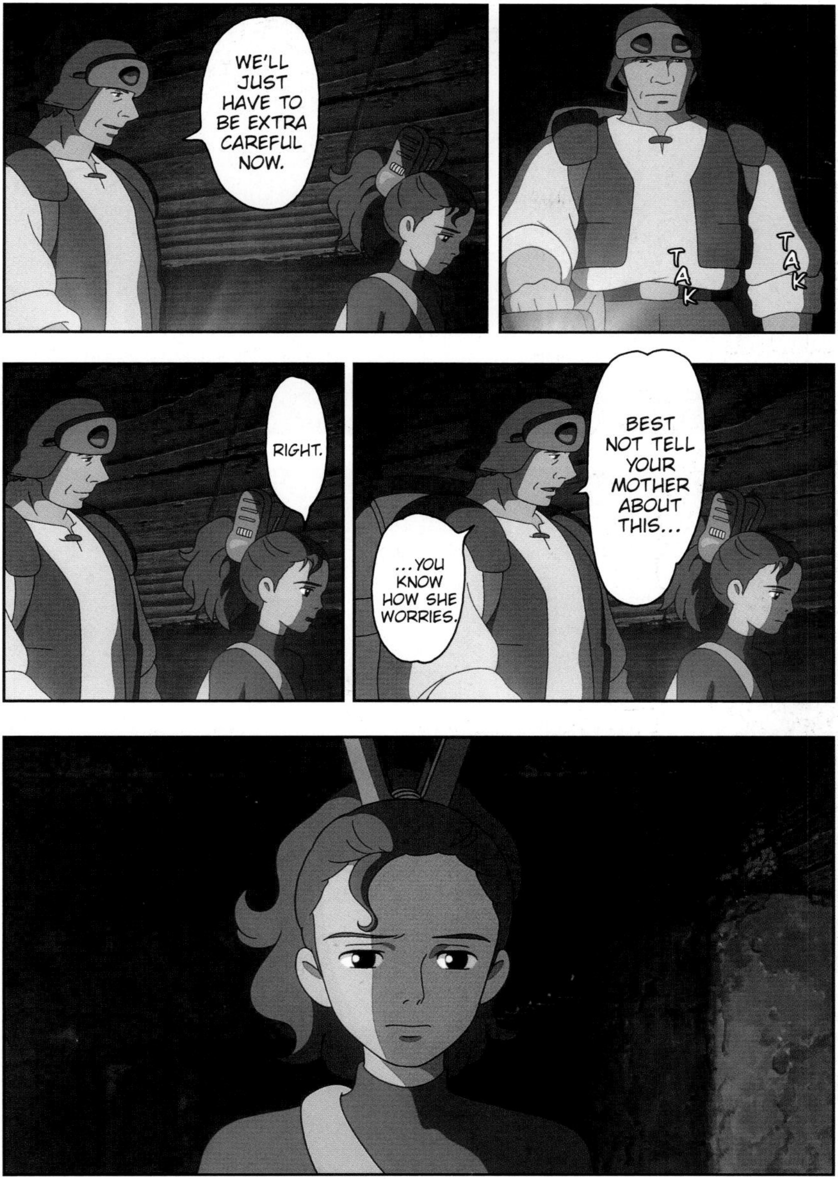
TAK
TAK
WE'LL JUST HAVE TO BE EXTRA CAREFUL NOW.
BEST NOT TELL YOUR MOTHER ABOUT THIS...
...YOU KNOW HOW SHE WORRIES.
RIGHT.

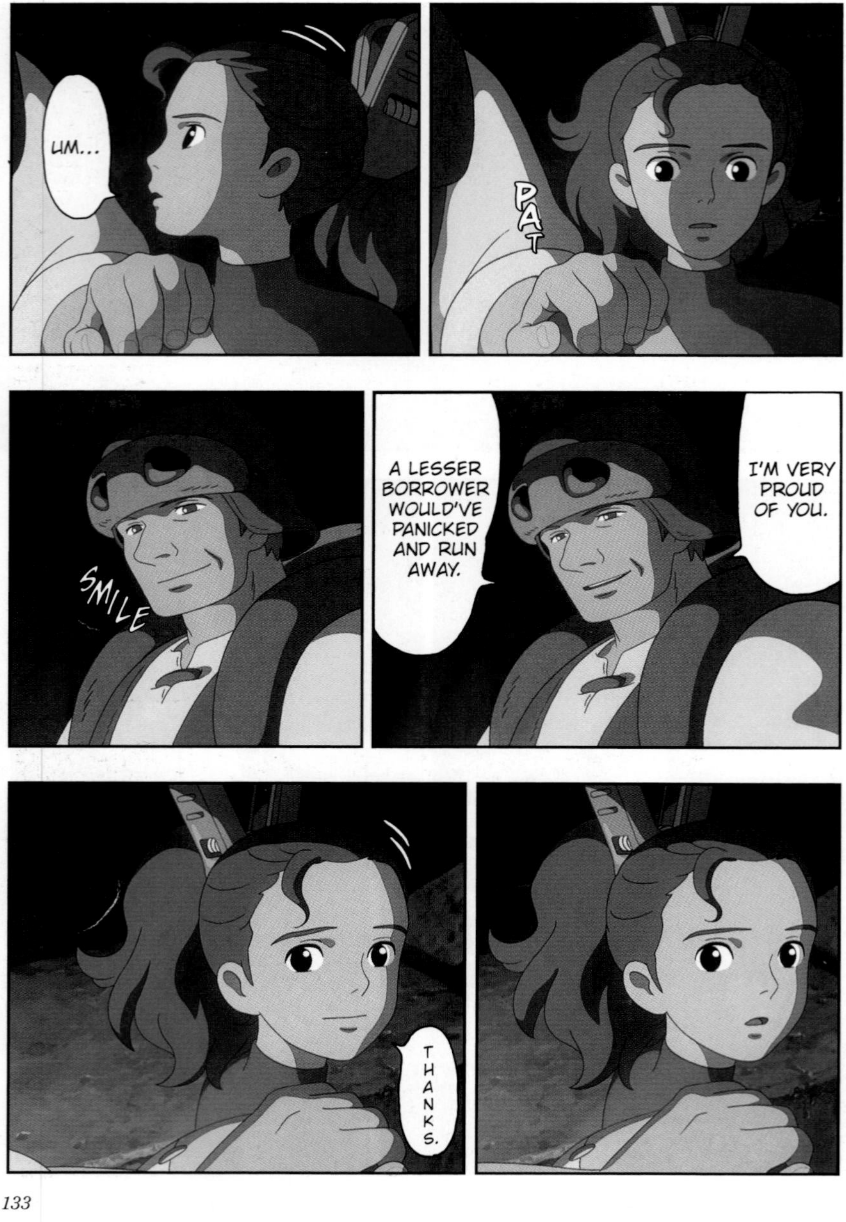
UM...
PAT
SMILE
A LESSER BORROWER WOULD'VE PANICKED AND RUN AWAY.
I'M VERY PROUD OF YOU.
THANKS.

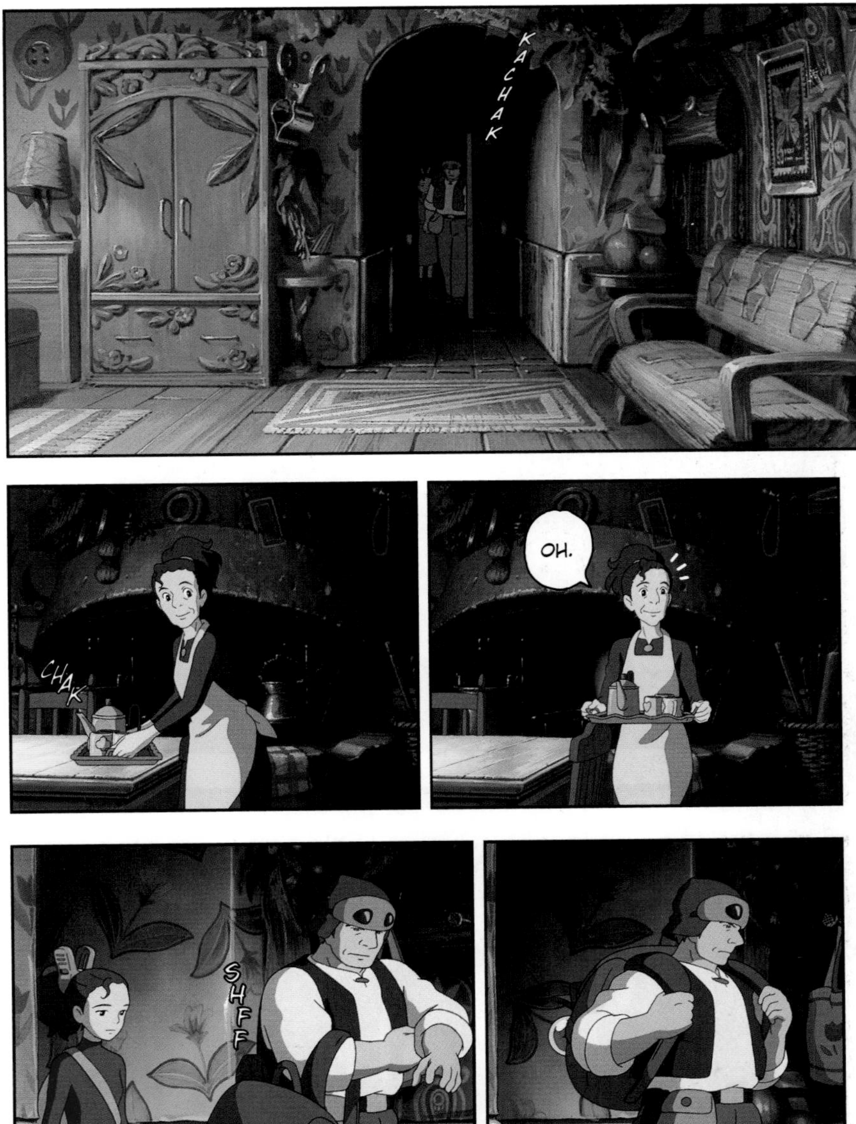
KACHAK
OH.
CHAK
SHFF

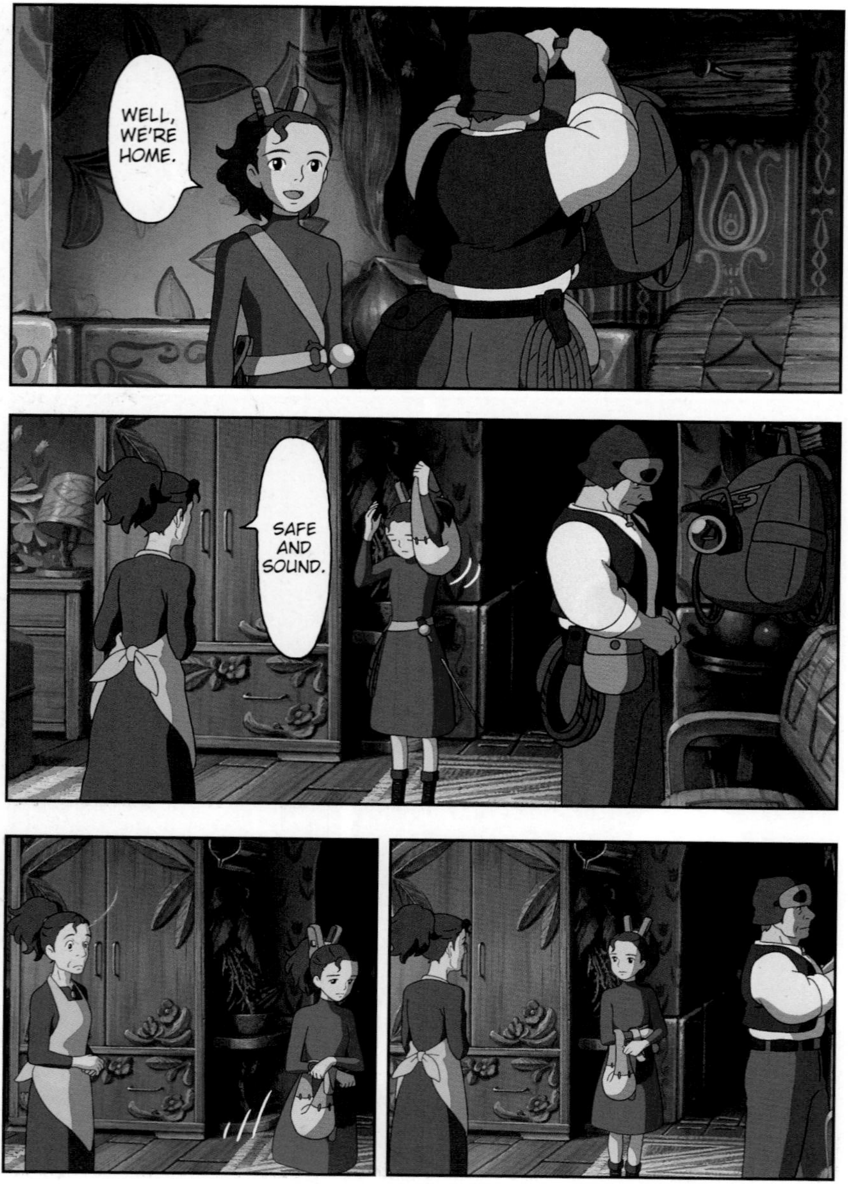
WELL, WE'RE HOME.
SAFE AND SOUND.

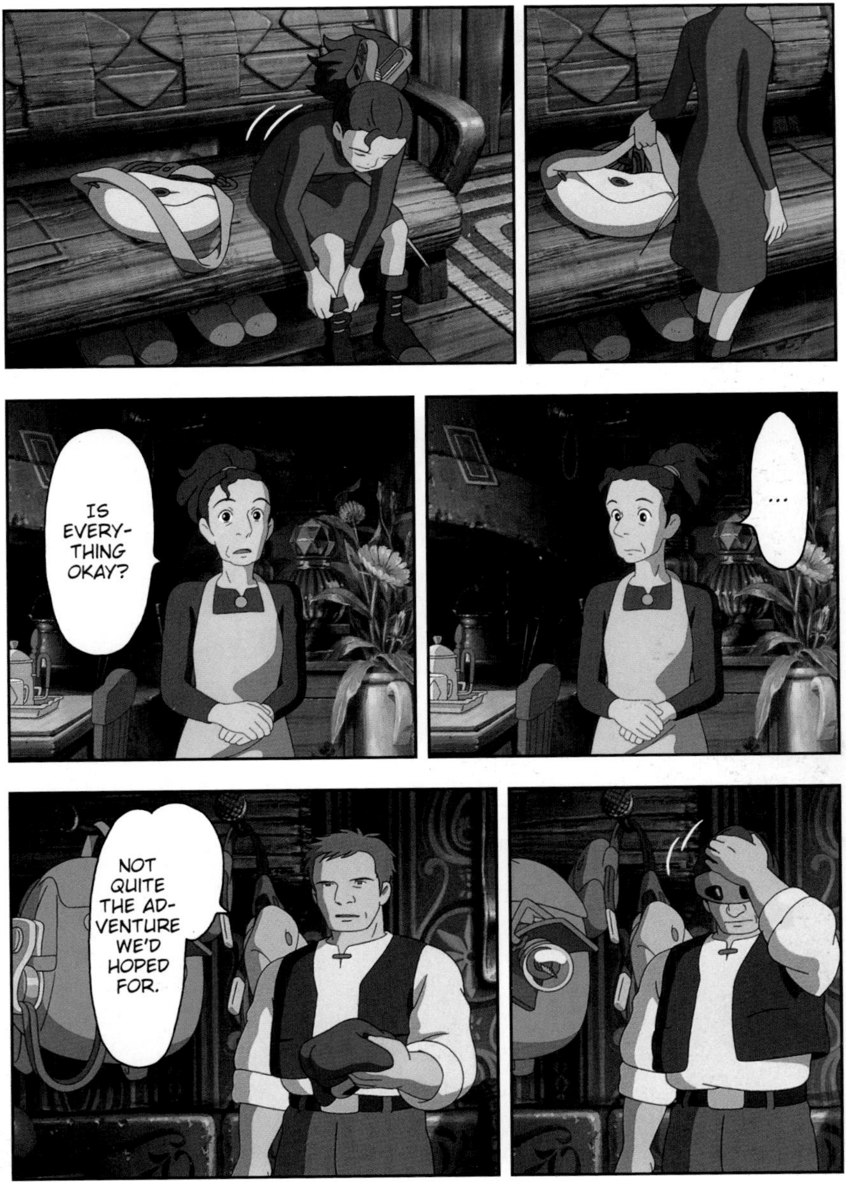
IS EVERY-THING OKAY?
...
NOT QUITE THE AD-VENTURE WE'D HOPED FOR.

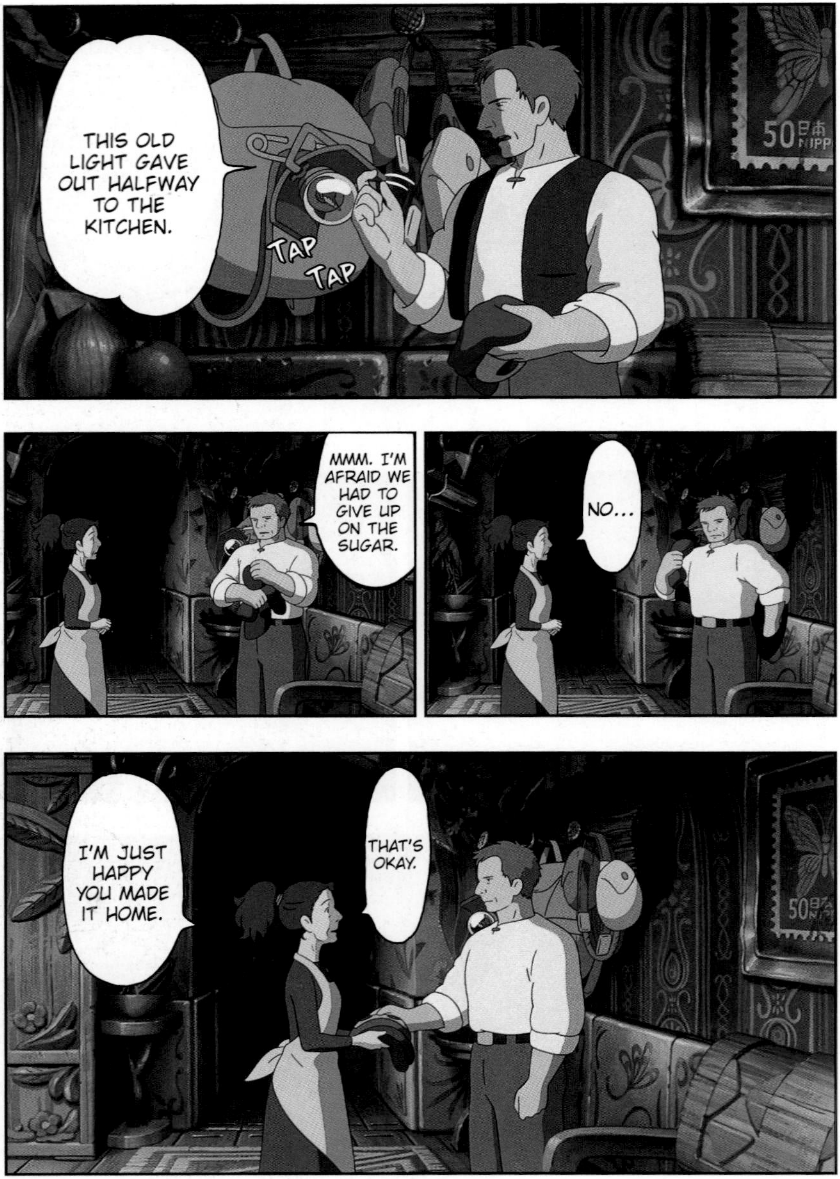
THIS OLD LIGHT GAVE OUT HALFWAY TO THE KITCHEN.
TAP TAP
MMM. I'M AFRAID WE HAD TO GIVE UP ON THE SUGAR.
NO...
THAT'S OKAY.
I'M JUST HAPPY YOU MADE IT HOME.

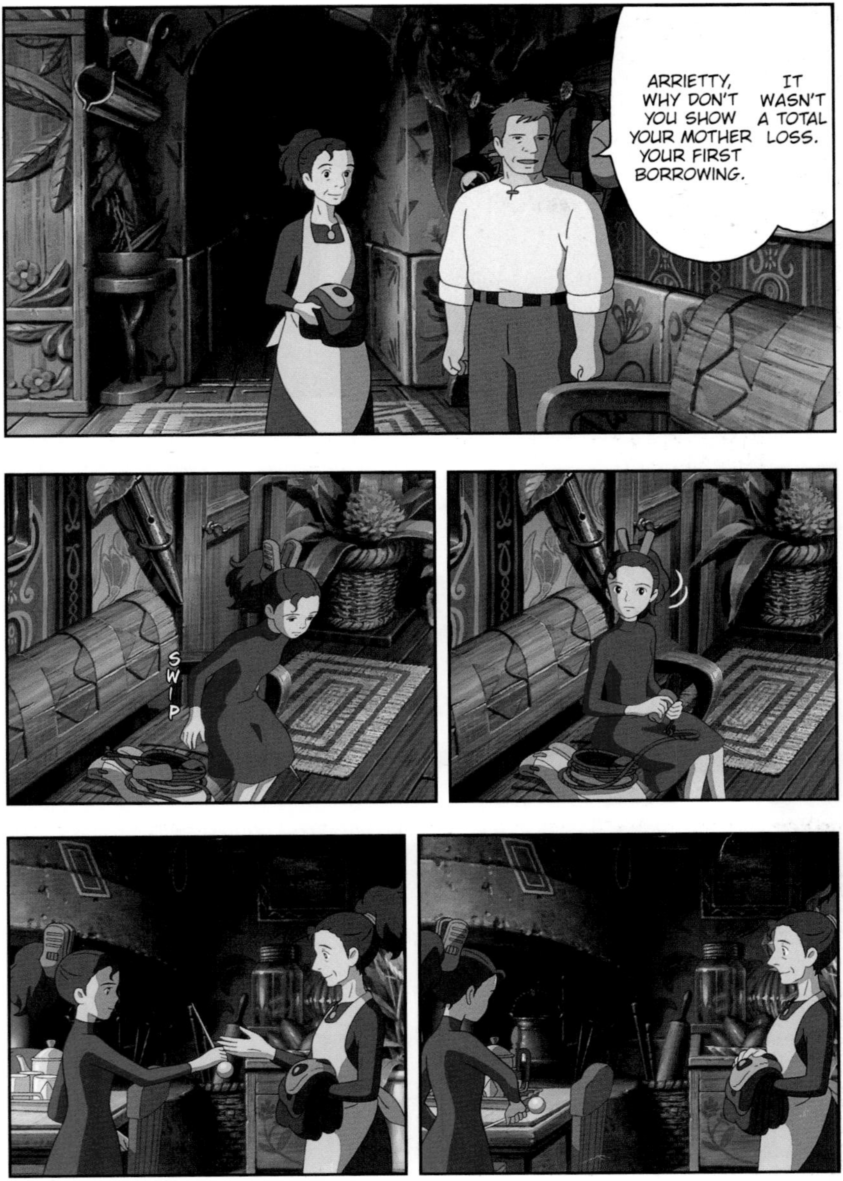
IT WASN'T A TOTAL LOSS.
ARRIETTY, WHY DON'T YOU SHOW YOUR MOTHER YOUR FIRST BORROWING.
SWIP

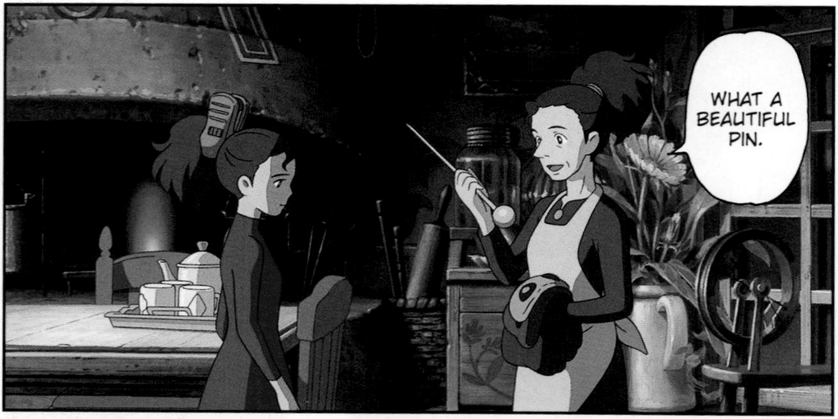
WHAT A BEAUTIFUL PIN.

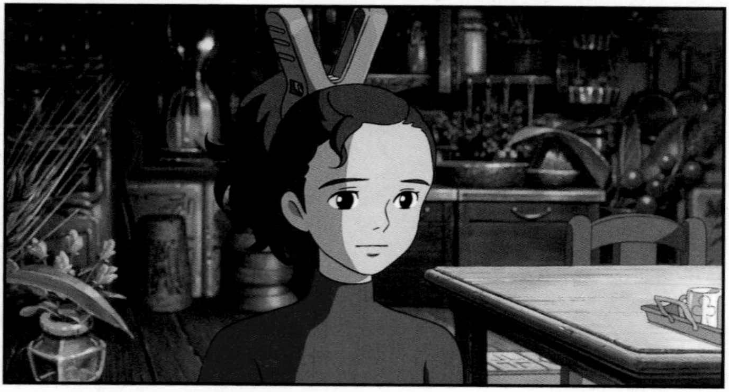

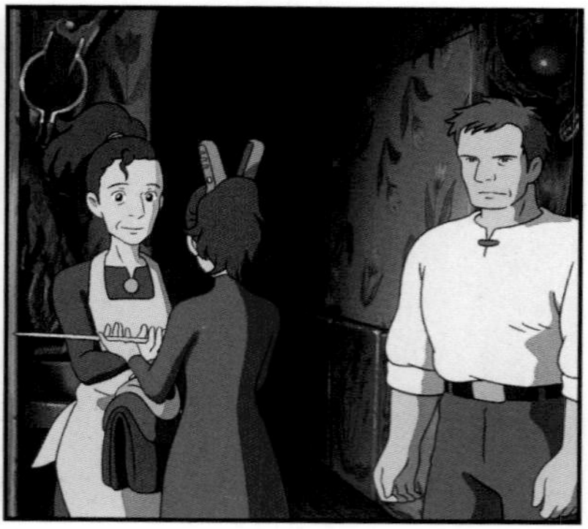

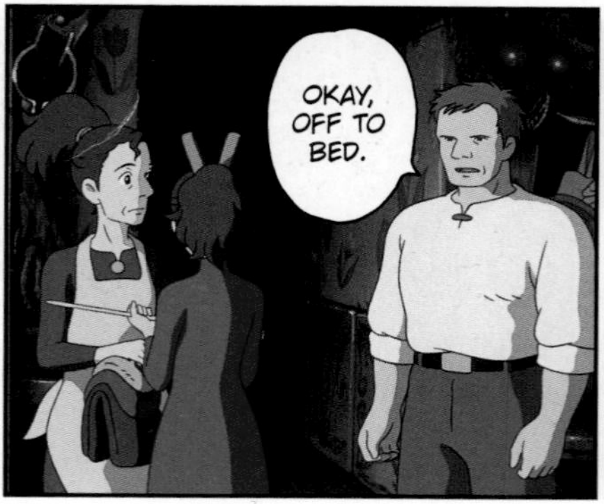
OKAY, OFF TO BED.

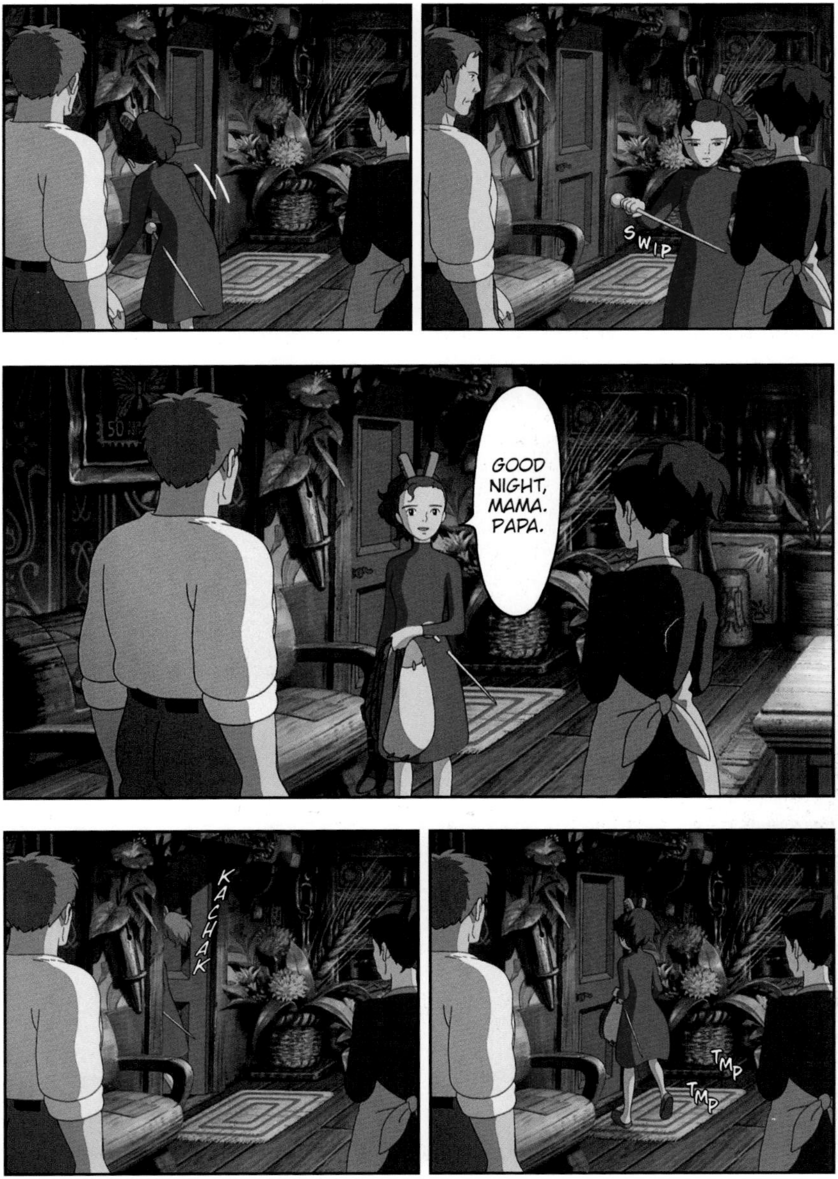
SWIP
GOOD NIGHT, MAMA. PAPA.
TMP
TMP
KACHAK

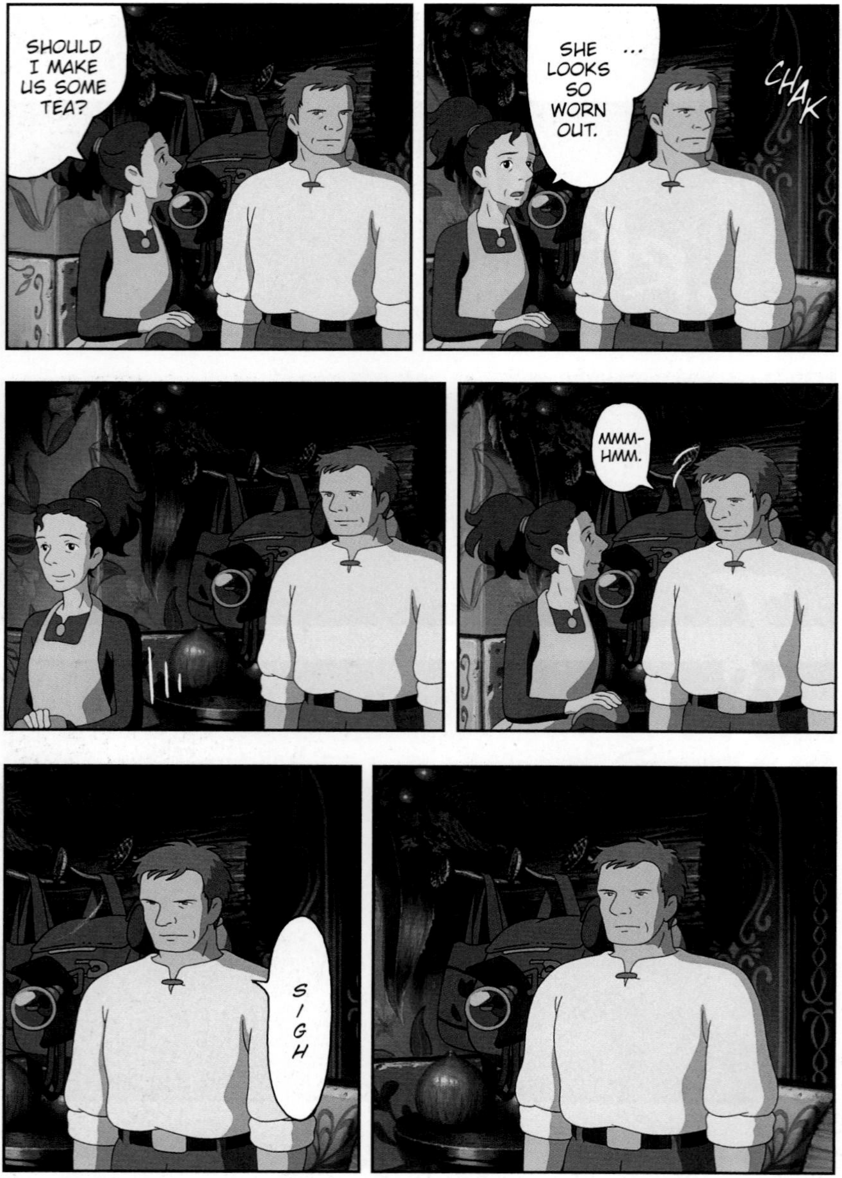
SHOULD I MAKE US SOME TEA?
SHE LOOKS SO WORN OUT. ...
CHAK
MMM-HMM.
SIGH

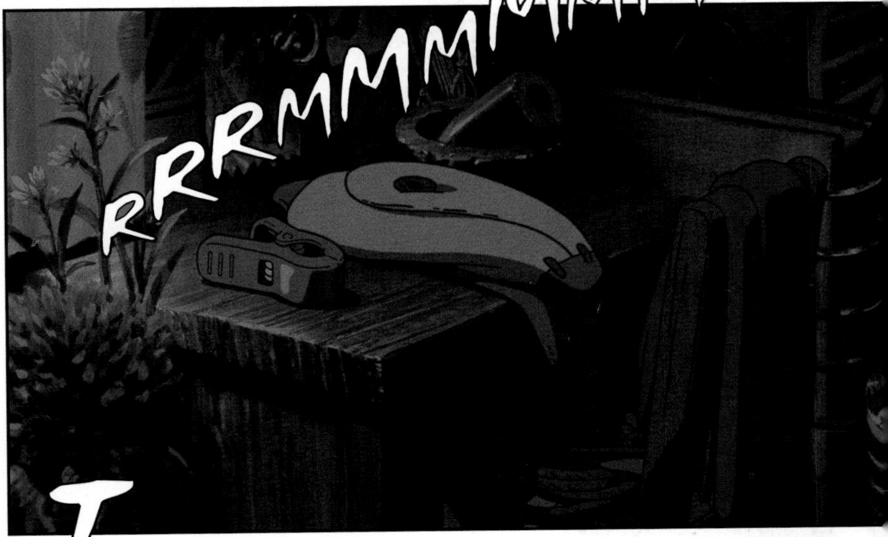
RRRMMMMMMM
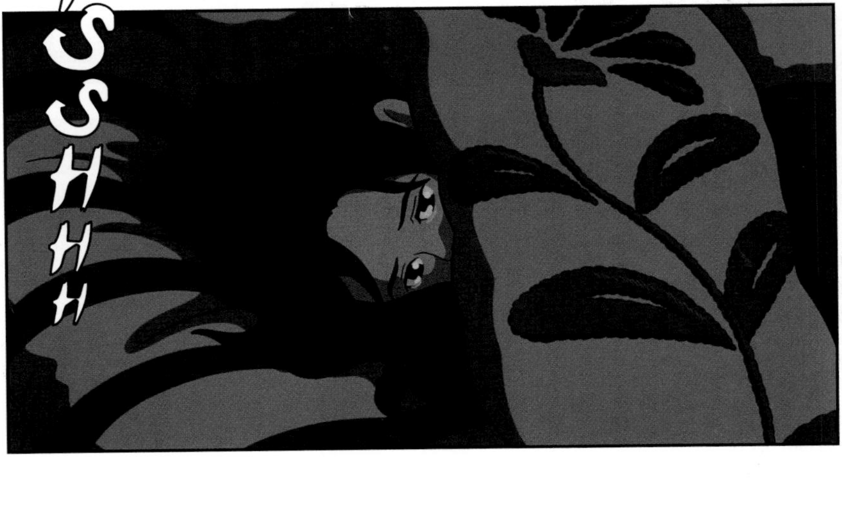
TSSHHH

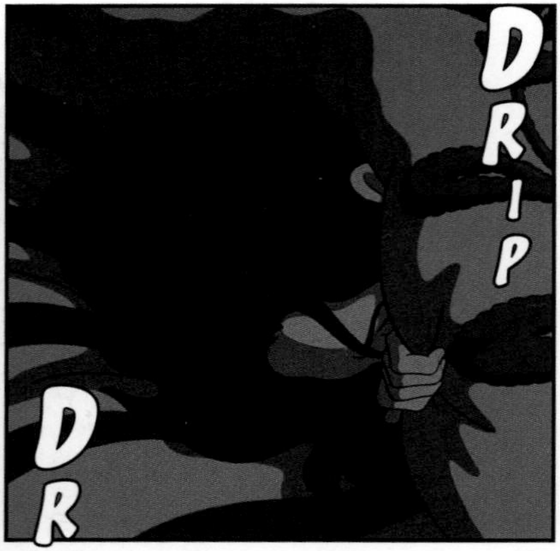
DRIP
DRIP
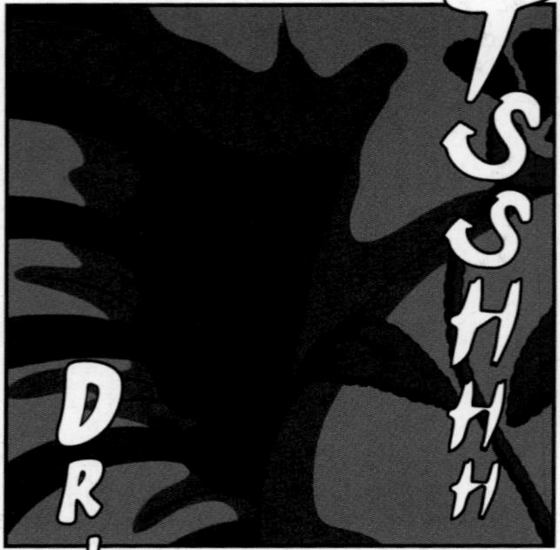
TSSHHH
DRIP
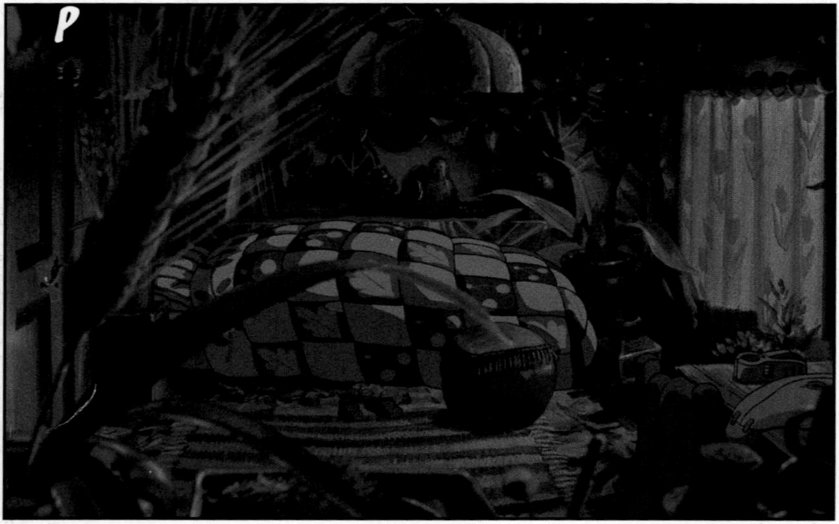

The Secret World of Arrietty

Planning by Hayao Miyazaki
Based on *The Borrowers* by Mary Norton
Original Screenplay by Hayao Miyazaki and Keiko Niwa
Directed by Hiromasa Yonebayashi

Chapter 2

スタジオジブリ作品
STUDIO GHIBLI

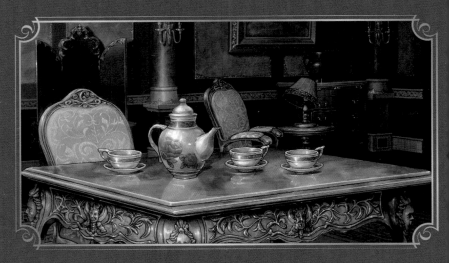

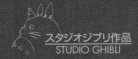

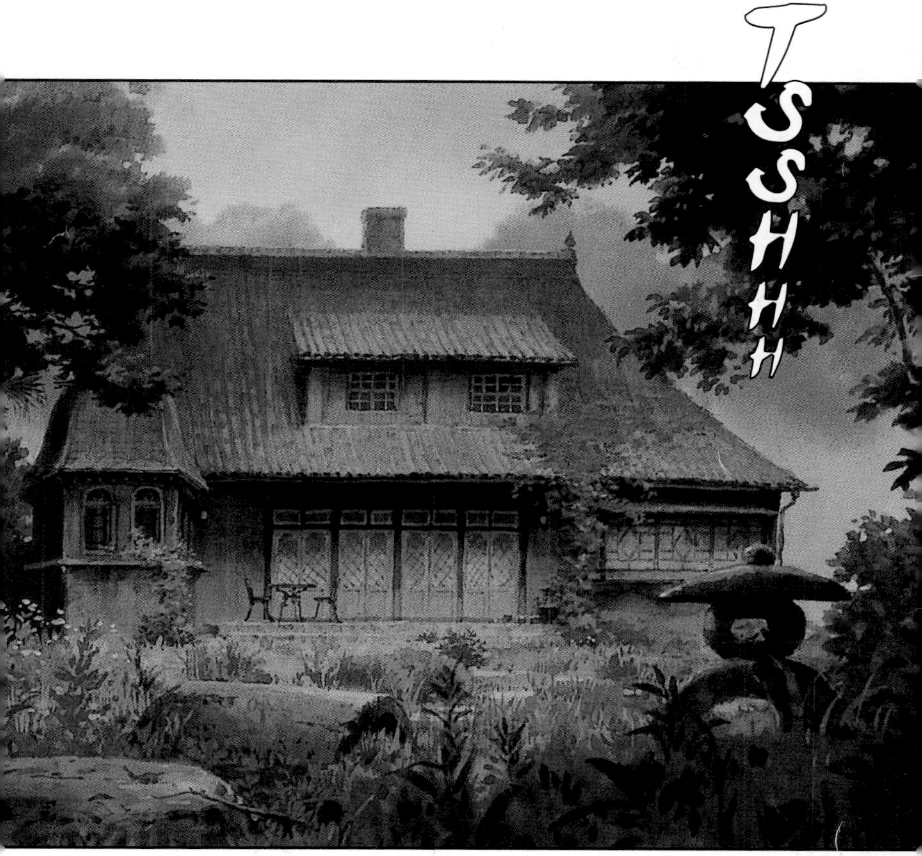
TSSHHH

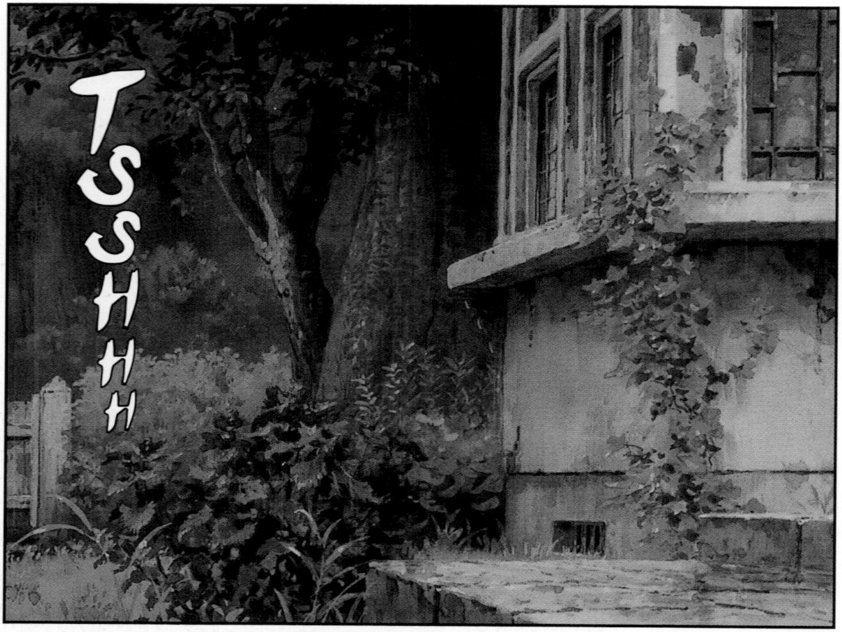
TSSHHH

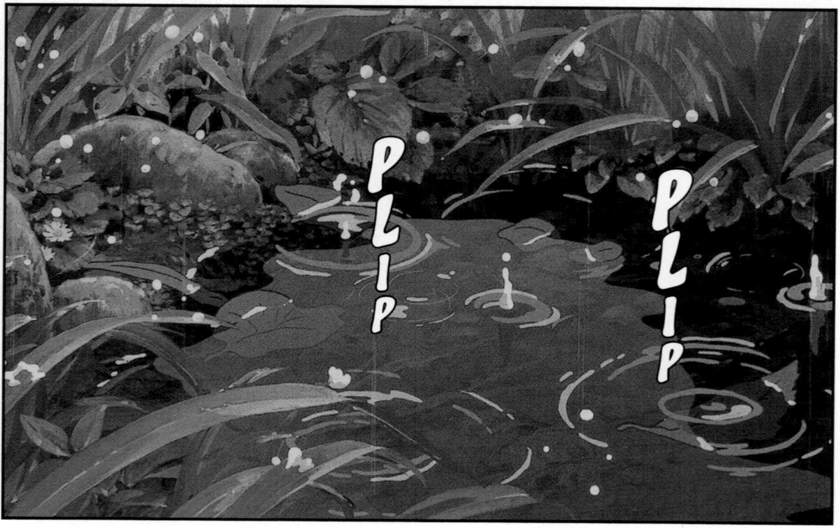
PLIP
PLIP

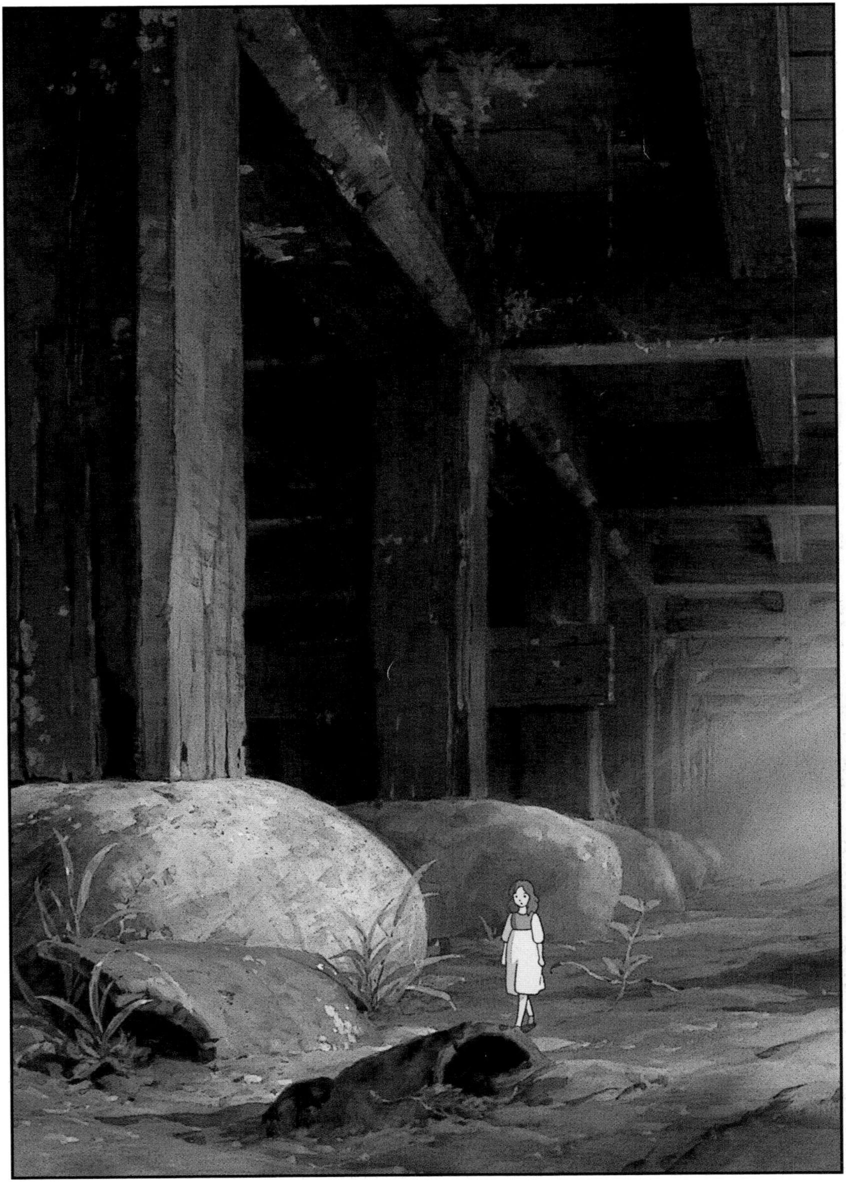

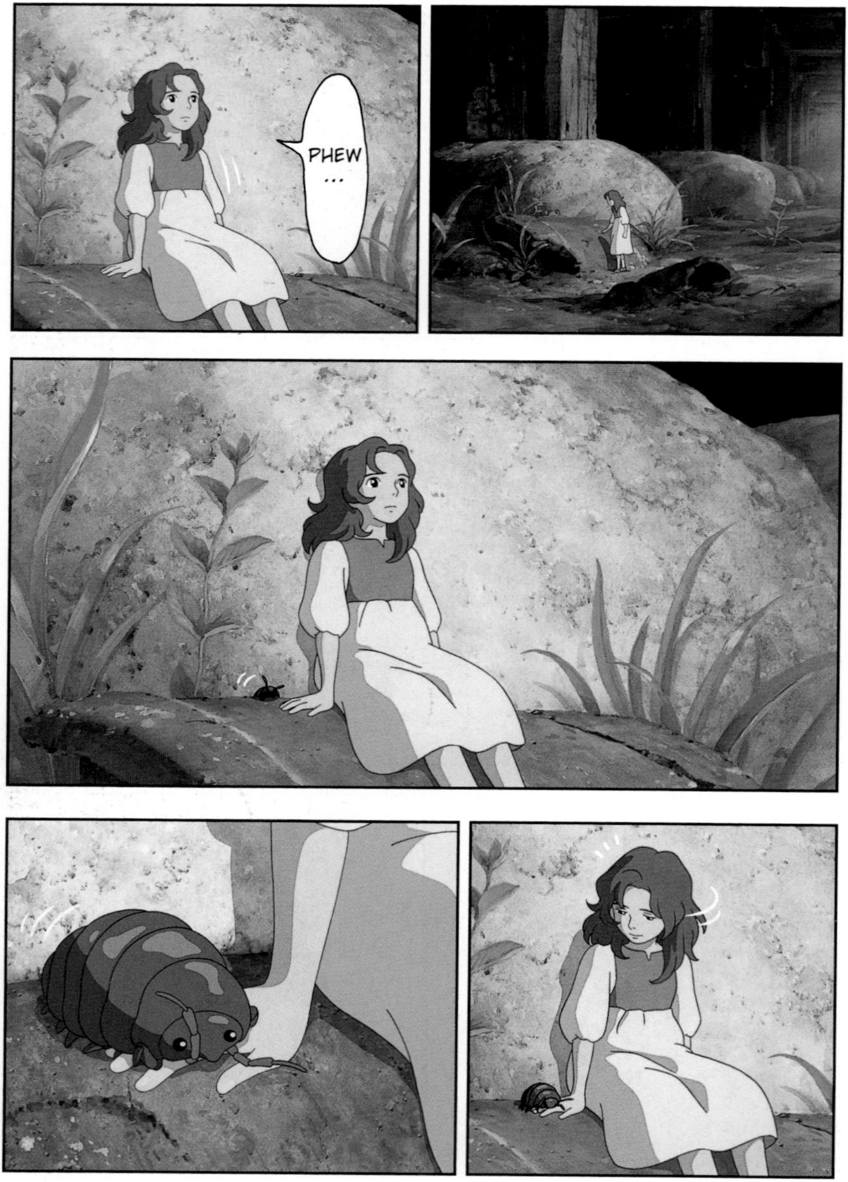
PHEW ...

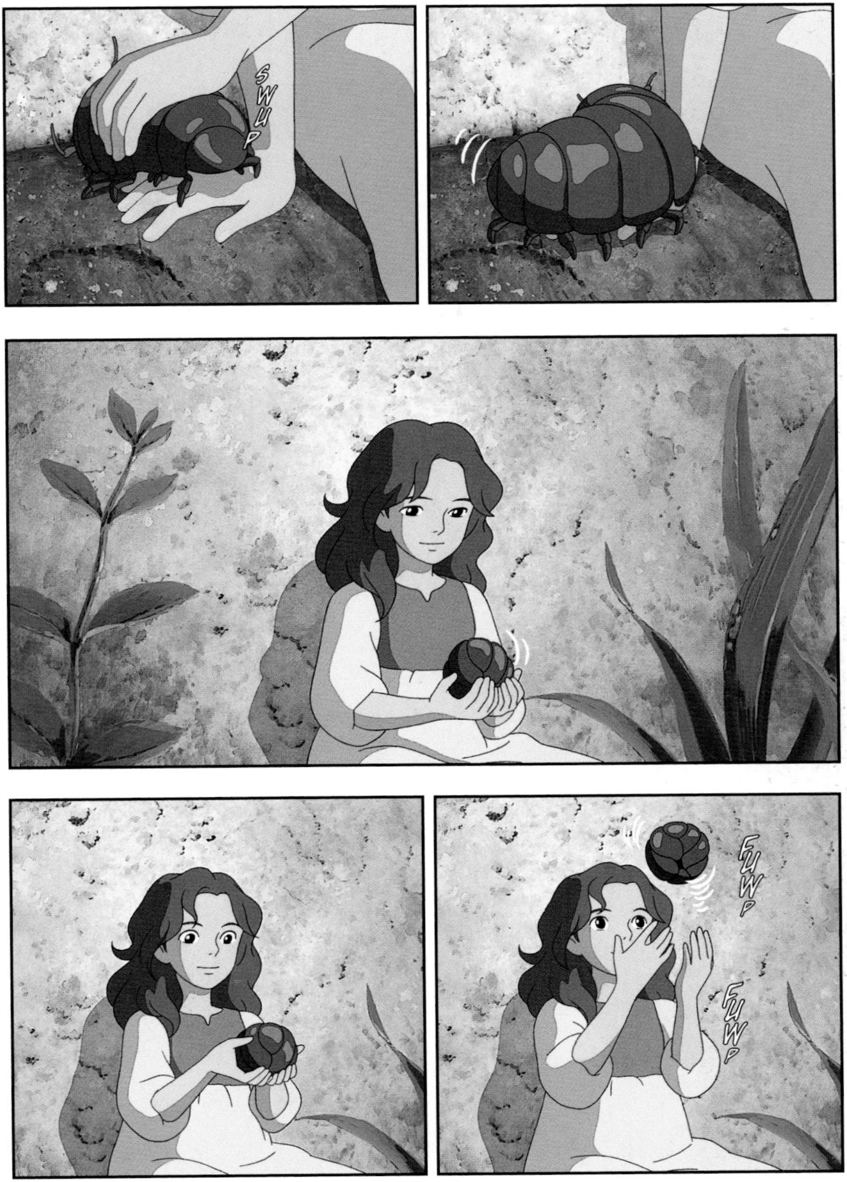
SWUP
FUWP
FUWP

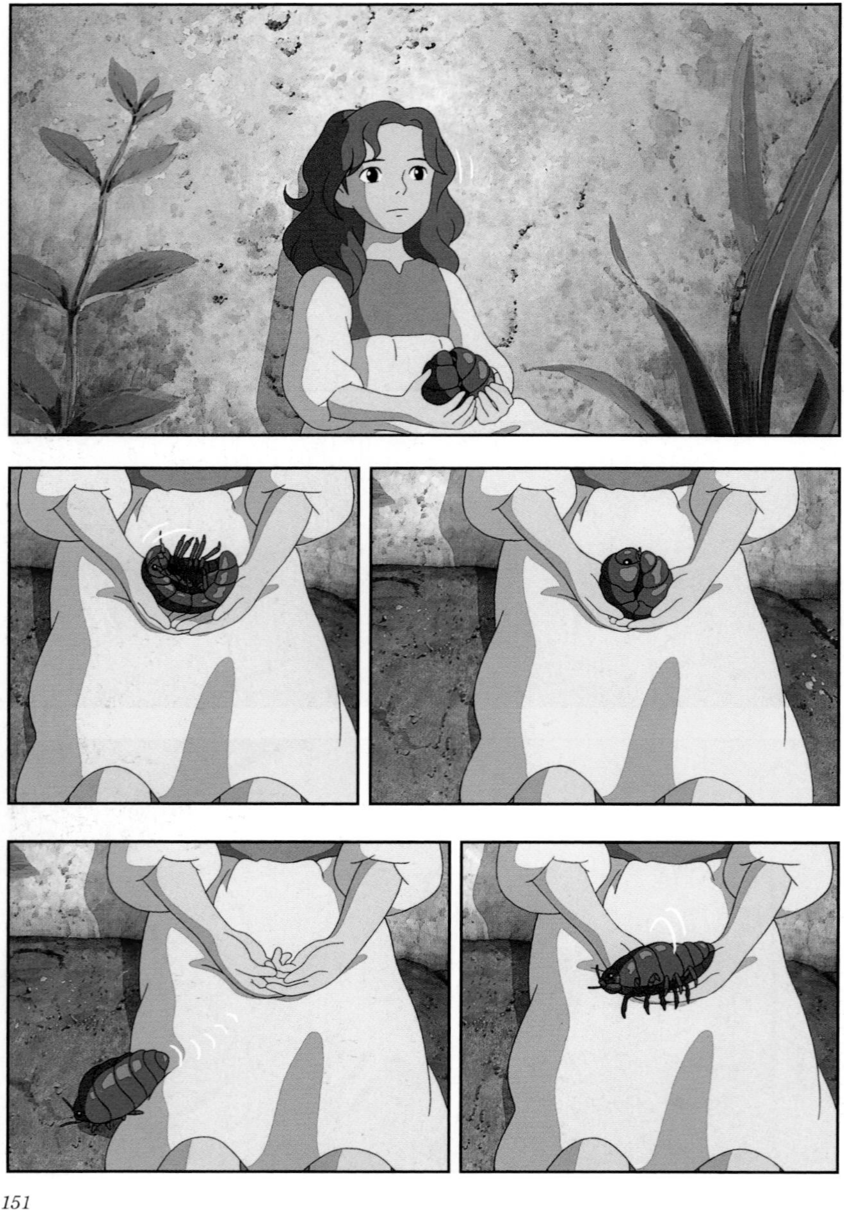

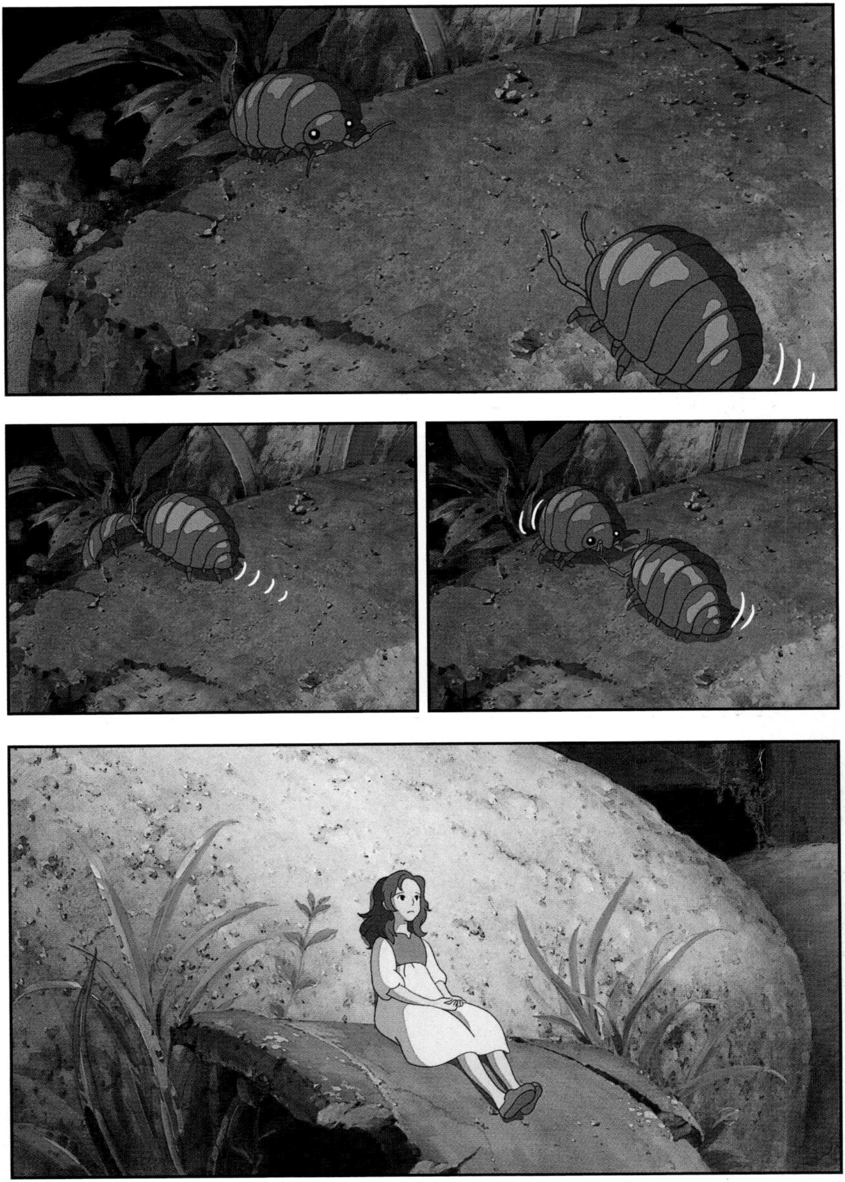

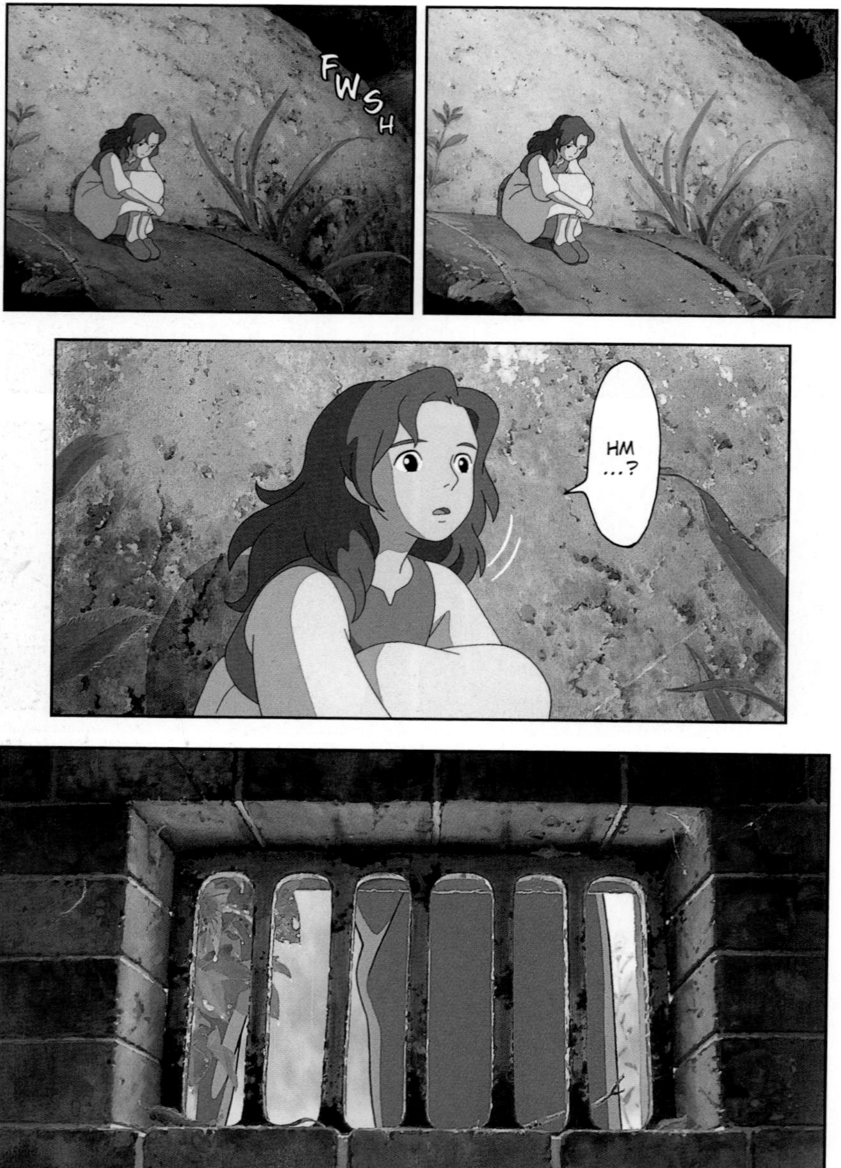
FWSH
HM ...?

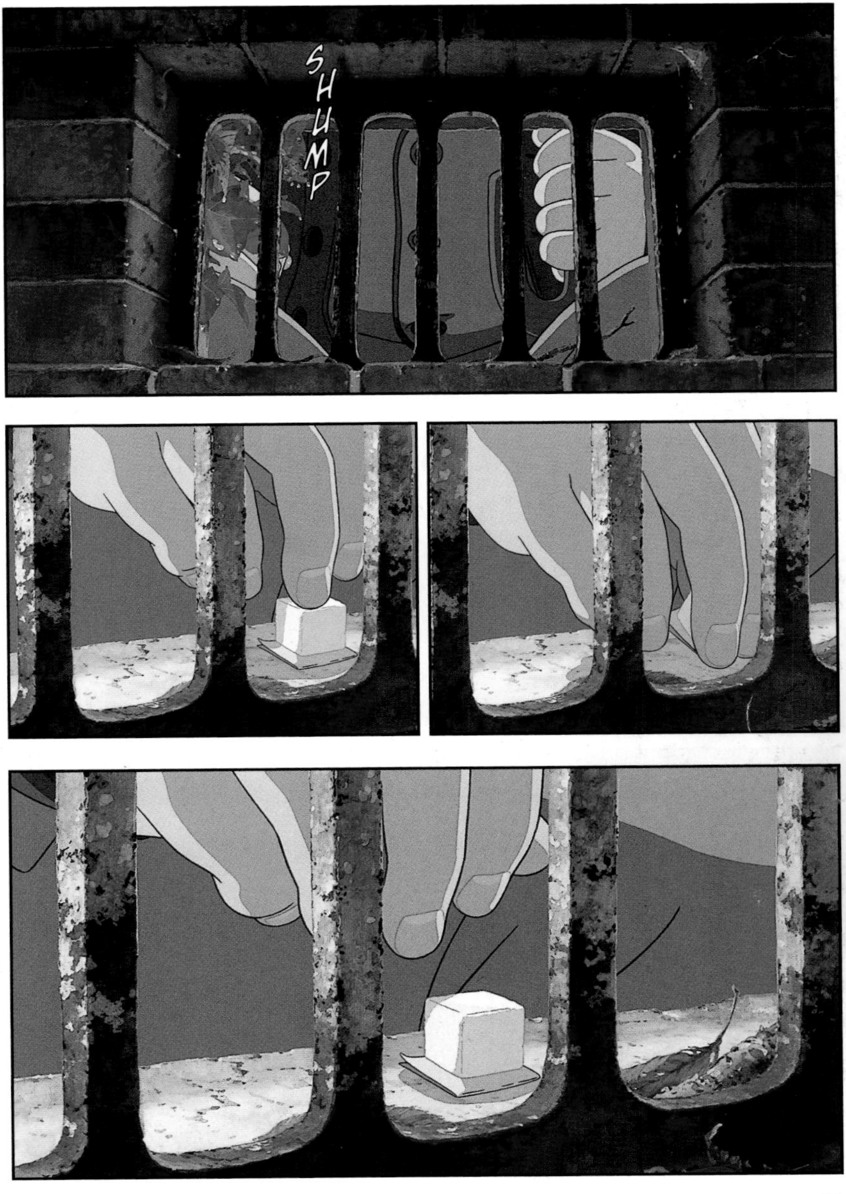
SHUMP

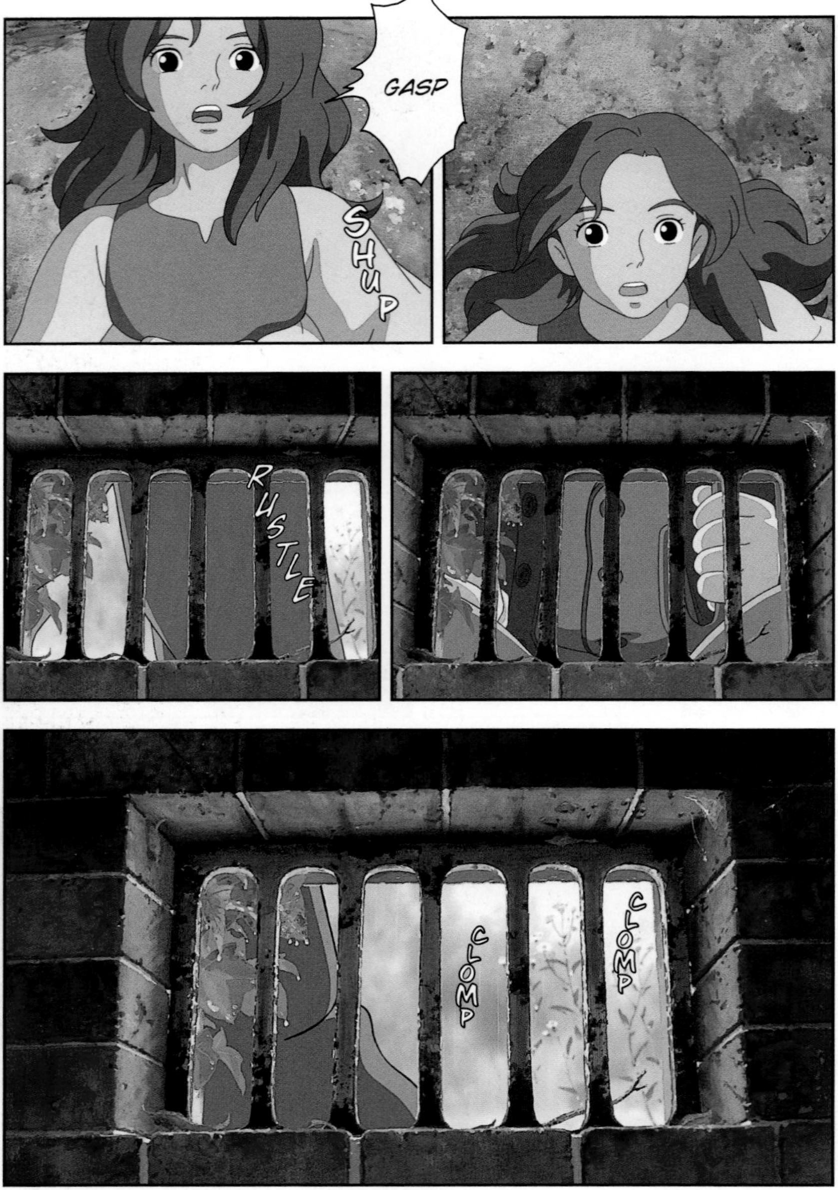
GASP
SHUP
RUSTLE
CLOMP
CLOMP

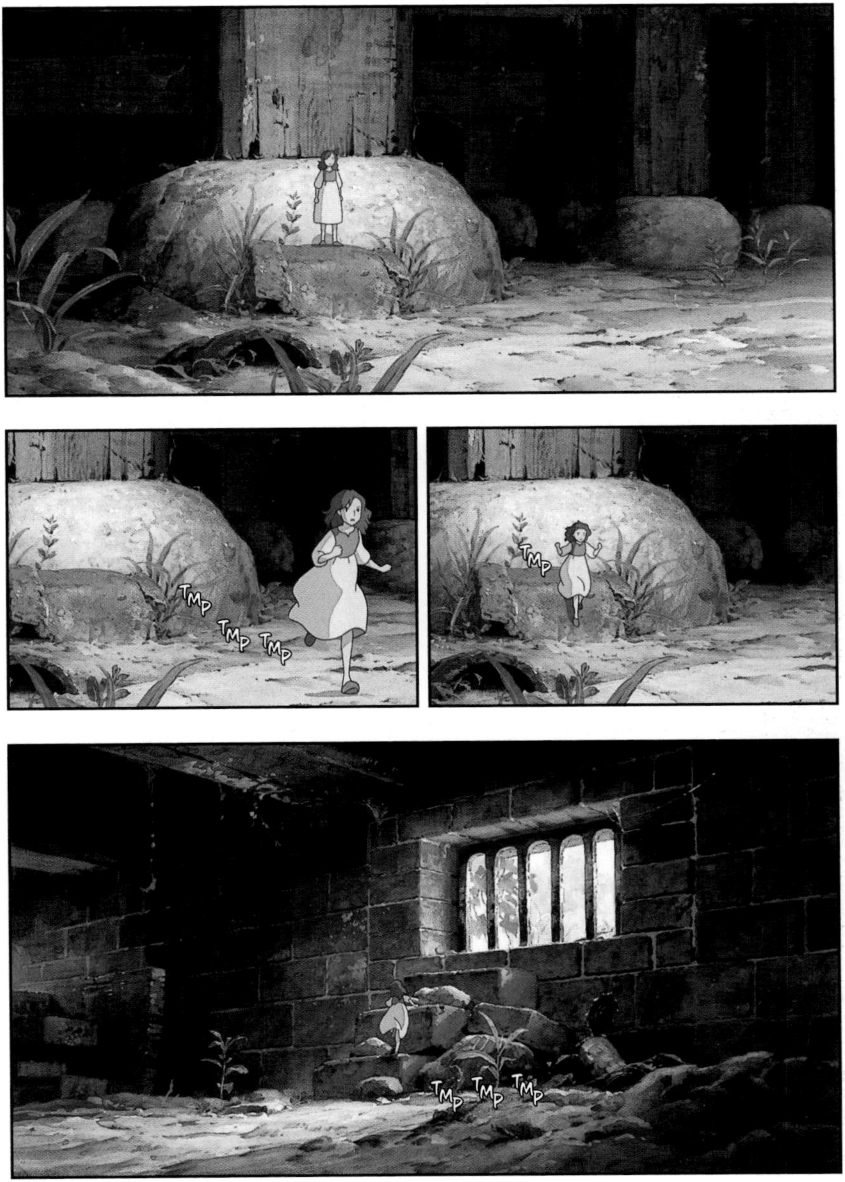
TMP
TMP
TMP
TMP
TMP
TMP
TMP

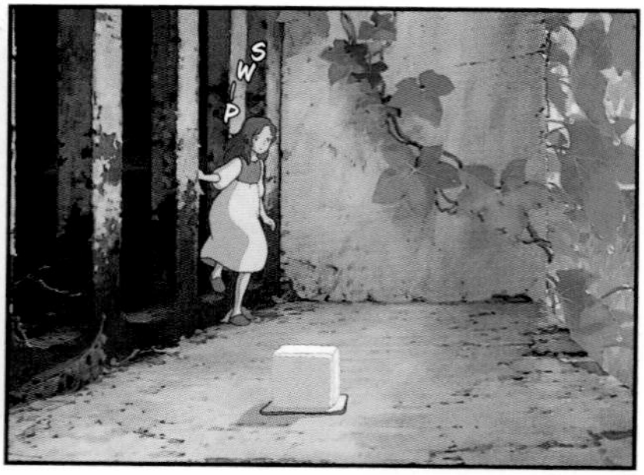
SWIP
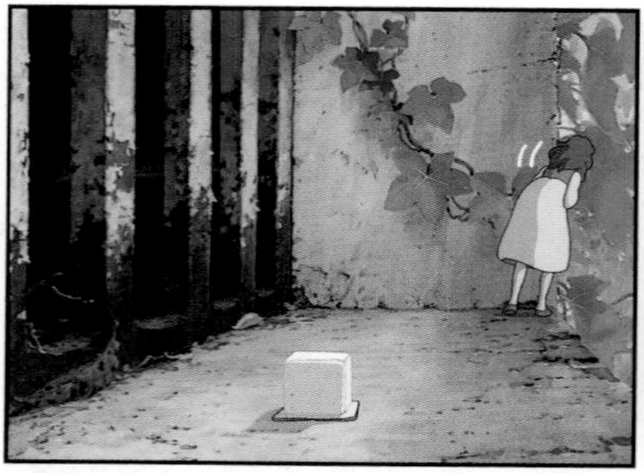
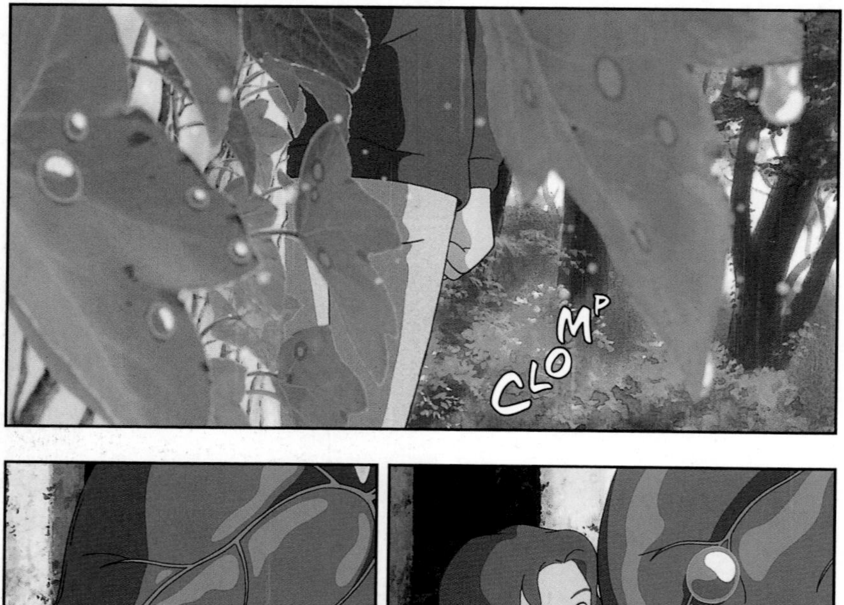
CLOMP
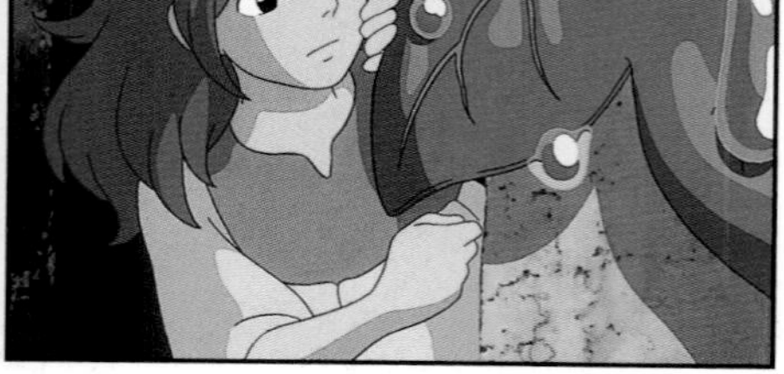
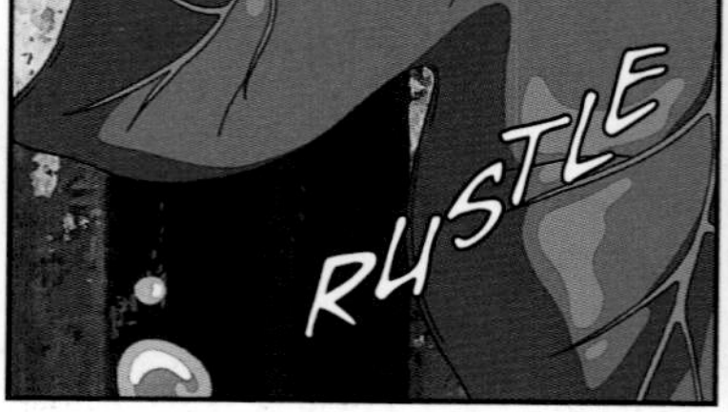
RUSTLE

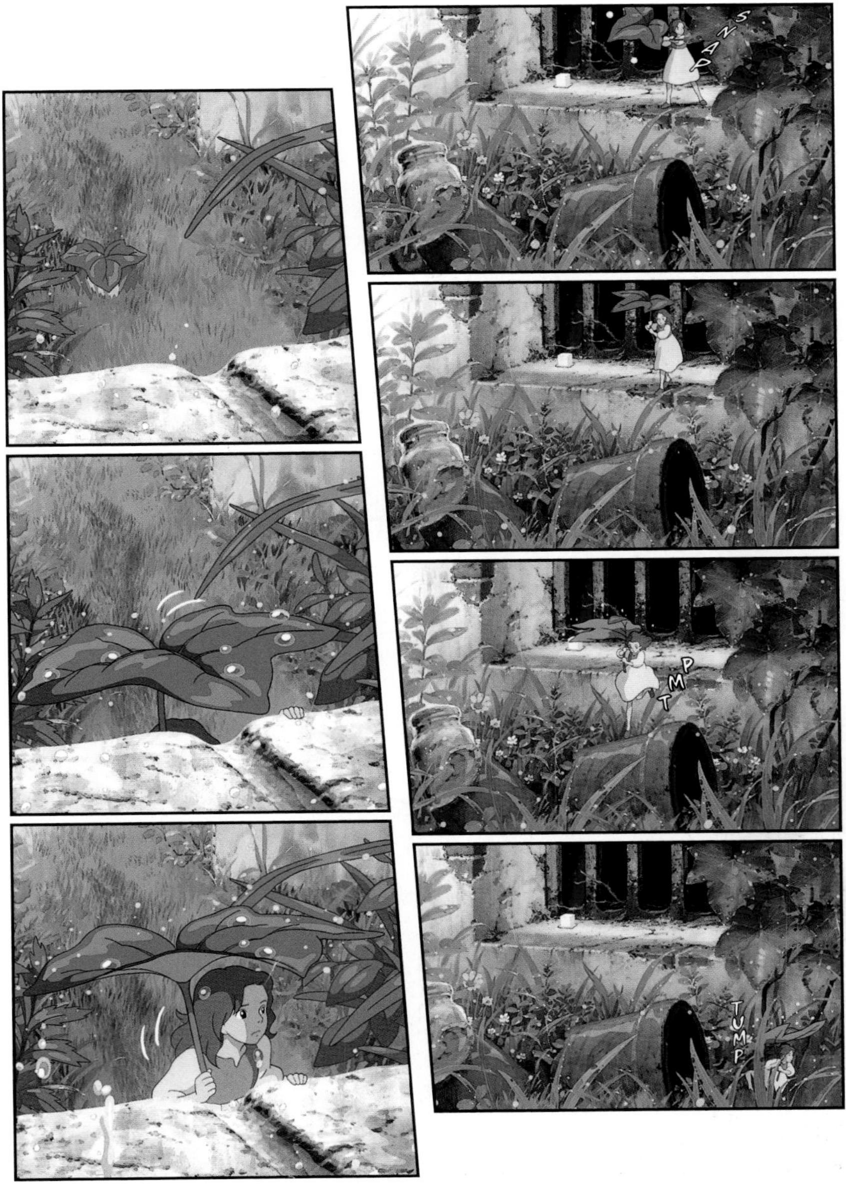
SNAP
TMP
TUMP

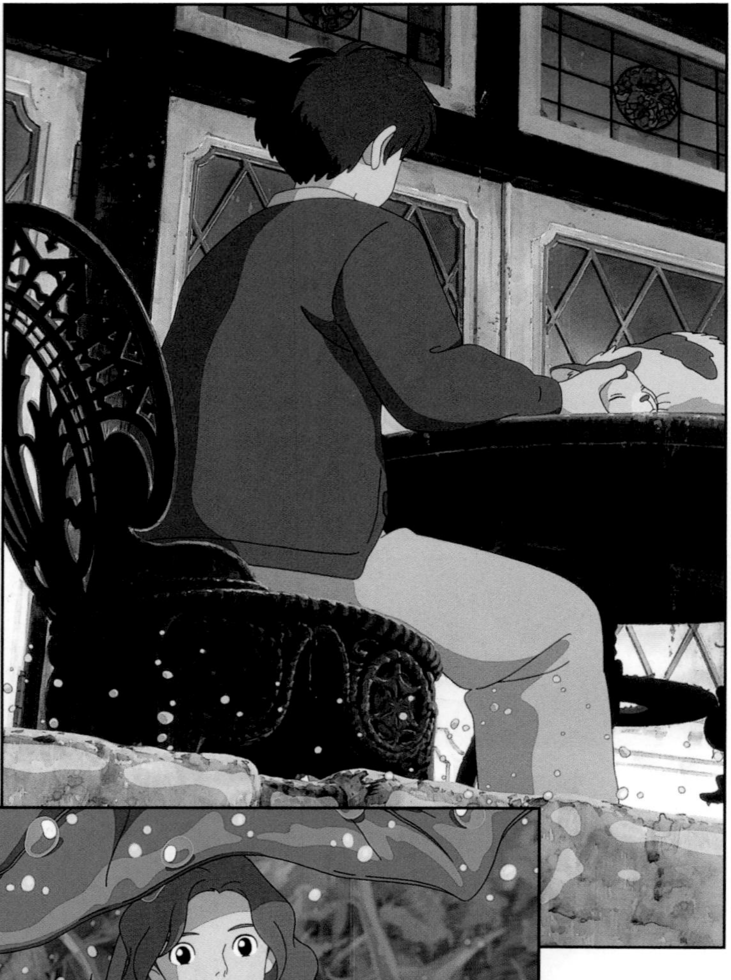

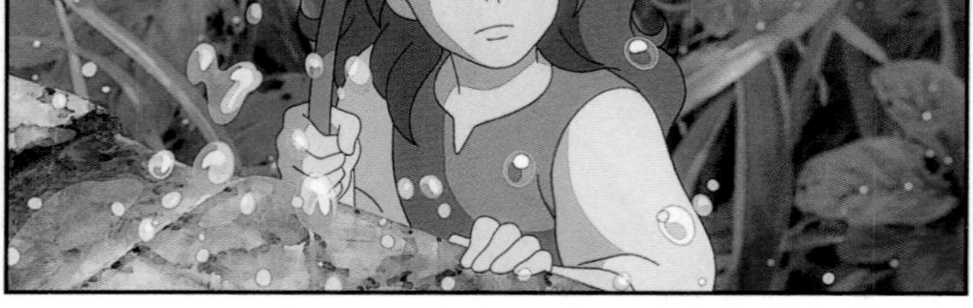

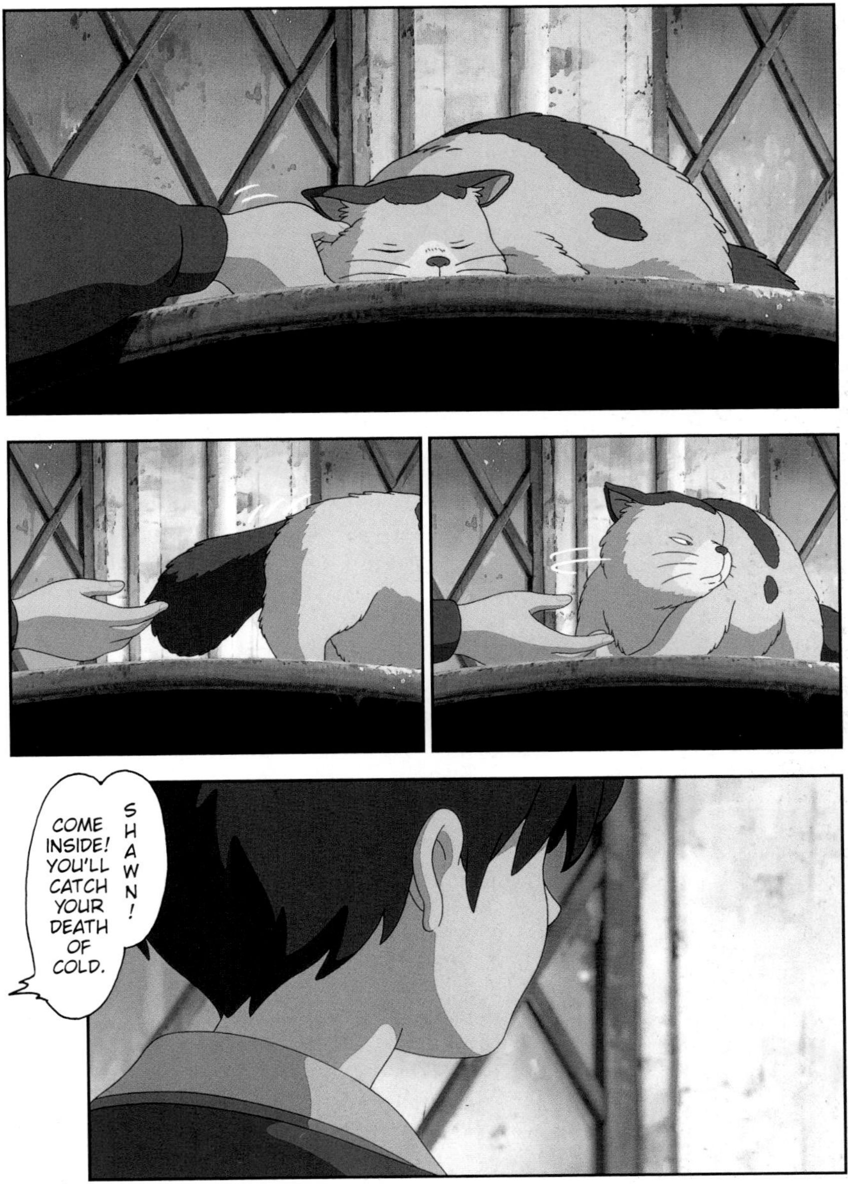
SHAWN!
COME INSIDE! YOU'LL CATCH YOUR DEATH OF COLD.

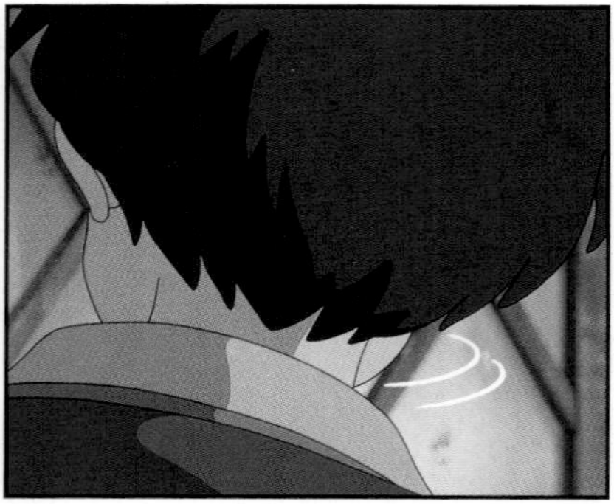
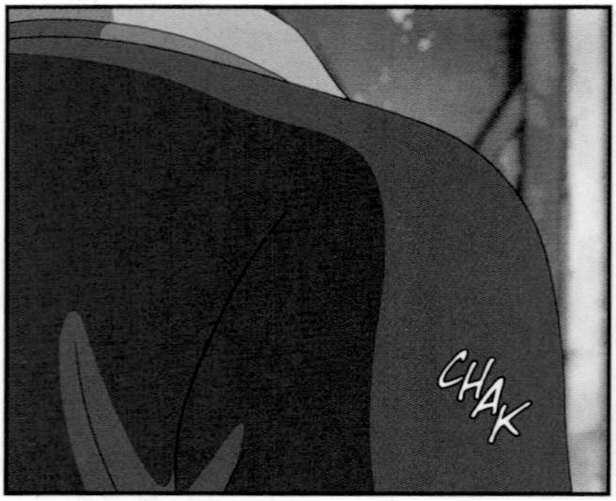
CHAK
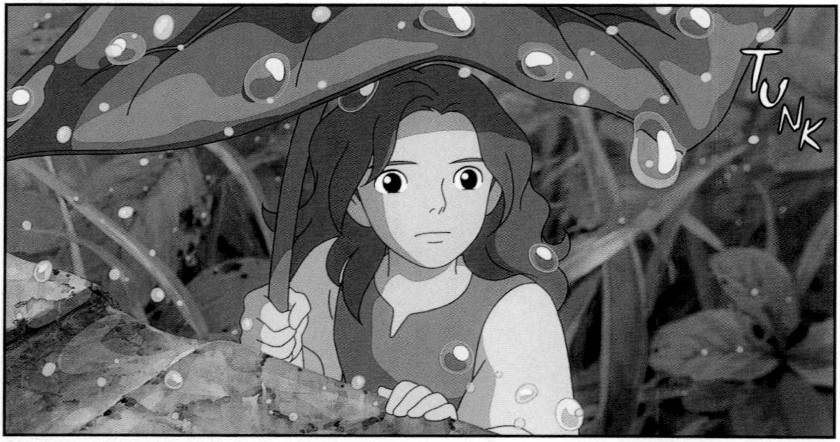
TUNK
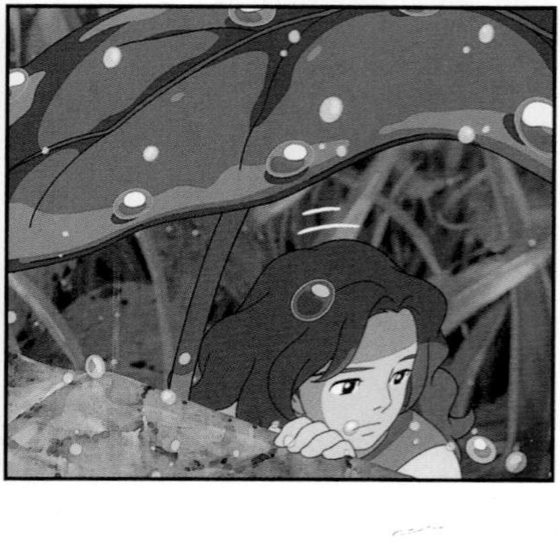
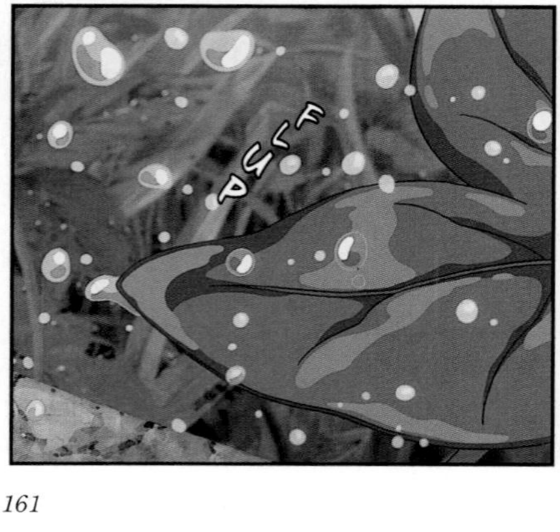
FLUP

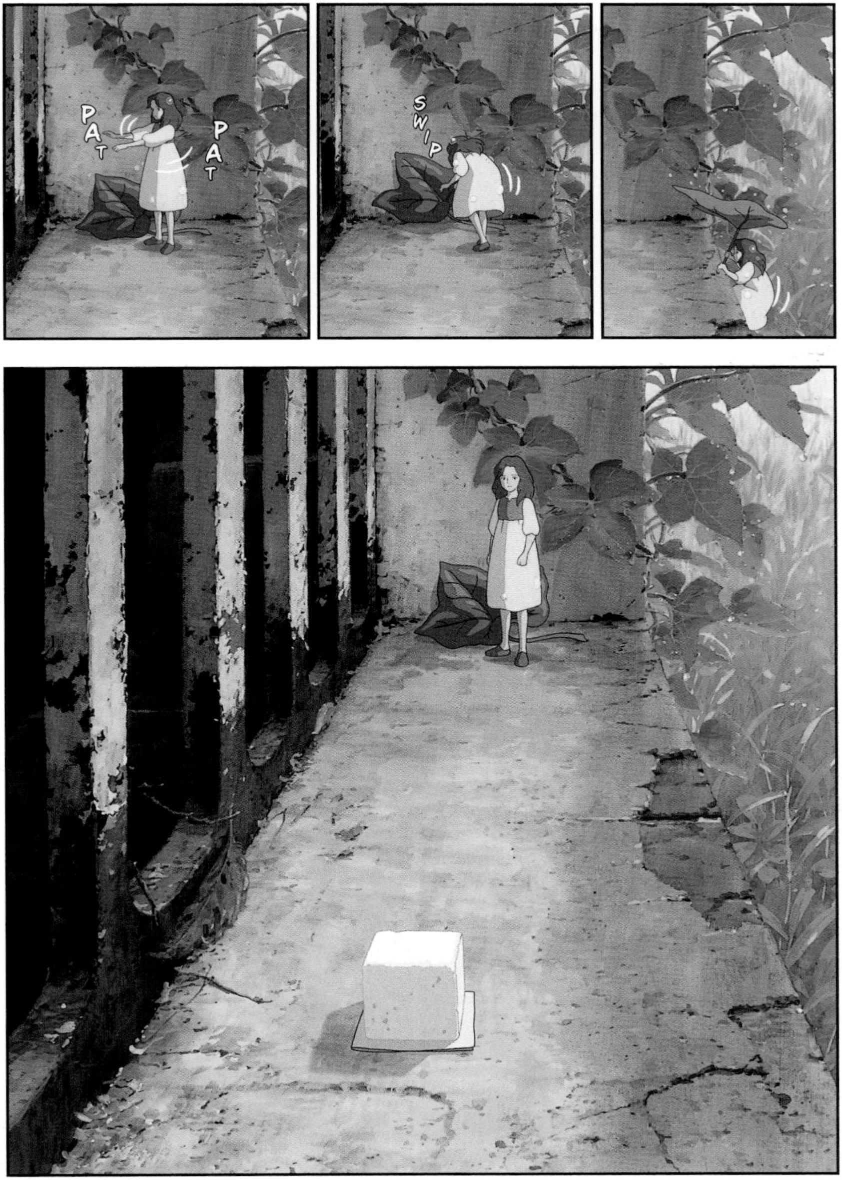
SWIP
PAT
PAT

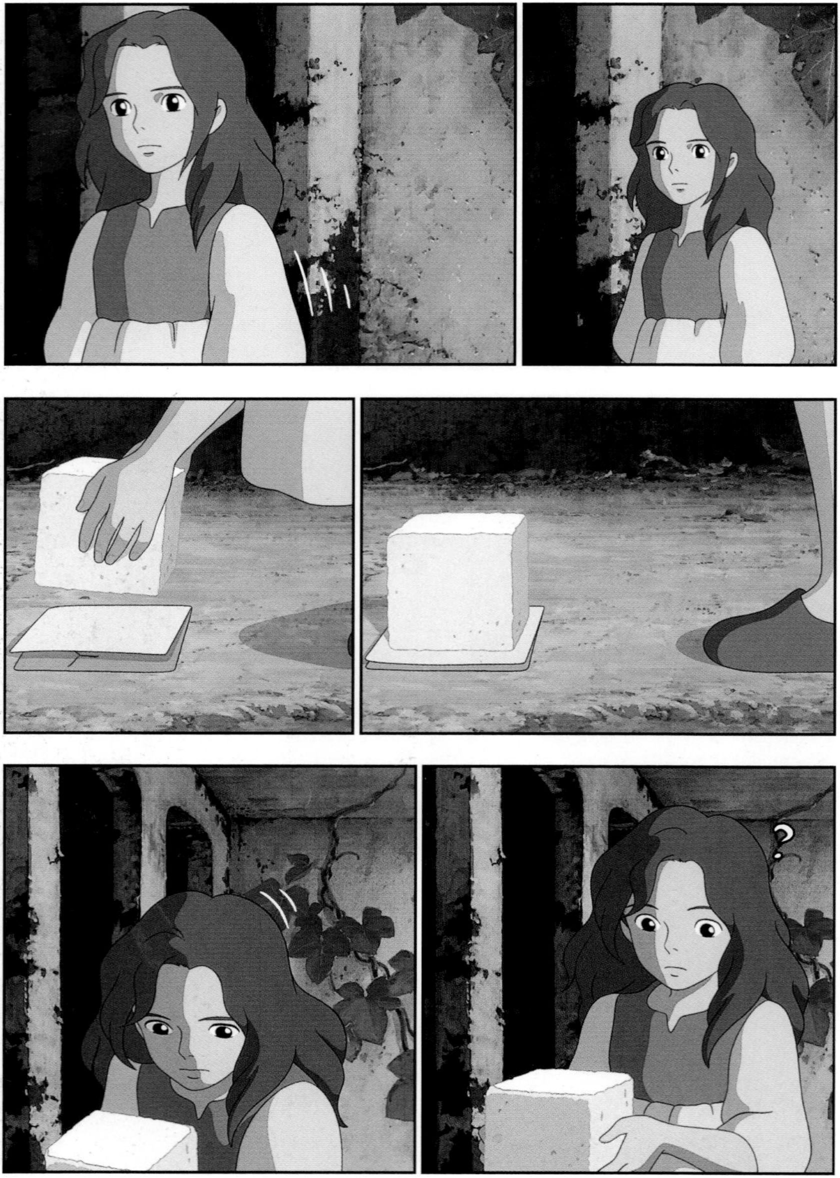
?

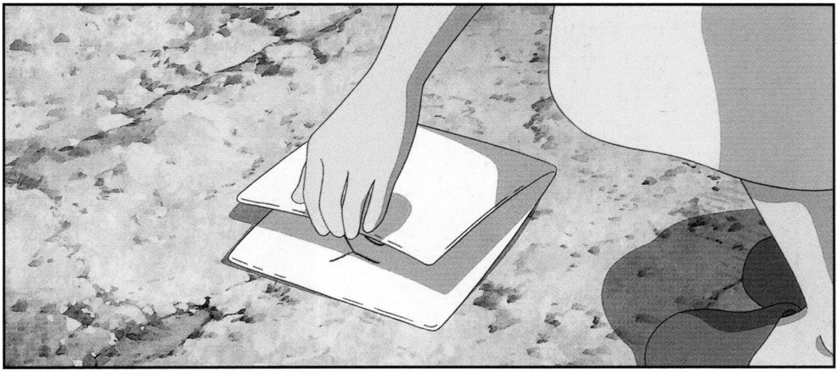
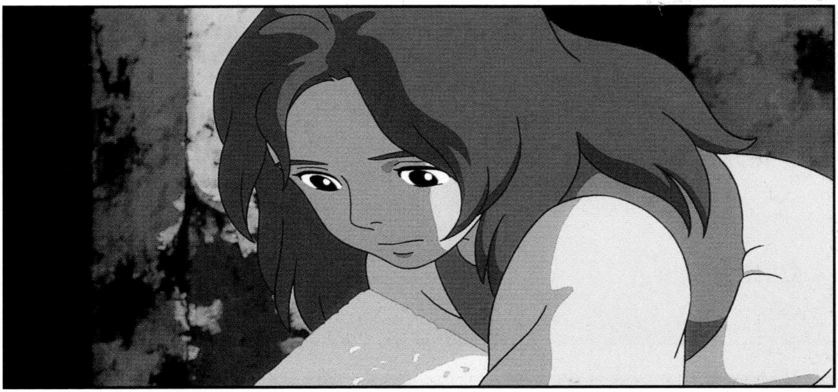
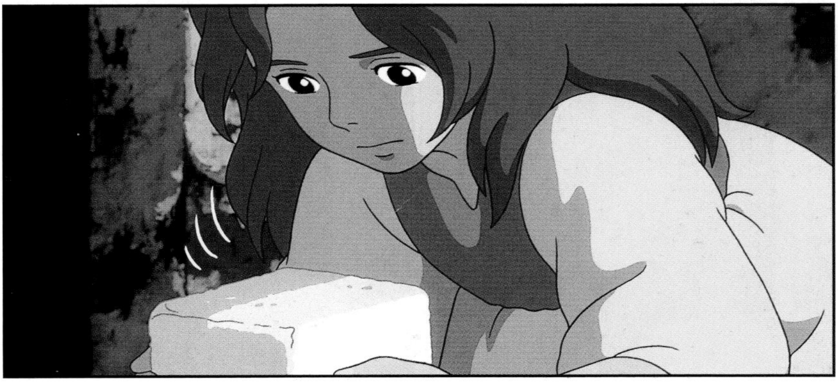

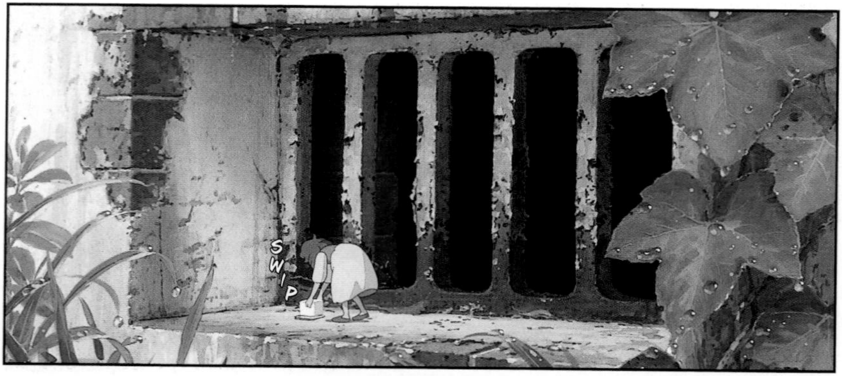
SWIP
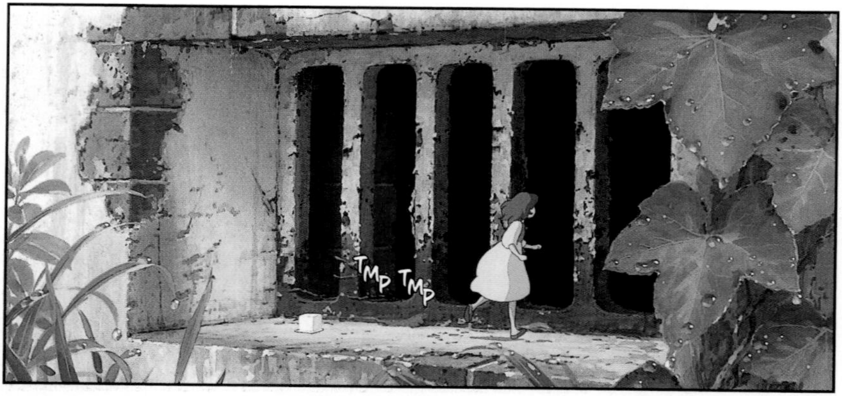
TMP TMP
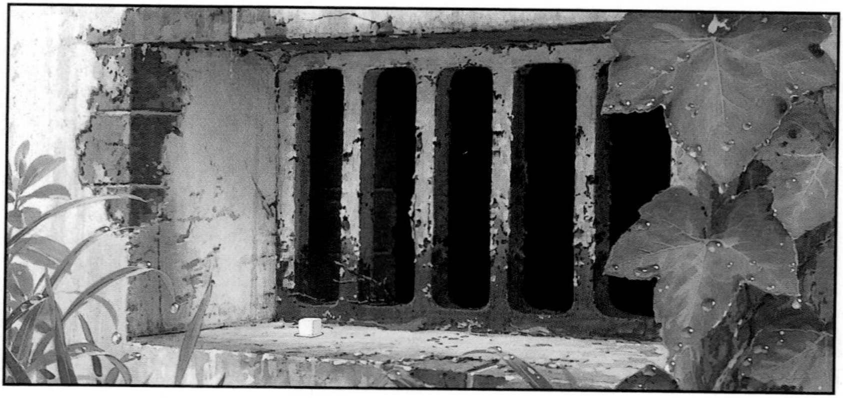

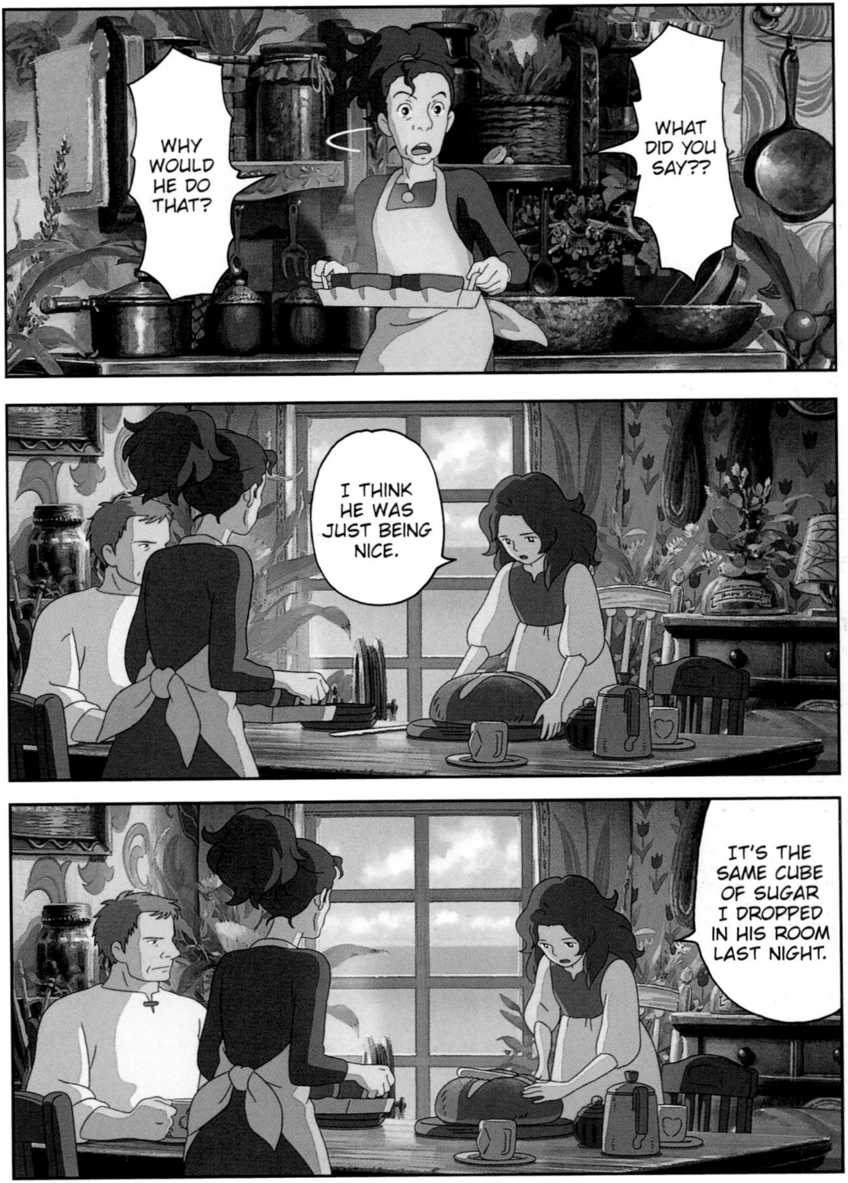
WHAT DID YOU SAY??
WHY WOULD HE DO THAT?
I THINK HE WAS JUST BEING NICE.
IT'S THE SAME CUBE OF SUGAR I DROPPED IN HIS ROOM LAST NIGHT.

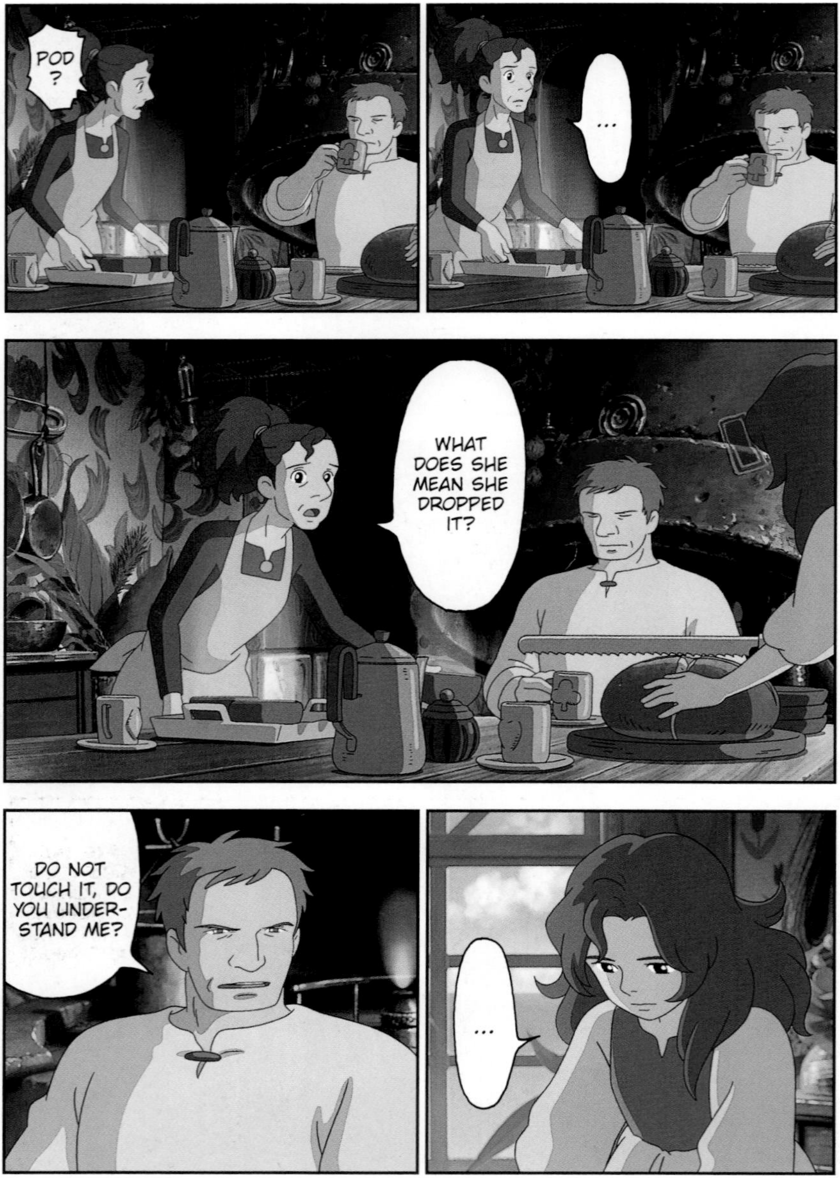

POD ?
...
WHAT DOES SHE MEAN SHE DROPPED IT?
DO NOT TOUCH IT, DO YOU UNDER-STAND ME?
...

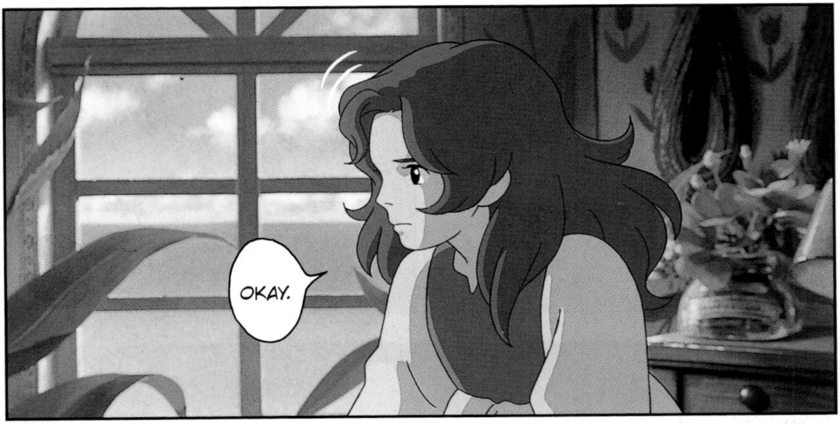
OKAY.

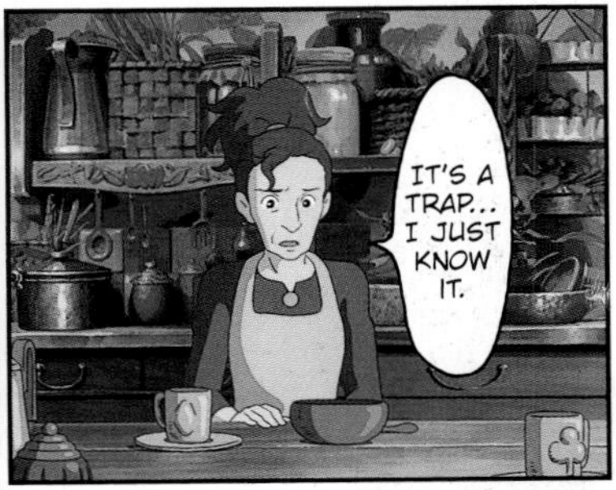
IT'S A TRAP... I JUST KNOW IT.

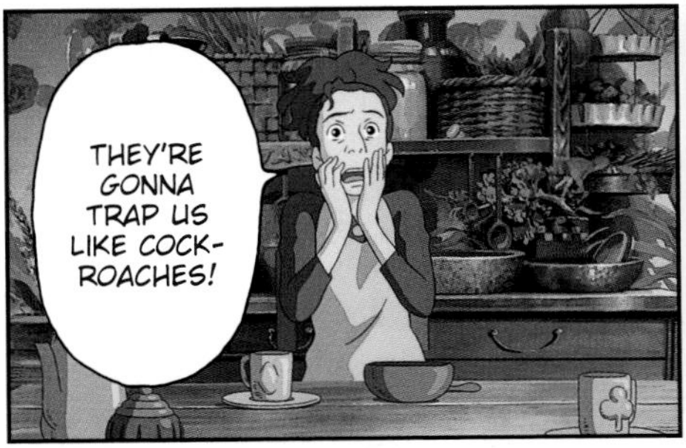
THEY'RE GONNA TRAP US LIKE COCK-ROACHES!

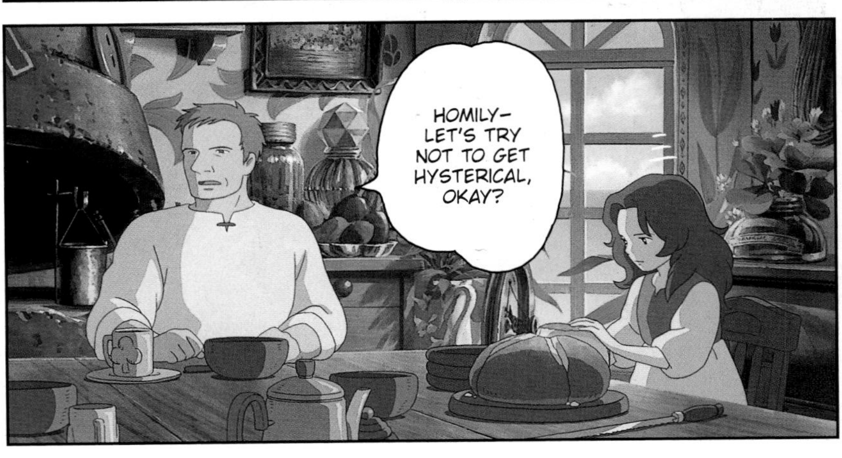
HOMILY-LET'S TRY NOT TO GET HYSTERICAL, OKAY?

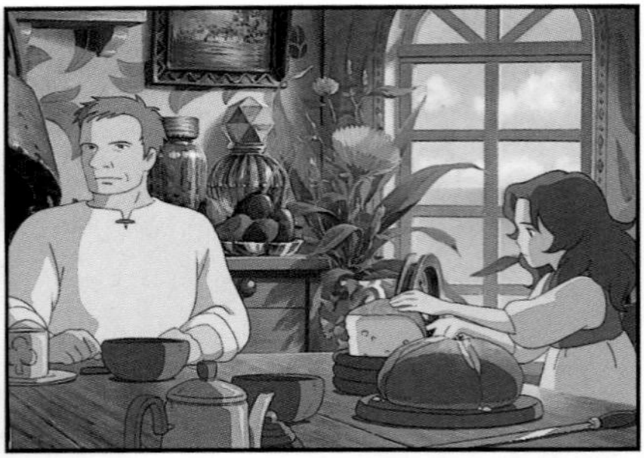
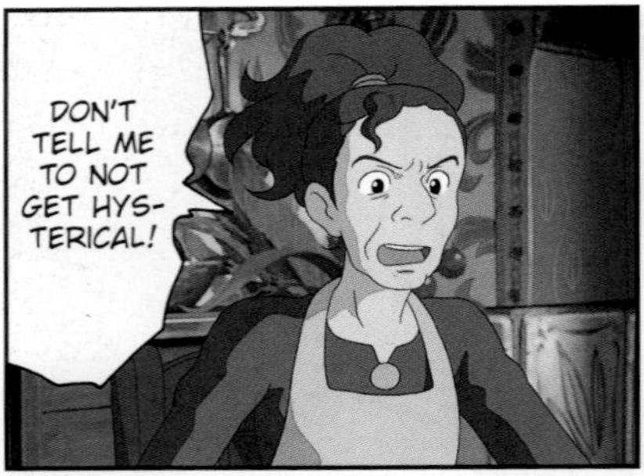
DON'T TELL ME TO NOT GET HYS-TERICAL!
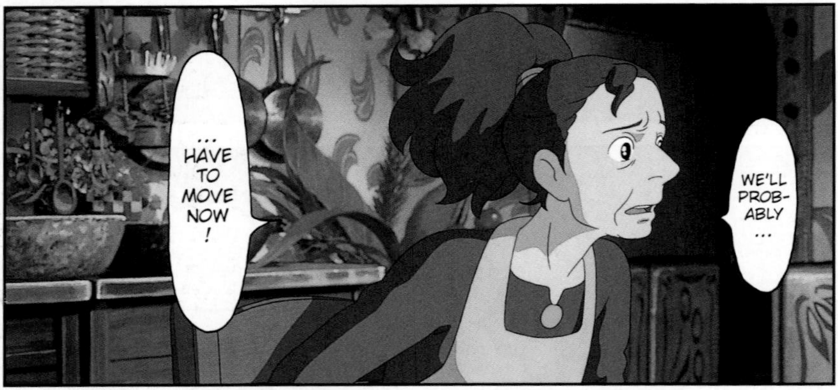
WE'LL PROB-ABLY ...
... HAVE TO MOVE NOW !
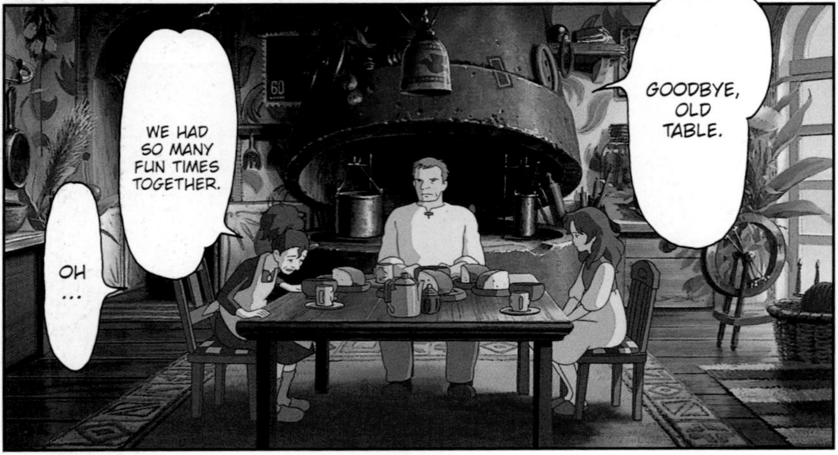
GOODBYE, OLD TABLE.
WE HAD SO MANY FUN TIMES TOGETHER.
OH ...

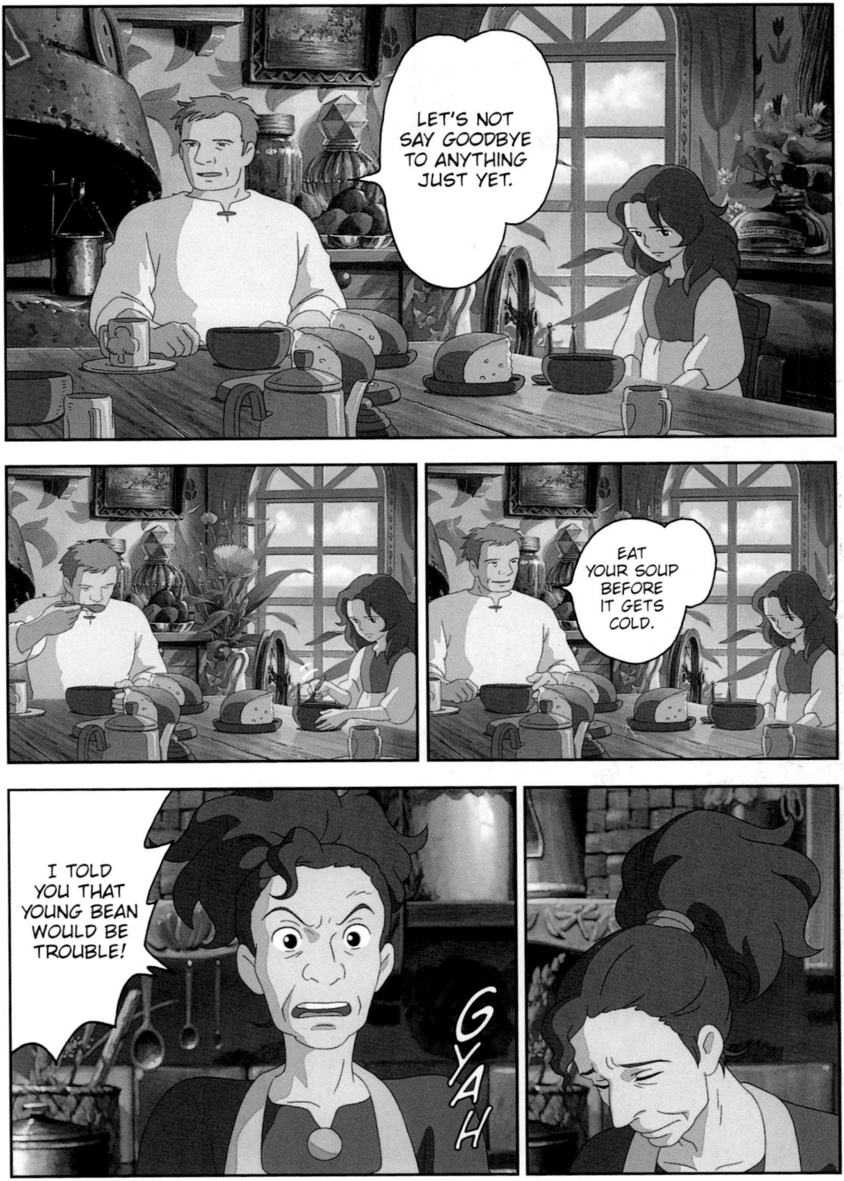
LET'S NOT SAY GOODBYE TO ANYTHING JUST YET.
EAT YOUR SOUP BEFORE IT GETS COLD.
I TOLD YOU THAT YOUNG BEAN WOULD BE TROUBLE!
GYAH

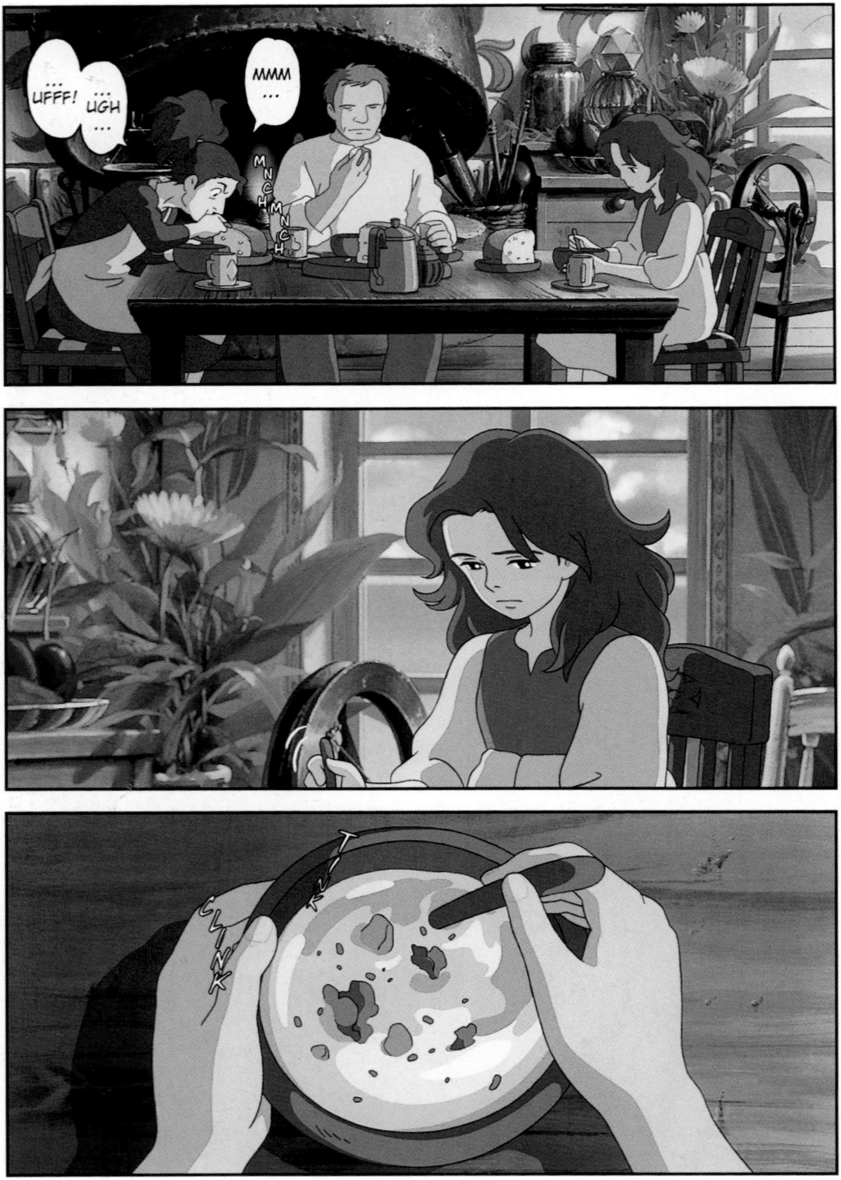
MMM ...
... UGH ...
... UFFF!
MNCH
MNCH
MNCH
TINK
CLINK

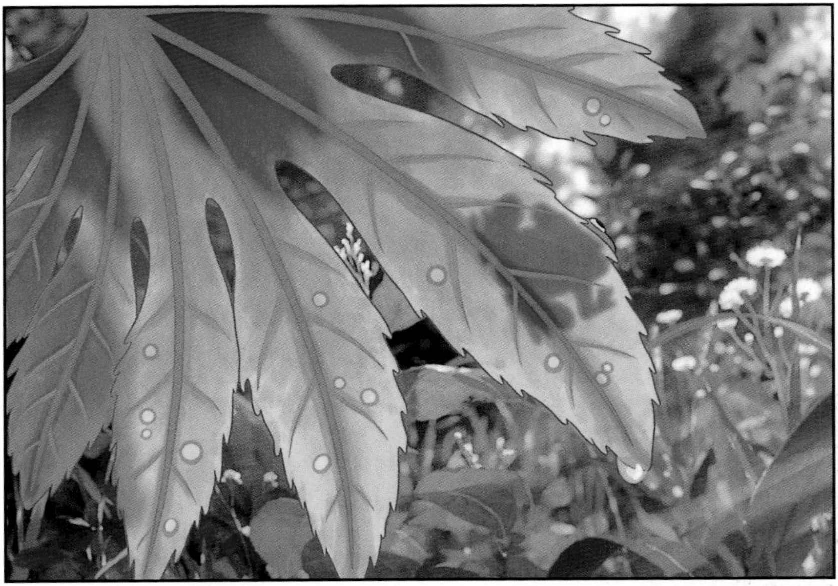
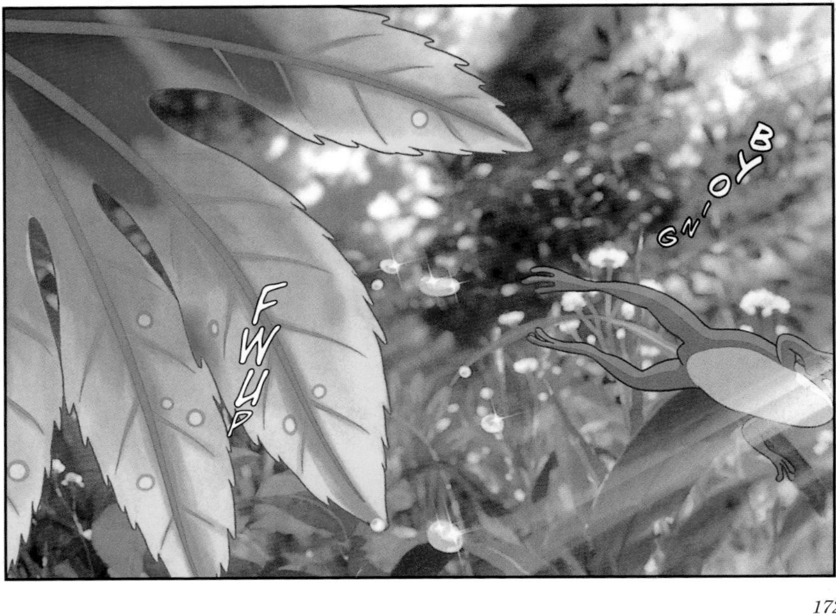
BYO-NG
FWUP

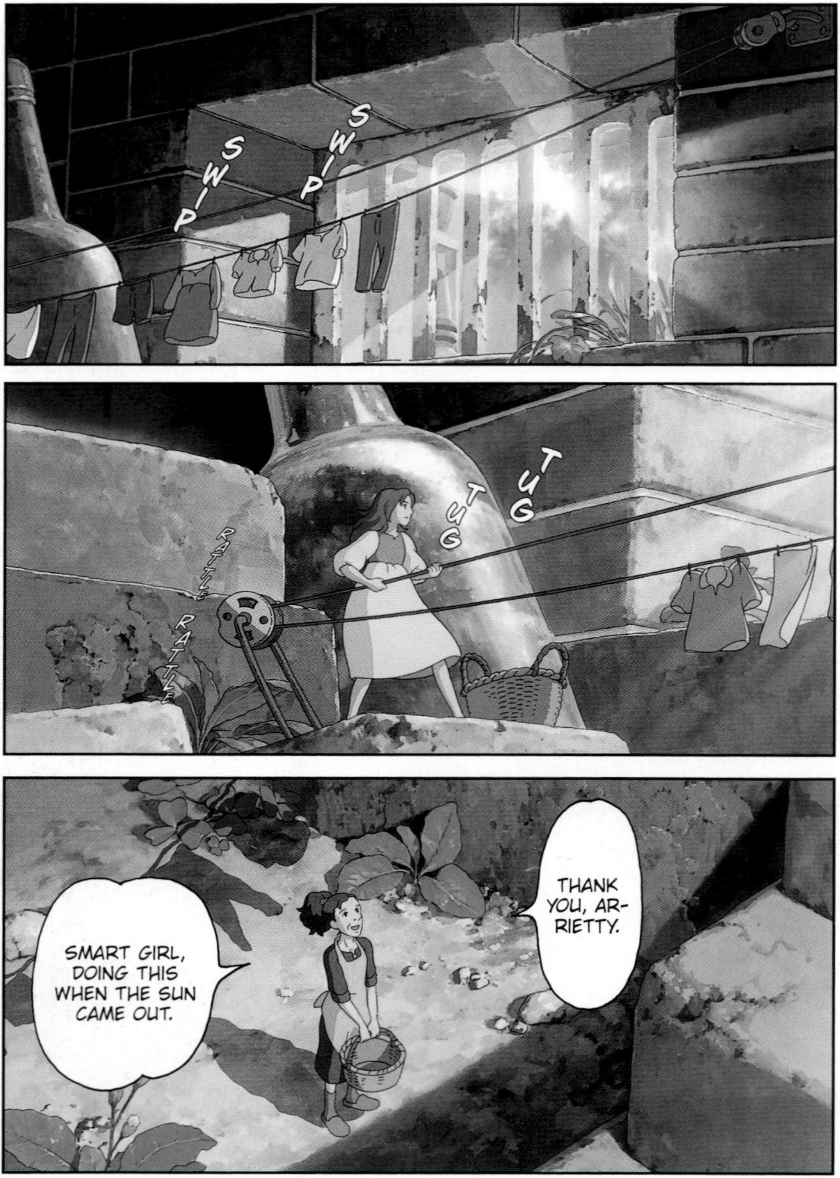
SWIP
SWIP
TUG
TUG
RATTLE
RATTLE
THANK YOU, AR-RIETTY.
SMART GIRL, DOING THIS WHEN THE SUN CAME OUT.

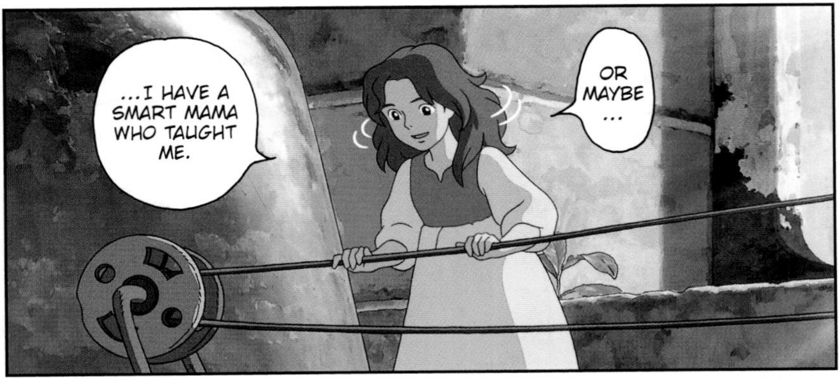
OR MAYBE ...
...I HAVE A SMART MAMA WHO TAUGHT ME.
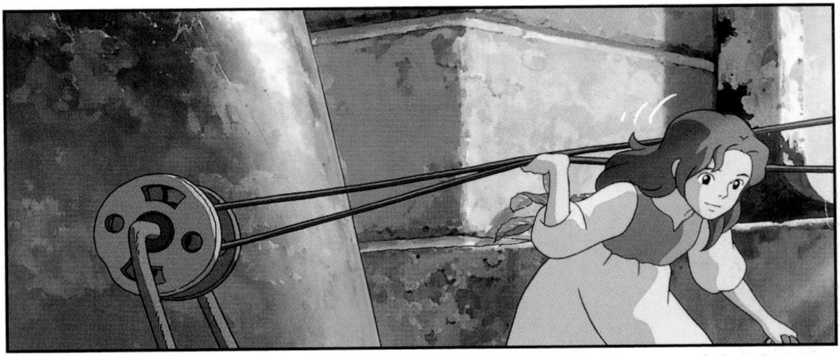
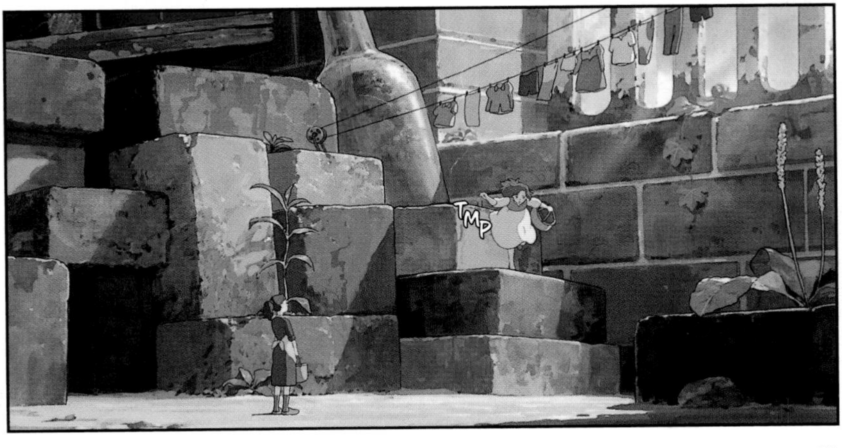
TMP

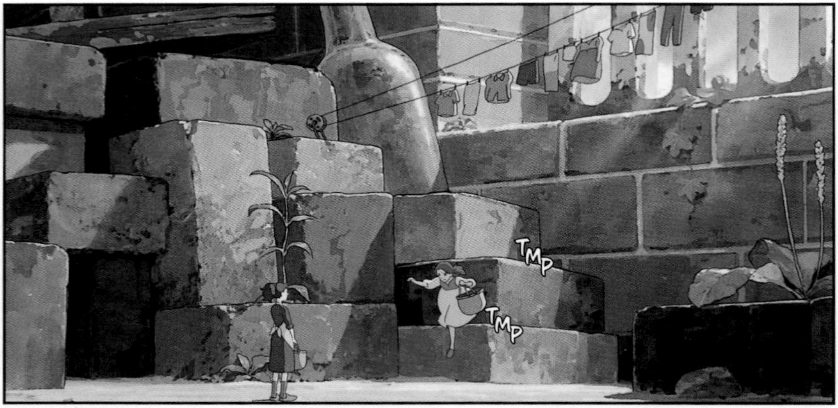
TMP
TMP

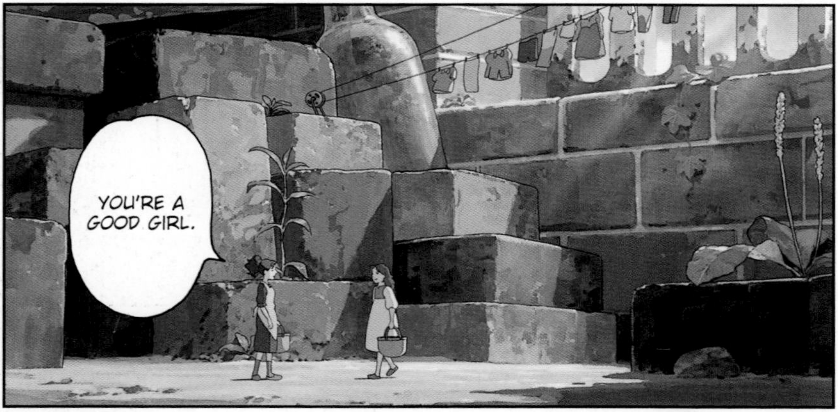
YOU'RE A GOOD GIRL.

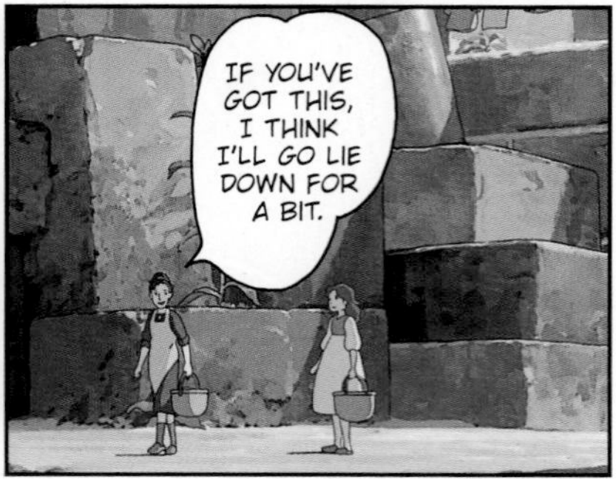
IF YOU'VE GOT THIS, I THINK I'LL GO LIE DOWN FOR A BIT.

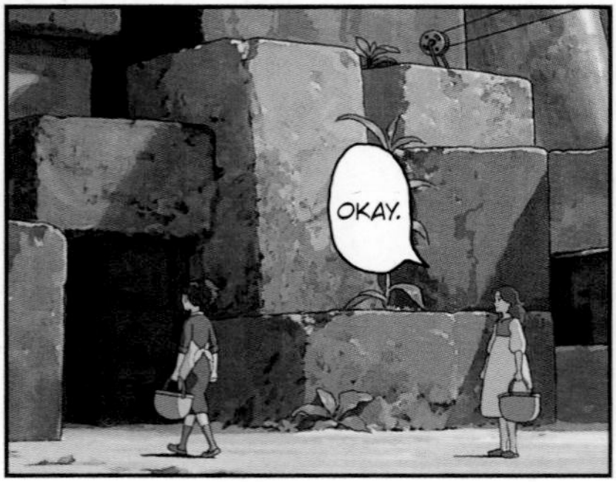
OKAY.

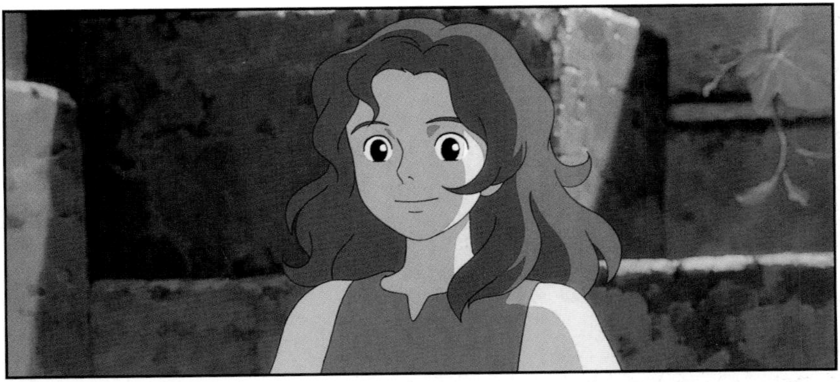

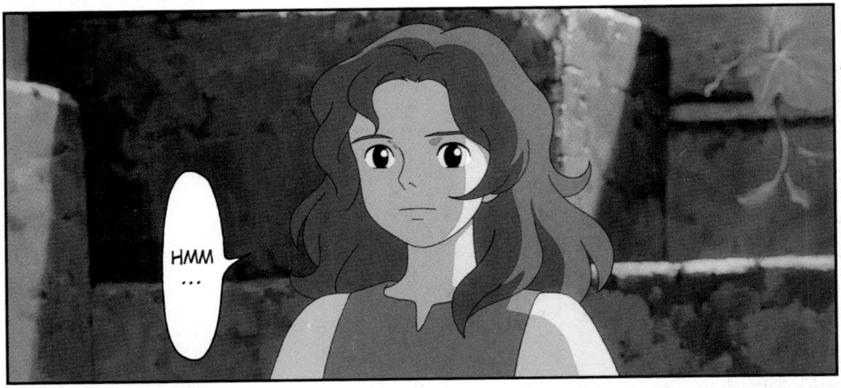
HMM ...

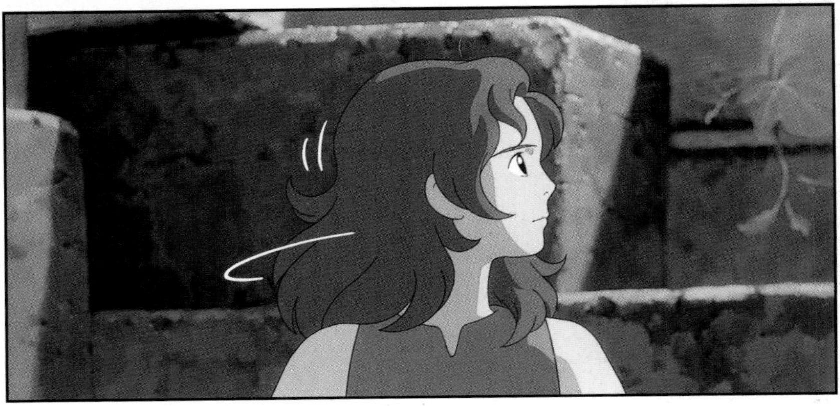

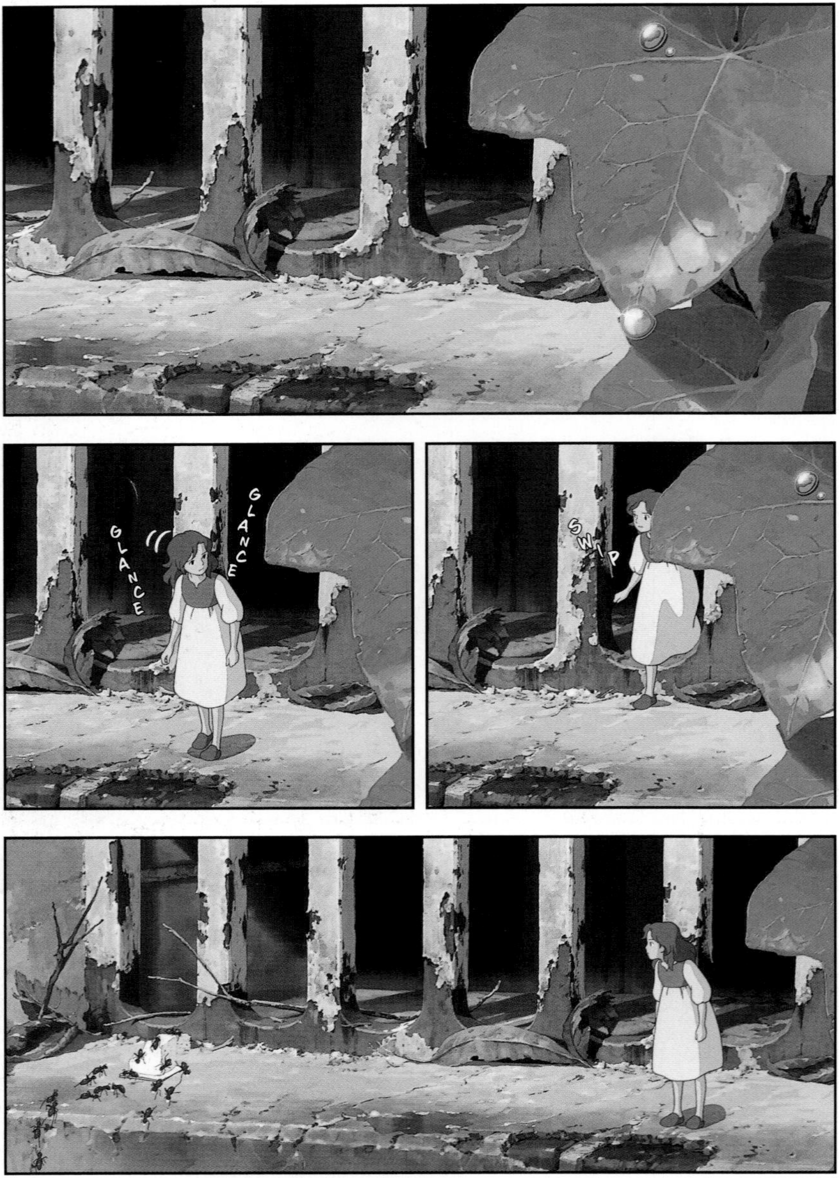
SWIP
GLANCE
GLANCE

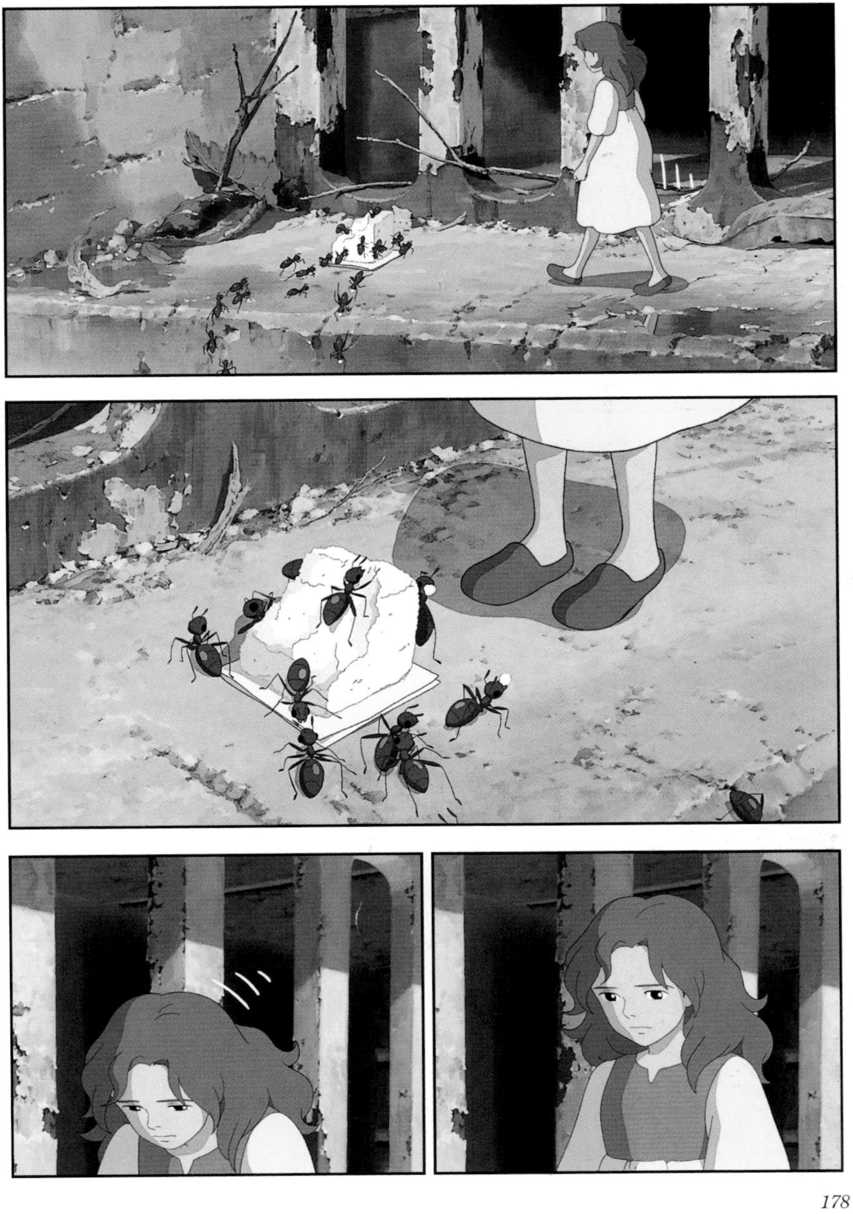

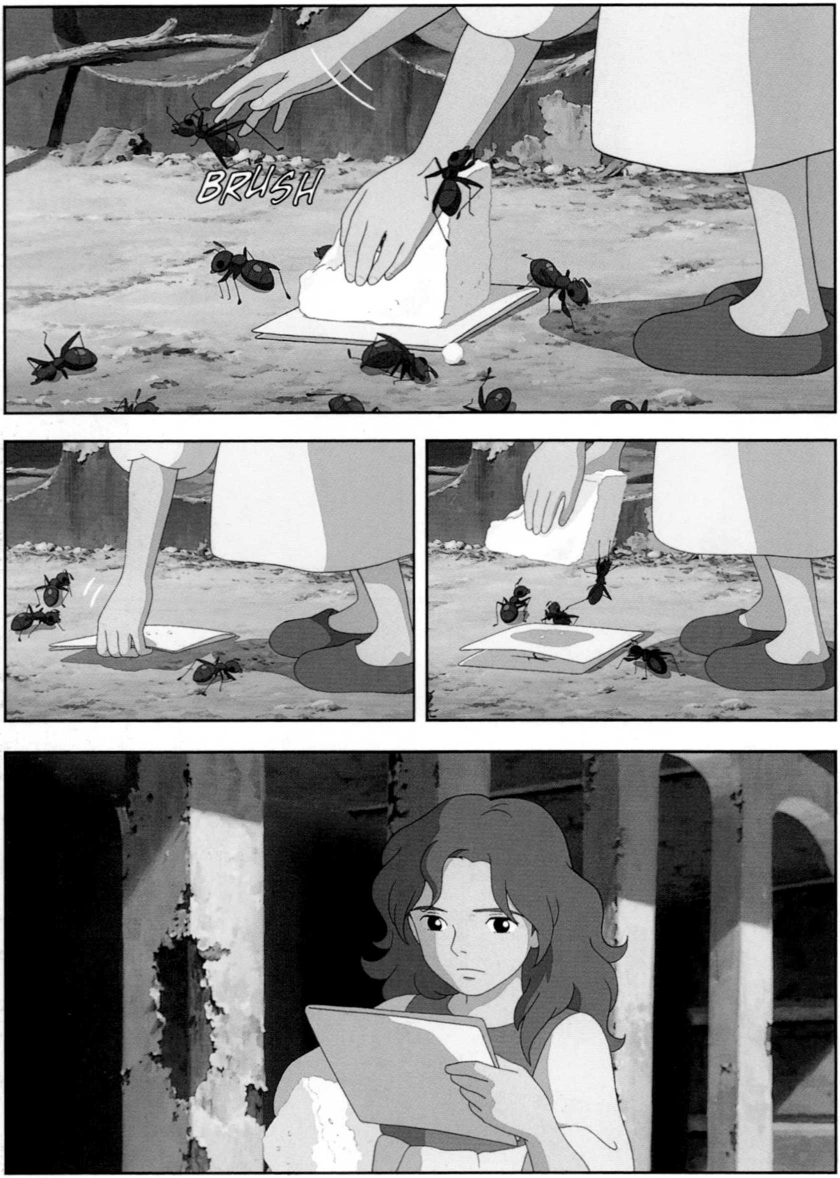
BRUSH

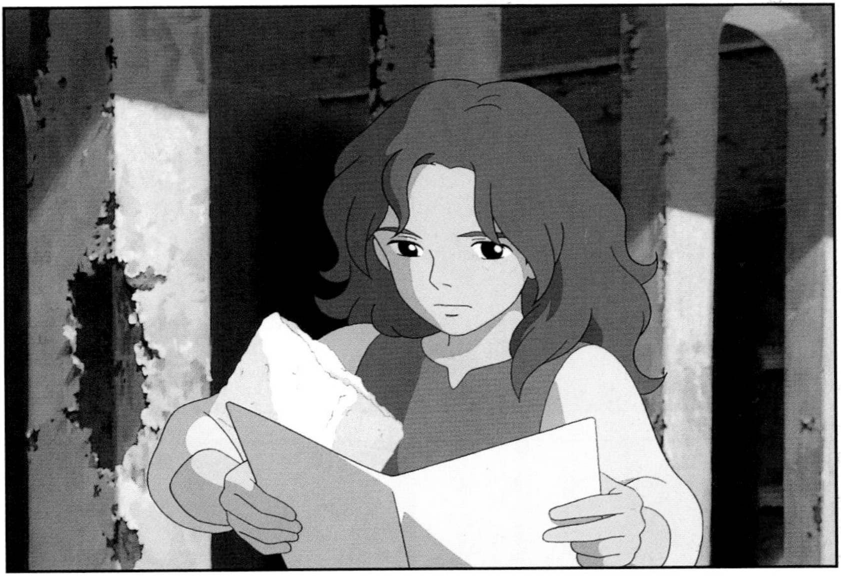

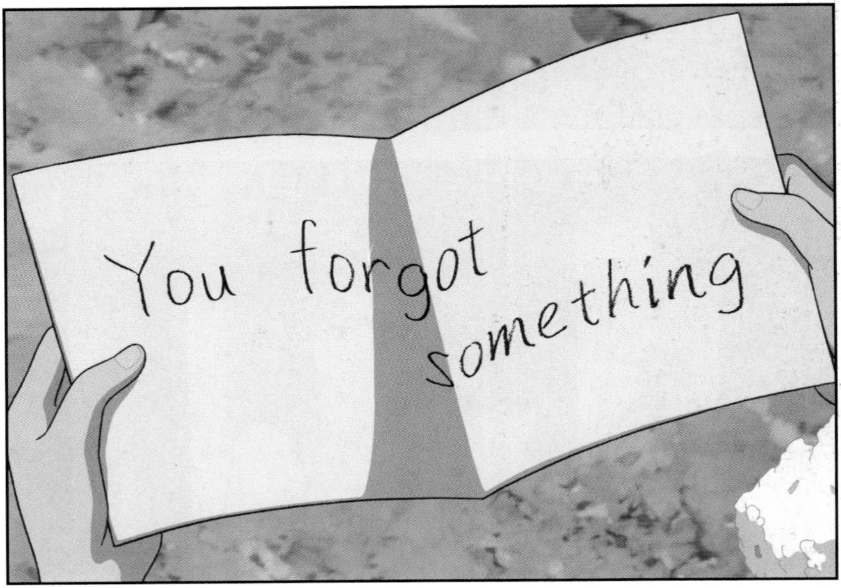
You forgot something

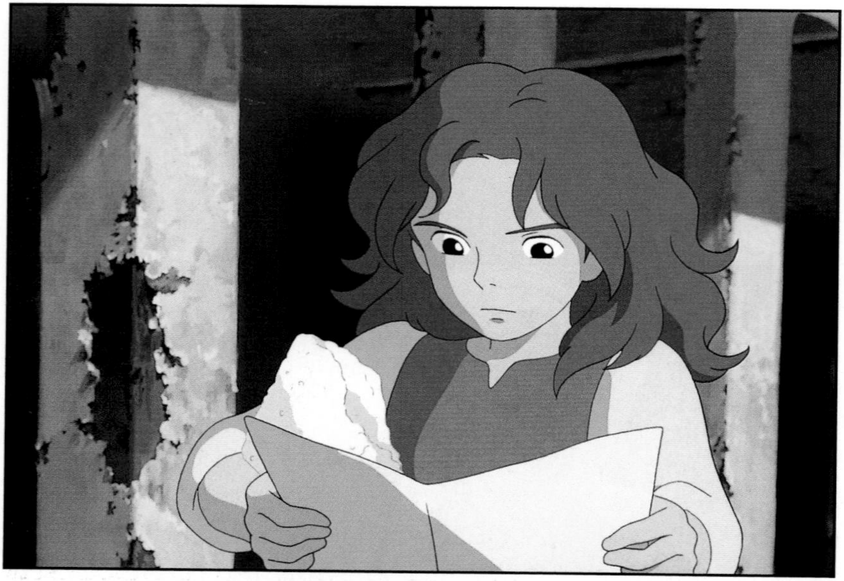

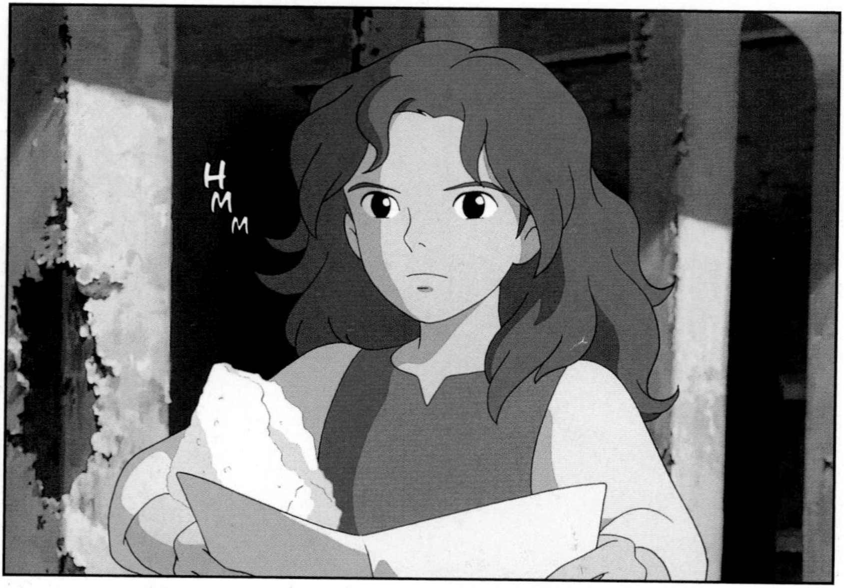
HMM

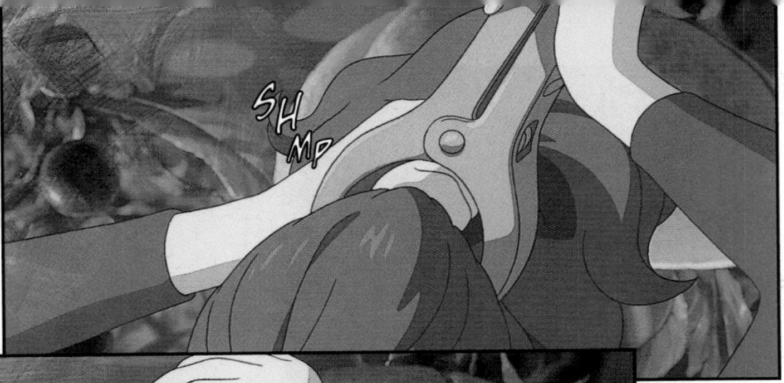
SHMP
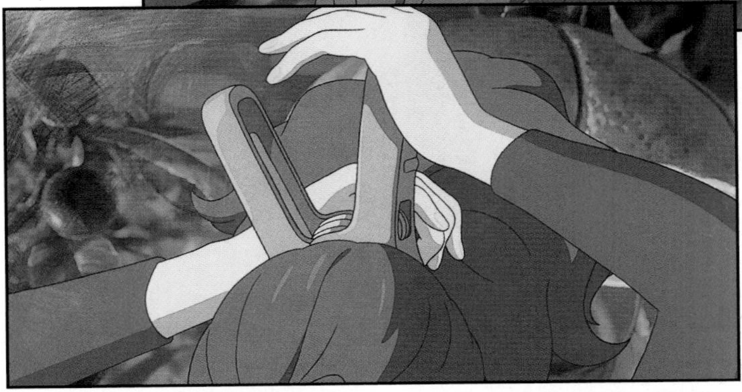
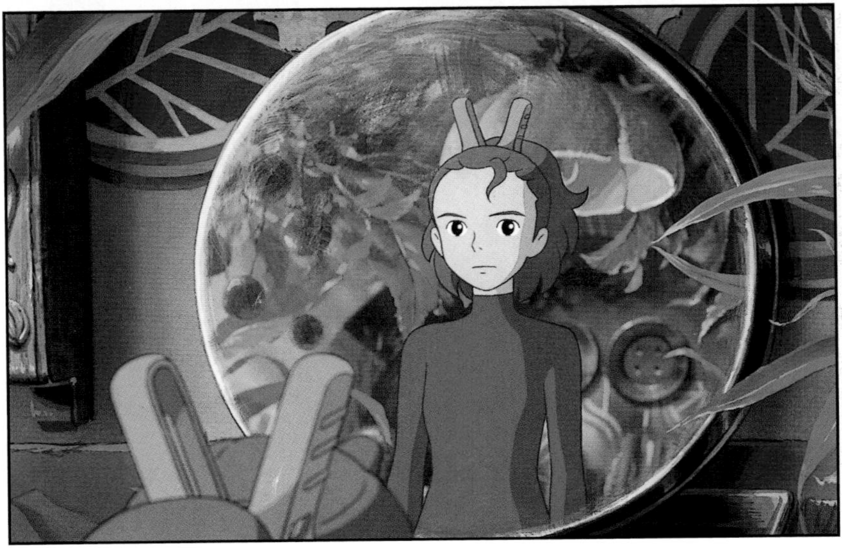

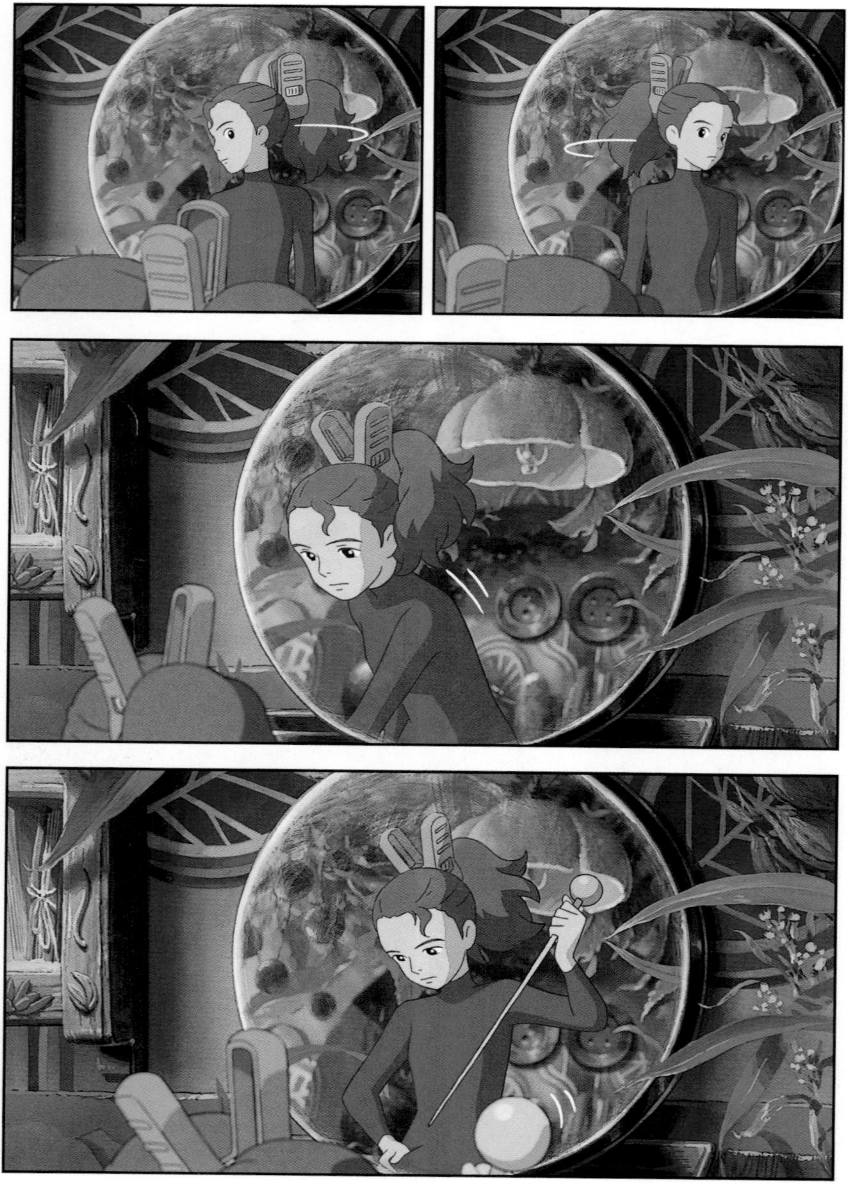

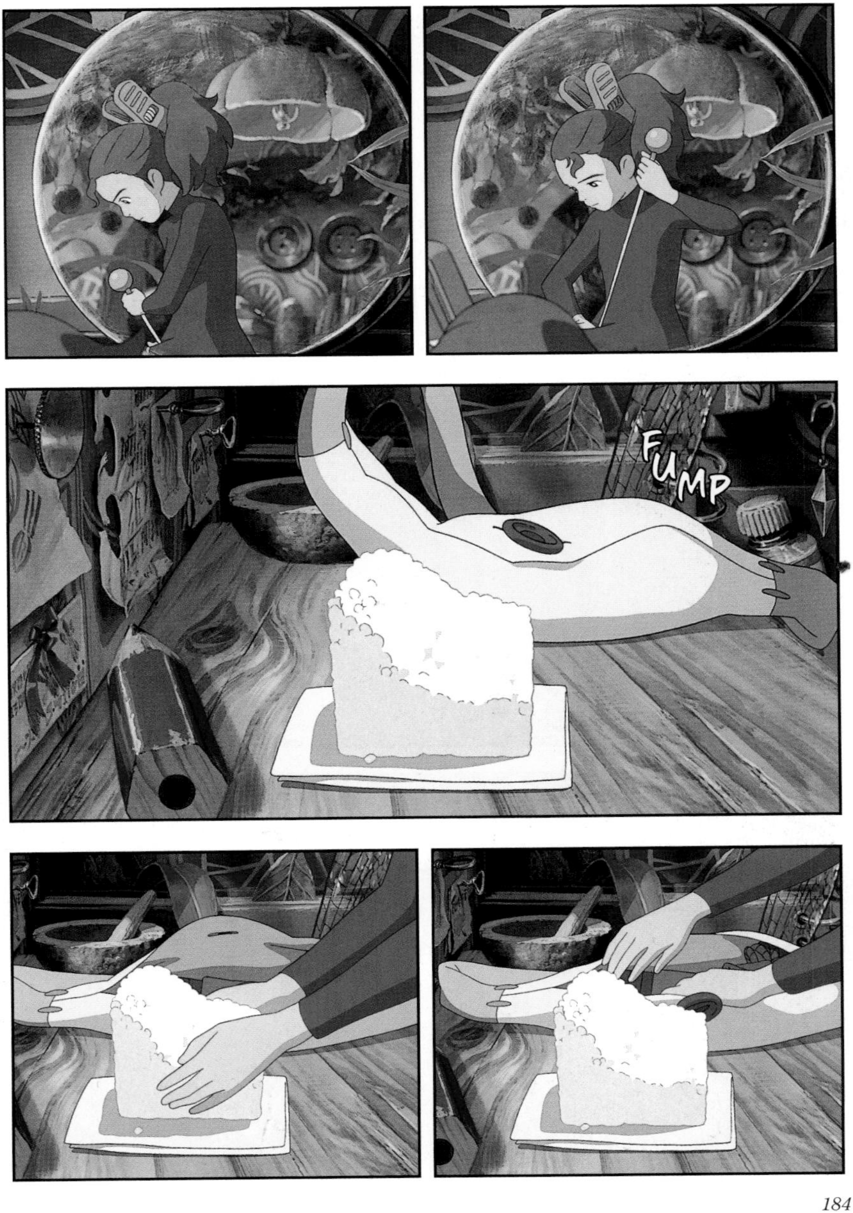
FUMP

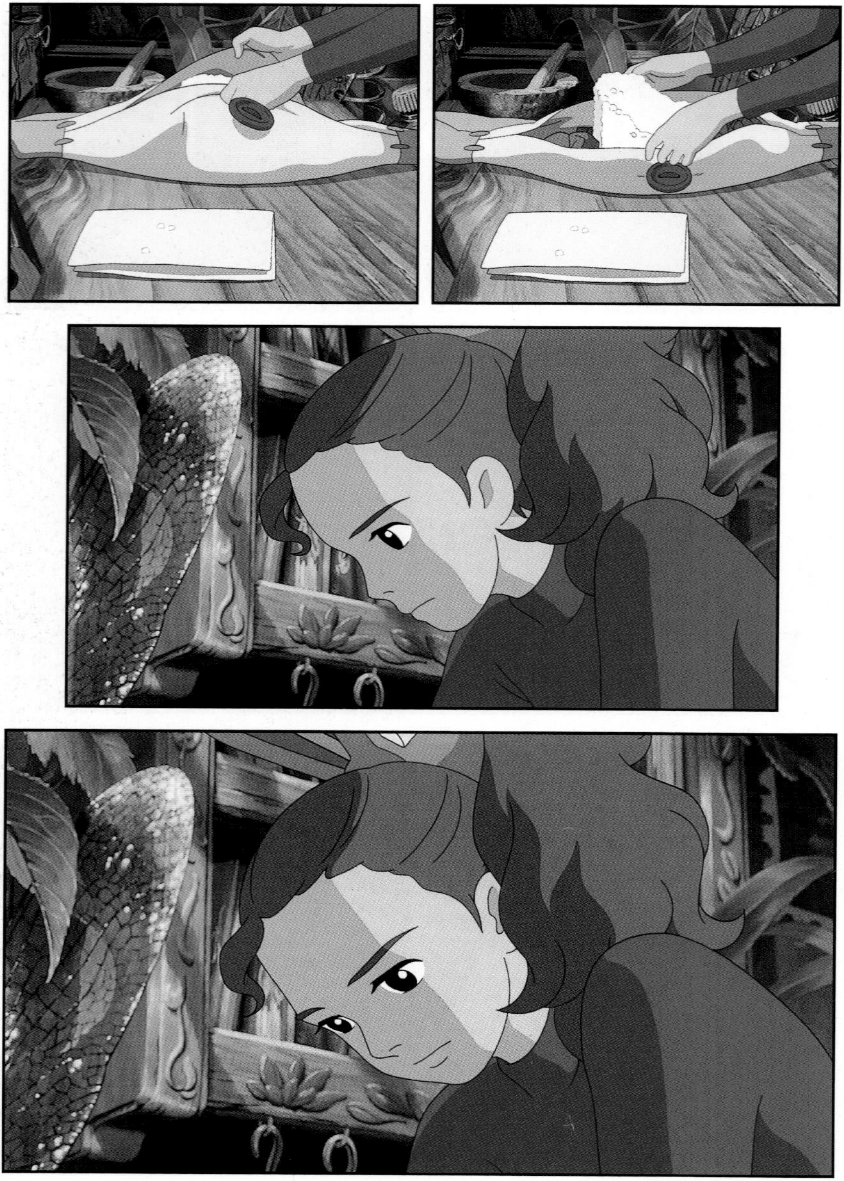

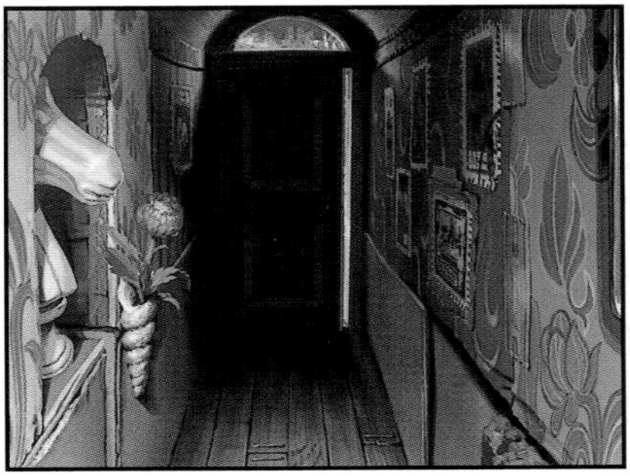
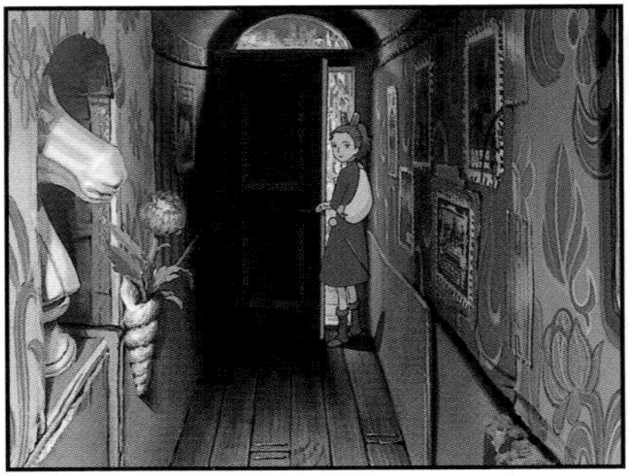
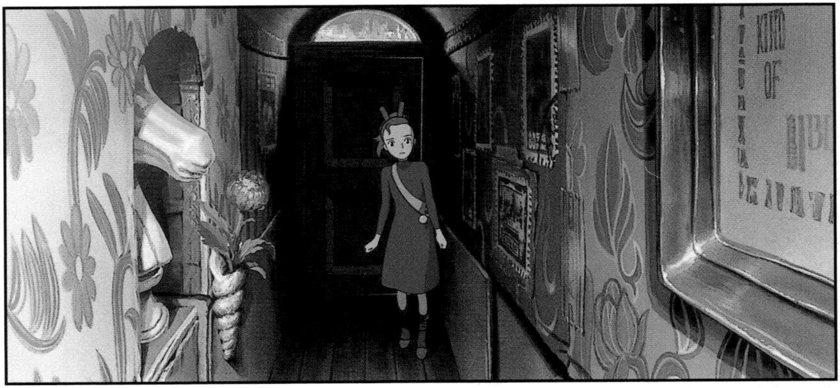
KIND
OF
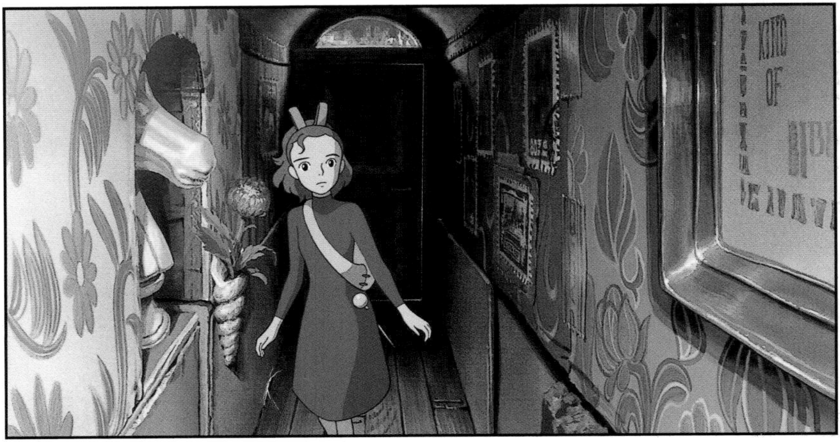
KIND
OF

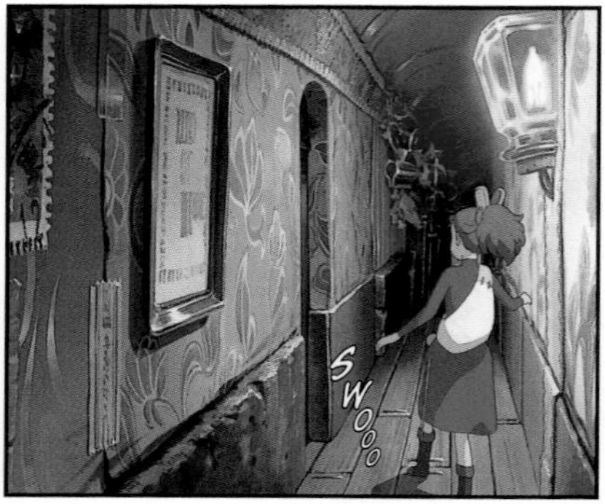
SWOOO
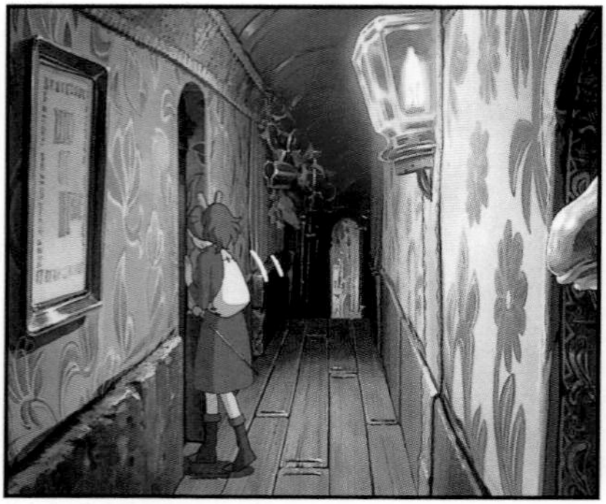
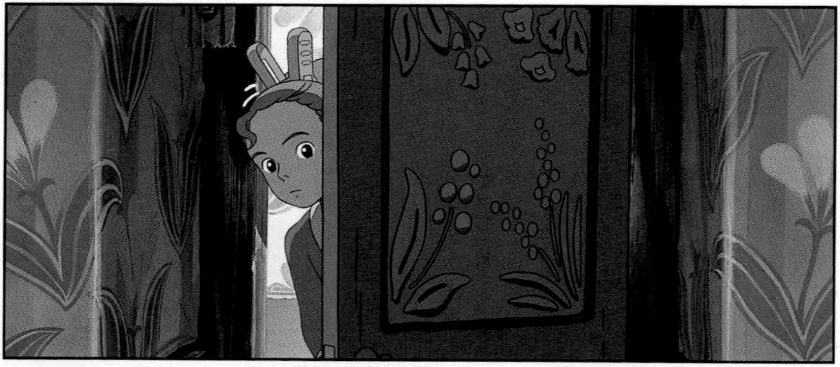
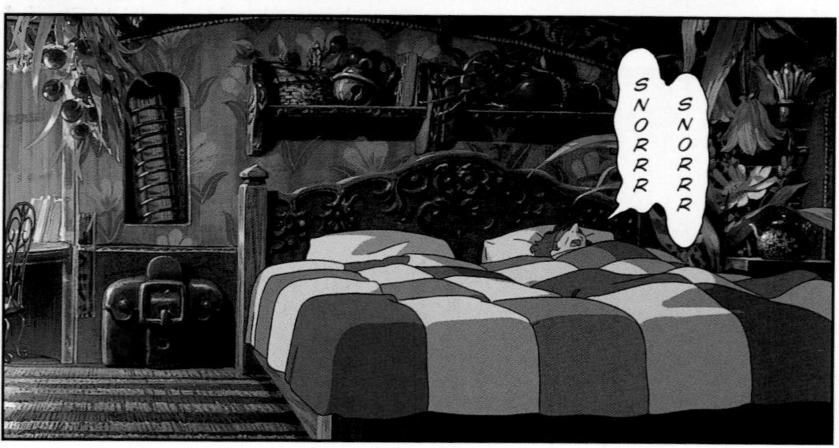
SNORRR SNORRR

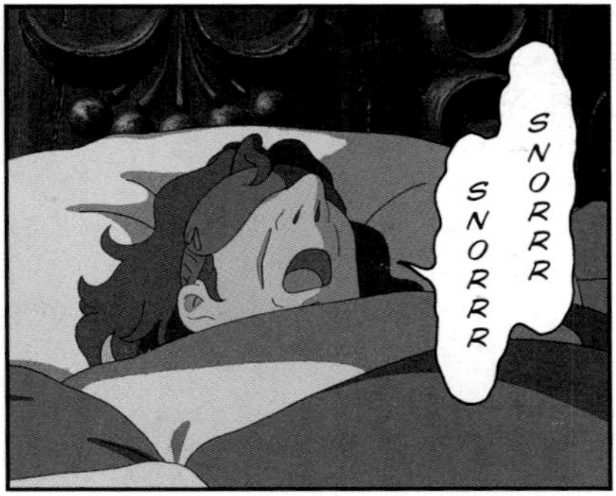
SNORRR
SNORRR
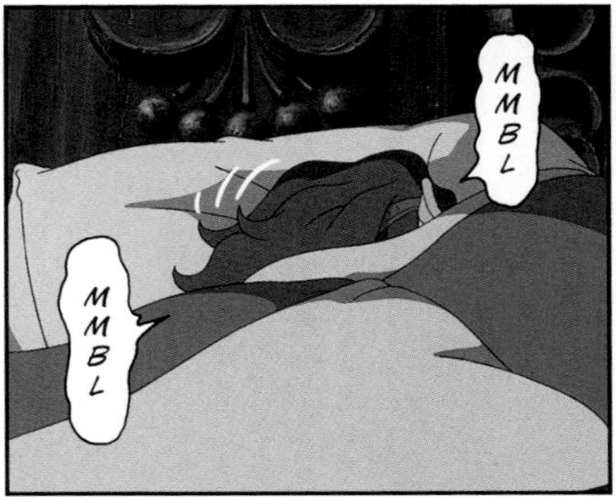
MMBL
MMBL
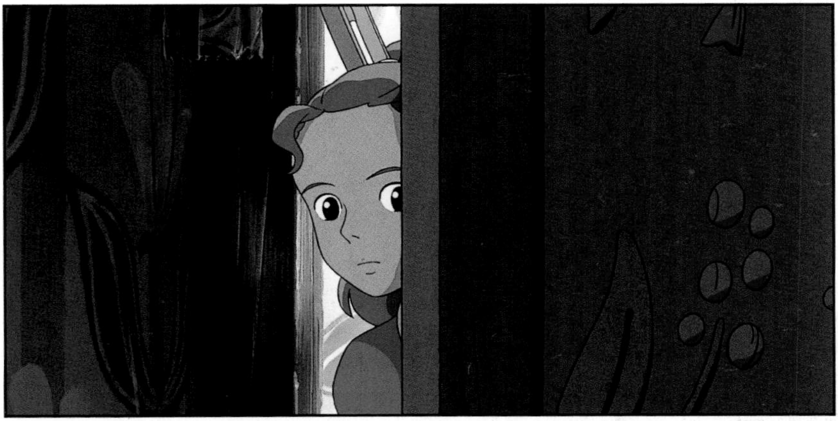
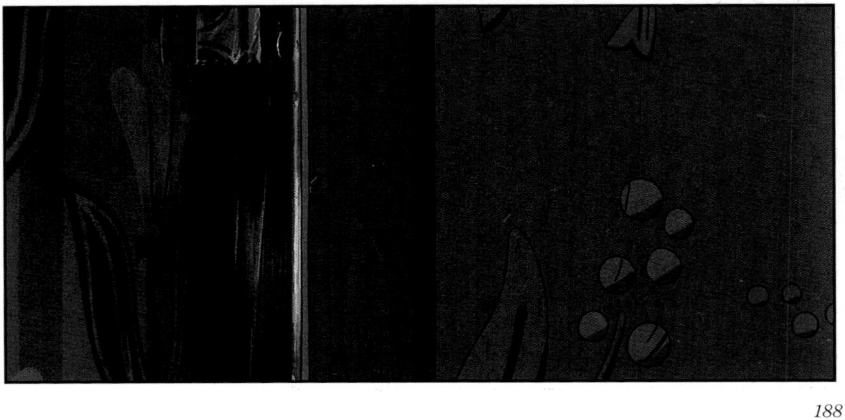

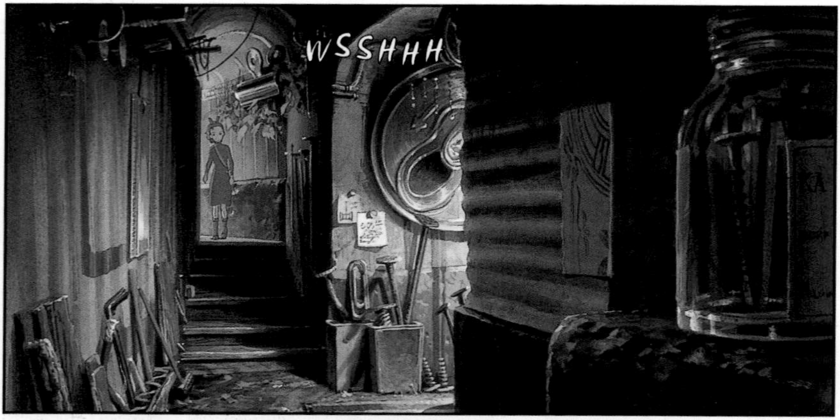
WSSHHH
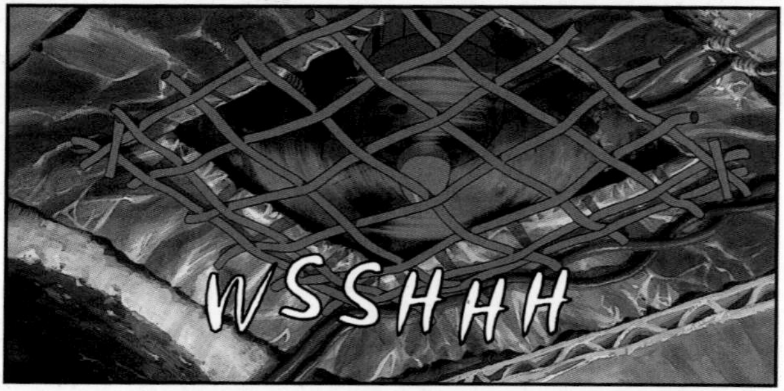
WSSHHH
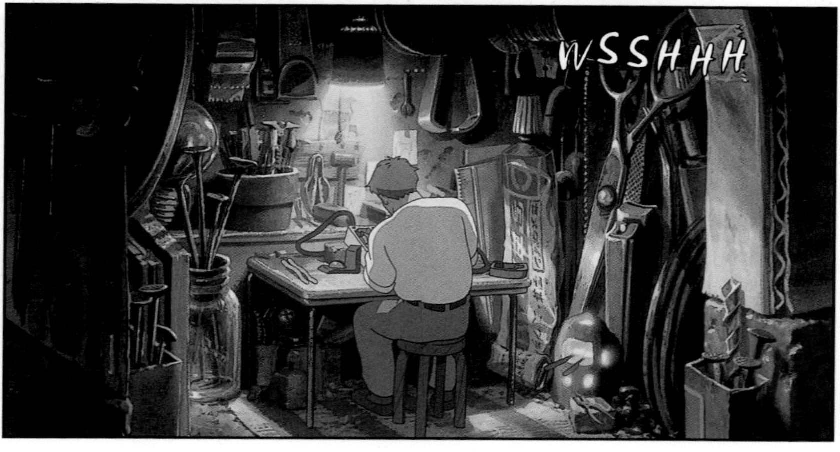
WSSHHH

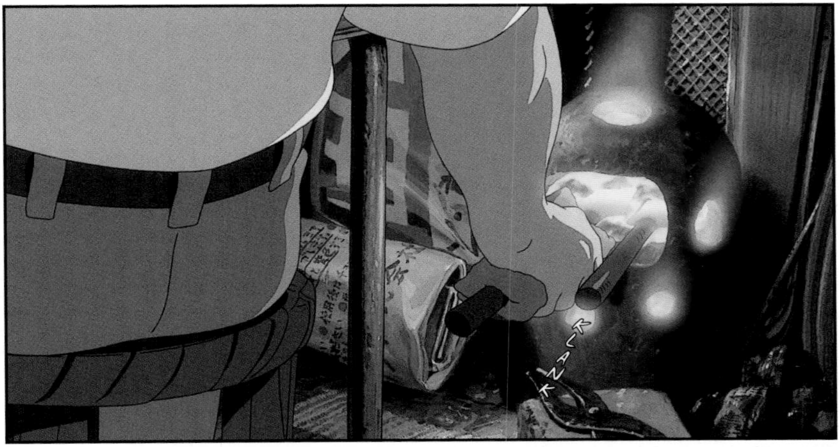
KLANK
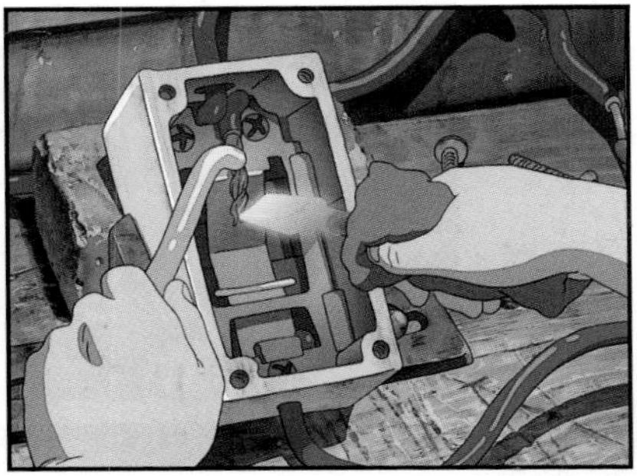
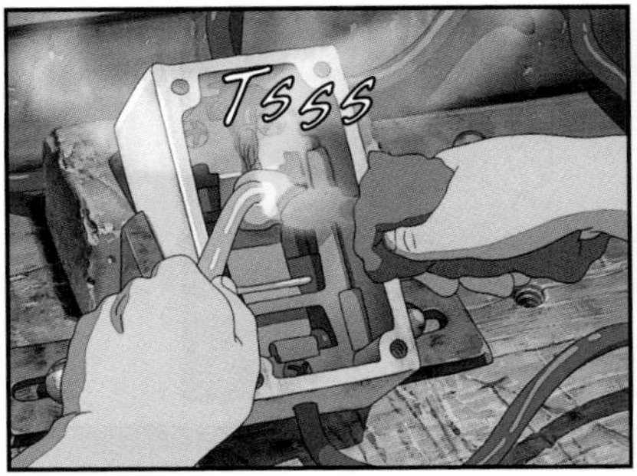
Tsss
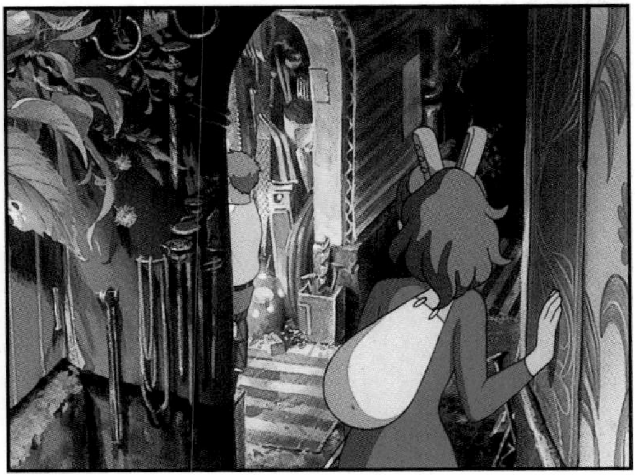
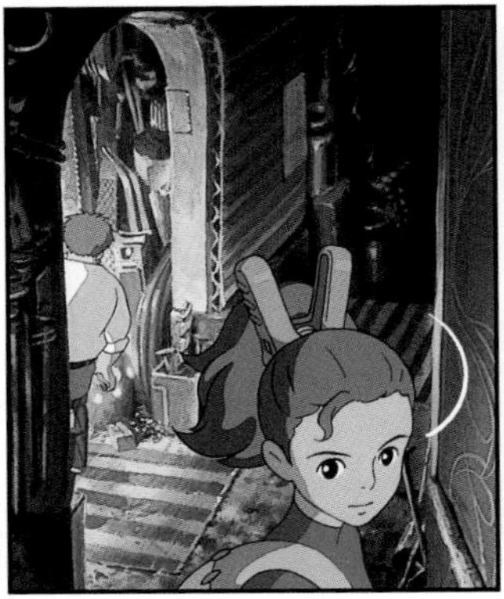

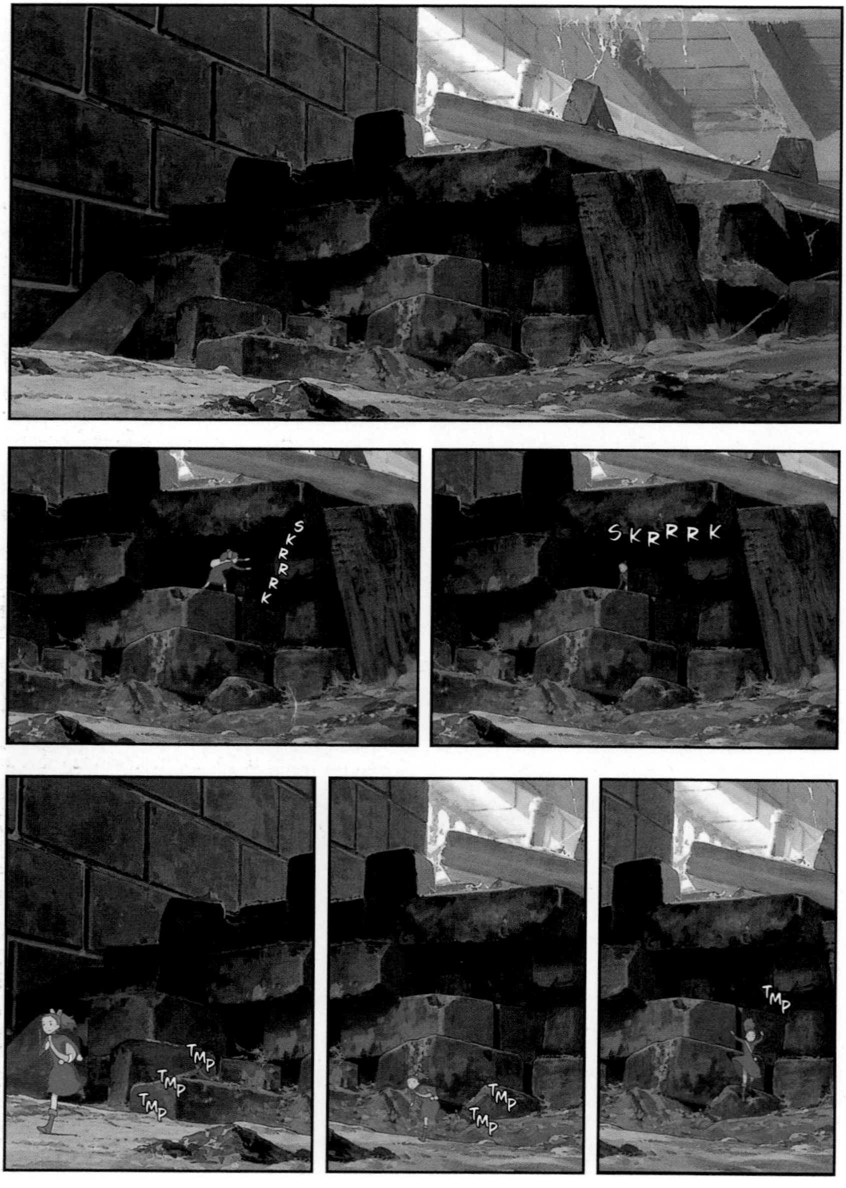
SKRRRK
SKRRRK
TMP
TMP
TMP
TMP
TMP
TMP

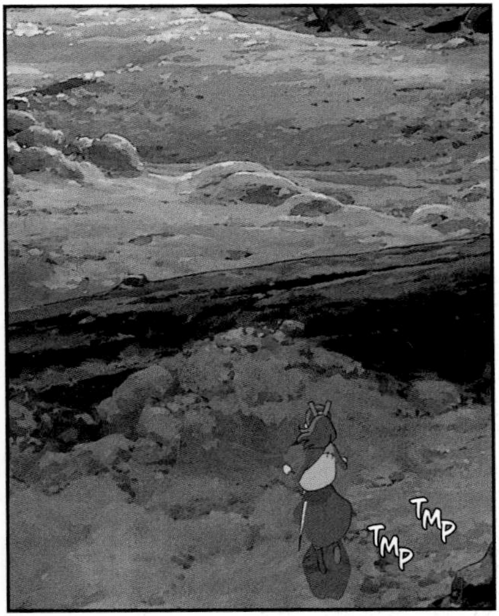
TMP
TMP
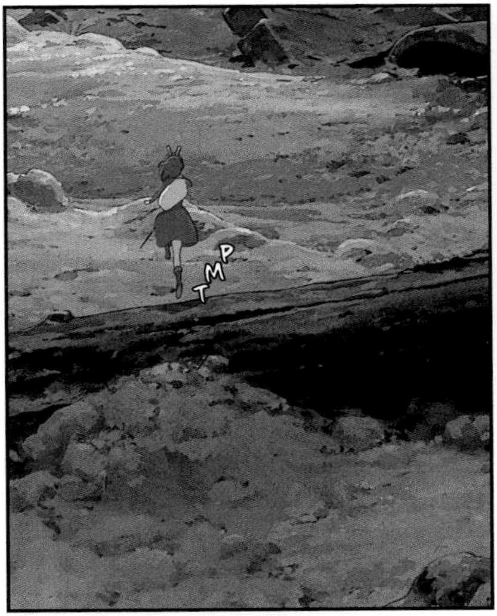
TMP
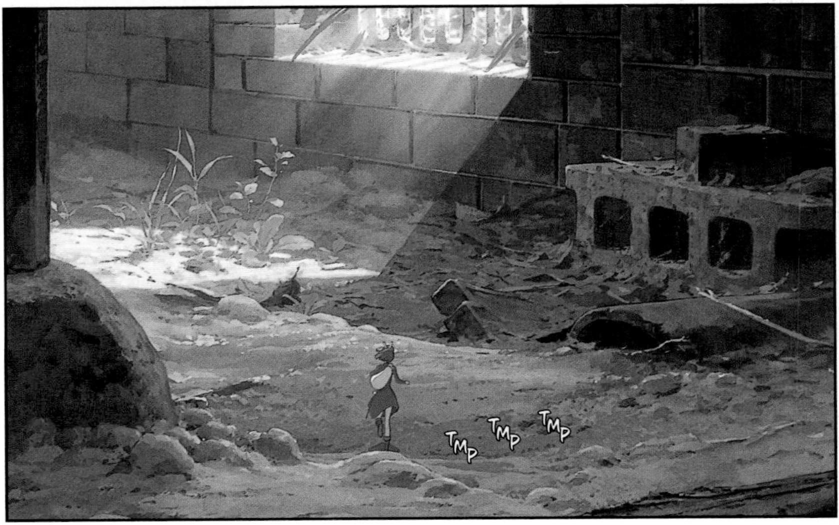
TMP
TMP
TMP

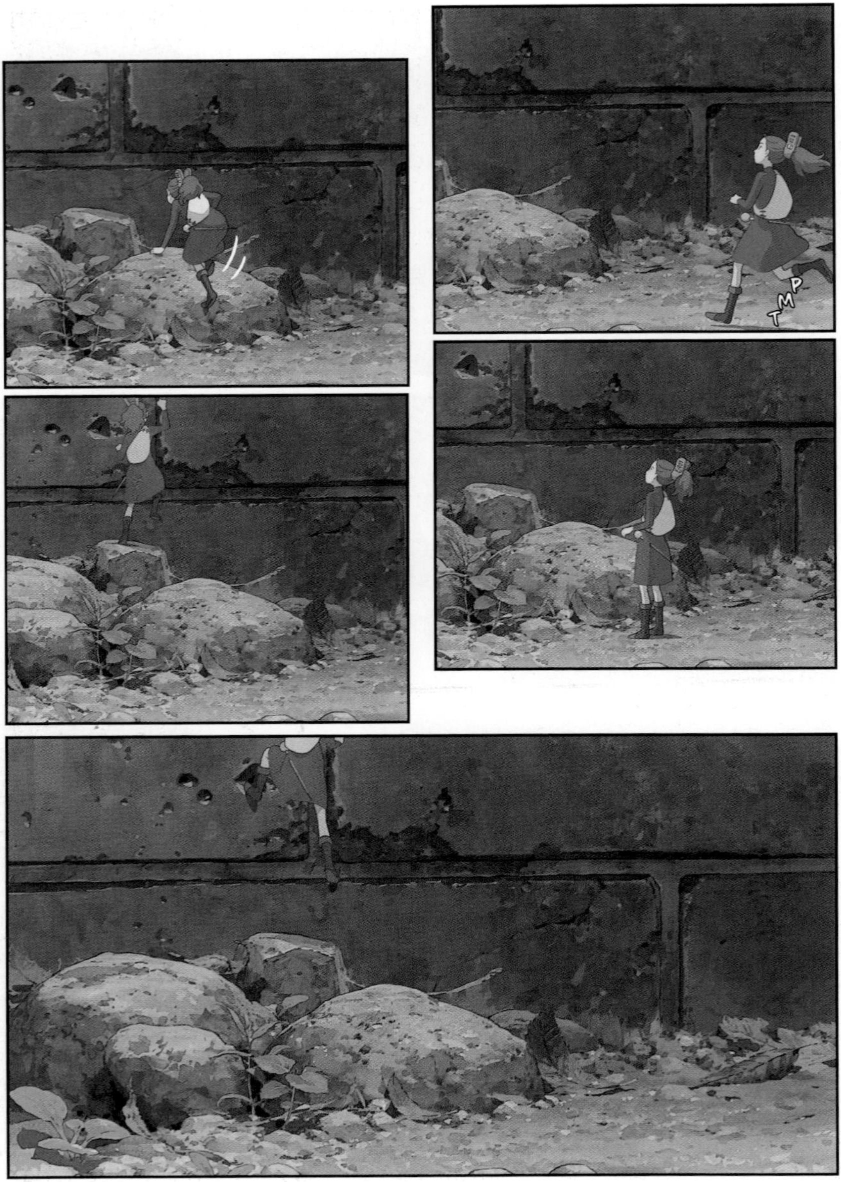
TMP

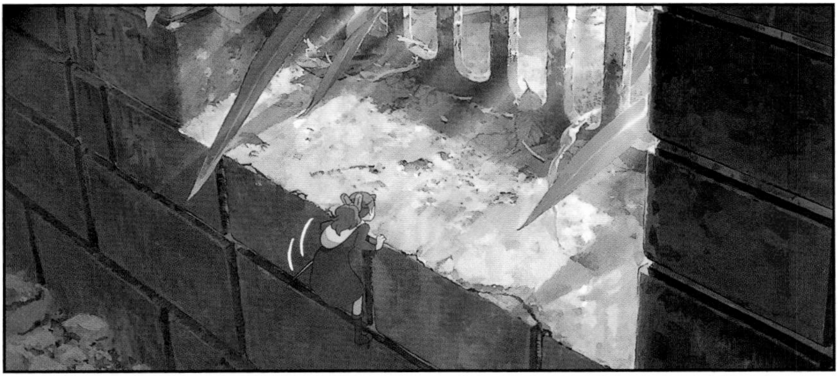
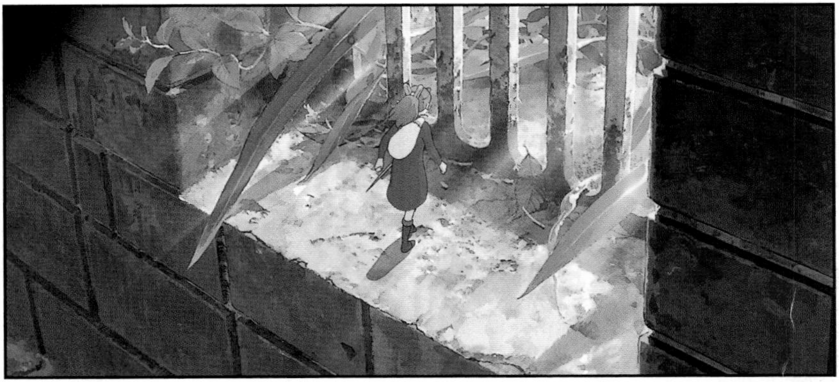
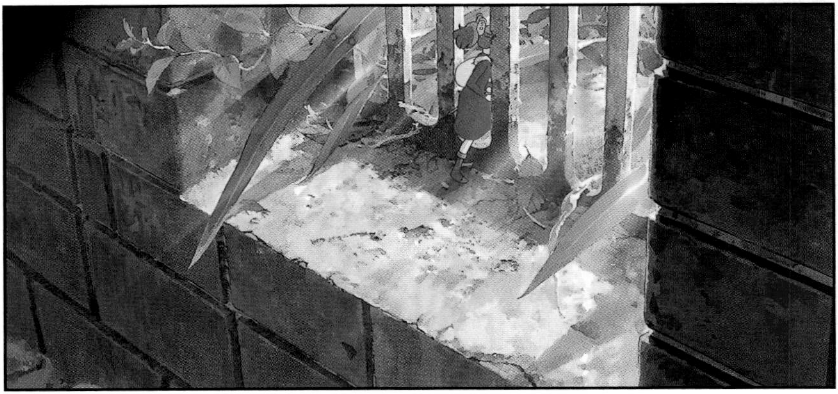

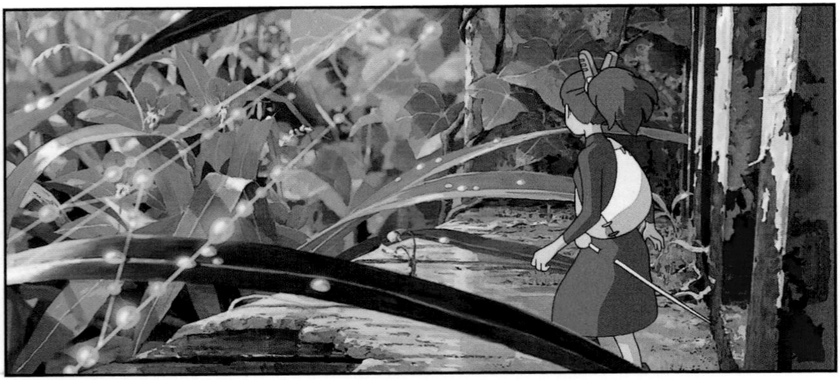
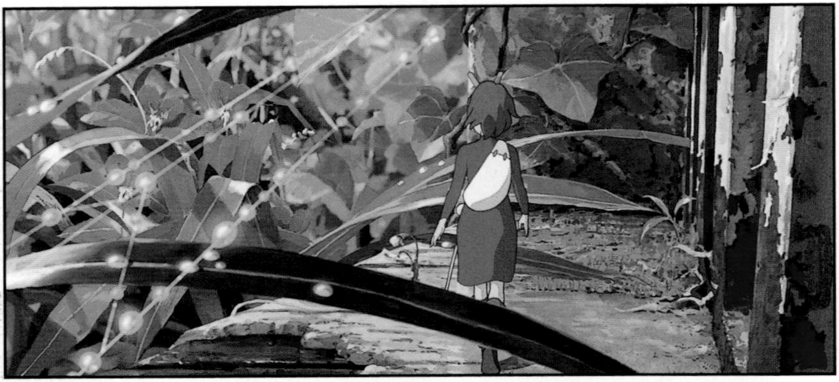
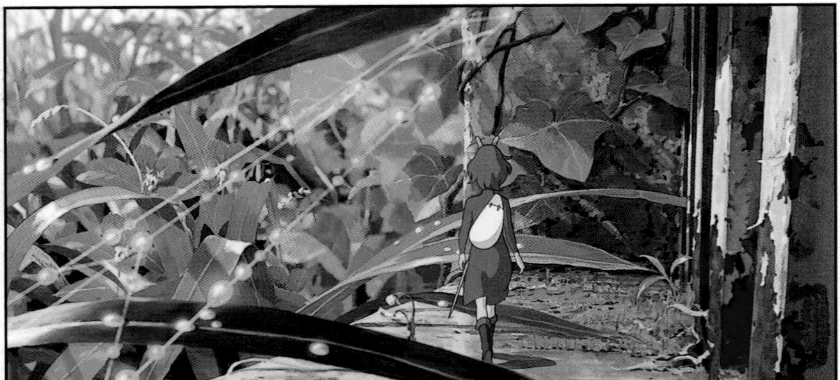

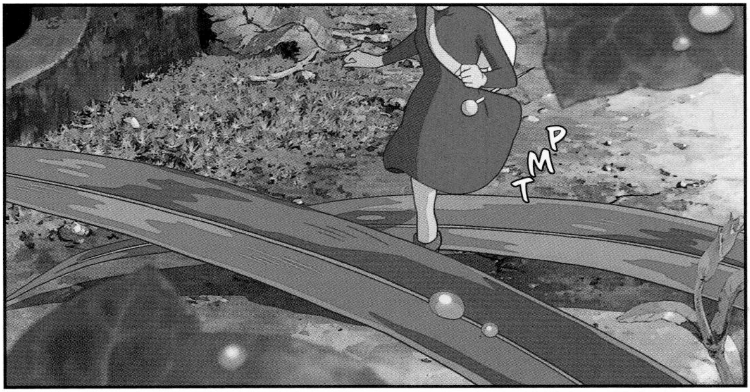
TMP
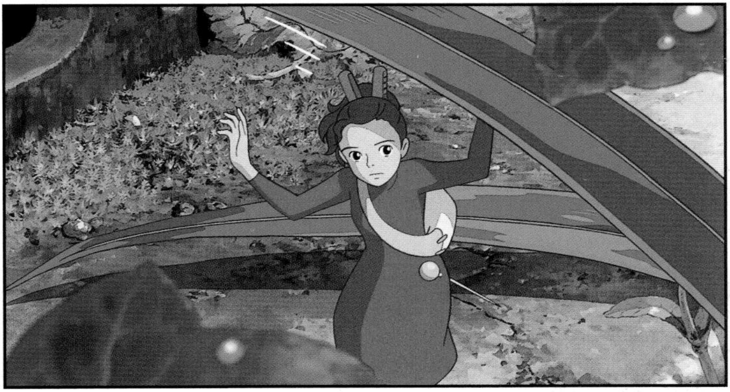
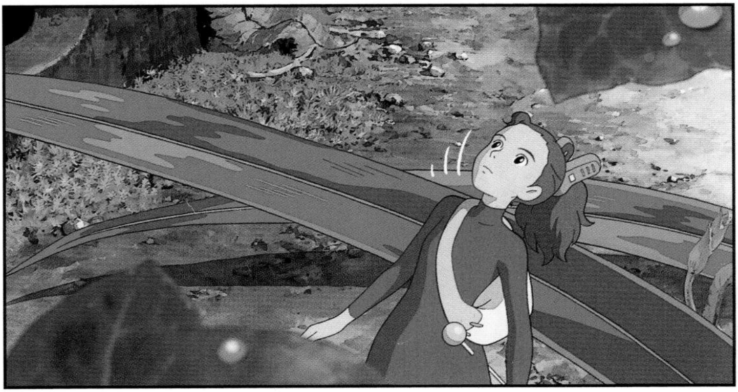

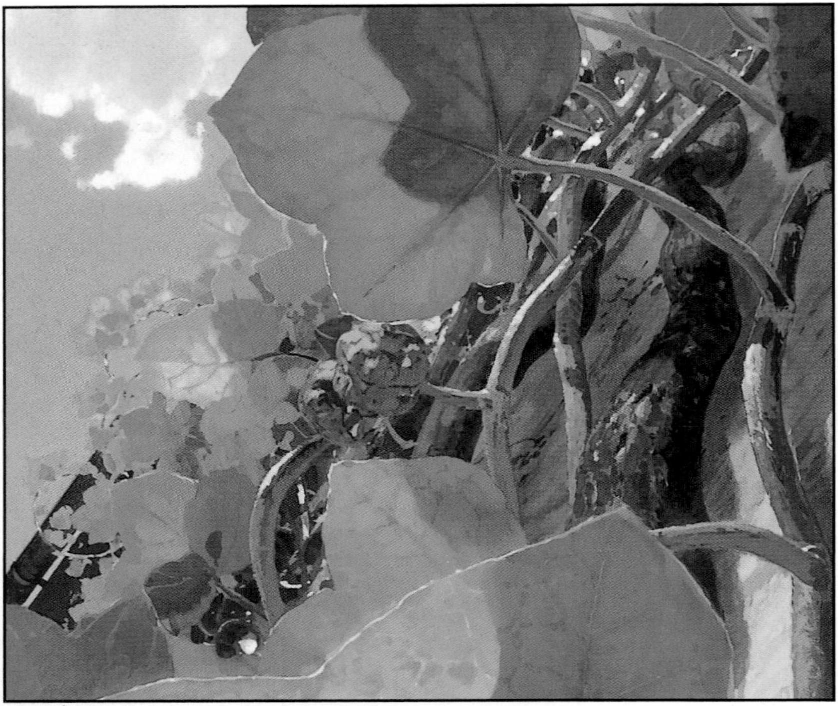

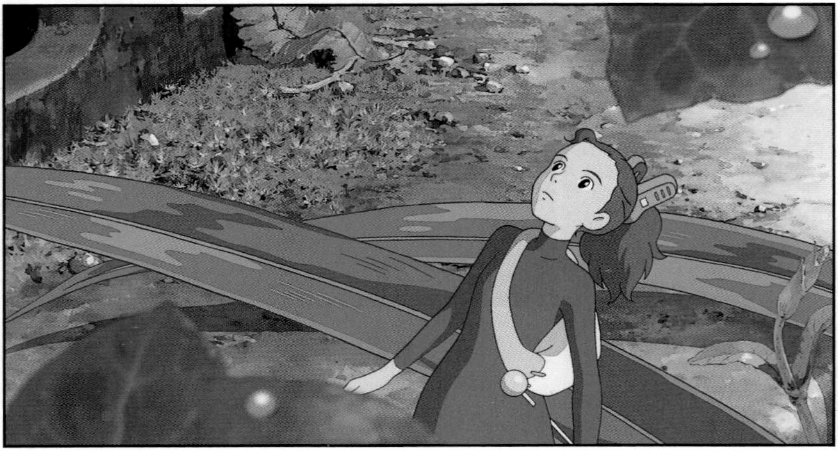

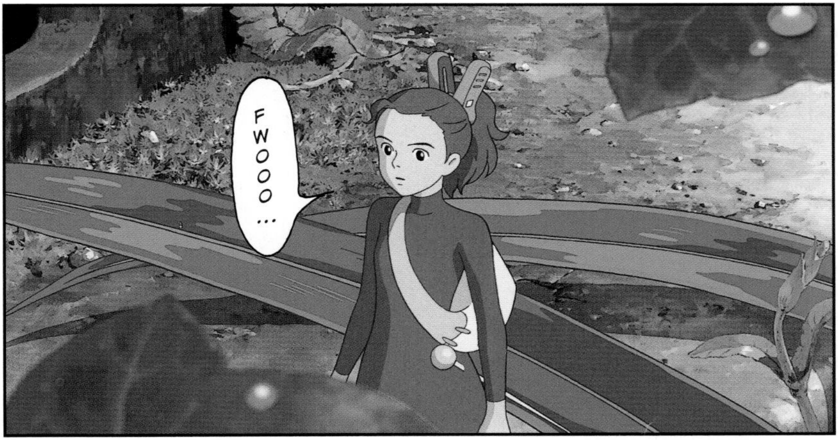
FWOOO...

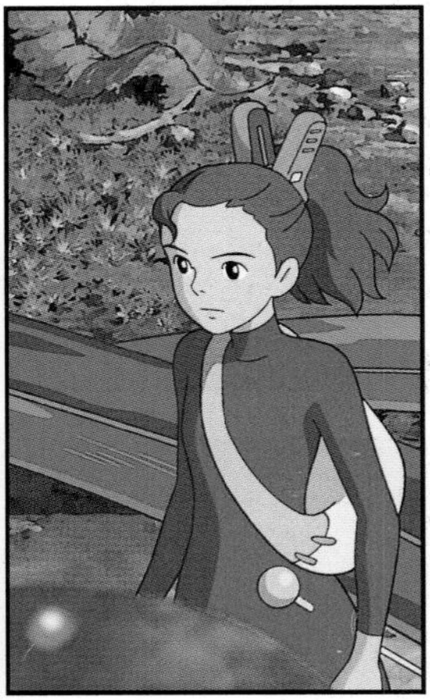

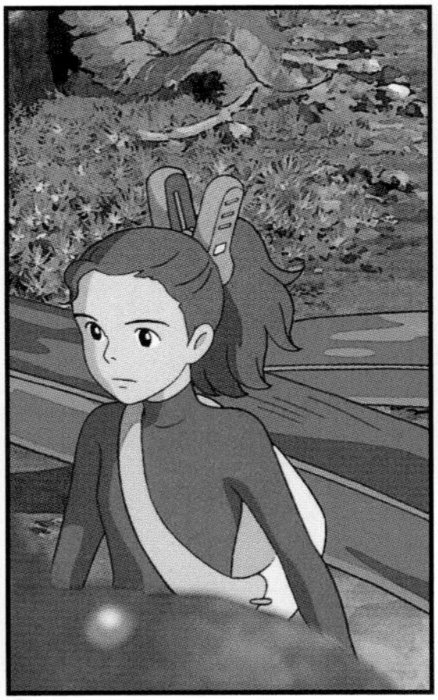

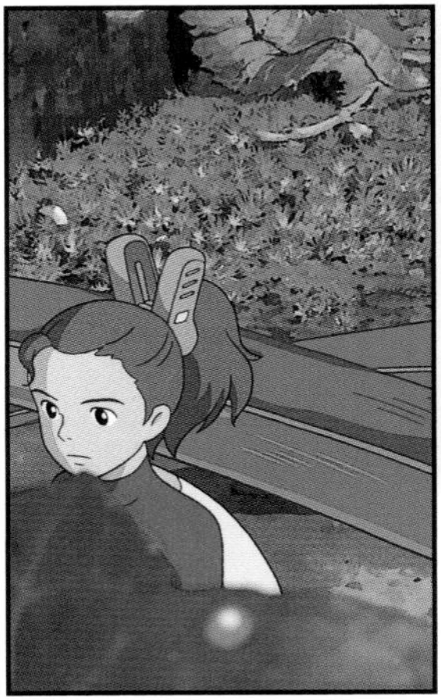

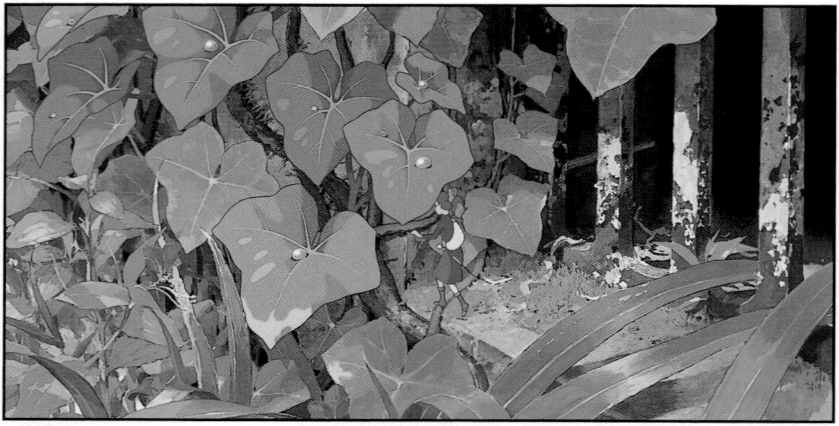

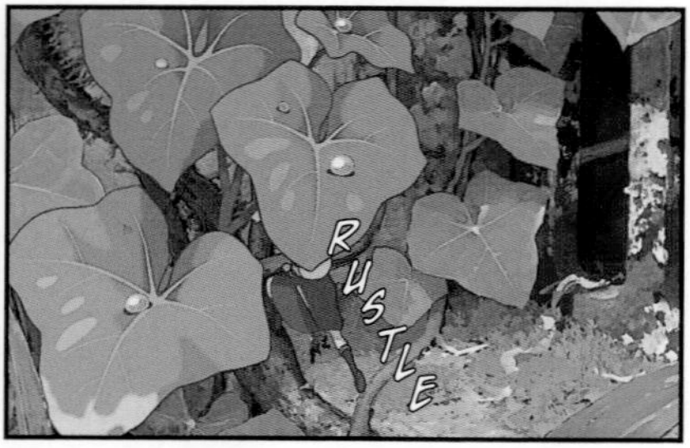
RUSTLE

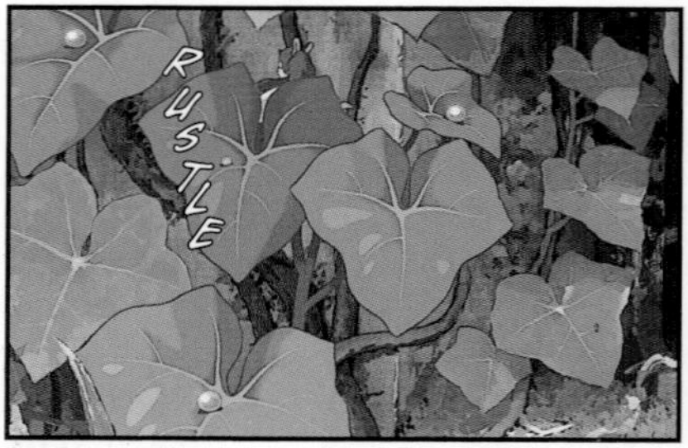
RUSTLE

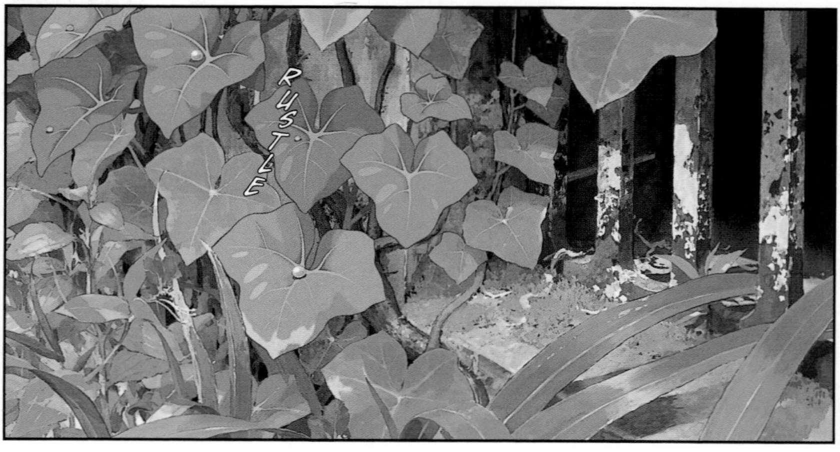
RUSTLE

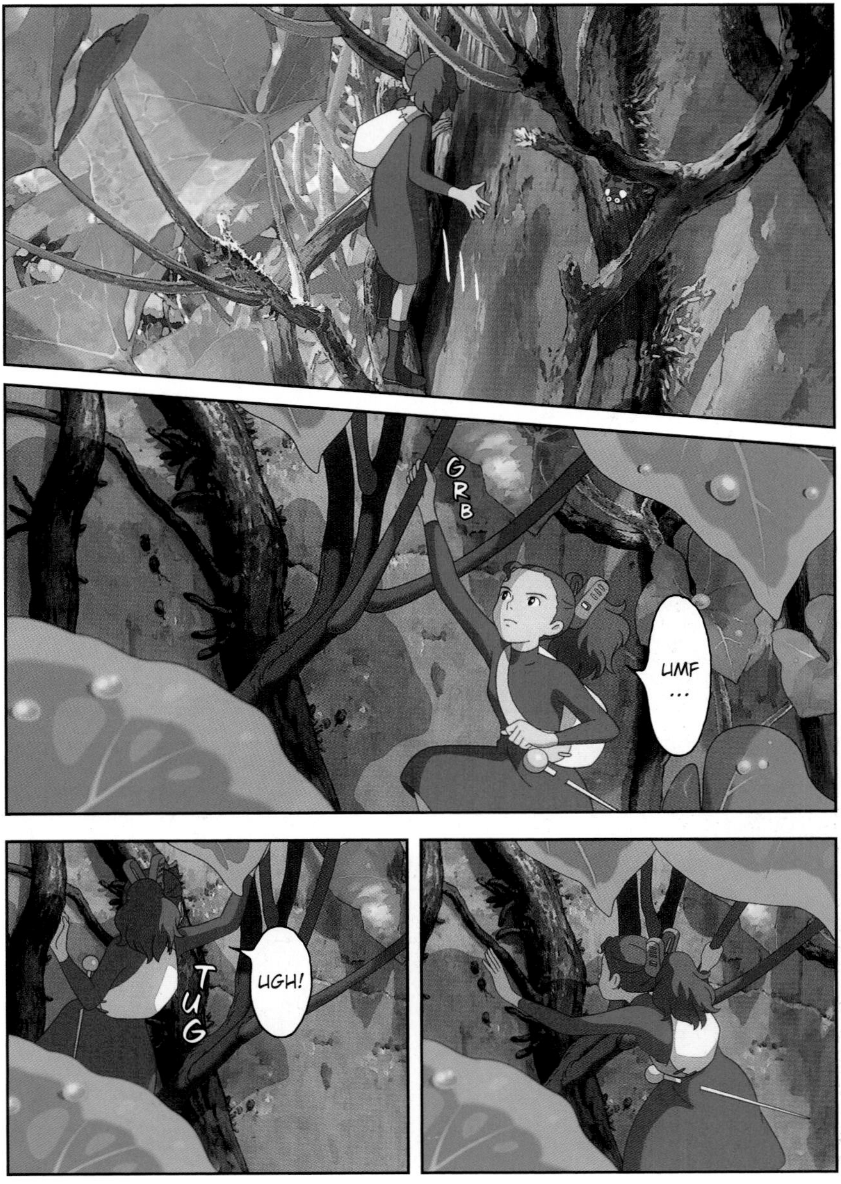
GRB
UMF ...
UGH!
TUG

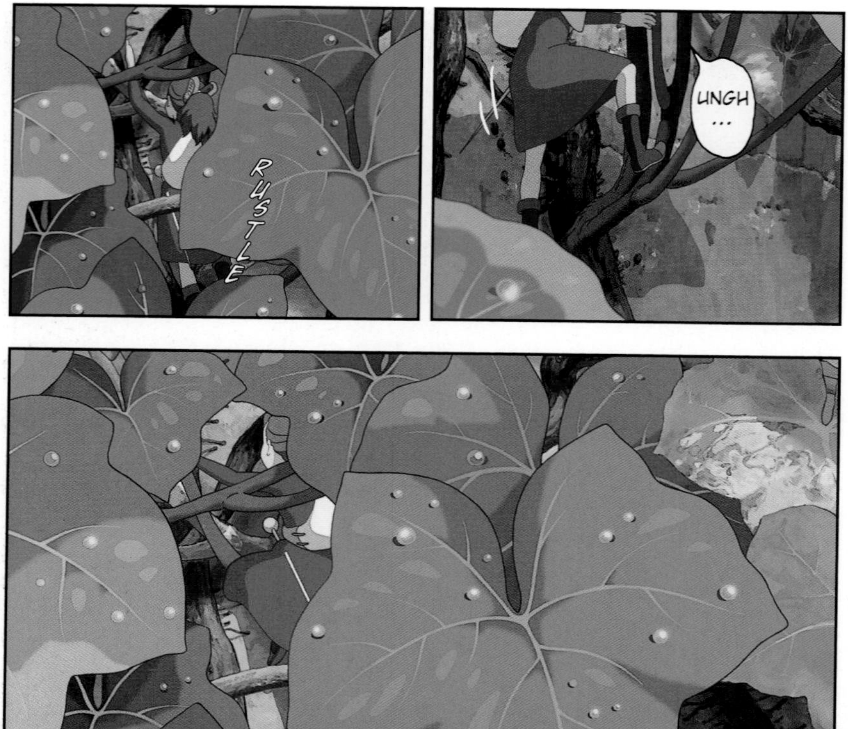
UNGH ...
RUSTLE
RUSTLE
RUSTLE

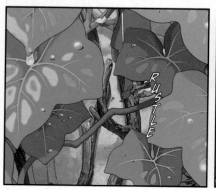

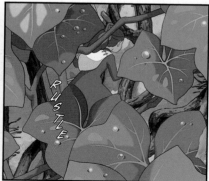

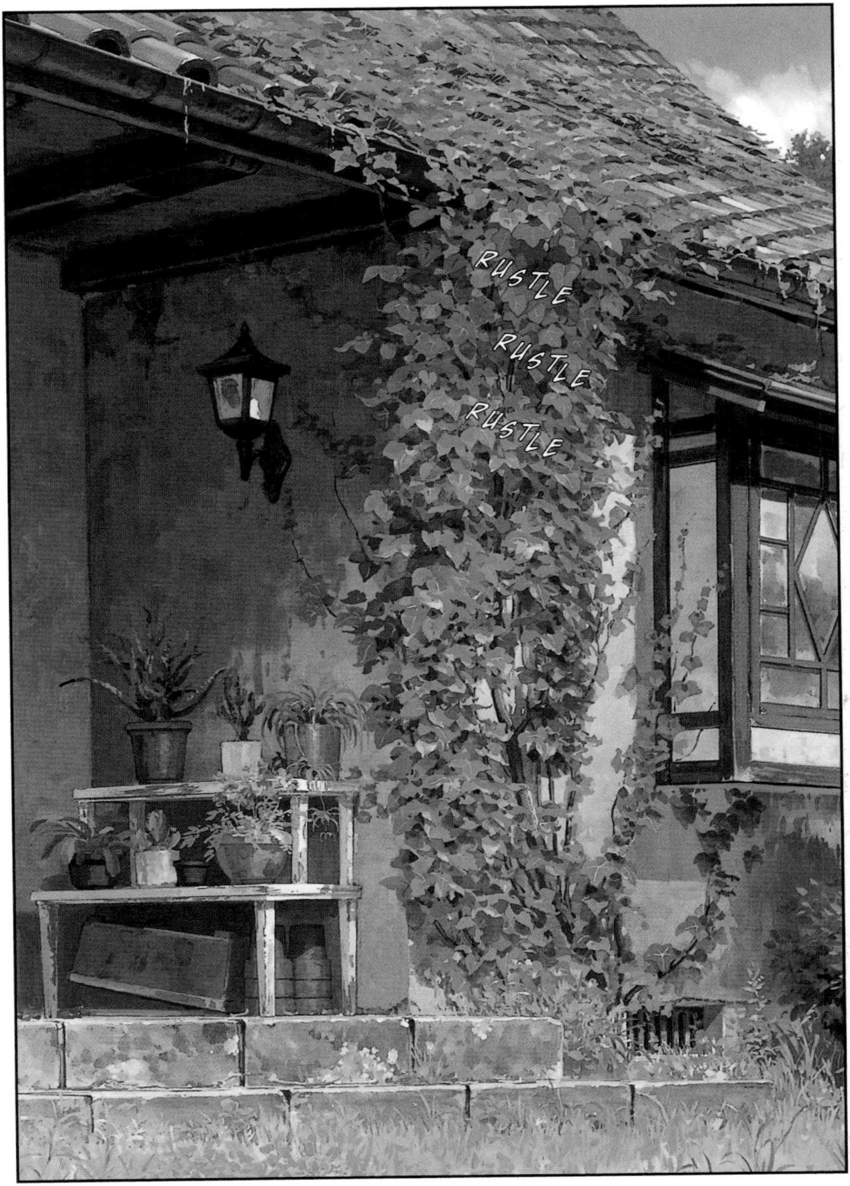
RUSTLE
RUSTLE
RUSTLE

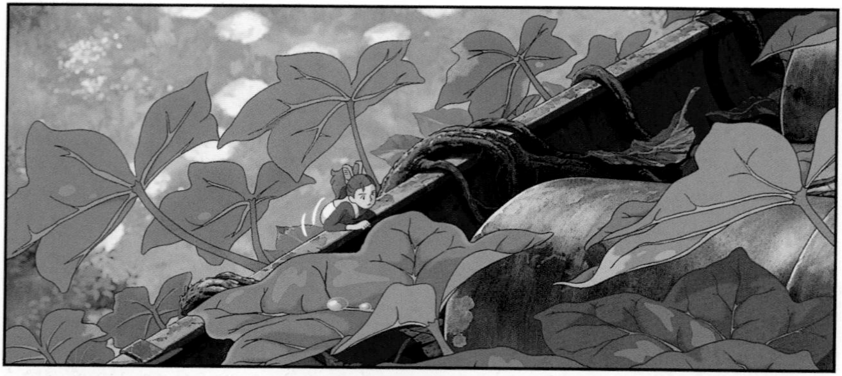

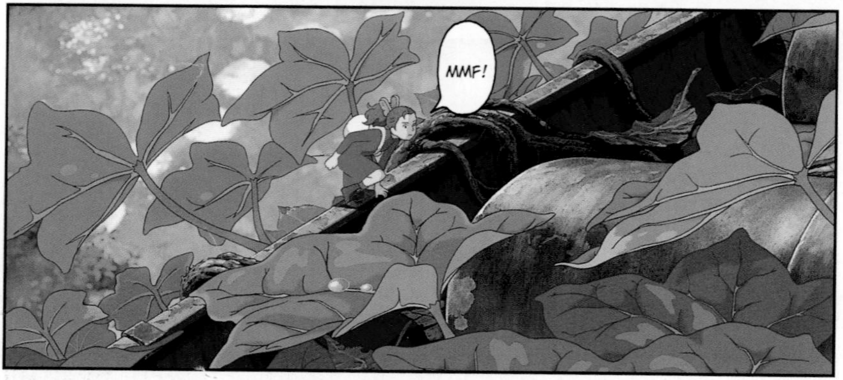
MMF!

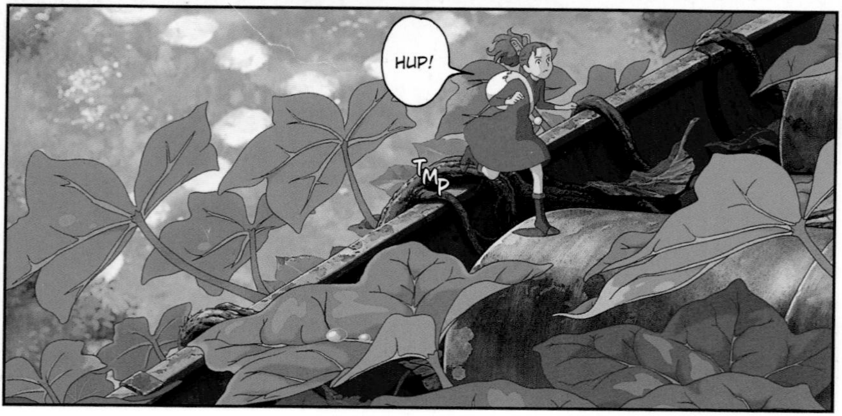
HUP!
TMP

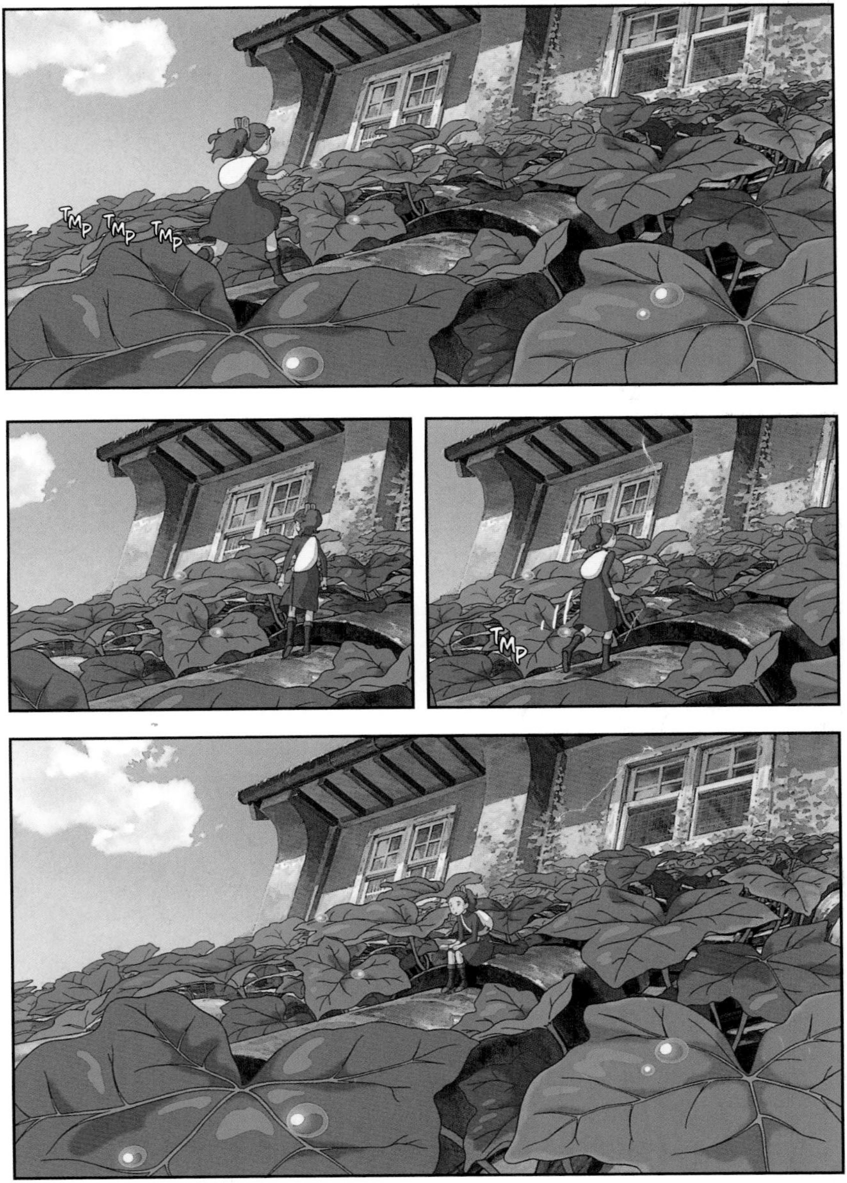
TMP TMP TMP
TMP

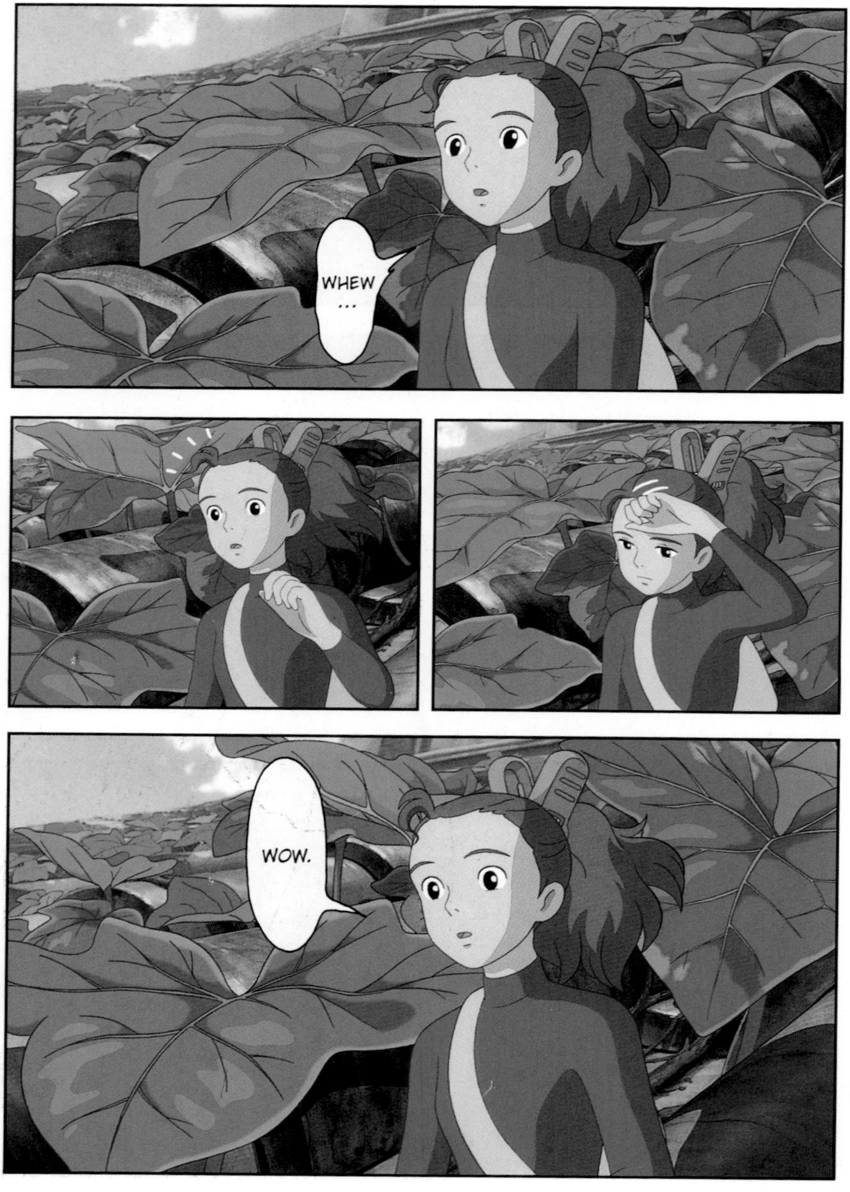
WHEW
...
WOW.

SWIP

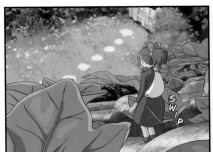

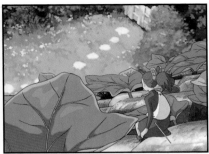

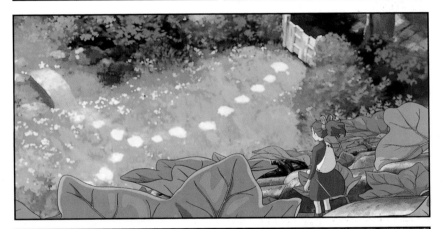

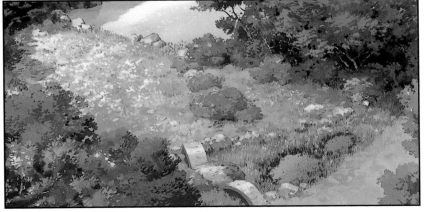

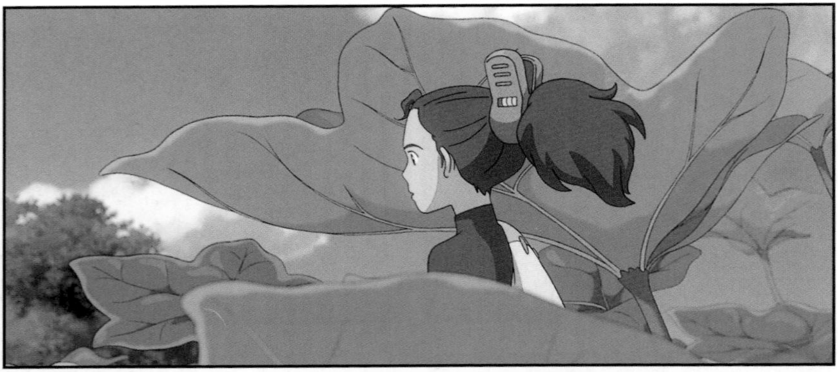

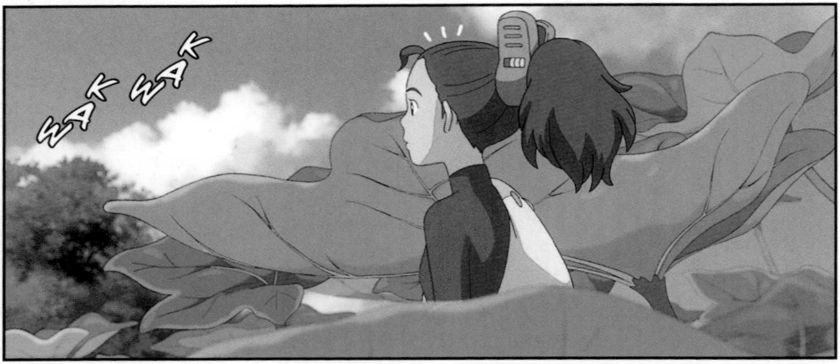
WAK WAK

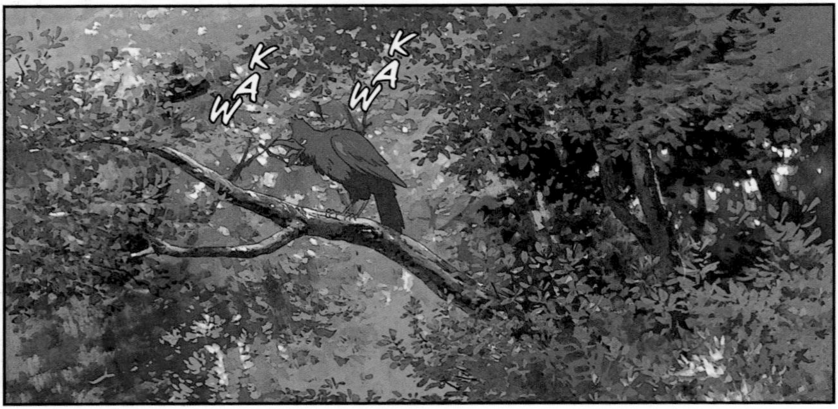
WAK WAK

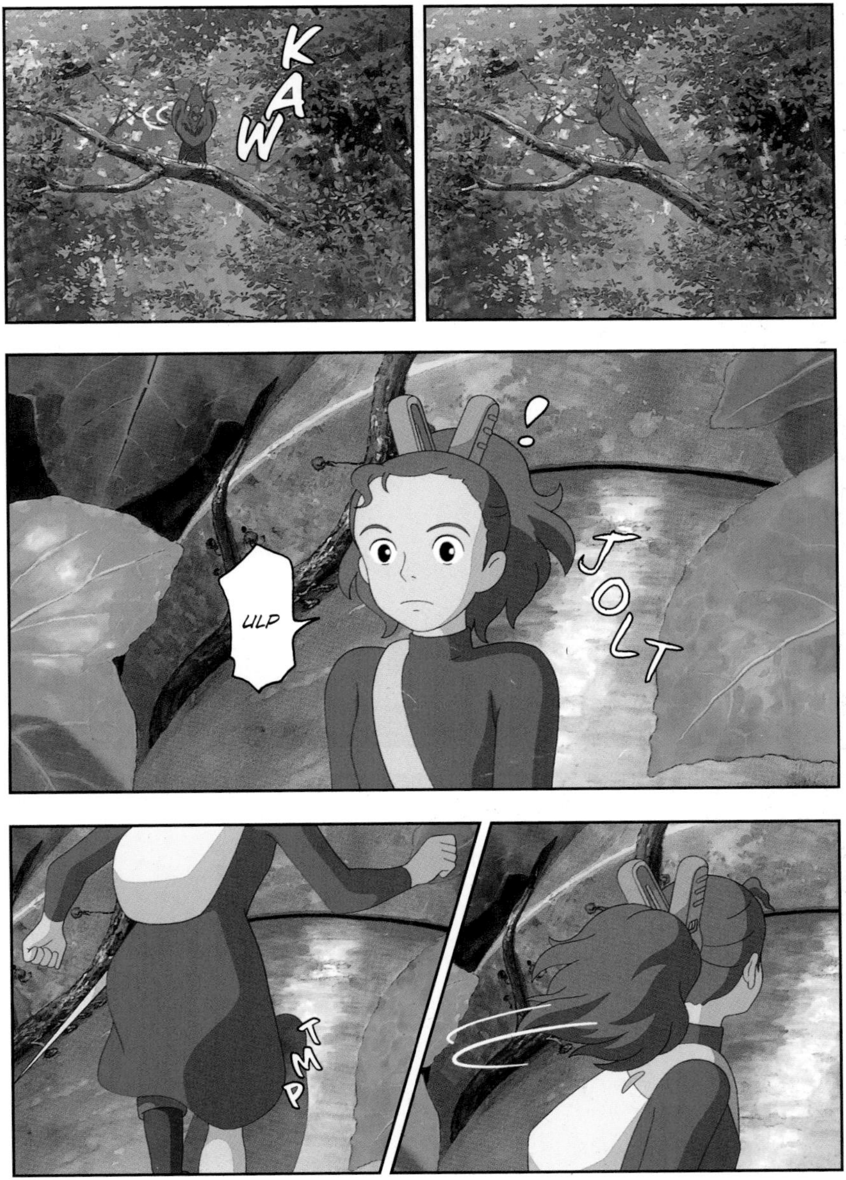
KAW
!
ULP
JOLT
TMP

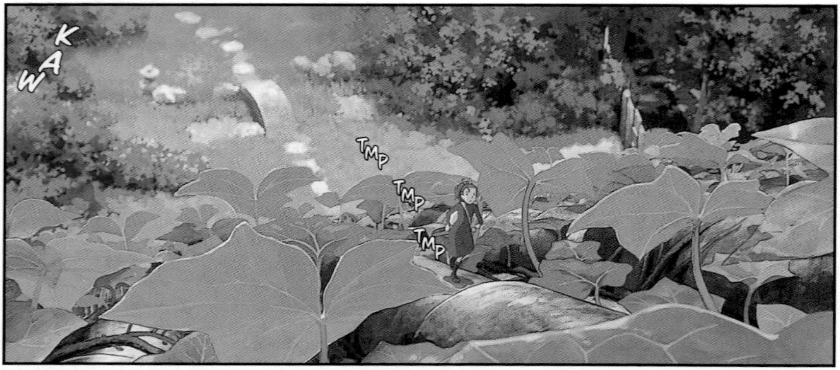
KAW
TMP
TMP
TMP
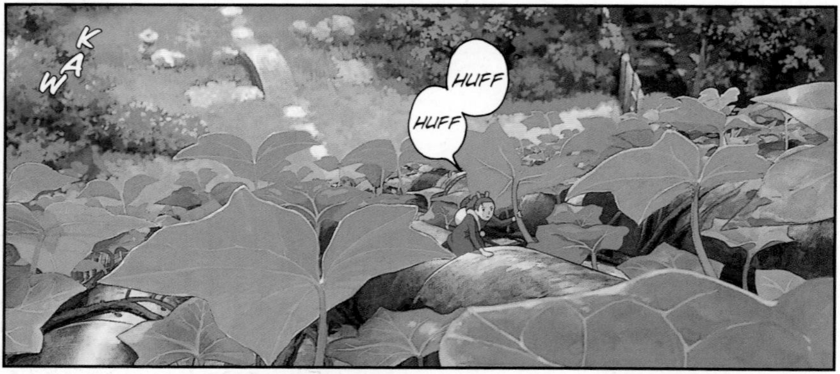
KAW
HUFF
HUFF
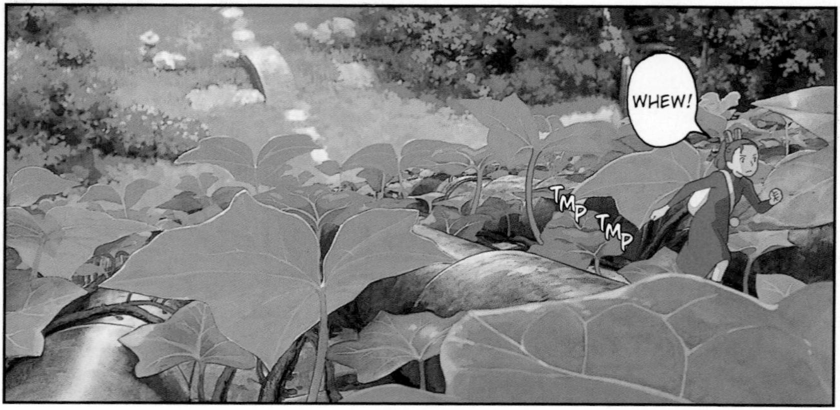
WHEW!
TMP
TMP

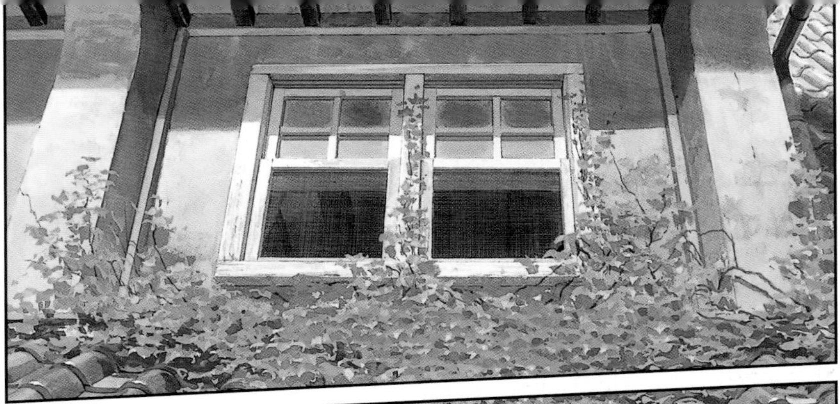
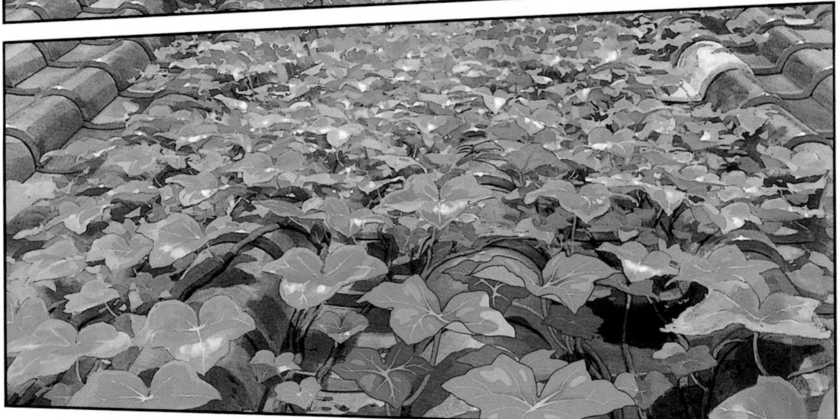
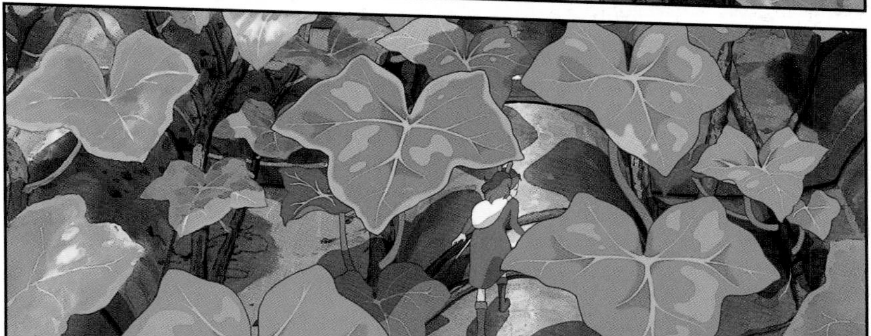

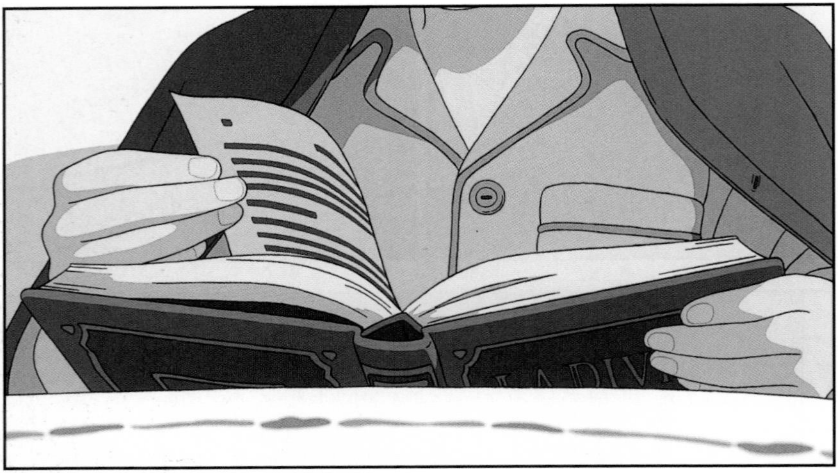
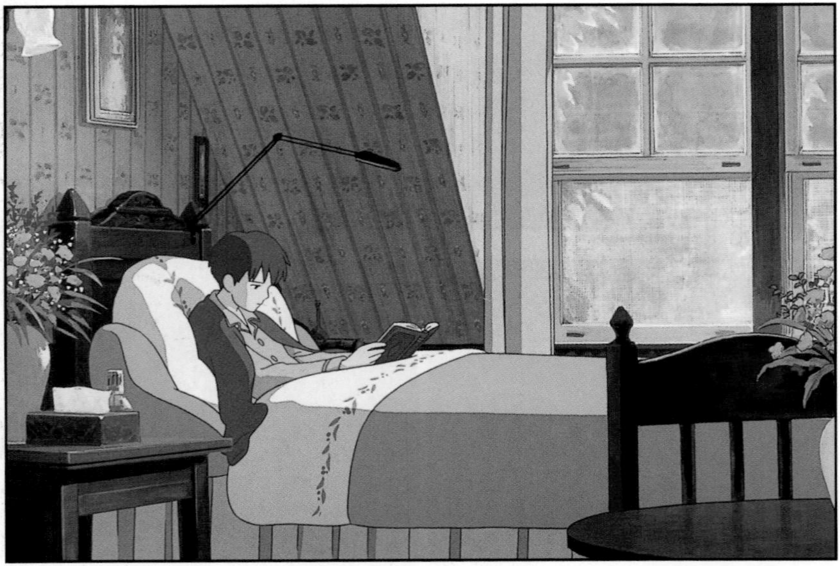

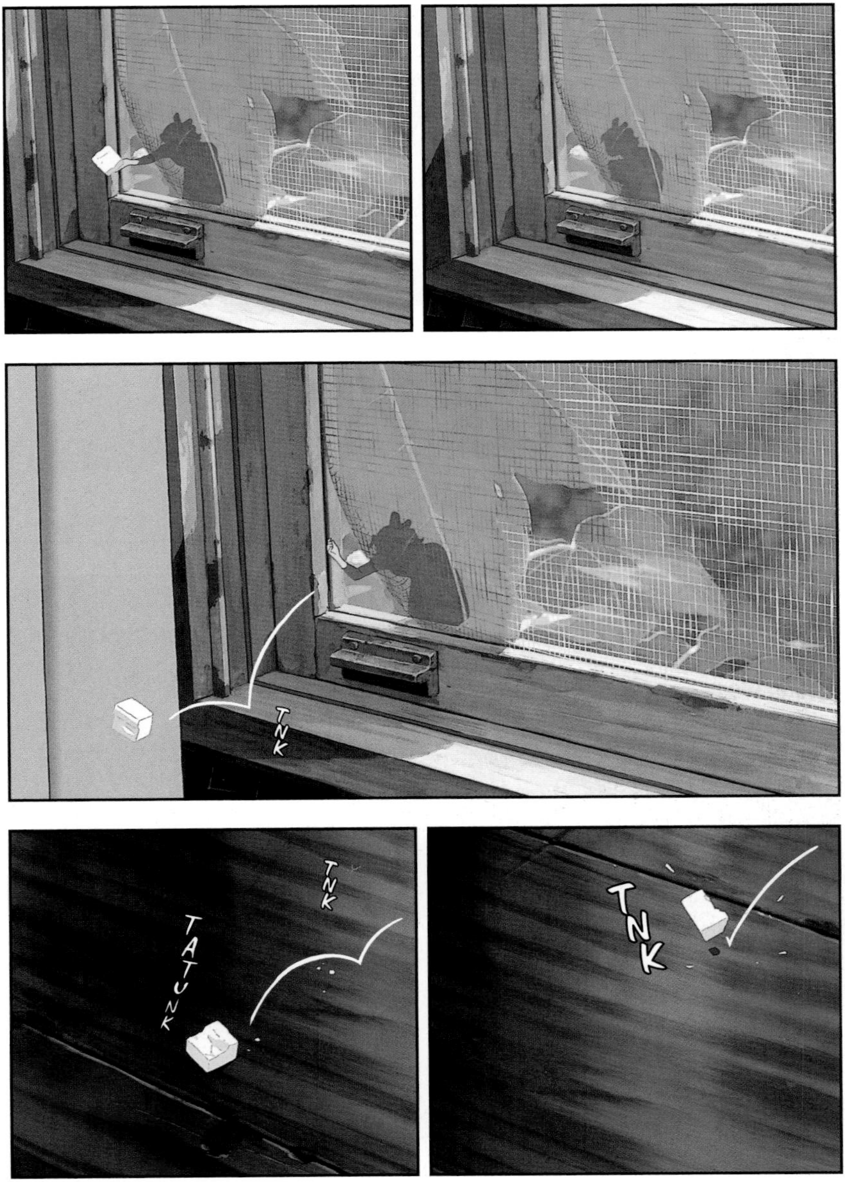
TNK
TNK
TNK
TATUNK

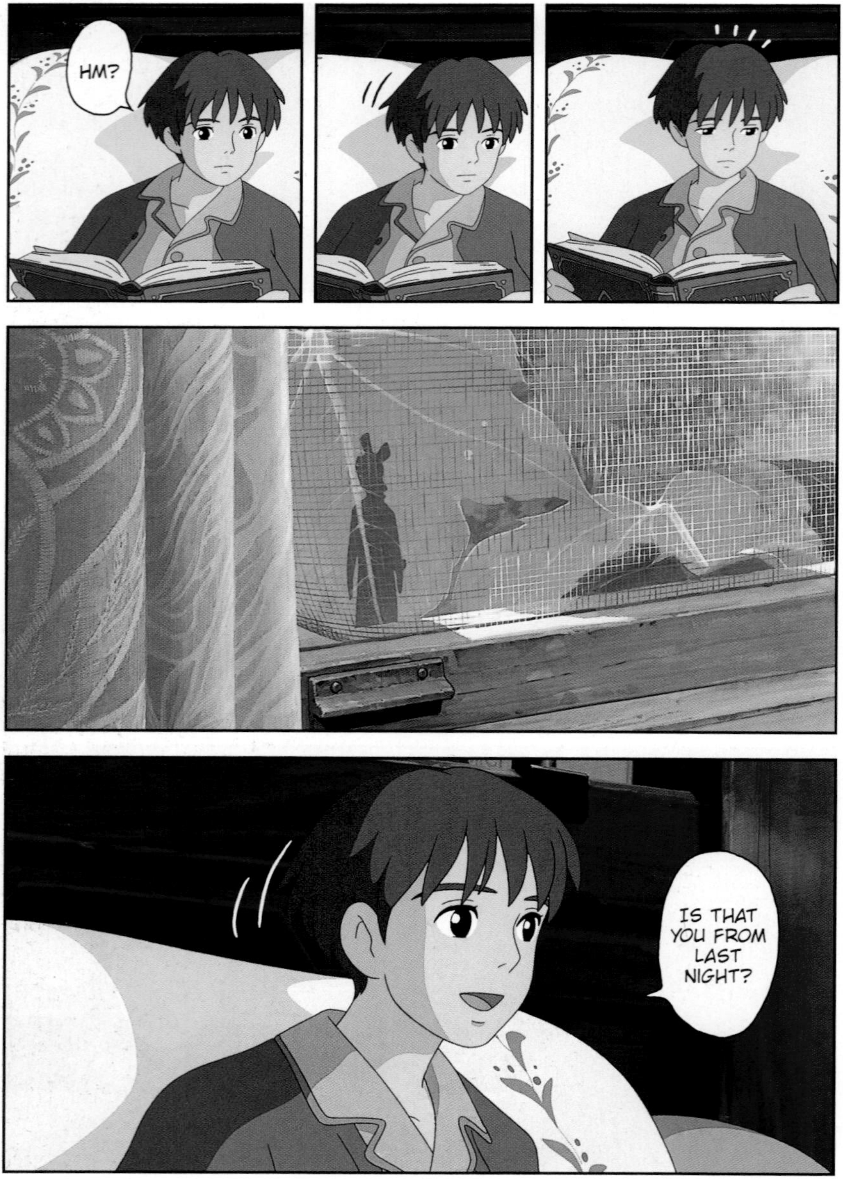
HM?
IS THAT YOU FROM LAST NIGHT?

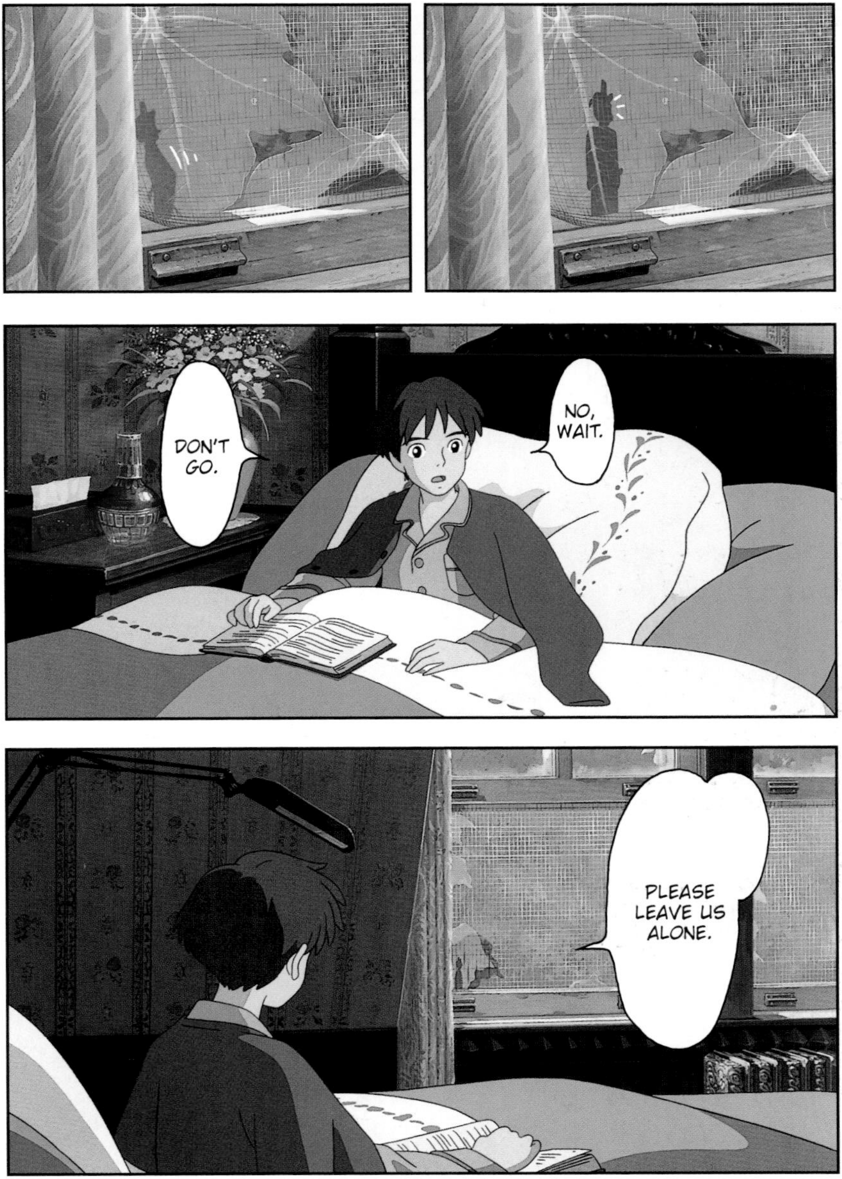
NO, WAIT.
DON'T GO.
PLEASE LEAVE US ALONE.

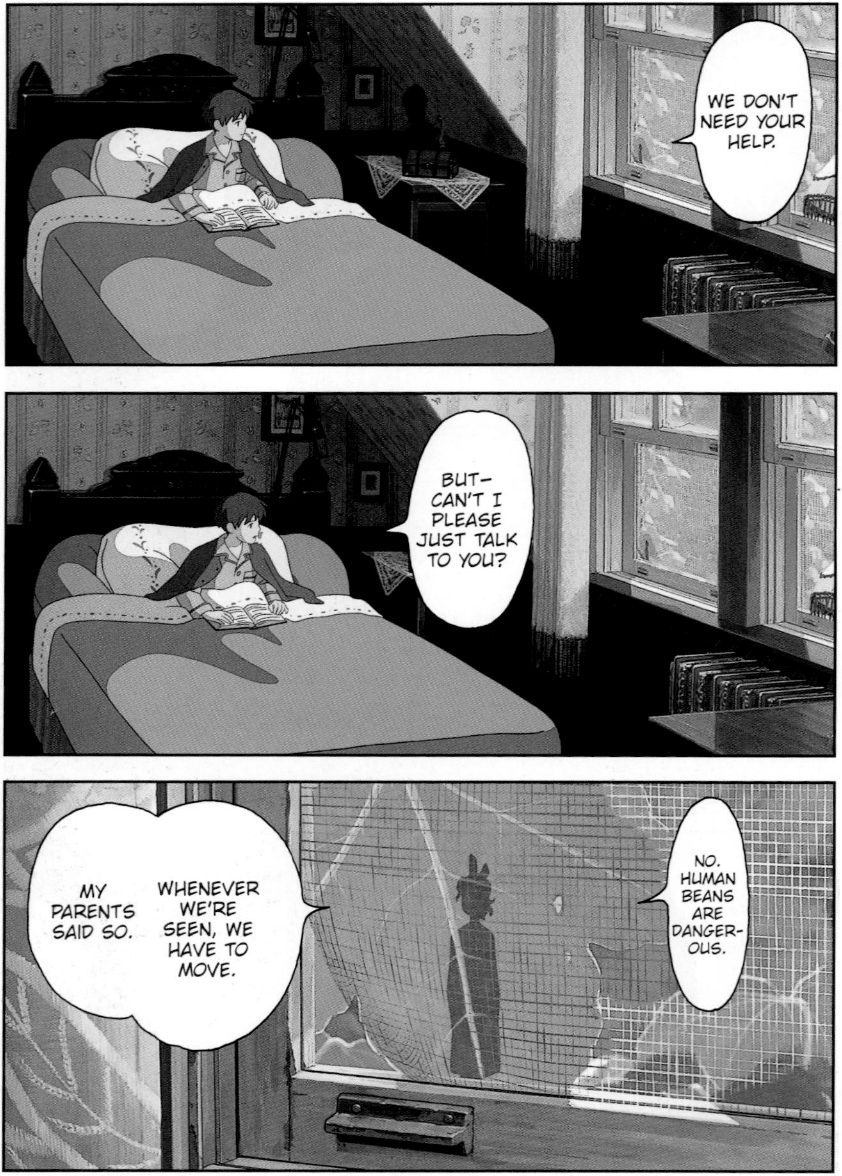
WE DON'T NEED YOUR HELP.
BUT— CAN'T I PLEASE JUST TALK TO YOU?
NO. HUMAN BEANS ARE DANGER-OUS.
WHENEVER WE'RE SEEN, WE HAVE TO MOVE.
MY PARENTS SAID SO.

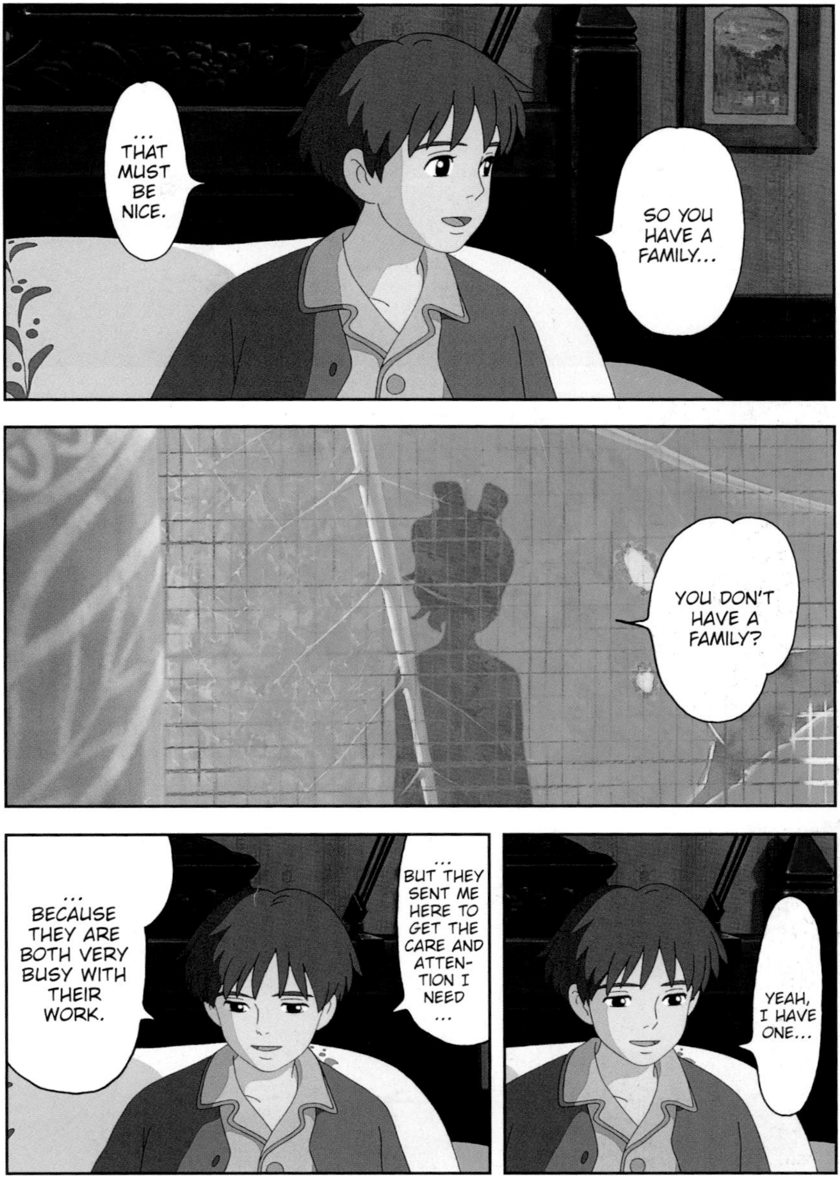
SO YOU HAVE A FAMILY...
... THAT MUST BE NICE.
YOU DON'T HAVE A FAMILY?
YEAH, I HAVE ONE...
... BUT THEY SENT ME HERE TO GET THE CARE AND ATTEN- TION I NEED ...
... BECAUSE THEY ARE BOTH VERY BUSY WITH THEIR WORK.

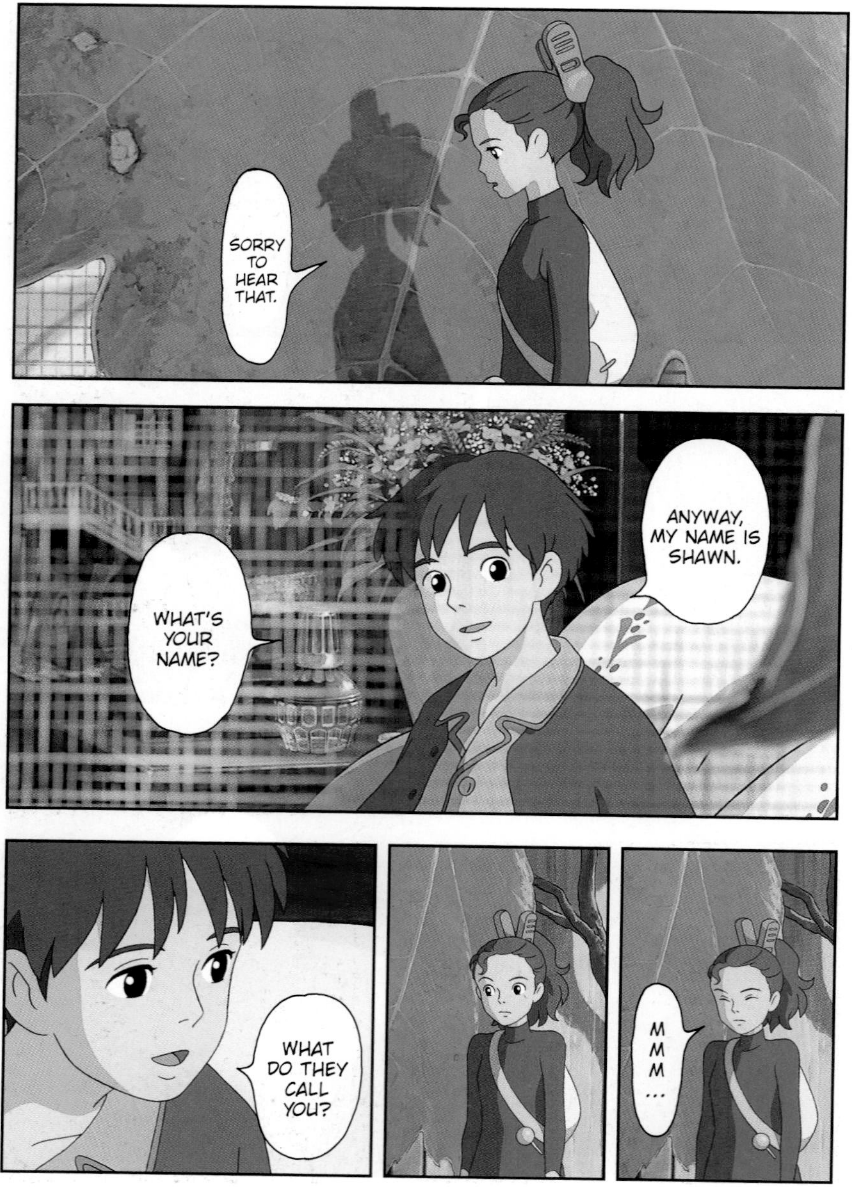
SORRY TO HEAR THAT.
ANYWAY, MY NAME IS SHAWN.
WHAT'S YOUR NAME?
WHAT DO THEY CALL YOU?
MMM...

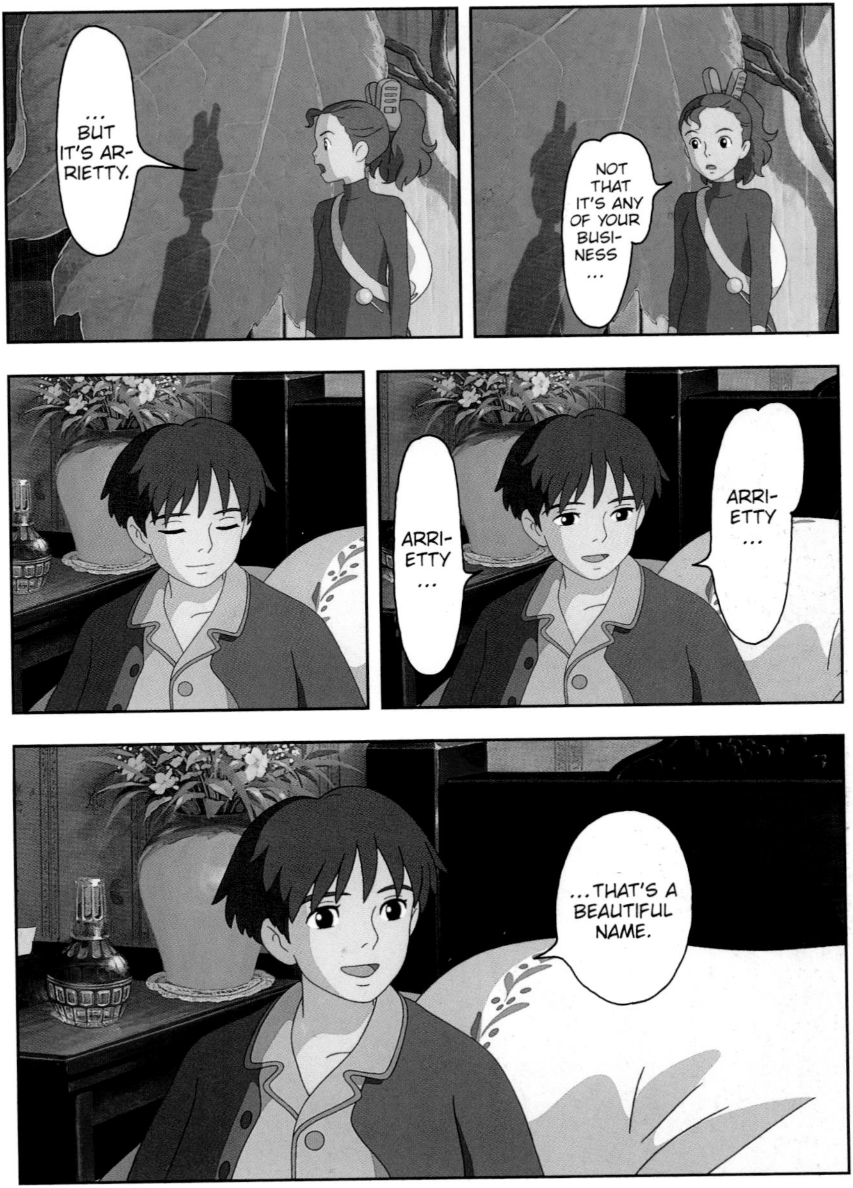
NOT THAT IT'S ANY OF YOUR BUSI- NESS ...
... BUT IT'S AR- RIETTY.
ARRI- ETTY ...
ARRI- ETTY ...
... THAT'S A BEAUTIFUL NAME.

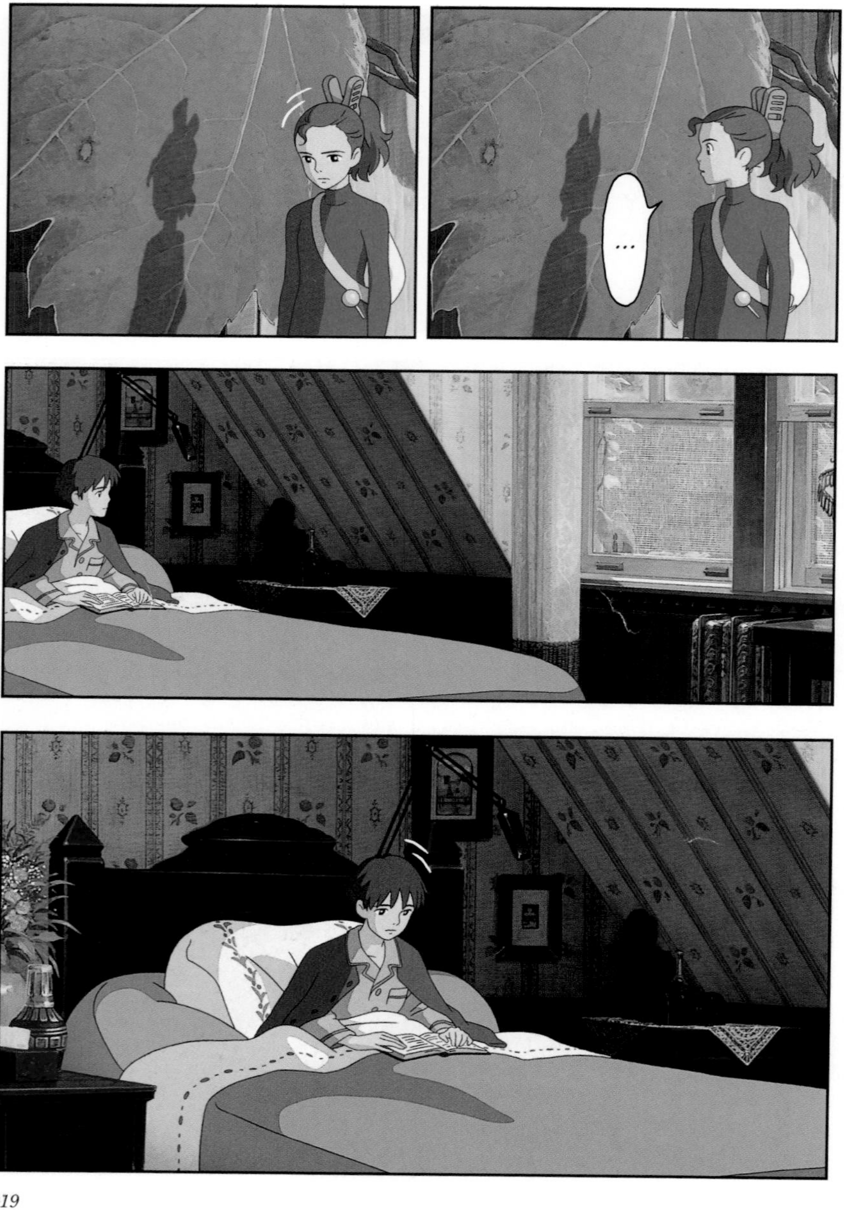
...

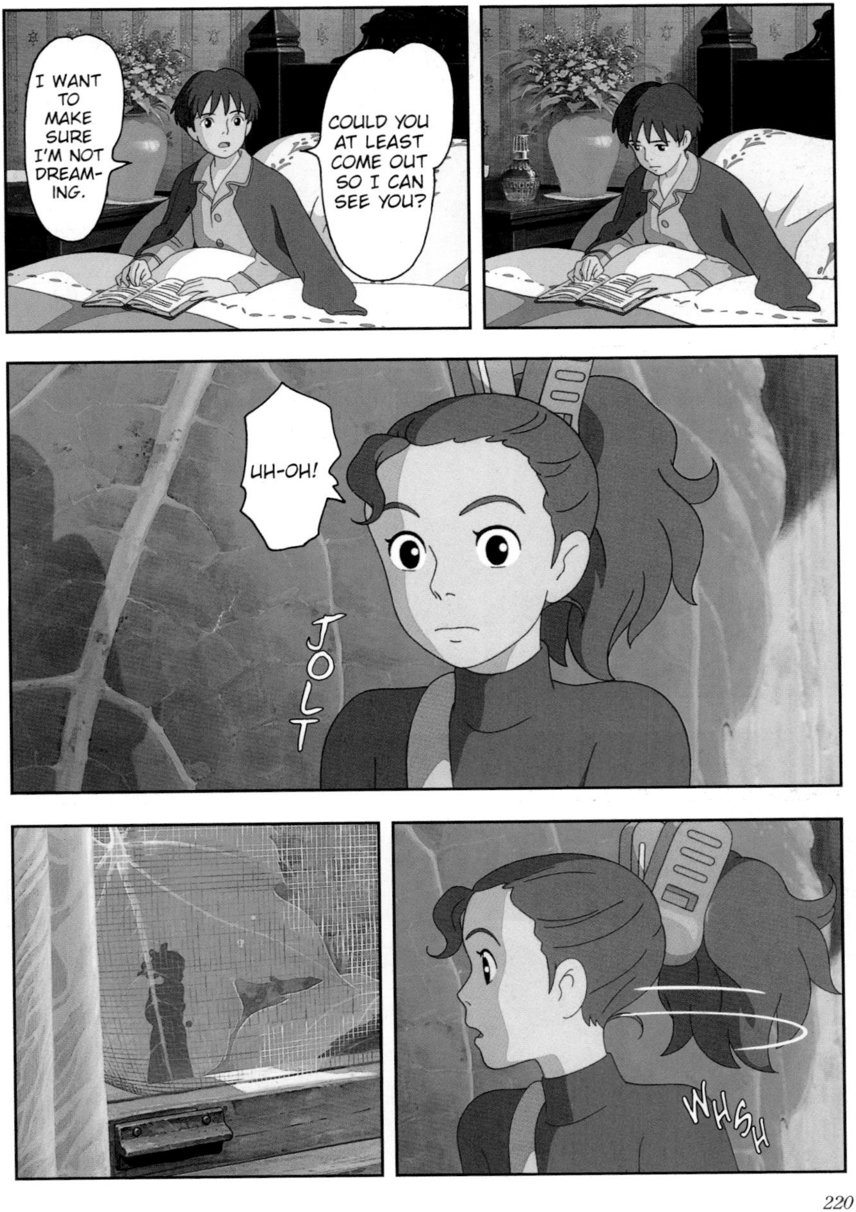
I WANT TO MAKE SURE I'M NOT DREAMING.
COULD YOU AT LEAST COME OUT SO I CAN SEE YOU?
UH-OH!
JOLT
WHSH

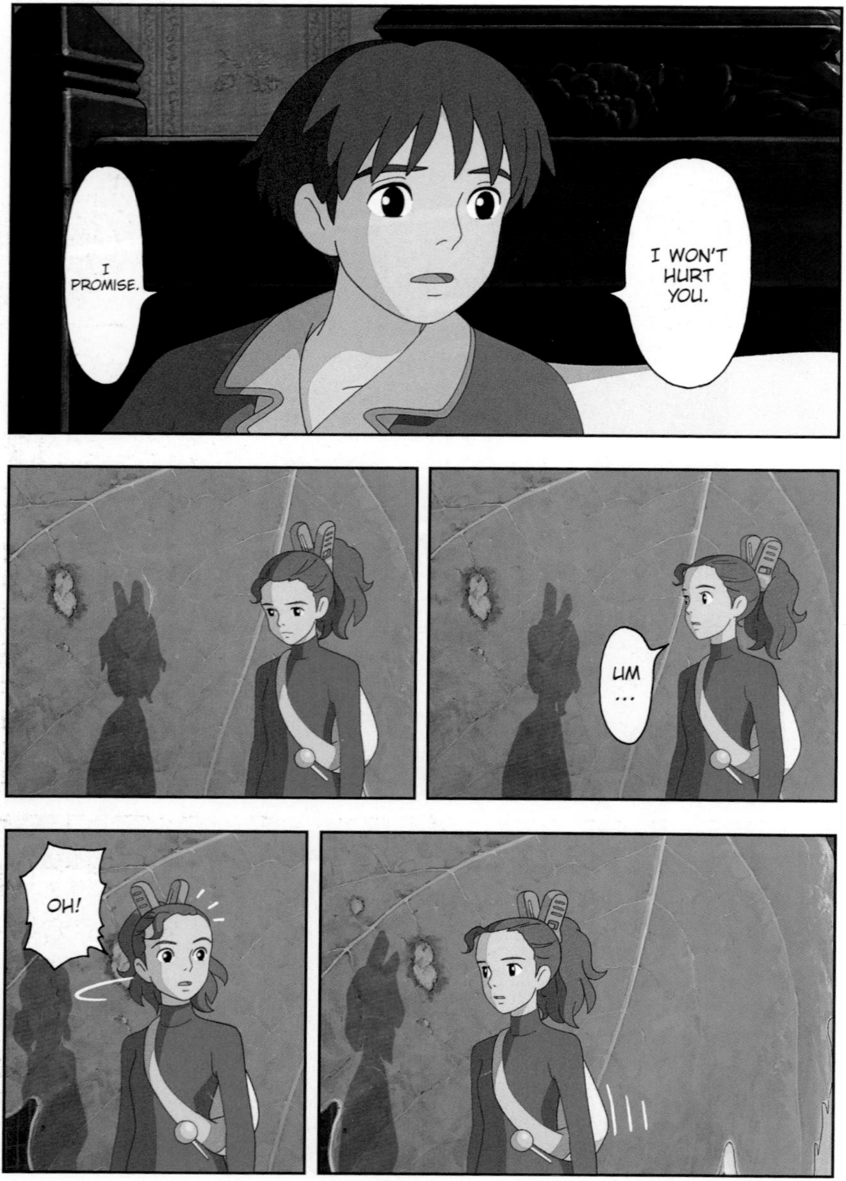
I WON'T HURT YOU.
I PROMISE.
UM ...
OH!

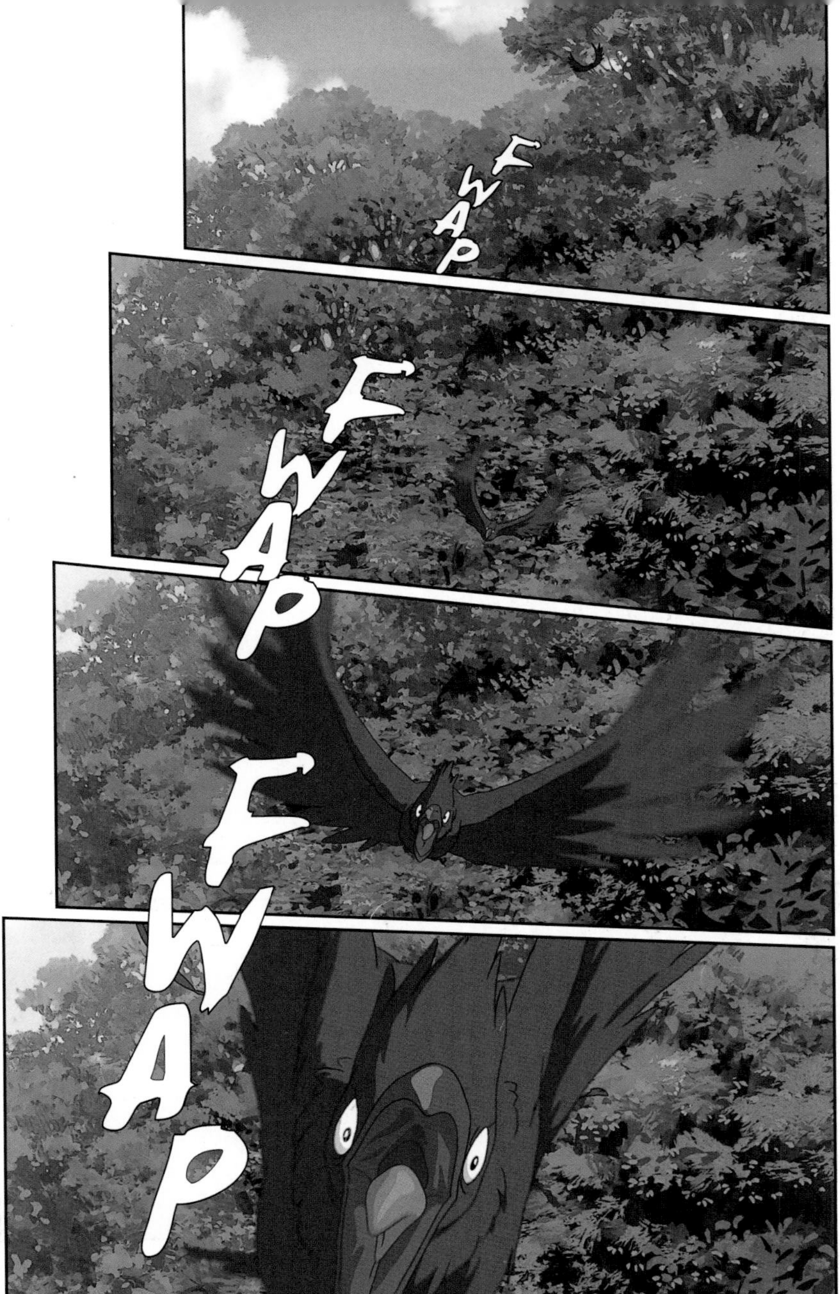
FWAP
FWAP
FWAP

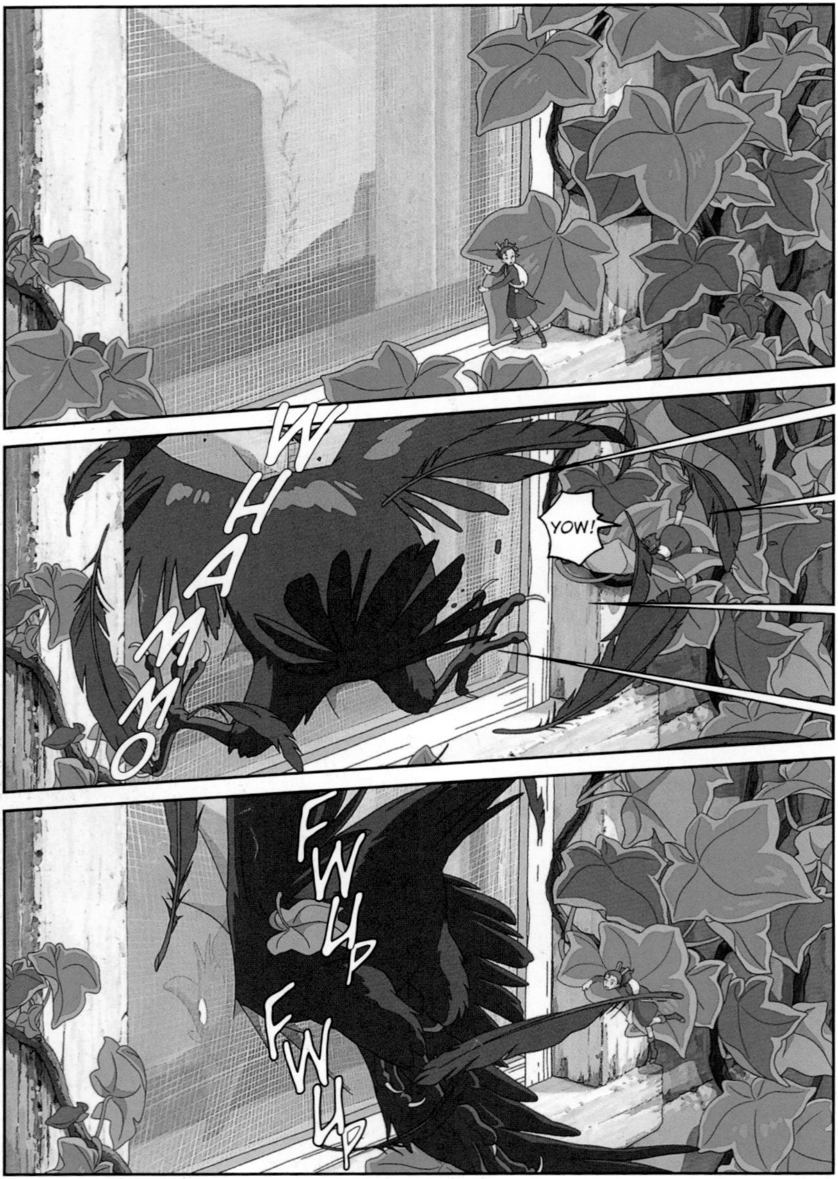
WHAMMO
YOW!
FWUP
FWUP

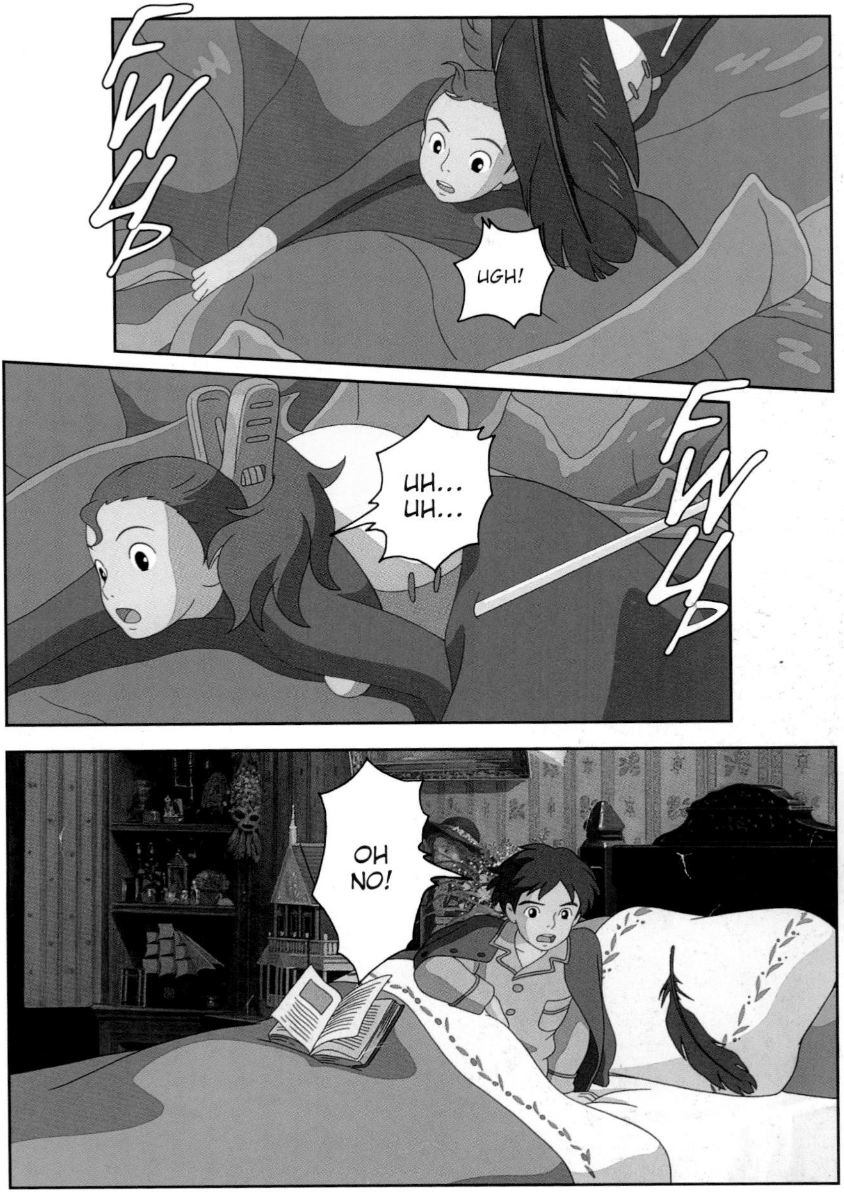
FWUP
UGH!
FWUP
UH... UH...
OH NO!

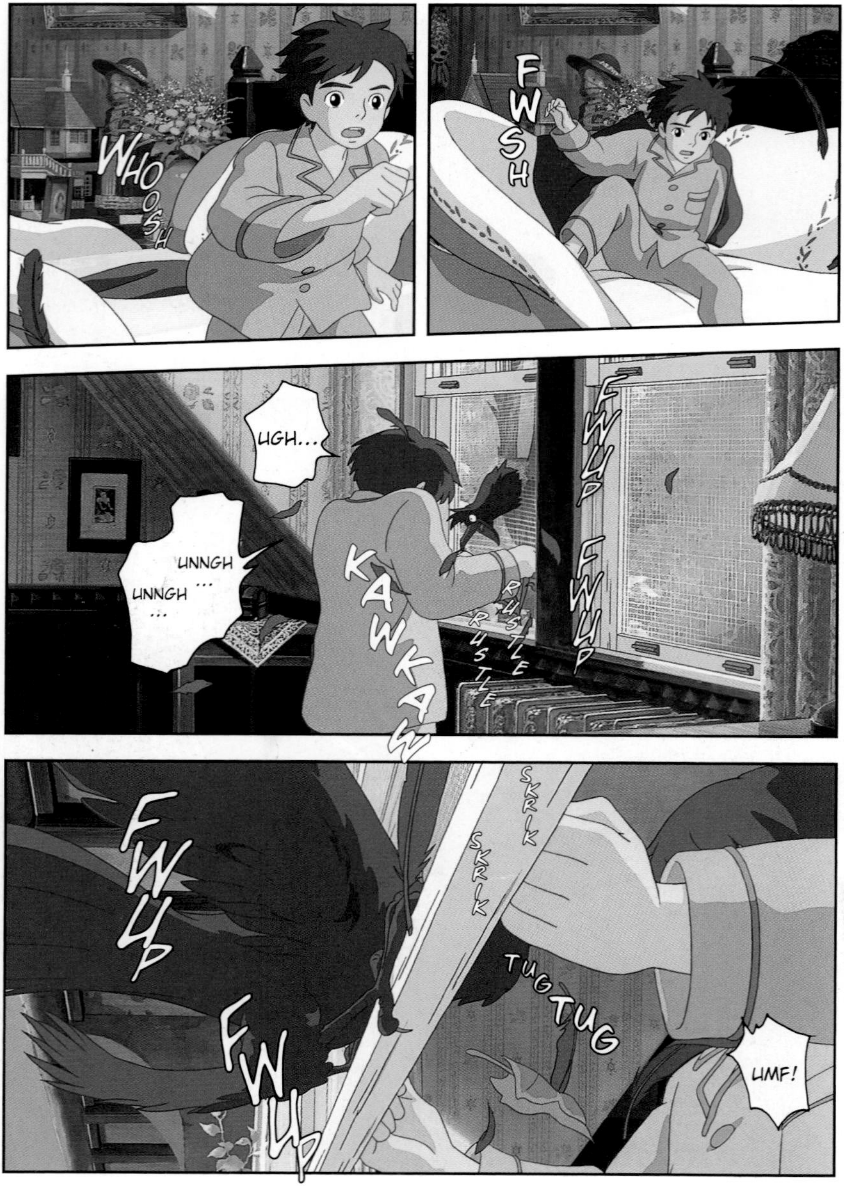
FWSH
WHOOSH
FWUP FWUP
RUSTLE RUSTLE
KAWKAW
UGH...
UNNGH... UNNGH...
UMF!
TUGTUG
SKRIK SKRIK
FWUP
FWUP

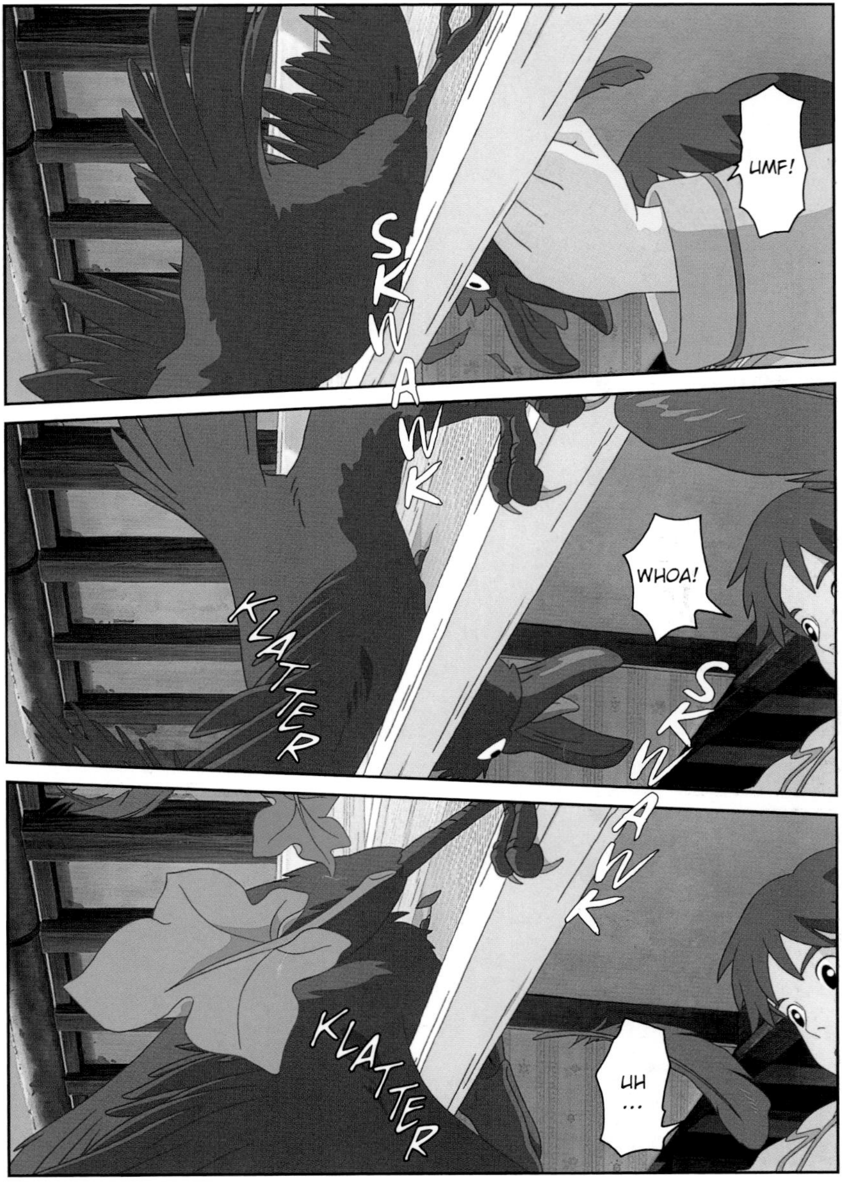
UMF!
SKWAWK
WHOA!
SKWAWK
KLATTER
UH ...
KLATTER

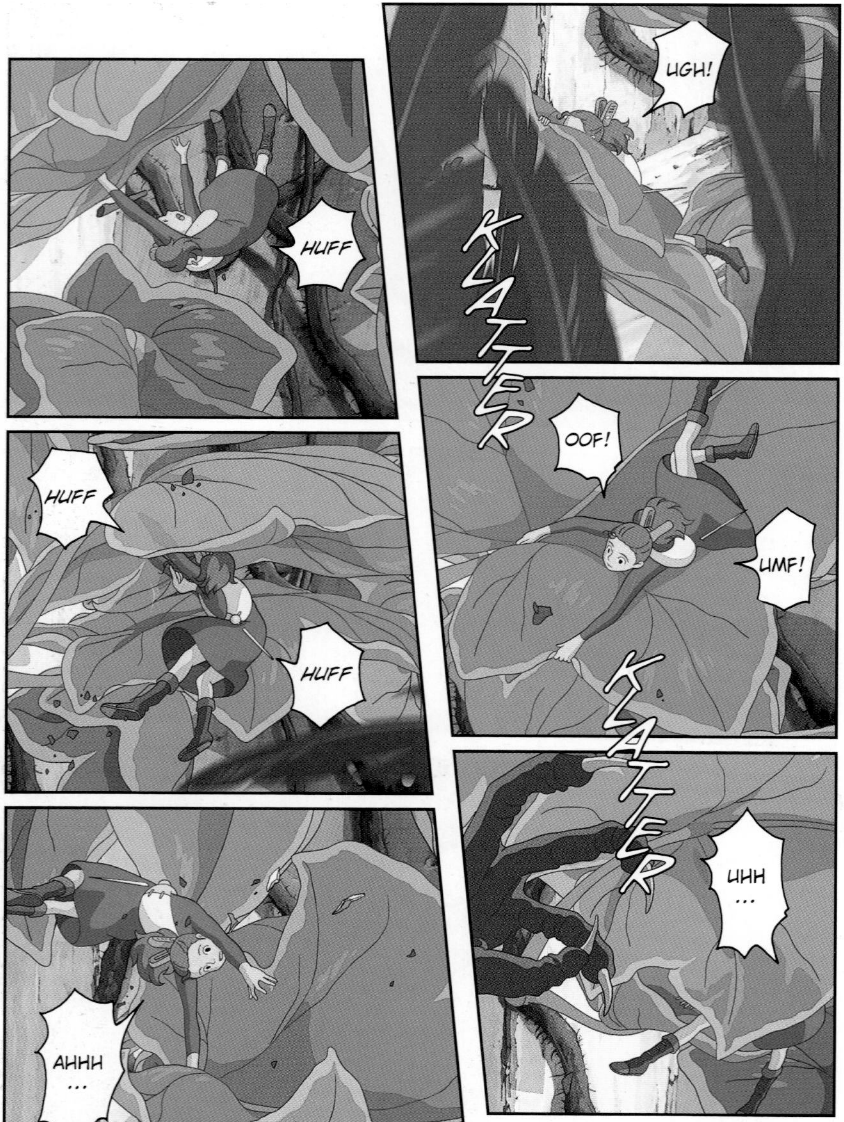
HUFF
HUFF
HUFF
AHHH ...
UGH!
KLATTER
OOF!
UMF!
KLATTER
UHH ...

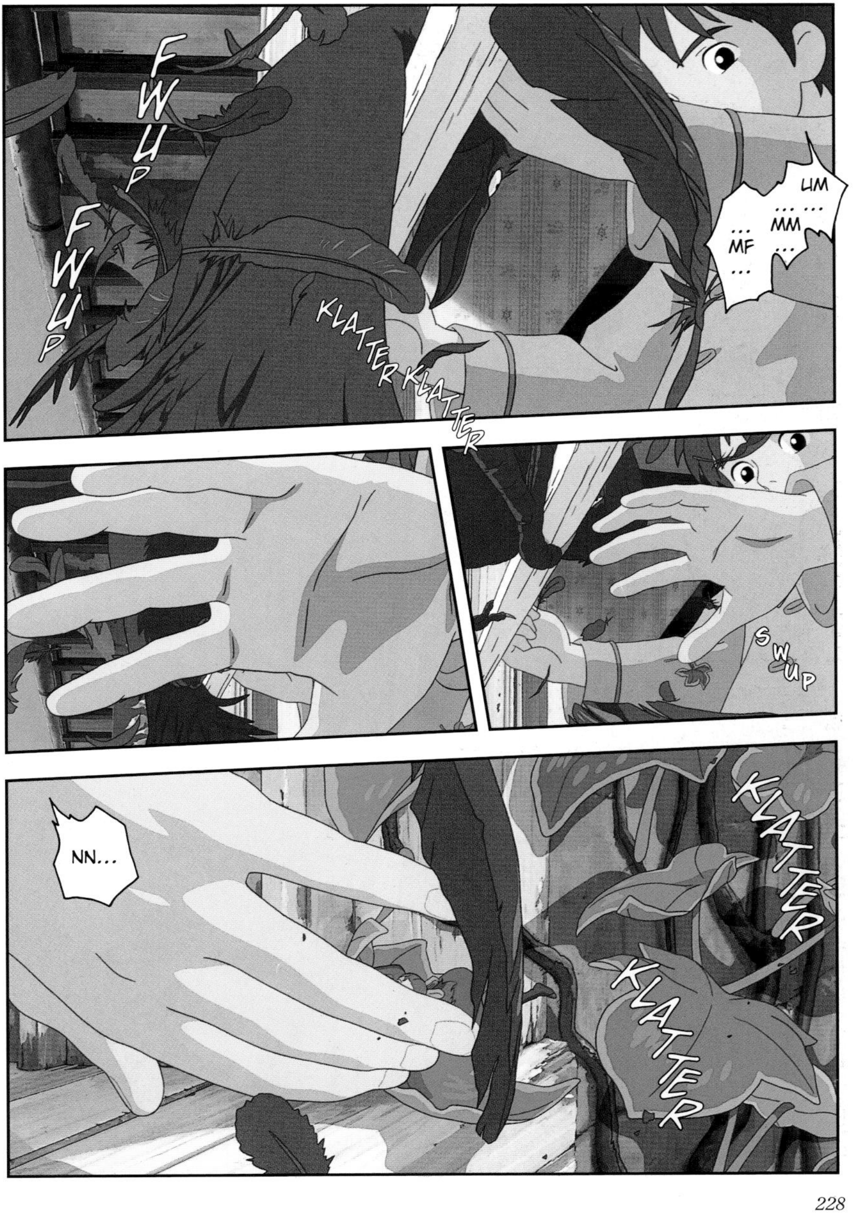
UM... ...MM... ...MF...
KLATTER KLATTER KLATTER
FWUP
FWUP
SWUP
KLATTER
KLATTER
NN...

... NN ...
FWUP
KLATTER
... NN ...
KLATTER
FWUP
... NN ...
... NN ...
... NN!

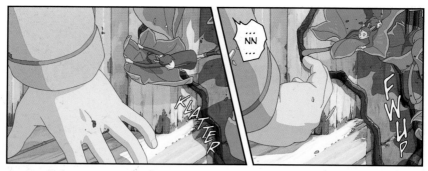

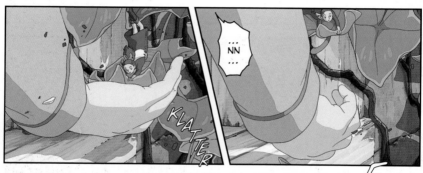

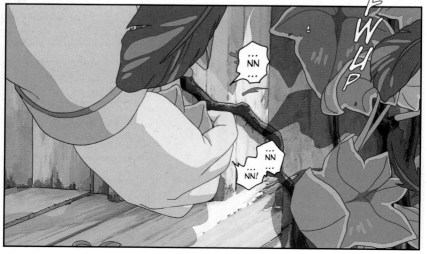

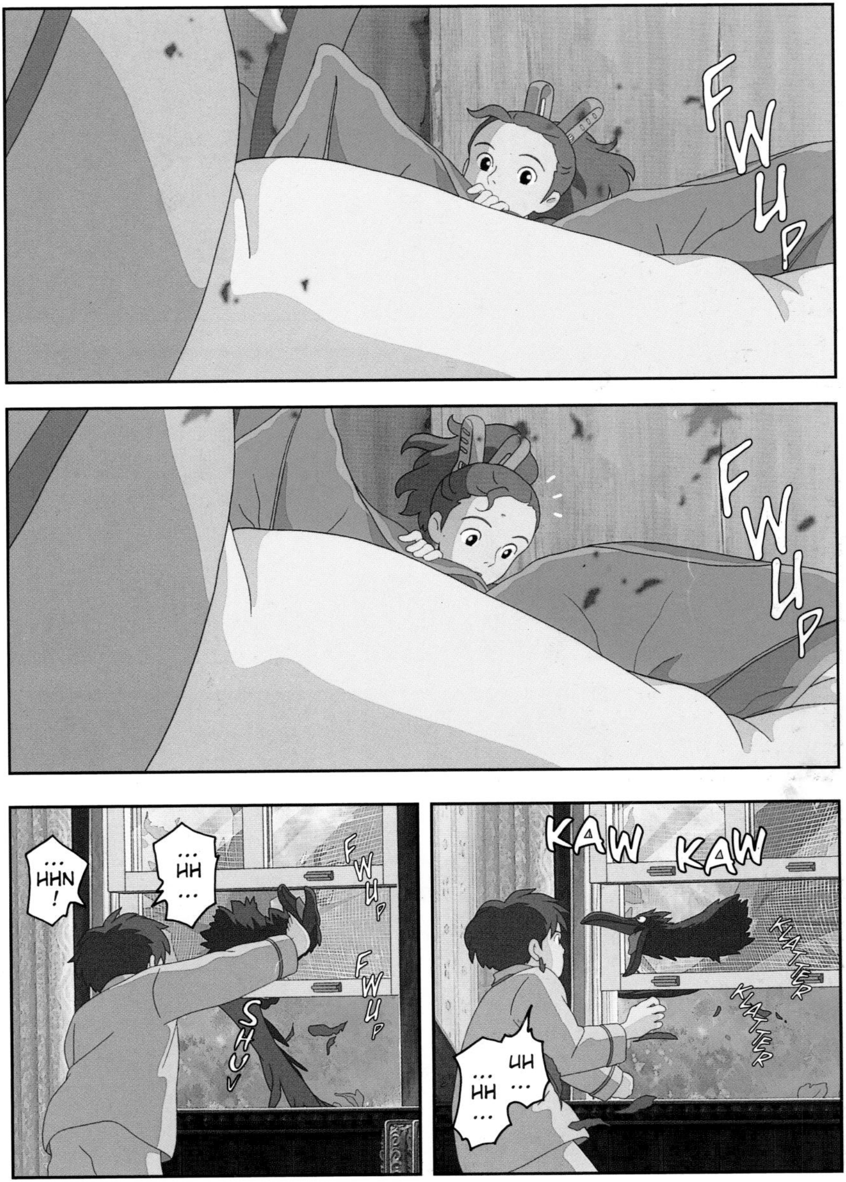
FWUP
FWUP
...HHN!
...HH...
FWUP
FWUP
SHUV
KAW KAW
KLATTER
KLATTER
UH...
...HH...

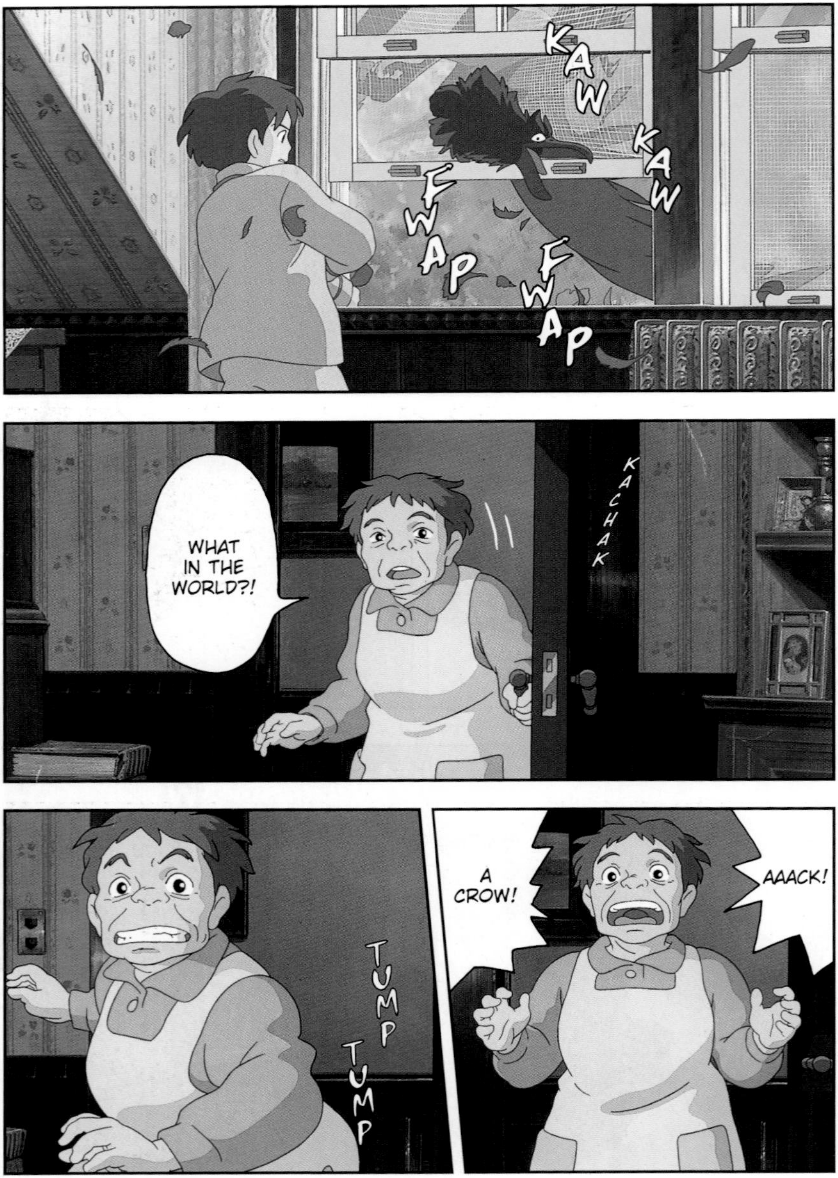
KAW
KAW
KAW
KAW
FWAP
FWAP
KACHAK
WHAT IN THE WORLD?!
AAACK!
A CROW!
TUMP
TUMP

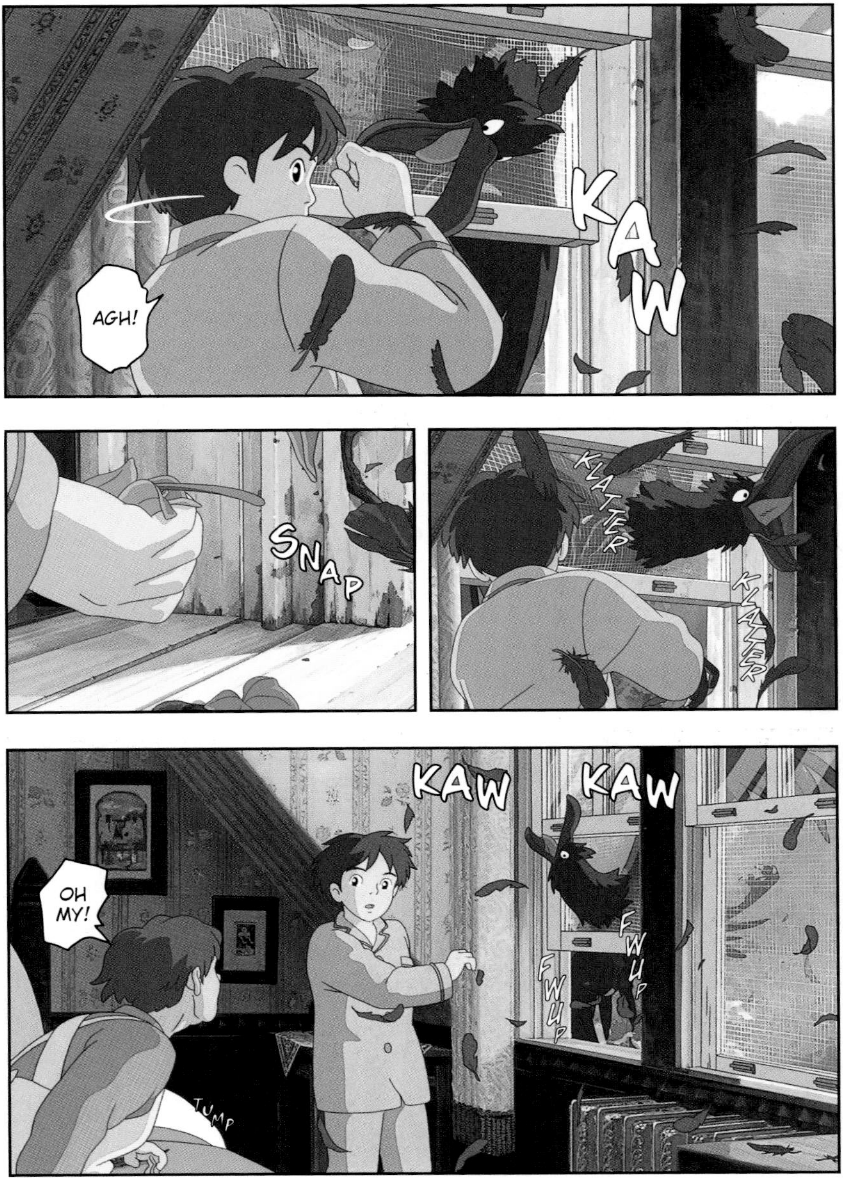
KAW
AGH!
KLATTER
KLATTER
SNAP
KAW
KAW
FWUP
FWUP
OH MY!
TUMP

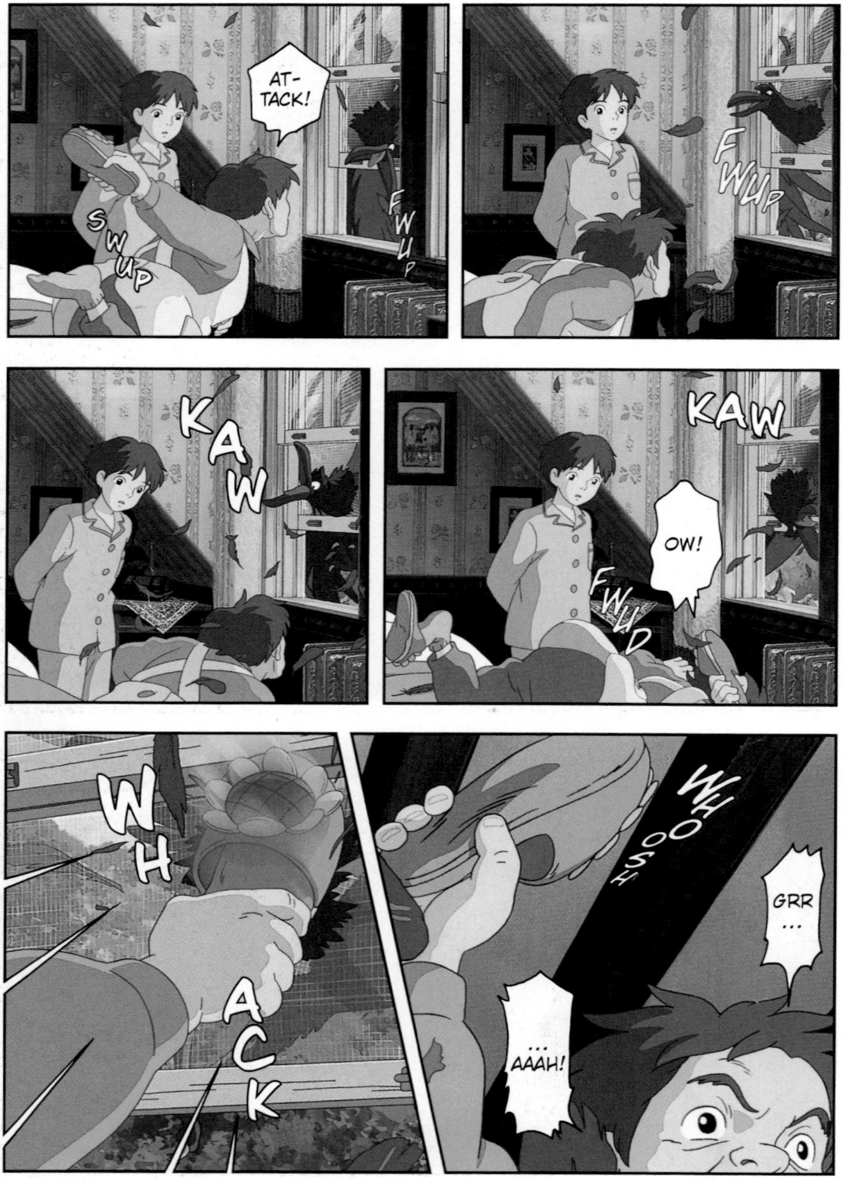
FWUP
AT-TACK!
FWUP
SWUP
KAW
OW!
FWUD
KAW
WHOOSH
GRR ...
... AAAH!
WHACK

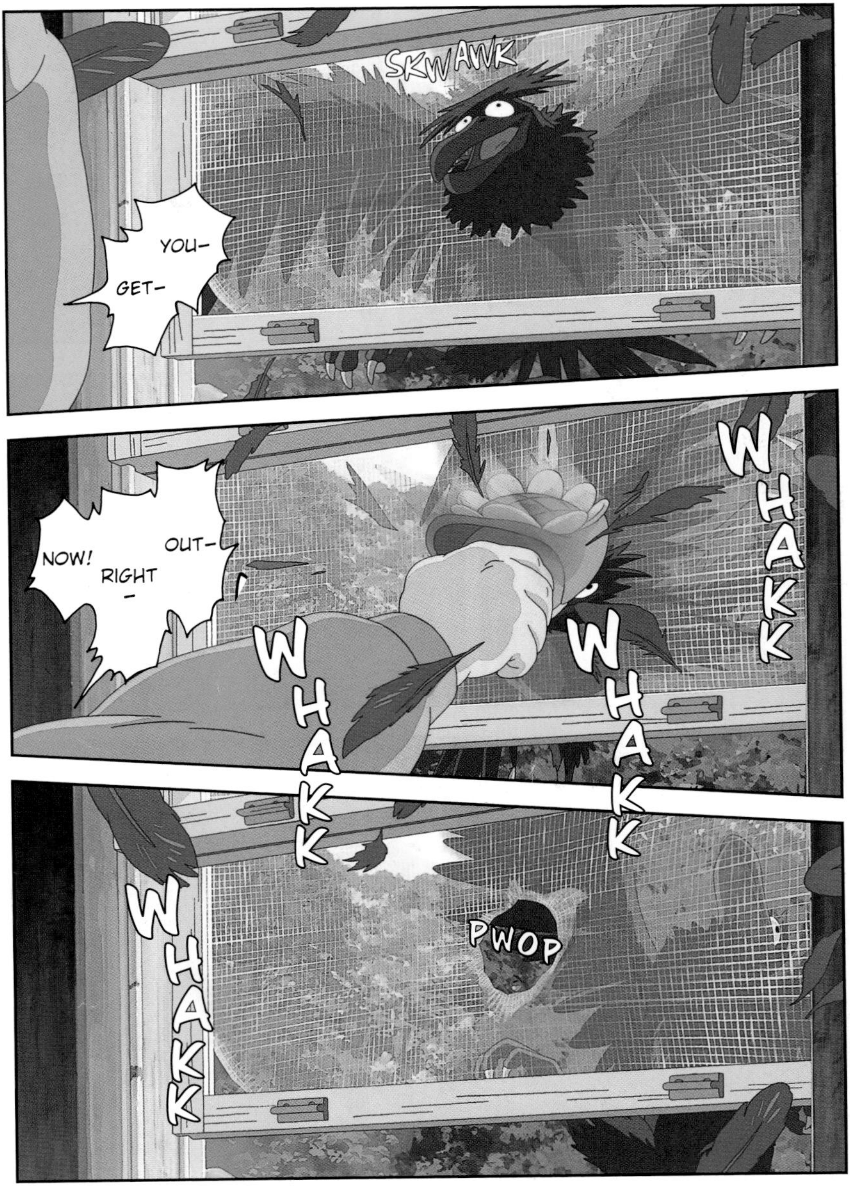
SKWAWK
YOU- GET-
WHAKK
OUT- RIGHT - NOW!
WHAKK
WHAKK
WHAKK
PWOP

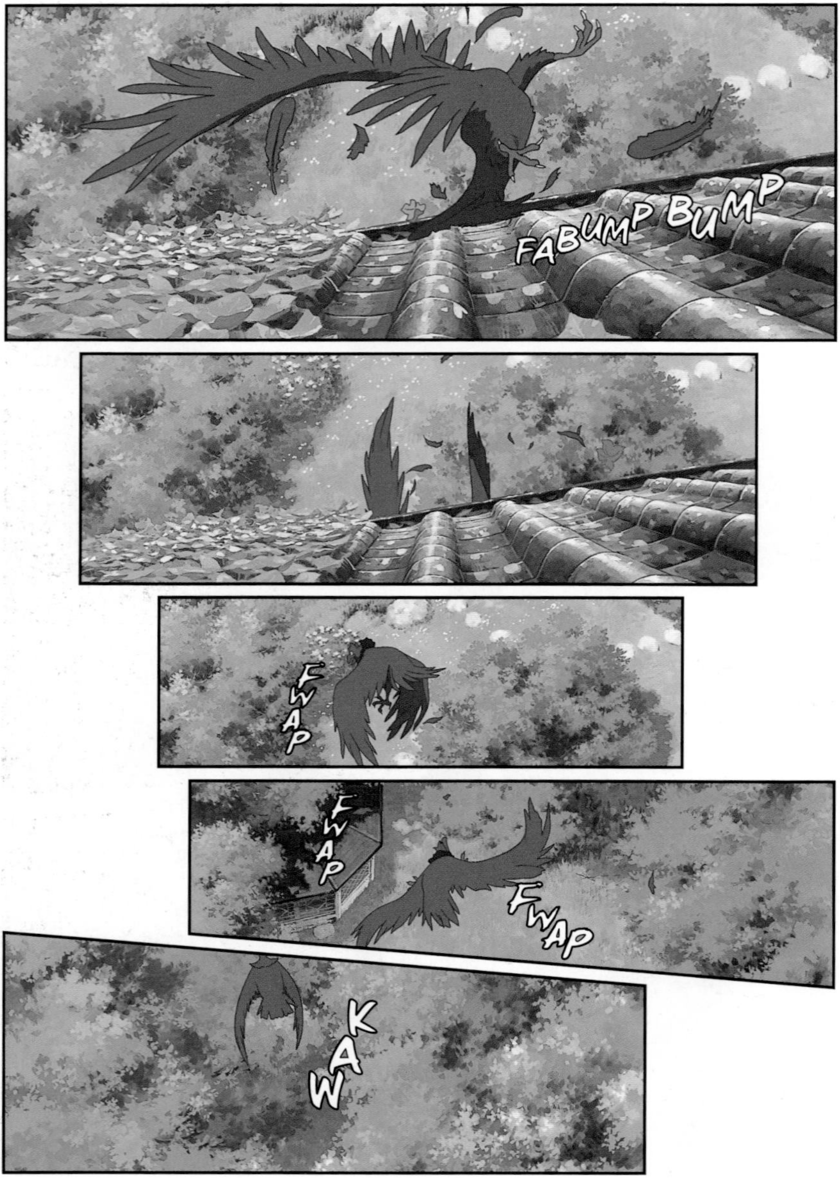
FABUMP BUMP
FWAP
FWAP
FWAP
WAK

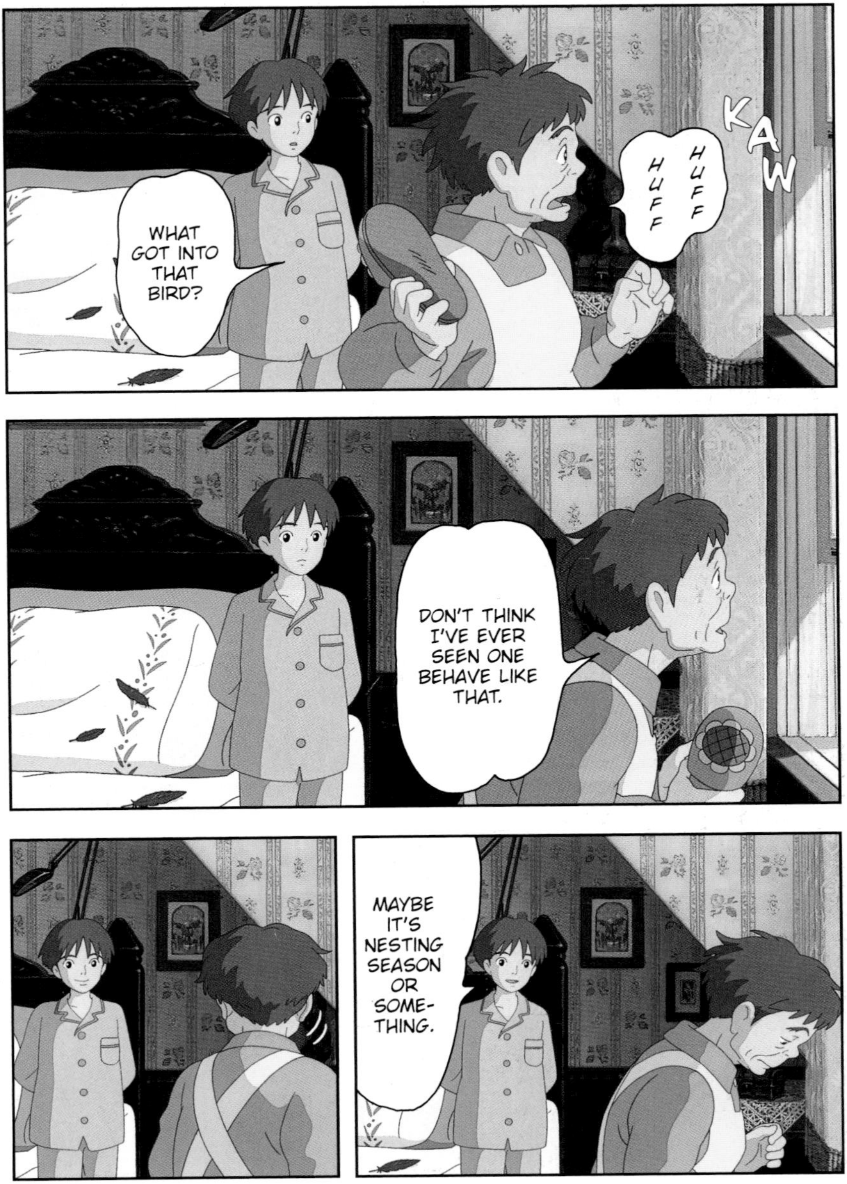
KAW
HUFF HUFF
WHAT GOT INTO THAT BIRD?
DON'T THINK I'VE EVER SEEN ONE BEHAVE LIKE THAT.
MAYBE IT'S NESTING SEASON OR SOME-THING.

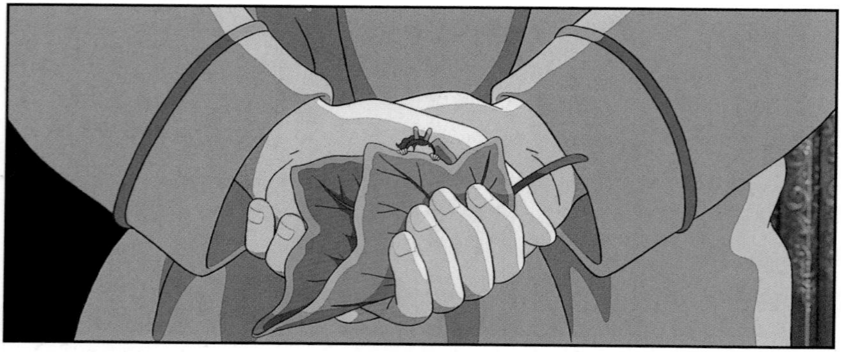
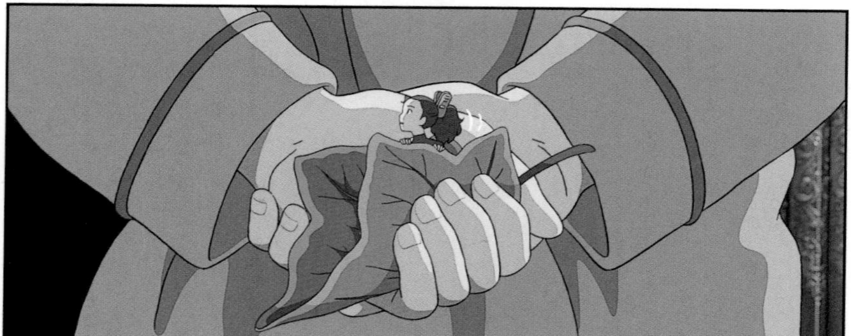
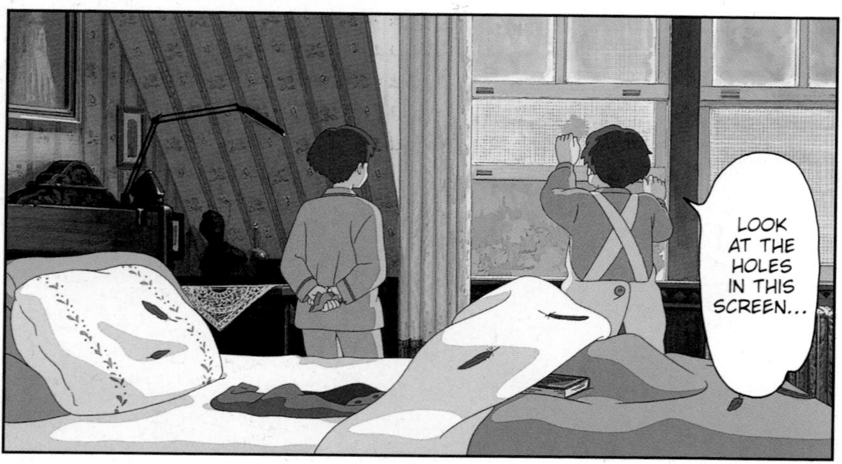
LOOK AT THE HOLES IN THIS SCREEN...

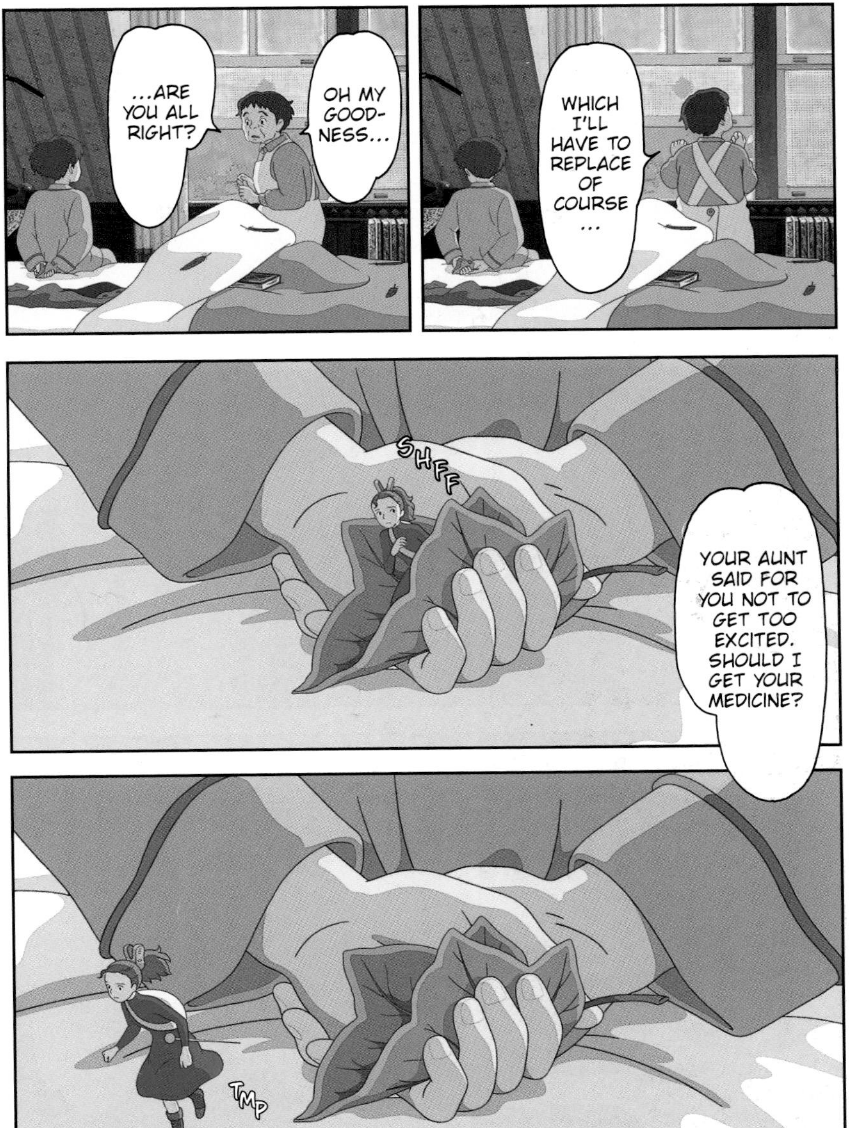
...ARE YOU ALL RIGHT?
OH MY GOODNESS...
WHICH I'LL HAVE TO REPLACE OF COURSE...
SHFF
YOUR AUNT SAID FOR YOU NOT TO GET TOO EXCITED. SHOULD I GET YOUR MEDICINE?
TMP

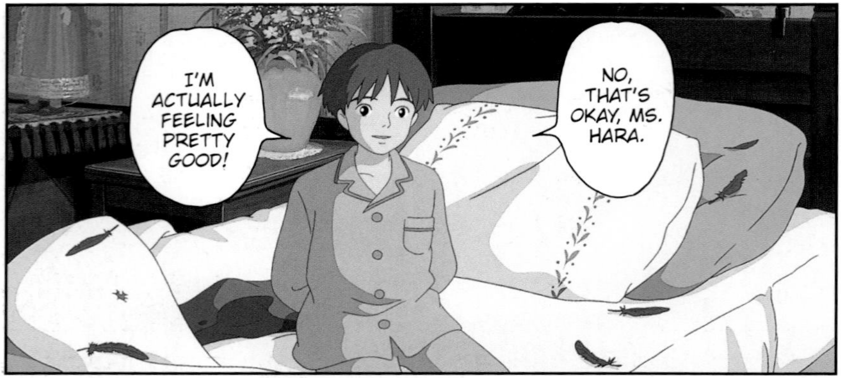
NO, THAT'S OKAY, MS. HARA.
I'M ACTUALLY FEELING PRETTY GOOD!

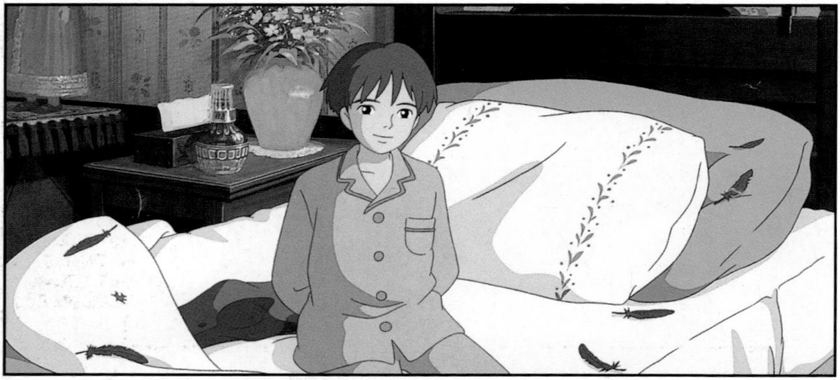

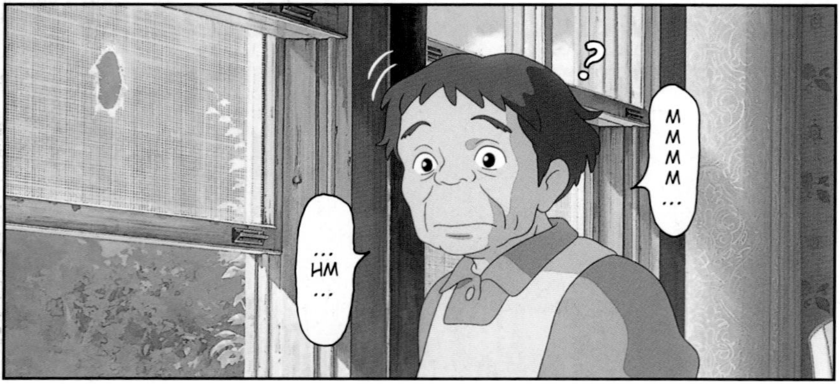
?
MMMM...
...HM...

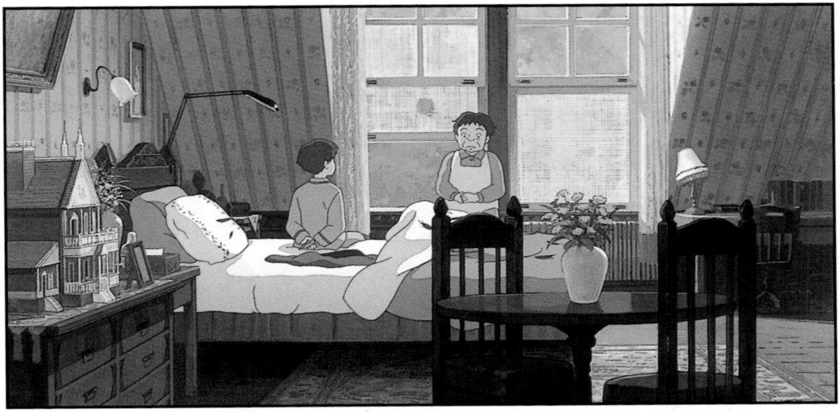

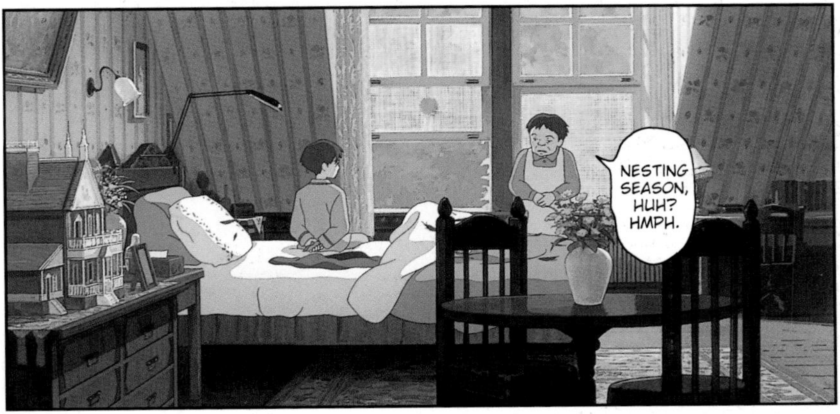
NESTING SEASON, HUH? HMPH.

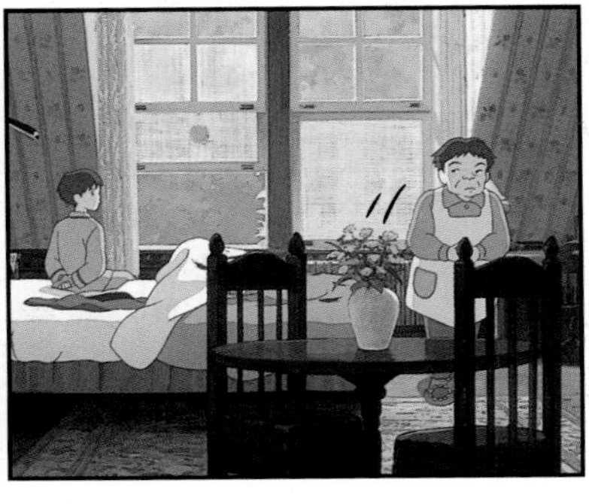

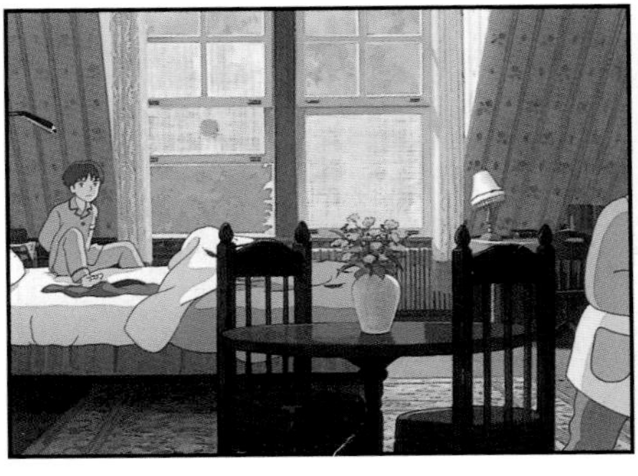

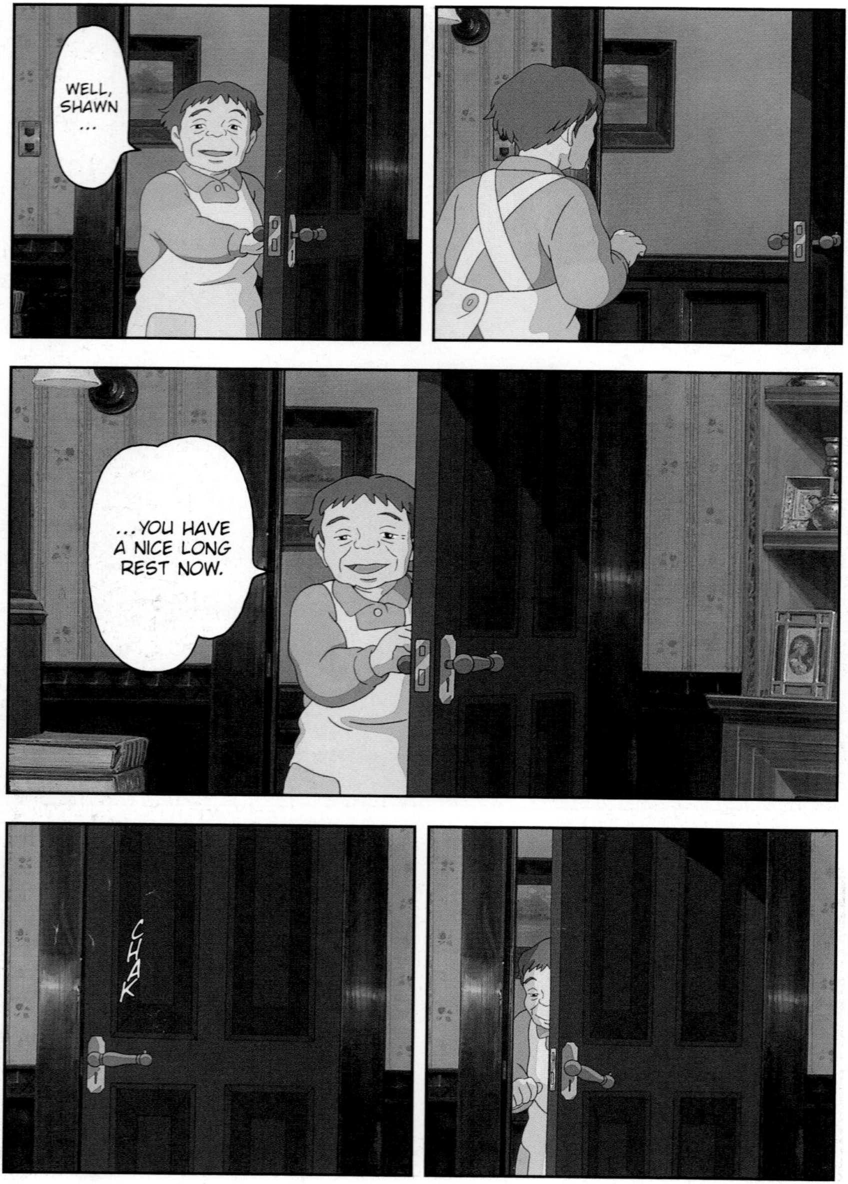
WELL, SHAWN ...
...YOU HAVE A NICE LONG REST NOW.
CHAK

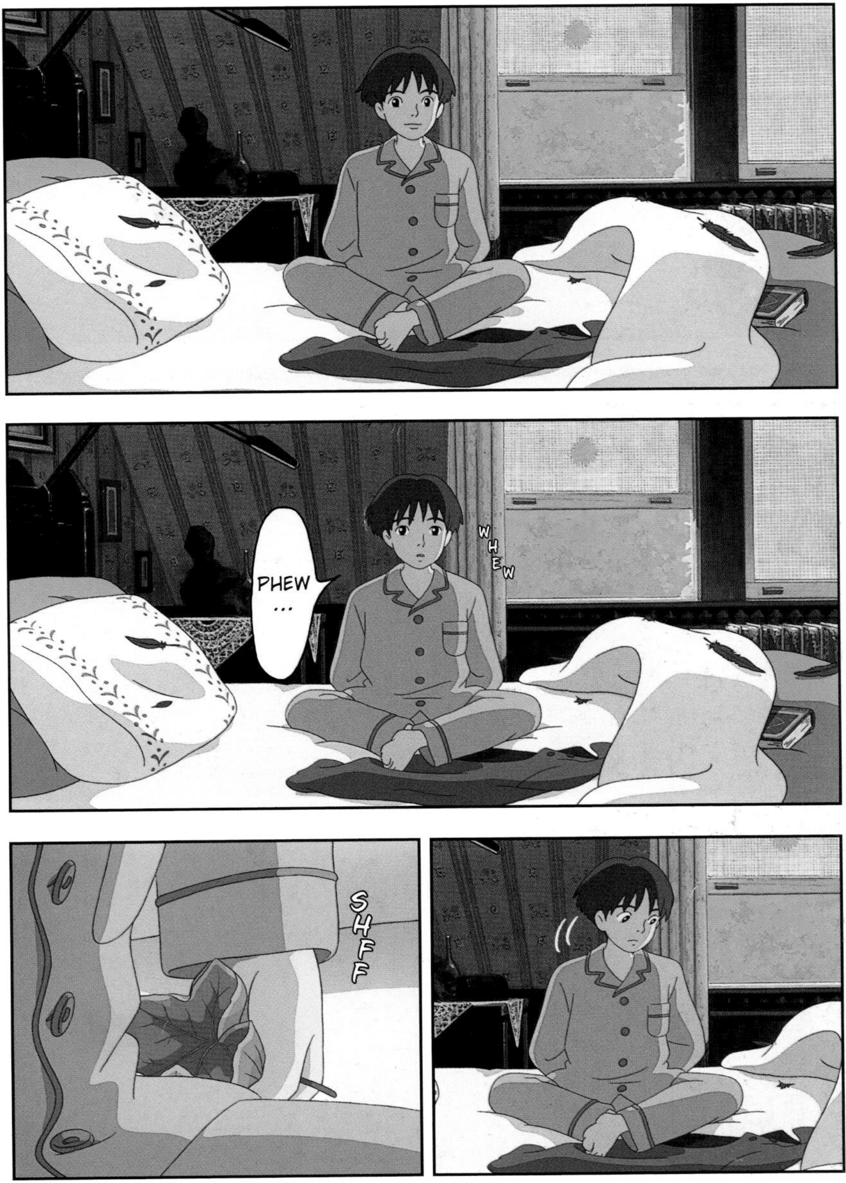
PHEW ...
WHEW
SHFF

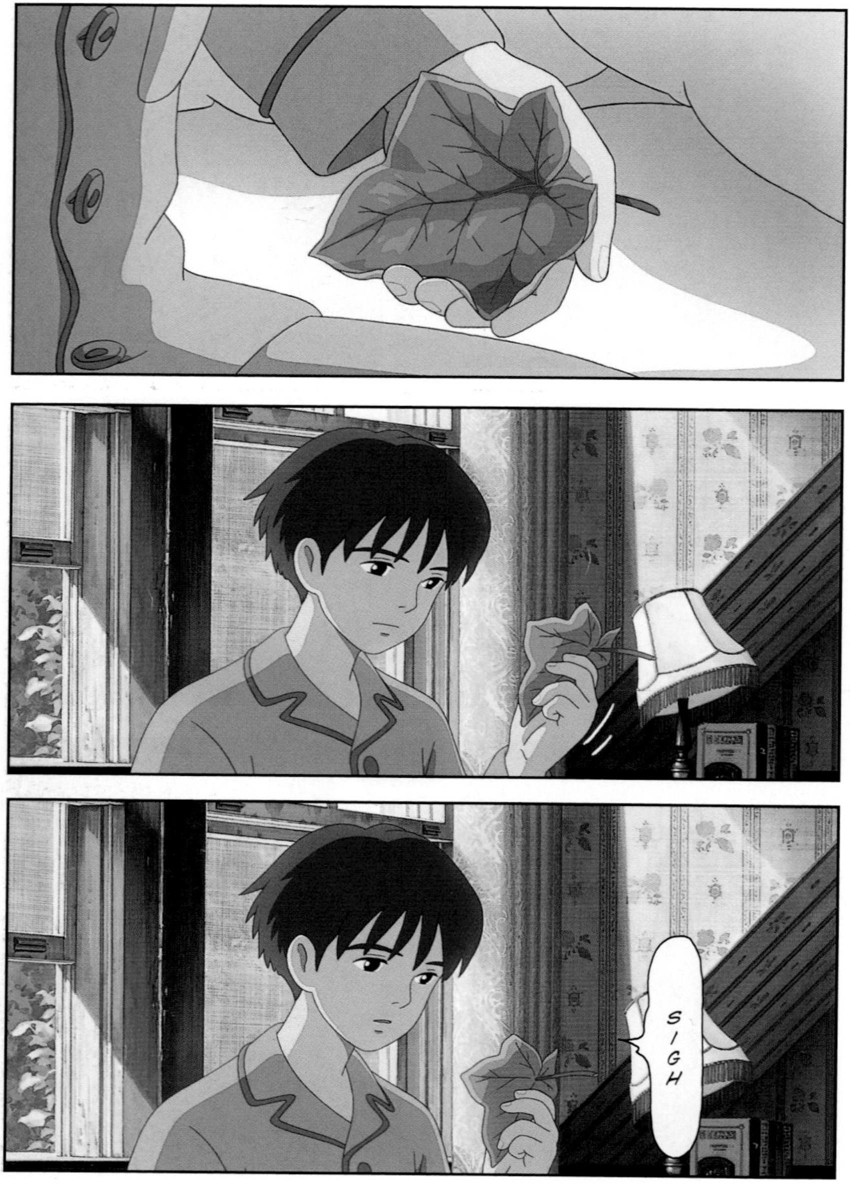
SIGH

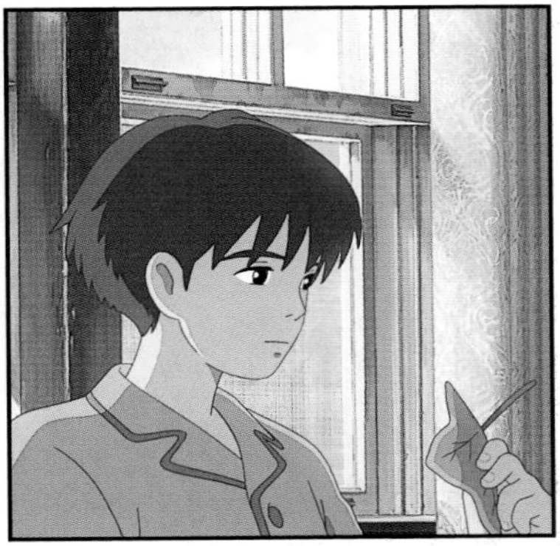
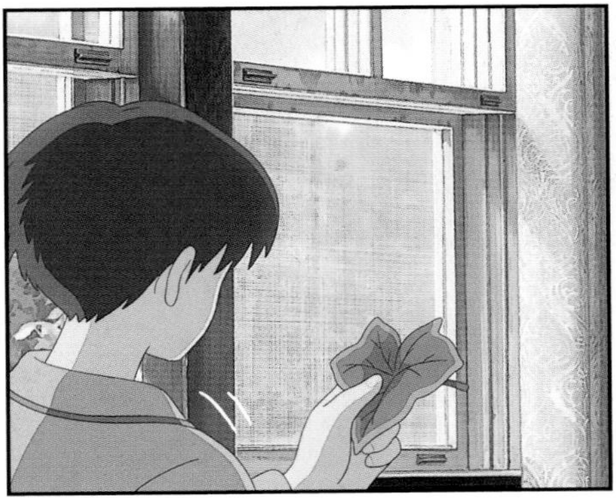
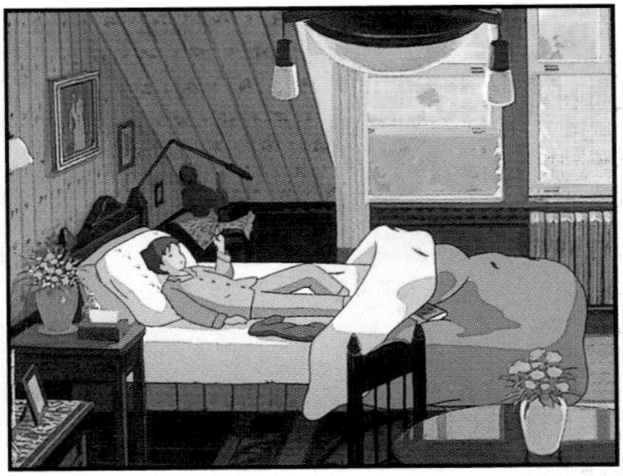
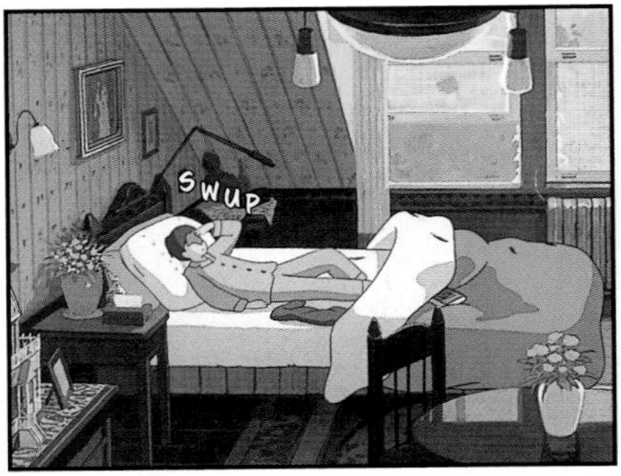
SWUP
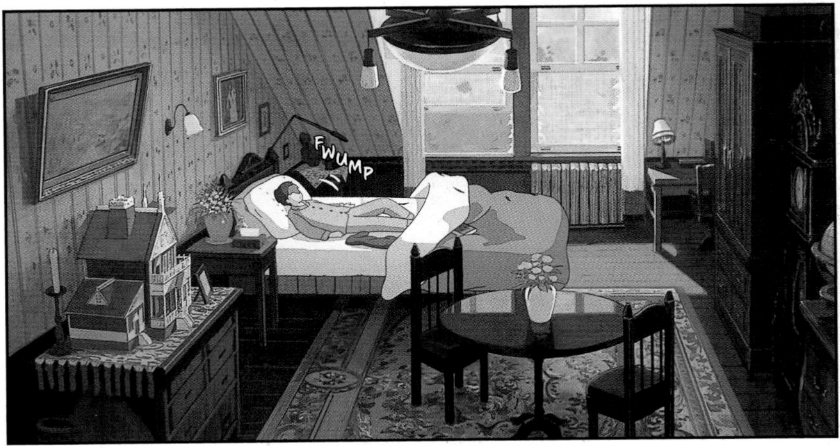
FWUMP

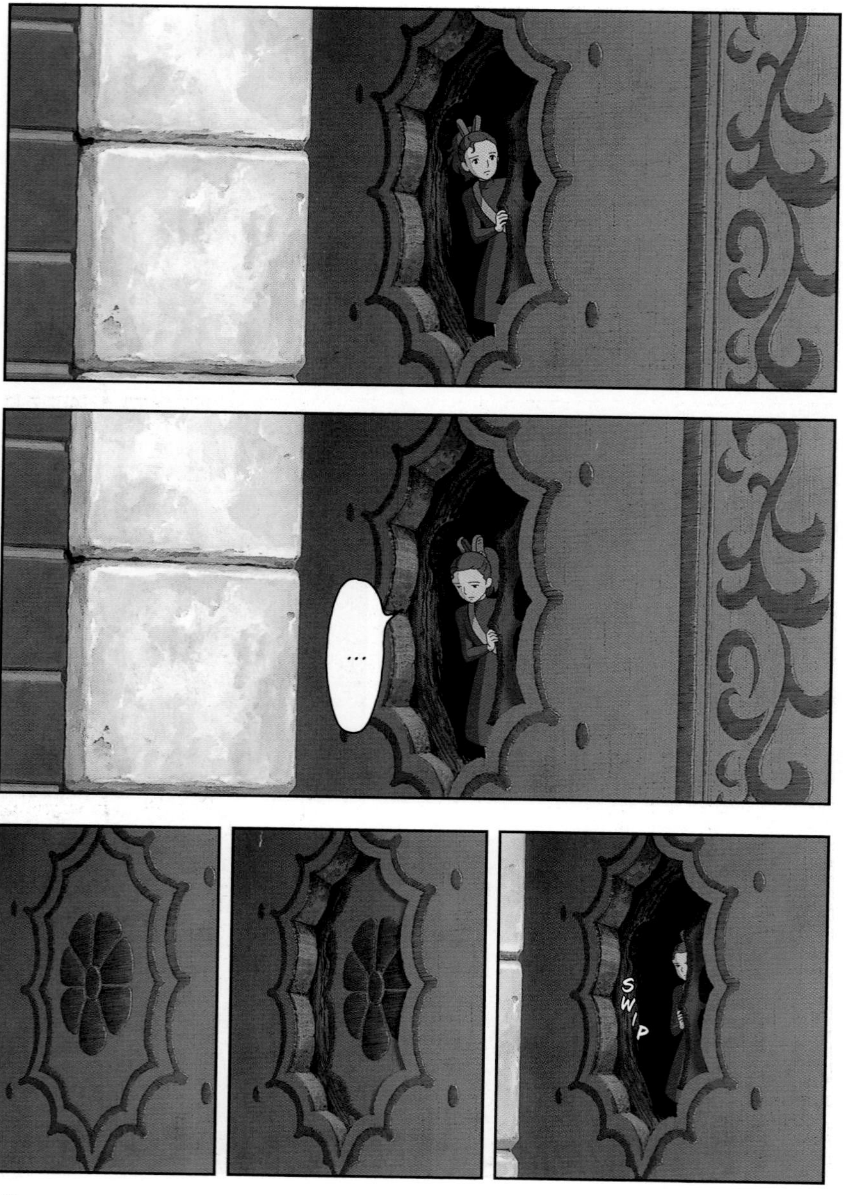
...
SWIP

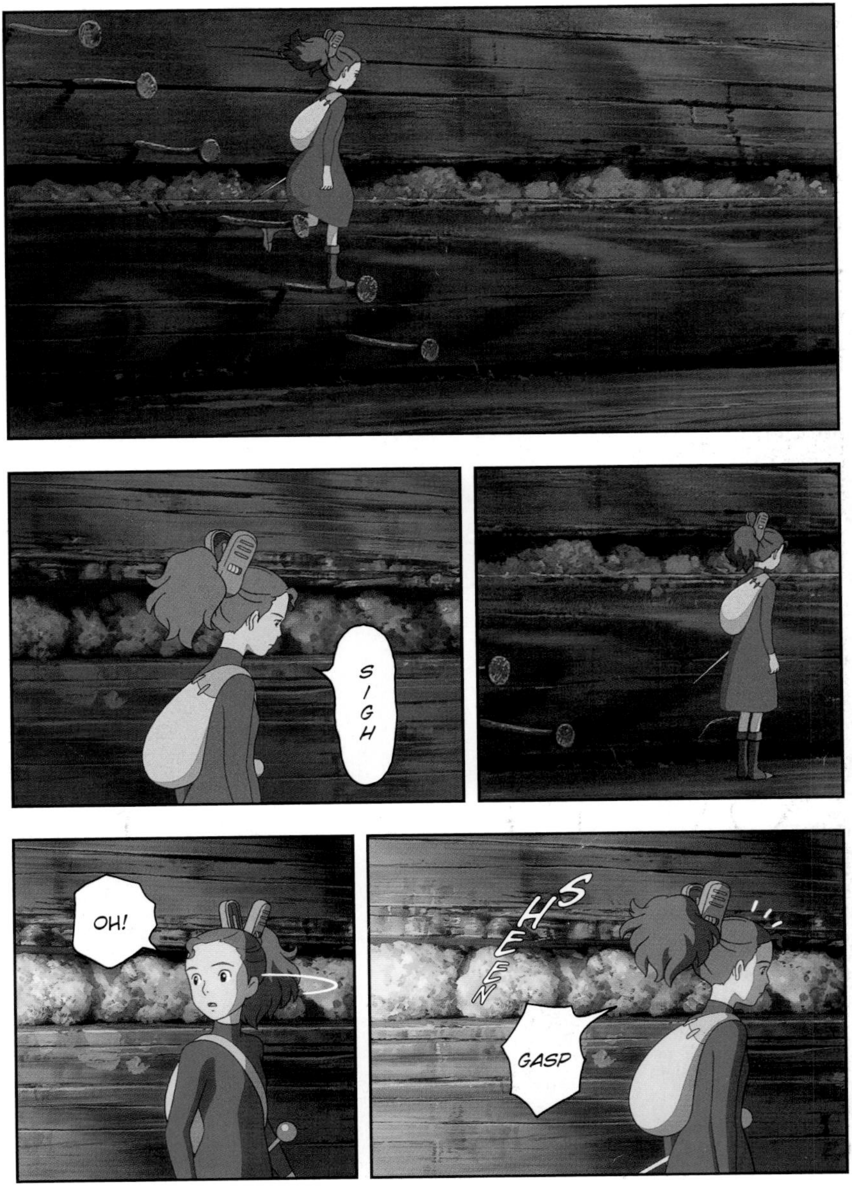
SIGH
SHEEN
GASP
OH!

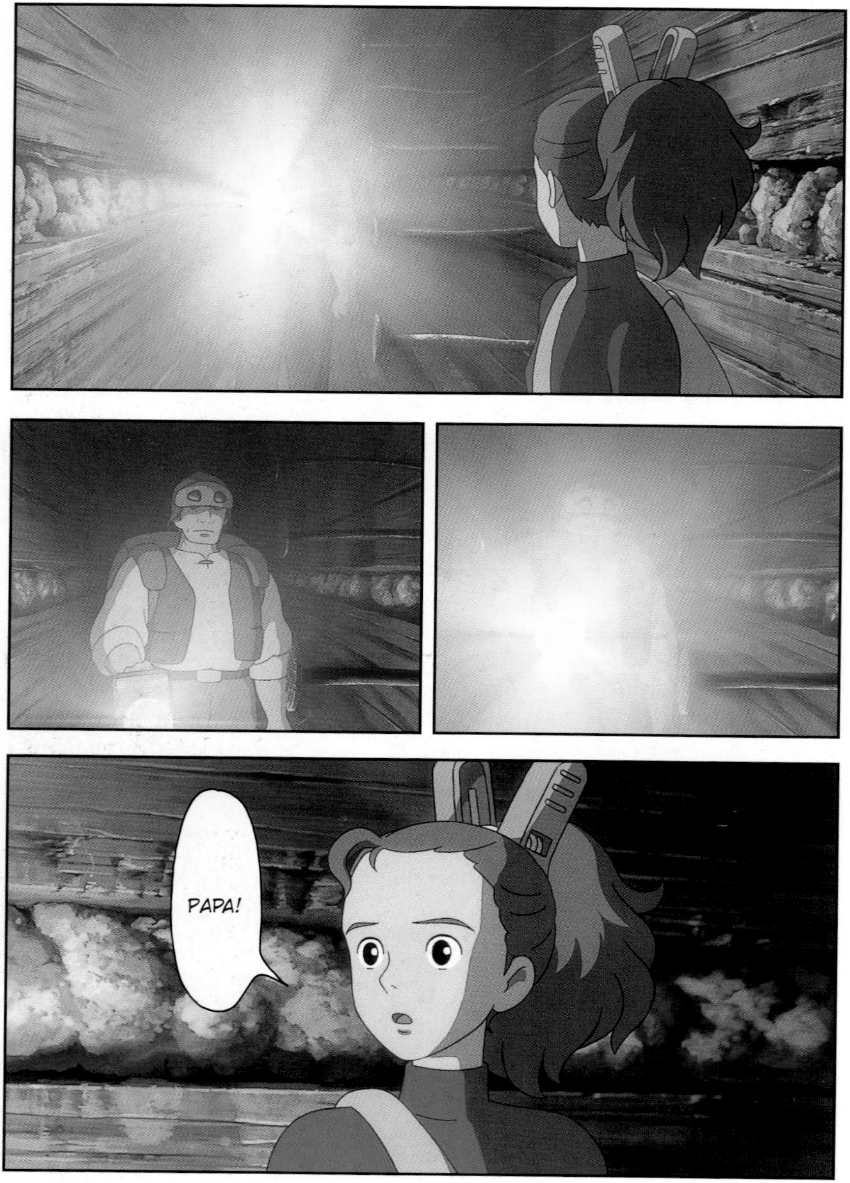
PAPA!

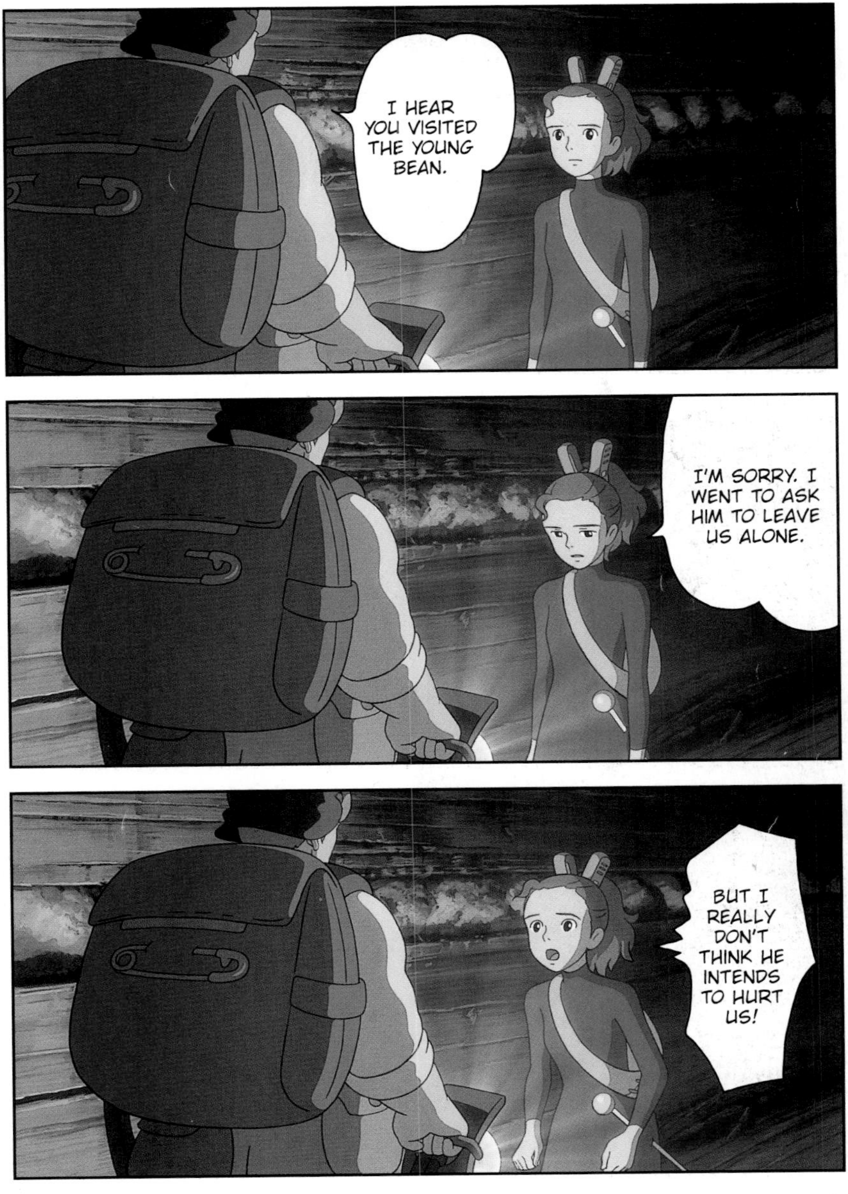
I HEAR YOU VISITED THE YOUNG BEAN.
I'M SORRY. I WENT TO ASK HIM TO LEAVE US ALONE.
BUT I REALLY DON'T THINK HE INTENDS TO HURT US!

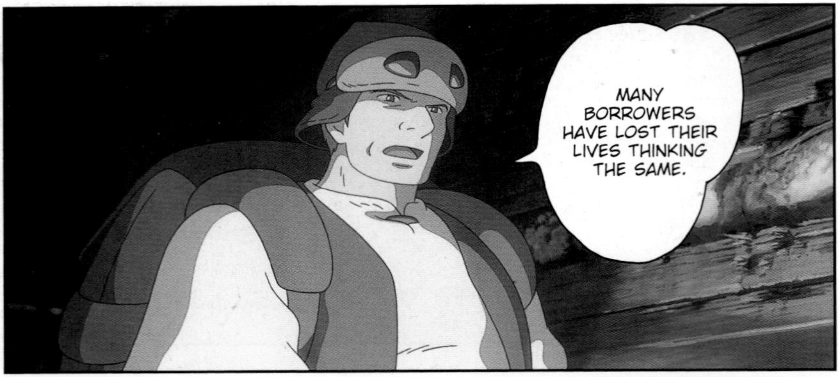
MANY BORROWERS HAVE LOST THEIR LIVES THINKING THE SAME.

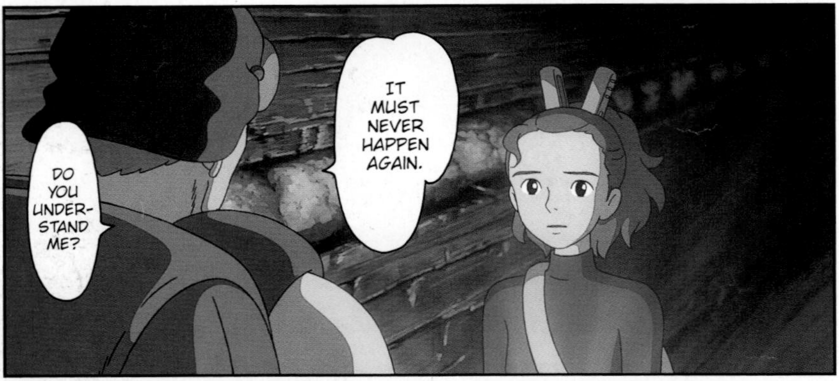
IT MUST NEVER HAPPEN AGAIN.
DO YOU UNDER-STAND ME?

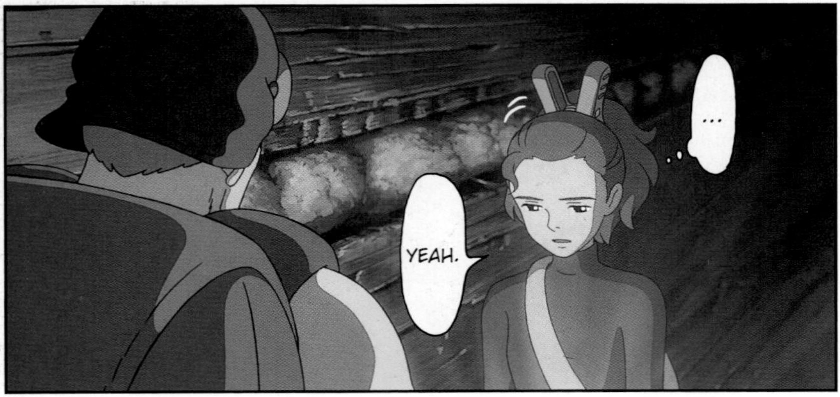
...
YEAH.

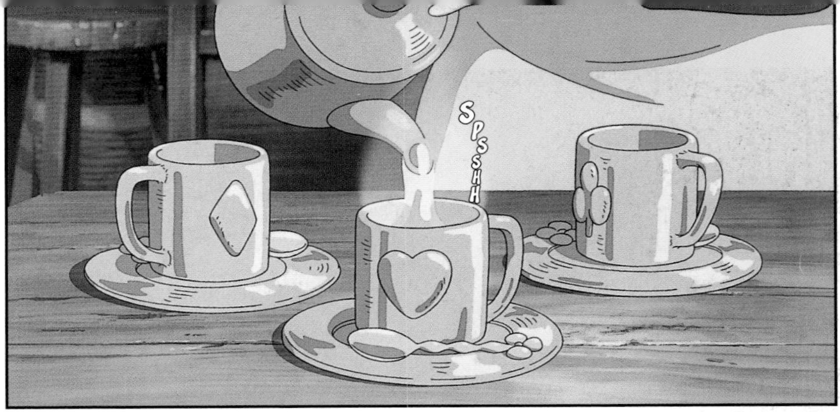
SPSSHH

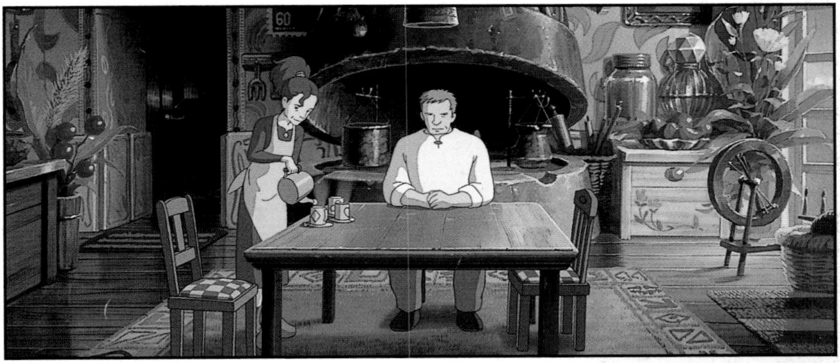

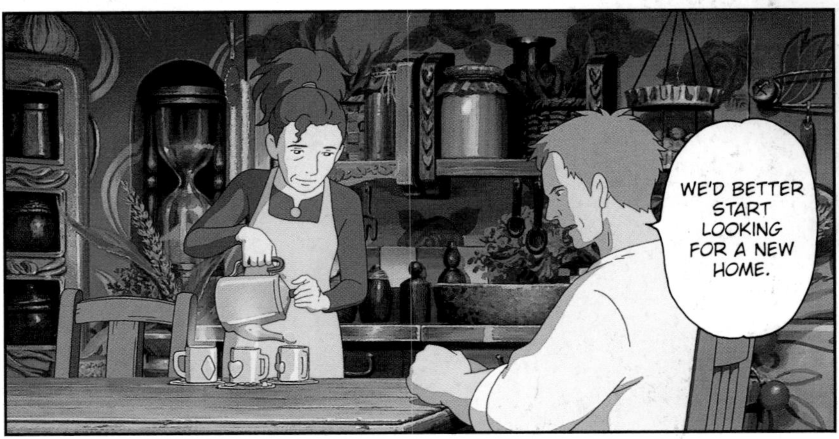
WE'D BETTER START LOOKING FOR A NEW HOME.

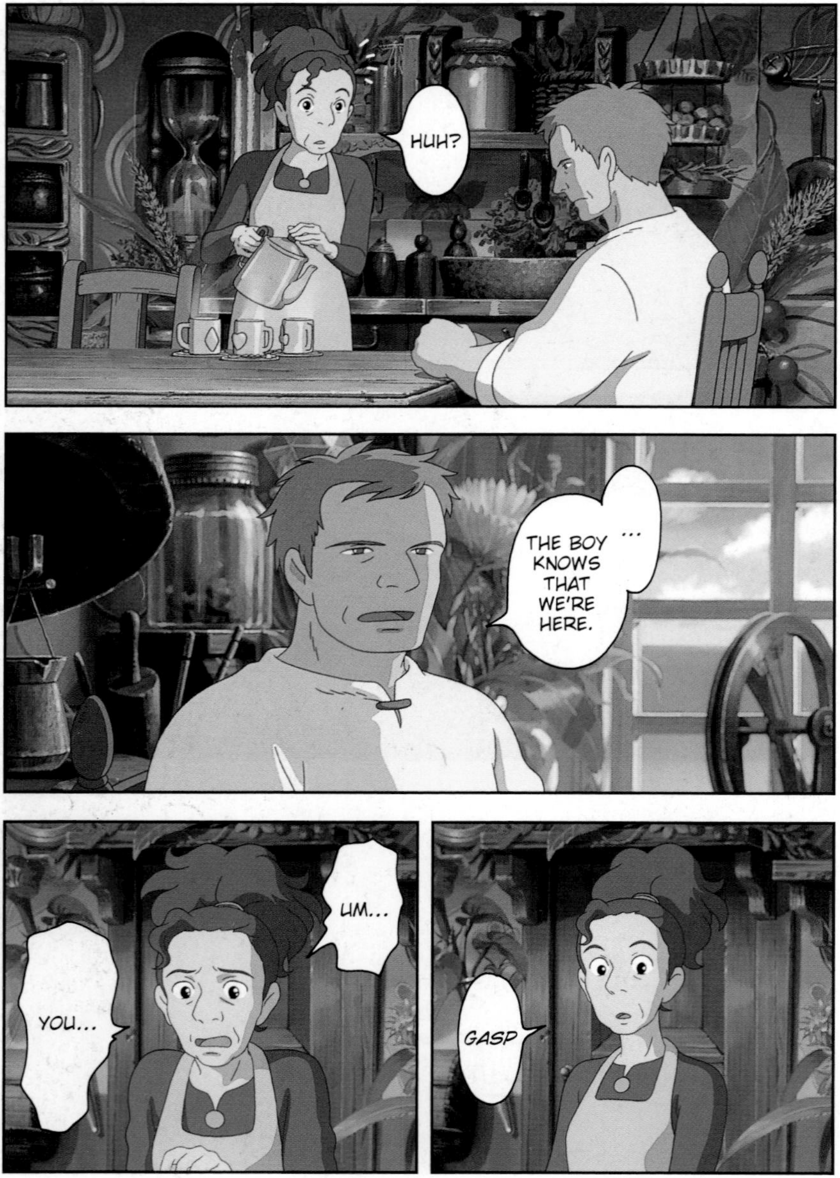
HUH?
... THE BOY KNOWS THAT WE'RE HERE.
GASP
UM...
YOU...

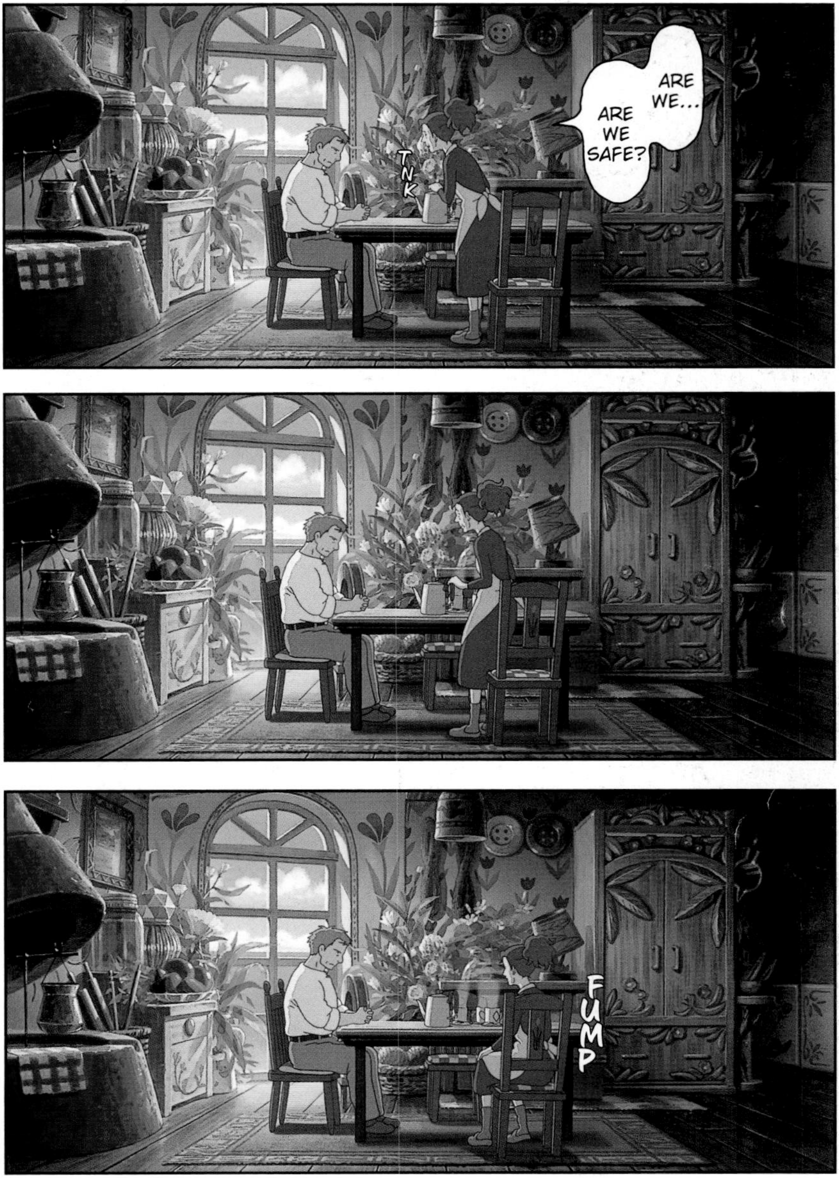
ARE WE...
ARE WE SAFE?
TNK
FUMP

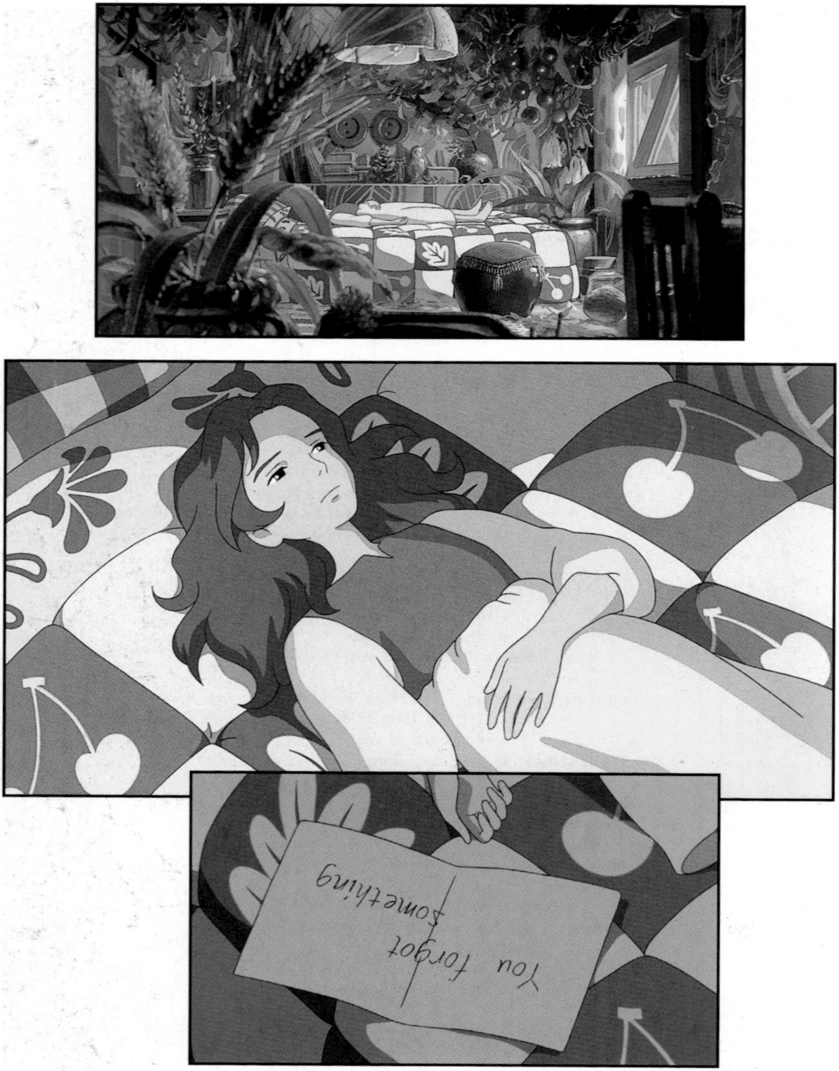
You forgot something

TO BE CONTINUED...

This book should be read in its original Japanese right-to-left format. Please turn it around to begin!

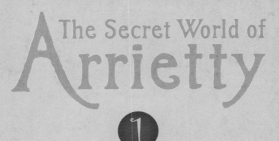

The Secret World of Arrietty

1

Volume 1 of 2

Planning by Hayao Miyazaki
Based on *The Borrowers* by Mary Norton
Directed by Hiromasa Yonebayashi
Original Screenplay by Hayao Miyazaki and Keiko Niwa
Translated from the Original Japanese by Rieko Izutsu-Vajirasarn and Jim Hubbert
English Language Screenplay by Karey Kirkpatrick

Film Comic Adaptation/HC Language Solutions, Inc.
Lettering/Erika Terriquez
Design/Yukiko Whitley
Editor/Josh Bettinger
Senior Editorial Director/Masumi Washington

Karigurashi no Arrietty (The Secret World of Arrietty)
© 2010 GNDHDDTW
All rights reserved.
First published in Japan by Tokuma Shoten Co., Ltd.
The Secret World of Arrietty title logo © 2012 GNDHDDTW

Printed in Singapore

Published by
VIZ Media, LLC
295 Bay St. San Francisco, CA 94133

First printing, January 2012
Second printing, May 2012

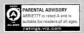

PARENTAL ADVISORY
ARRIETTY is rated A and is
suitable for readers of all ages.
ratings.viz.com

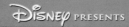
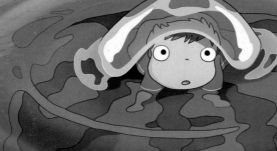

ne Jones
ao Miyazaki

HOWL'S MOVING CASTLE

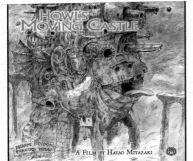

A hardcover book generously packed with concept sketches, character and background drawings, paintings, and cell images!

208 FULL COLOR & 48 B/W pages $34.99!

HOWL'S MOVING CASTLE
Picture

An attractive hardcover fo
whole family with scene-b
film footage and character

$19.99

Buy yours today at
store.viz.com!

www.viz.com

Breathtaking. Visual. Magical.